AF606852

DOODLE EVERYTHING

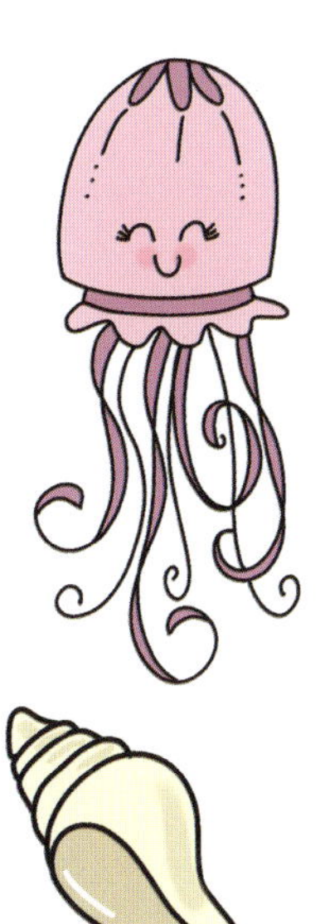
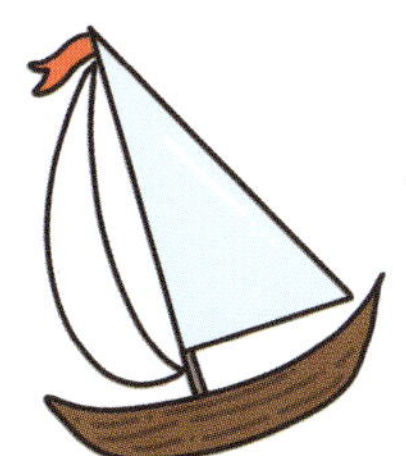
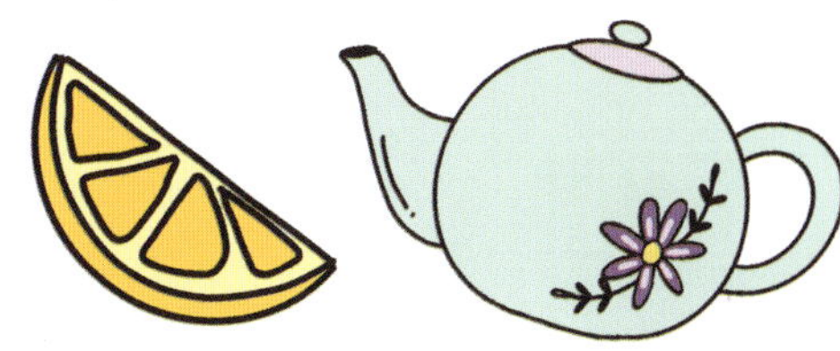
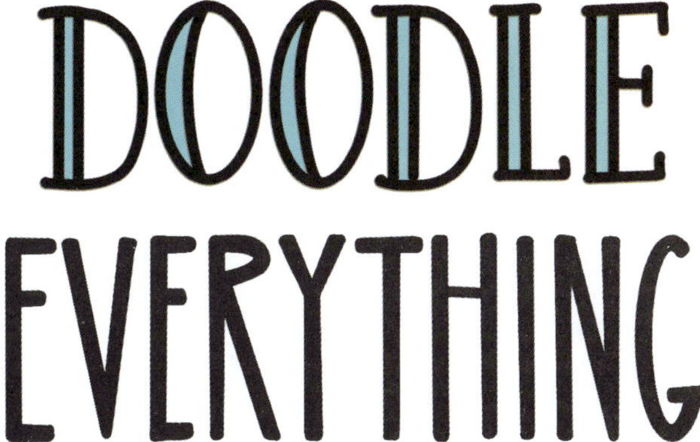

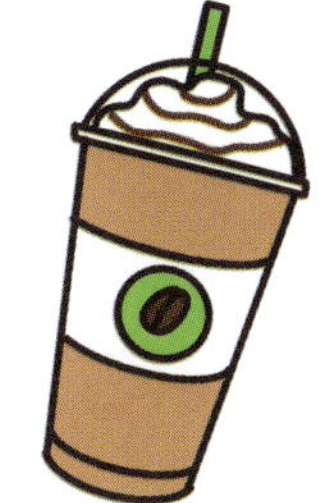
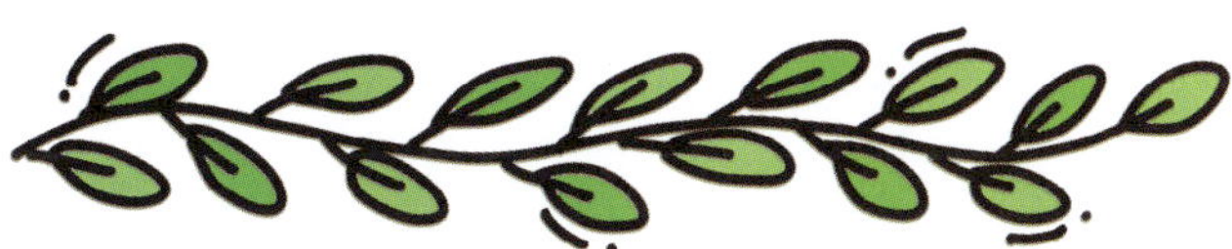

Learn to Draw with 400+ Easy, Adorable Designs

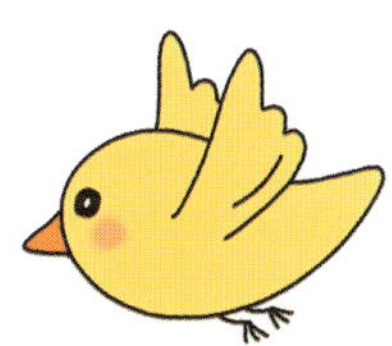
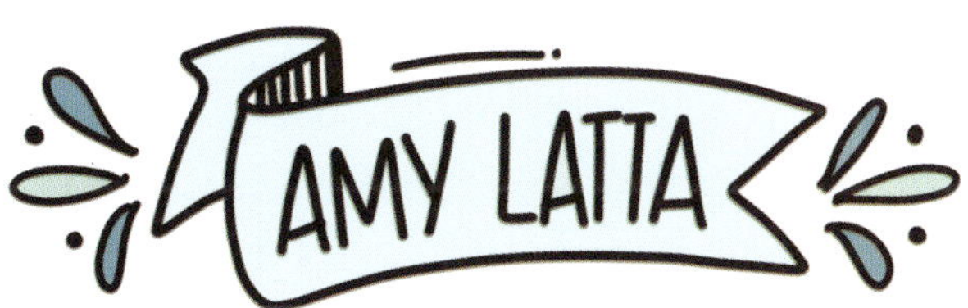

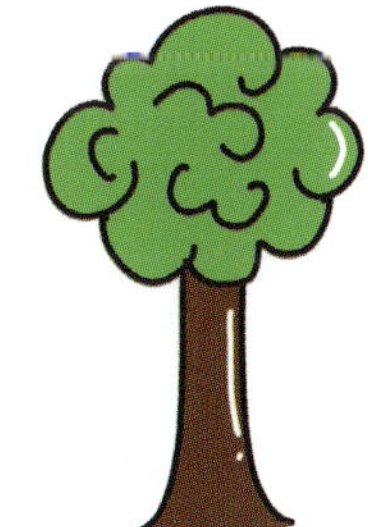
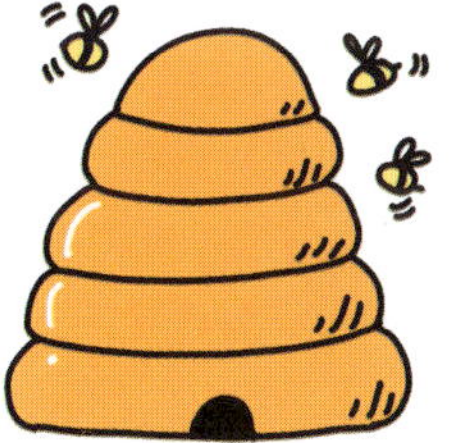
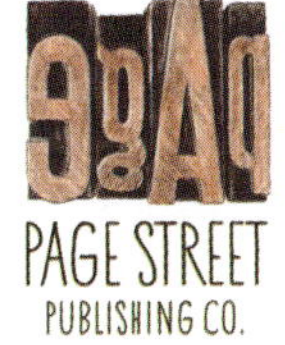

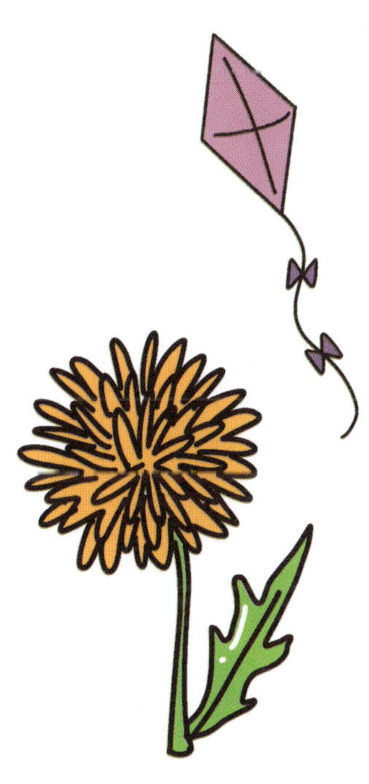

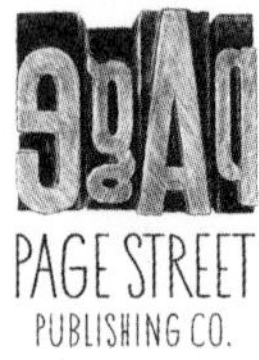

First published in 2022 by

Page Street Publishing Co.

27 Congress Street, Suite 1511

Salem, MA 01970

www.pagestreetpublishing.com

Distributed by Macmillan, sales in Canada by The Canadian Manda Group.

26 25 7

ISBN-13: 978-1-64567-632-4

ISBN-10: 1-64567-632-3

Library of Congress Control Number: 2022930177

Cover design by Amy Latta. Book design by Meg Baskis for Page Street Publishing Co.

Illustrations by Amy Latta

Printed and bound in China

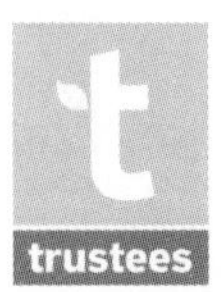

Page Street Publishing protects our planet by donating to nonprofits like The Trustees, which focuses on local land conservation.

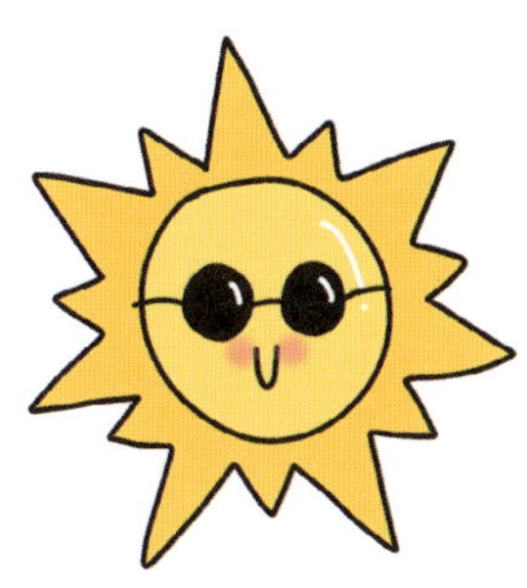

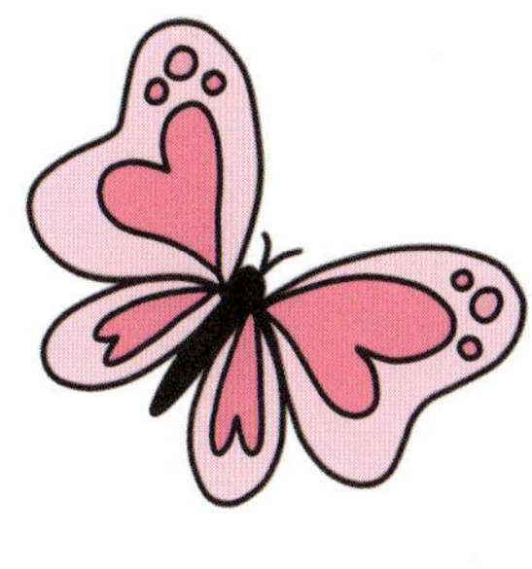

FOR ERIN, THE SISTER OF MY HEART,
THE MOCHA TO MY CARAMEL,
WHO BELIEVED IN MY LITTLE DOODLES BEFORE I DID.

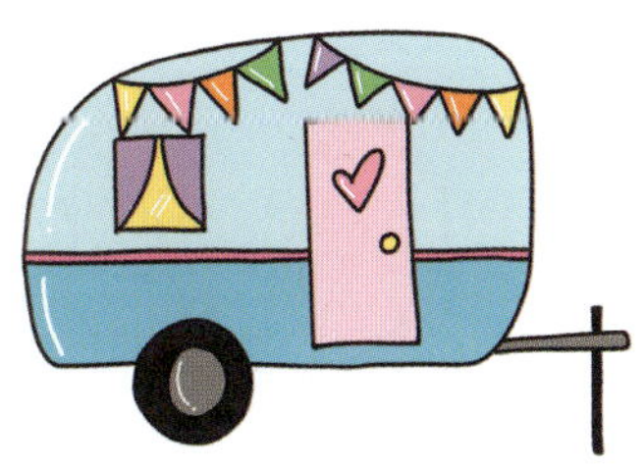

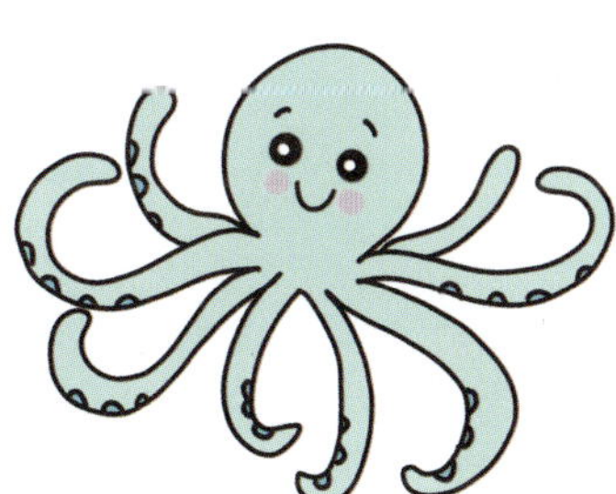

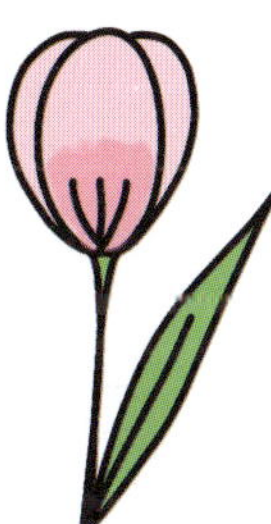

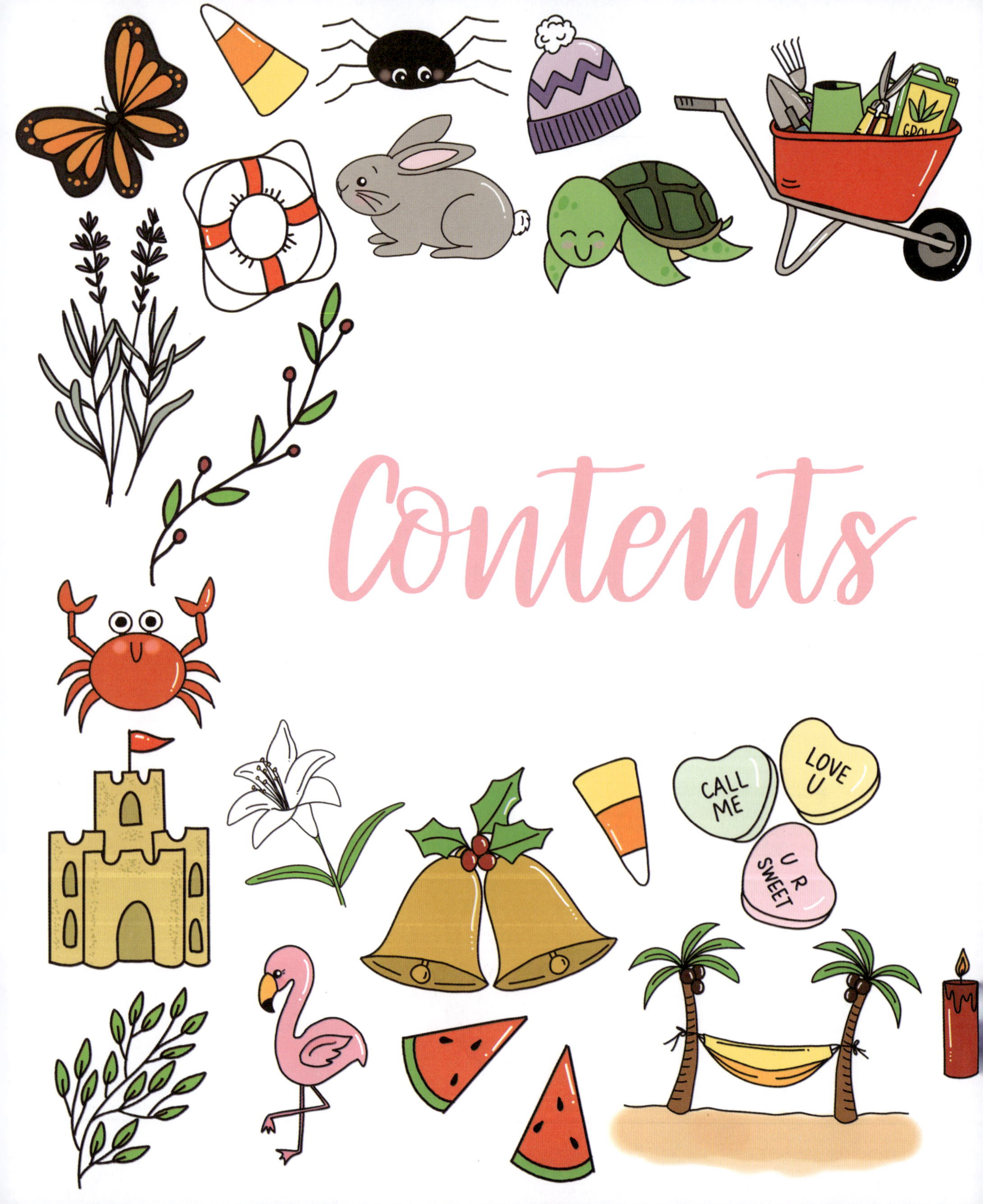
Contents
CALL ME
LOVE U
U R SWEET

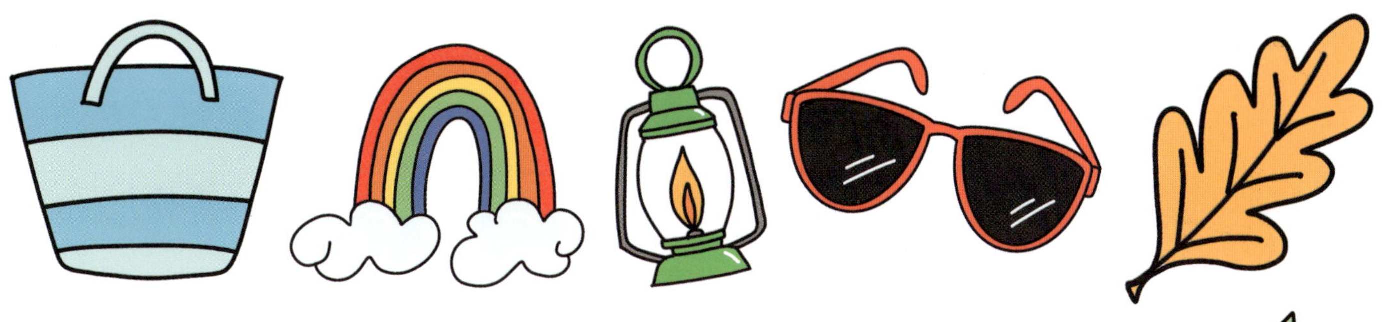

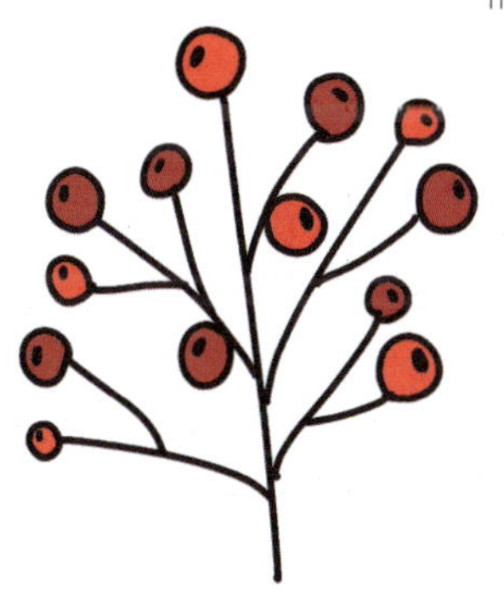

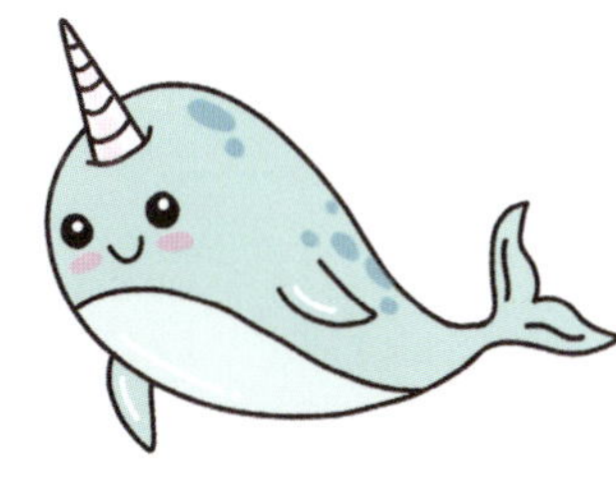

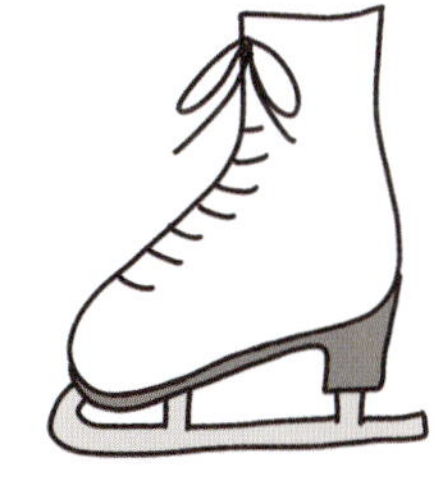

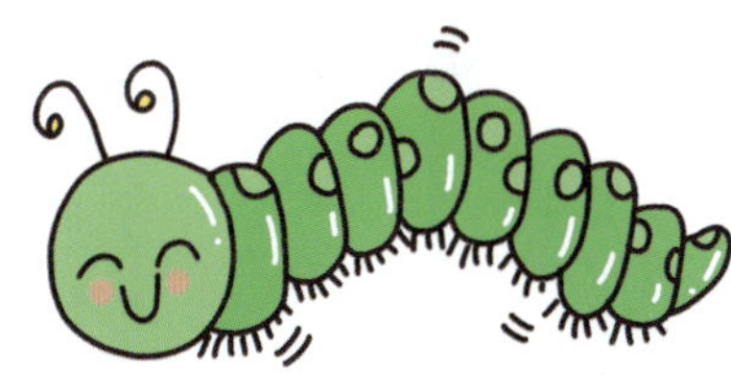

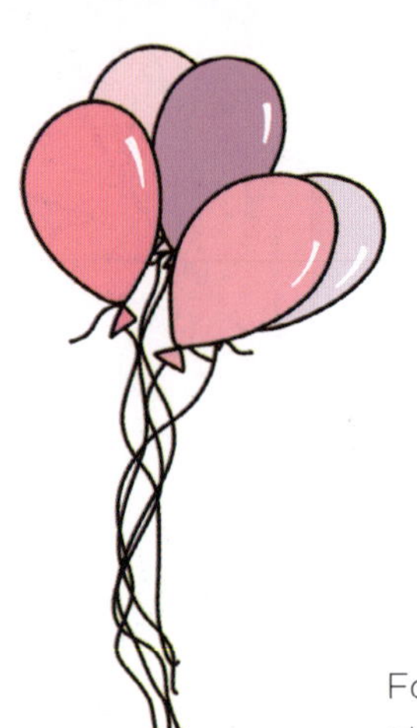

INTRODUCTION

For as long as I can remember, I have loved to doodle. If you were to look at my notebooks from elementary school all the way through college, you'd find pages filled with flowers, sketches of my teachers and all kinds of other images. Even now, I doodle while I talk on the phone or when I'm listening to a speaker. Since you picked up this book, I'm guessing you do too! So why is it that we enjoy the art of doodling? In part, I think it's relaxing, even therapeutic. Also, this kind of drawing can actually help us remember things, like when we're taking notes on a topic. Doodles can also be a great way to connect with others, such as when we draw a handmade card or gift tag or decorate an envelope.

Doodles are a fun and easy way to learn to draw as well. Maybe you'd like to dip your toes into the world of art and want to start drawing the things around you, but aren't sure where to start. This is the perfect place! These doodles show simple ways to draw all kinds of cute animals, plants and objects, and they'll get you started with a new hobby.

Whatever your reasons for doodling are, I hope you find this book to be a fun source of inspiration. Feel free to work through it from front to back—learning everything it has to offer, to pick and choose your favorite illustrations—or to search for specific topics as you need them for your projects. The drawings are separated into chapters based on where you might find them, such as At the Beach (page 31), In the Snow (page 64), Around Town (page 122) or At the Stadium (page 136), but some images could fit into more than one category. If you're looking for a particular doodle and can't find it right away, check out the full index in the back (page 187) and it will quickly guide you to the page(s) you need.

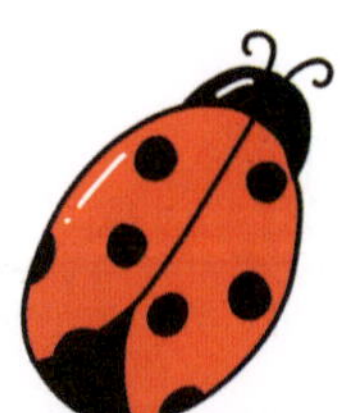

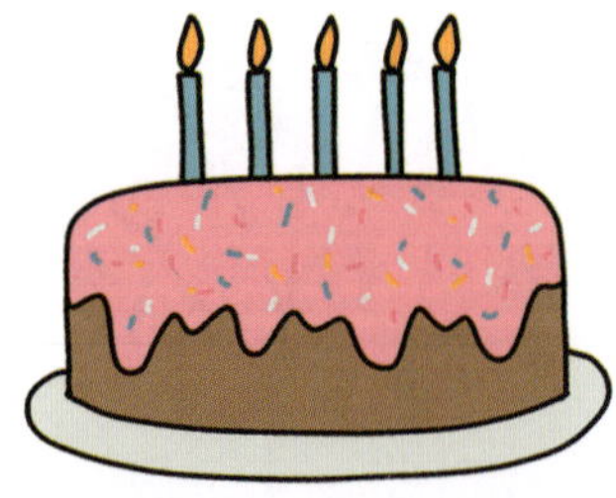

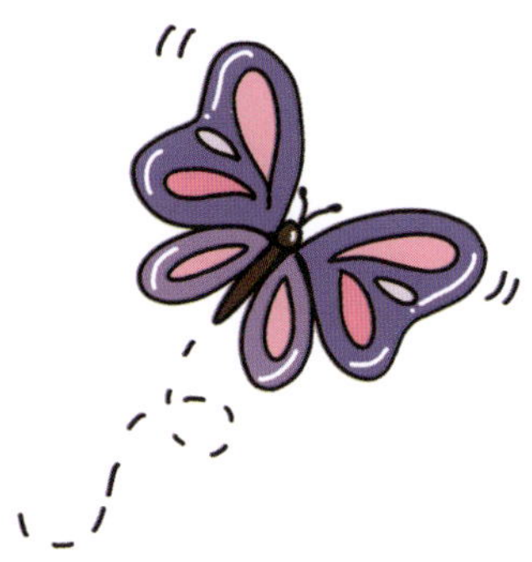

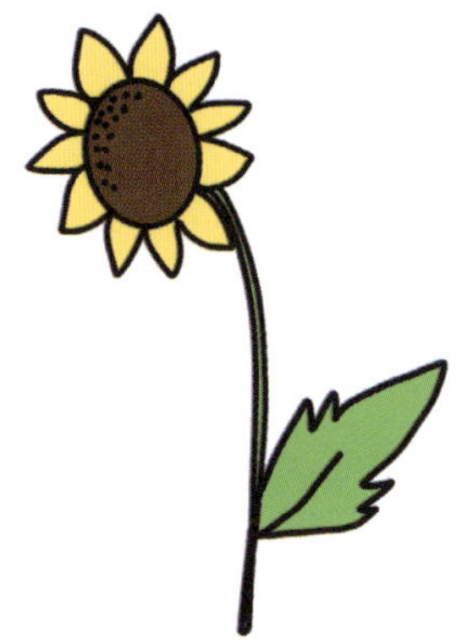

As we begin, I want to encourage you not to be intimidated by the look of a finished drawing or the idea of sketching a particular thing. The reality is that every image is made up of lines and simple shapes, and that's exactly how we are going to approach our doodles. Each one is broken down visually into a series of steps that will walk you through the process from start to finish. You can follow my steps exactly or put your own spin on an image, making it your unique creation.

I highly suggest sketching all of your doodles in pencil first while you're learning, then tracing over them with markers, pens or any other material of your choice. Not only will this allow you to fix any mistakes as you go, it will also give you the opportunity to erase unnecessary lines when one part of a doodle overlaps another.

Are you ready to get creative with me? Grab a pencil, a good eraser and your favorite markers, colored pencils or crayons and let's doodle everything!

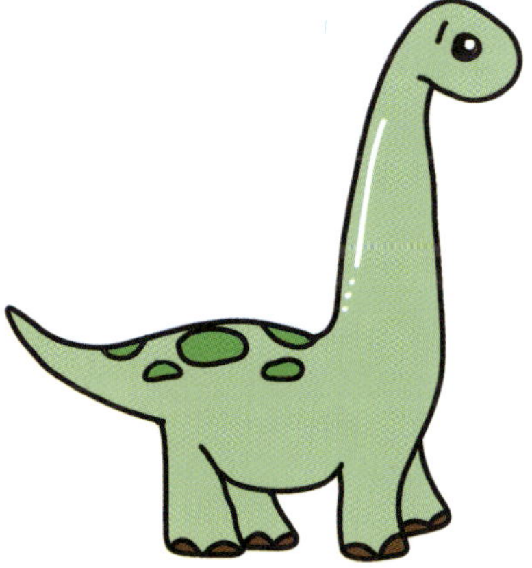

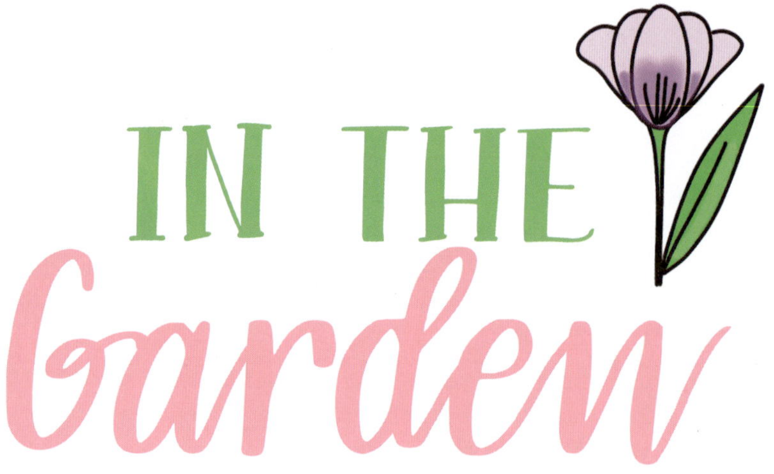

IN THE Garden

A garden is an artistic masterpiece, with each flower, plant, leaf and herb adding to its natural beauty. In fact, nature is so beautiful that we often bring it indoors to adorn our homes and even, at times, ourselves. Giving, receiving, carrying or wearing flowers often marks the milestone celebrations in our lives because the blooms add to the beauty of those moments. In the same way, we can use garden-inspired doodles in our artwork. They can adorn an envelope, decorate a card or enhance a hand-lettered quote. These natural doodles are never out of place, and no matter which ones you choose, they're sure to be a lovely addition.

FLOWERS, VINES & PRETTY BOTANICALS

SIMPLE LEAF

Many of the flowers and the vines we draw will incorporate leaves, so learning to draw these is a great place to start. The most basic leaf shape is similar to the shape of a teardrop: rounded on the bottom and pointed at the top. Add a stem and some color, and voilà, you have a leaf!

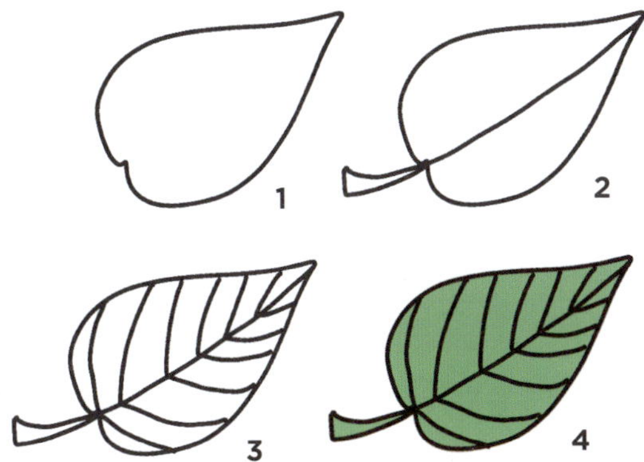

ROUNDED LEAF

For an easy variation on the basic leaf, simply draw an oval shape instead of a teardrop, then add a curving line for the stem. This gives the effect of coming from a different kind of plant or tree than the first type of leaf.

1 2 3

OAK LEAF

To draw an oak leaf, start with a slightly curving line for the stem, then draw several "V" shapes going down the line. These will be the veins. Next, draw a loose outline of the shape made by those veins. I like coloring this style of leaf in bold fall shades.

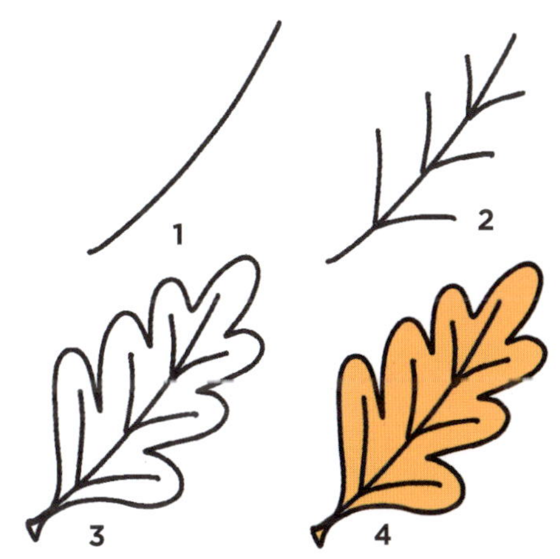

DETAILED LEAF

If you want a leaf that looks more complex, try this variation. Start with a slightly curving line for the stem, then draw a rounded diamond shape at the top. Next, draw a semicircle under the diamond and connect it to the diamond on both sides. Continue drawing semicircles going down the stem at regular intervals and connect each one to the semicircle above it. Add some color to finish your sketch.

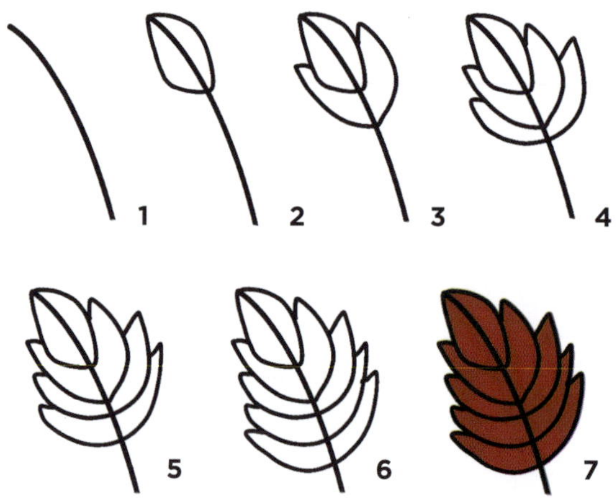

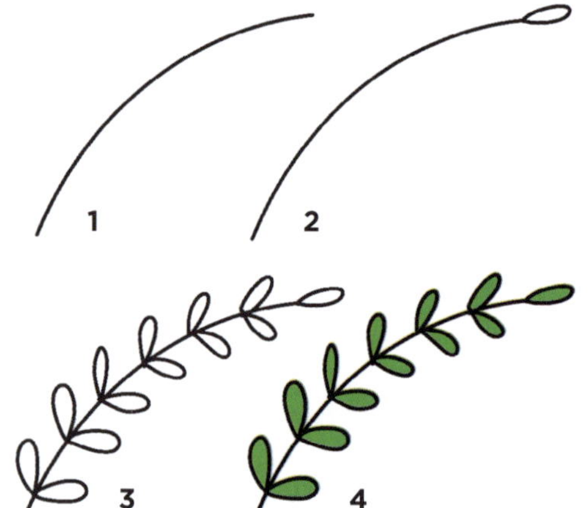

SIMPLE VINE

A leafy vine is a great accent to any design. In fact, it's one of the most common embellishments I use when I'm making a hand-lettered project. Not only is it pretty as a stand-alone doodle, it also creates a wonderful border. To draw a simple one, start with a curving line, then add a teardrop shape to one end. Continue down the line, adding teardrop-shaped leaves, then color them in.

POINTED LEAF VINE

To create a variation on the simple vine, we can change the leaf shape. Instead of rounded leaves, this time let's draw them with points on the ends. Another way to change things up is to alternate the position of the leaves along the stem.

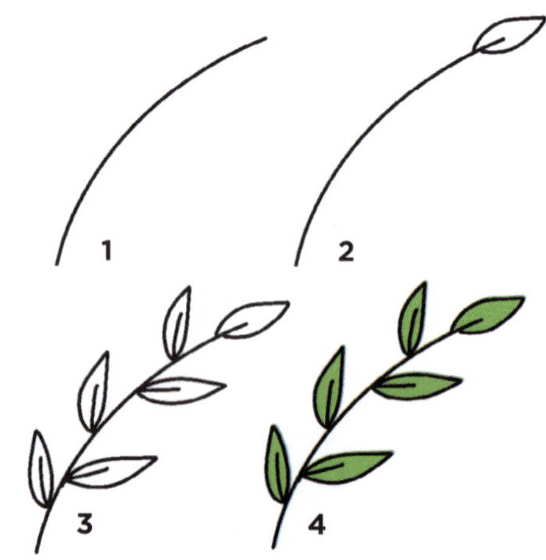

BRANCH

A branch starts with a series of lines. Start with a long line for the main branch, then sketch a few shorter lines coming off it. Then, add even shorter lines on each of those secondary branches. Finally, add leaf shapes at the end of each line and anywhere else along the branch you like.

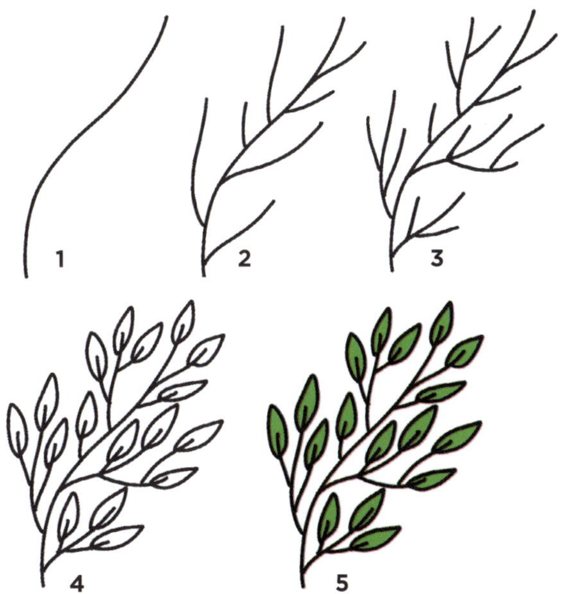

ROSEBUD

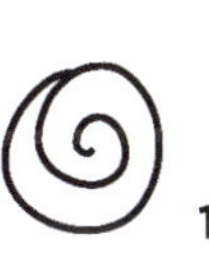

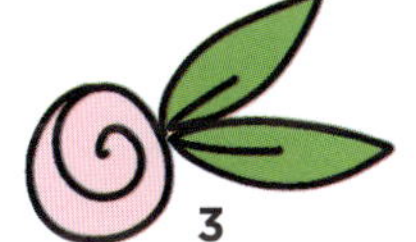

The simplest flower to doodle is a sweet little rosebud. It's nothing more than a spiral! Color it in, add a couple leaves, and voilà, you have a tiny flower.

LARGE SIMPLE FLOWER

Drawing a large flower can be as simple as sketching a circle! Start with a circular shape, then trace over it several more times, allowing your lines to overlap one another. Then, add dots to the flower's center. Add some leaves on opposite sides (an odd number like three helps it look more natural and visually balanced). Coloring the center and the outside edges a darker shade than the rest of the flower helps add dimension.

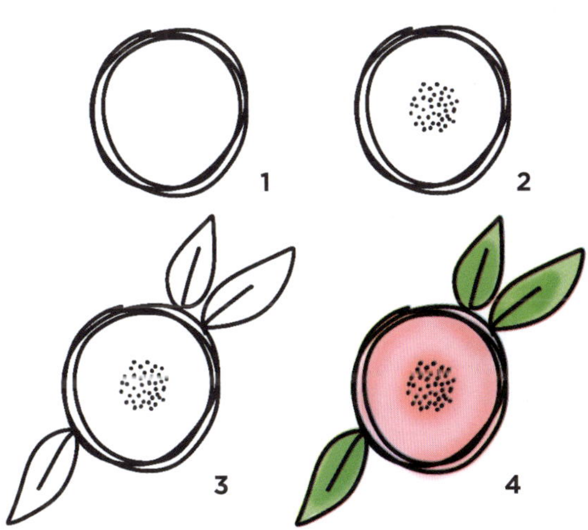

SMALL ACCENT FLOWER

A tiny petaled flower is as easy to draw as one-two-three. Without picking up your pen, make three upside-down teardrop shapes right next to each other. Let the center one be slightly larger than the others to provide a focal point. Then, draw a short detail line inside the bottom of each petal.

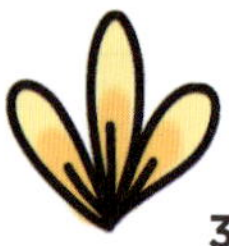

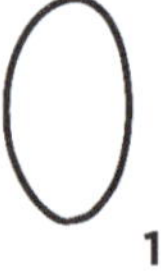

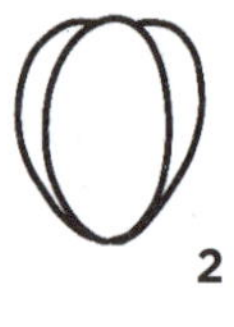

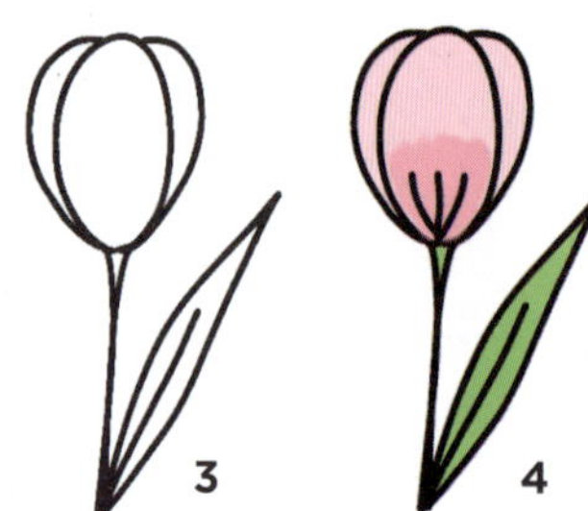

FLOWER BUD

To draw this cute little bud, start with an oval, then make shapes similar to parentheses on the sides. Adding color, detail lines and a stem gives it the perfect finishing touches. These buds can stand alone or as part of a vine or cluster of flowers.

OPENING BUD

One way to add variation to your floral drawings is to incorporate buds that are in various stages of opening. For example, by taking the simple flower bud doodle and adding one extra petal on each side, we get the illusion of a flower that's just about to be fully opened.

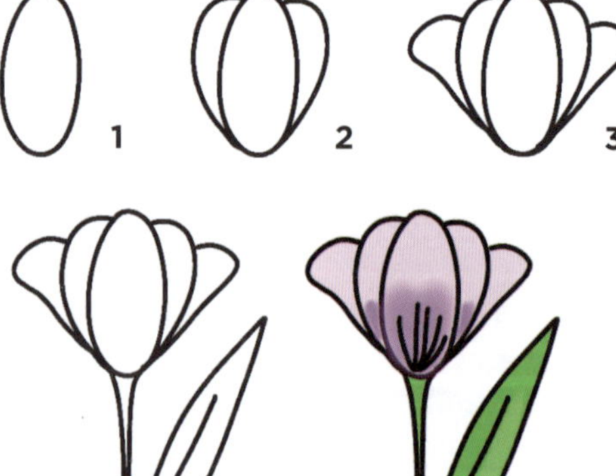

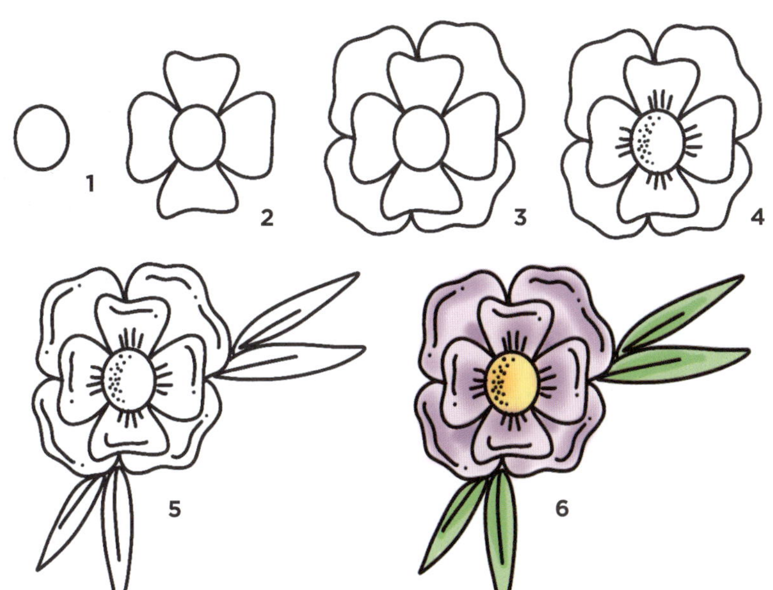

PETALED FLOWER

Simple shapes and lines make up this pretty petaled flower. Start with a circle in the center, then add four petals. Draw a second row of petals and finish it off with some detail lines and dots. Feel free to sketch some leaves to go with the flower, or even to group a few of these together, along with some buds.

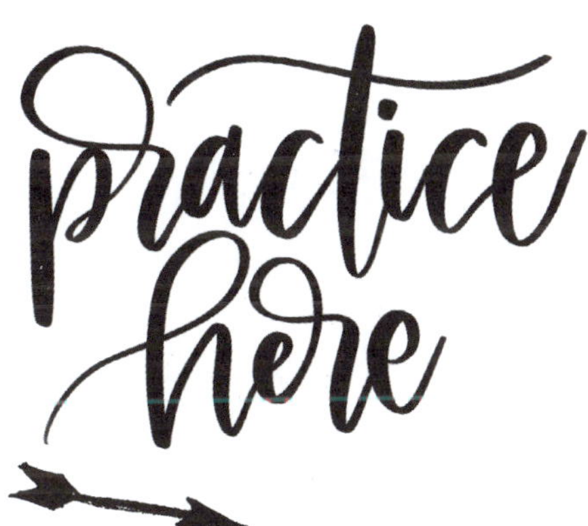

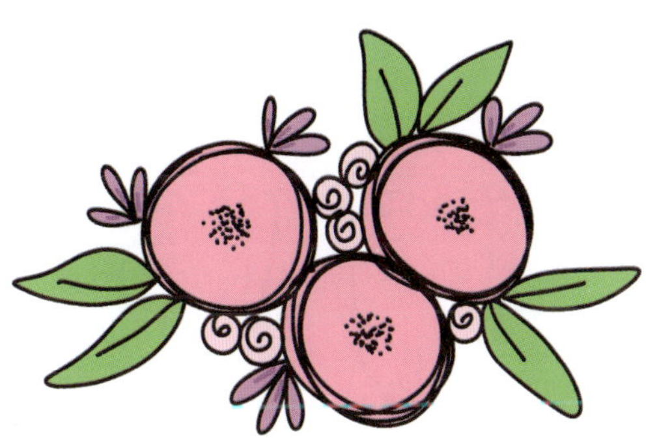

SIMPLE TULIP

Sketch an easy tulip by drawing a "U" shape and adding a "W" shape across the top. Add a stem with a leaf or two coming from the base of the shape. Then, add three short lines with dots on the end coming out from the top of the flower, along with a few detail lines inside the shape itself.

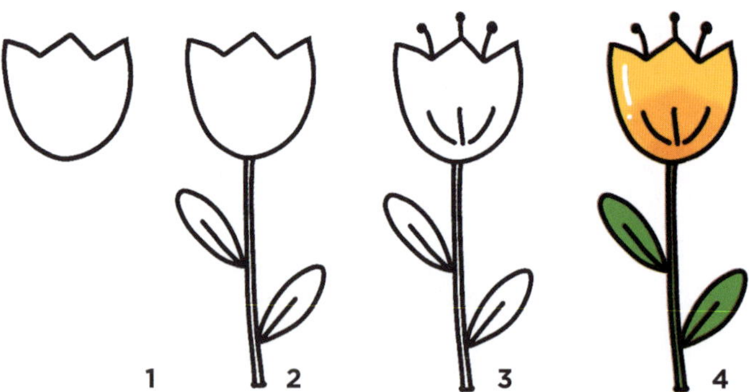

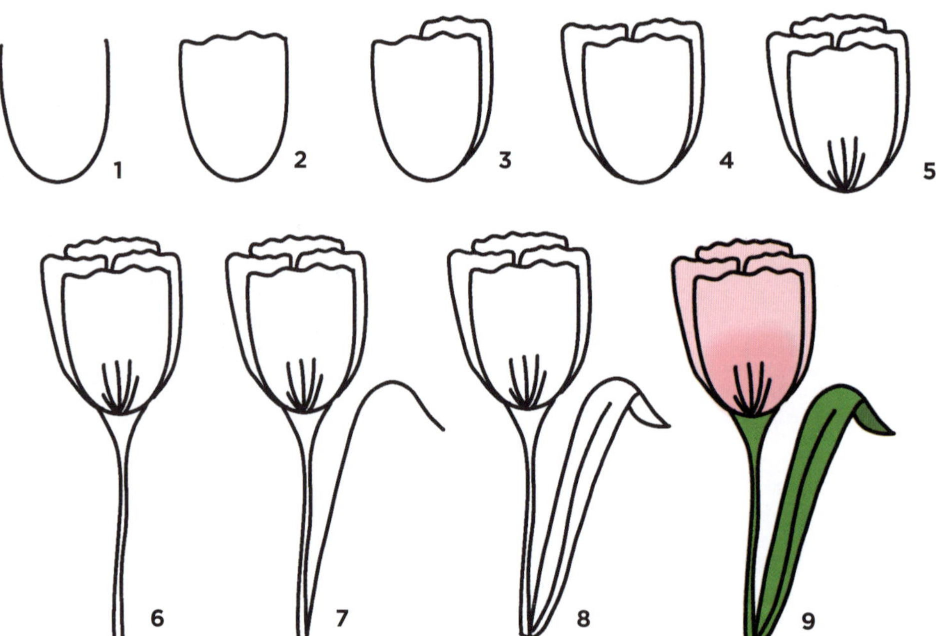

DETAILED TULIP

This more detailed variation on the tulip starts with a "U" shape that has a wavy line across the top. Next, draw two short wavy lines behind it and connect each one to the side of the "U." Finally, draw a fourth petal in the back. Add a stem, a leaf and detail lines for more complexity.

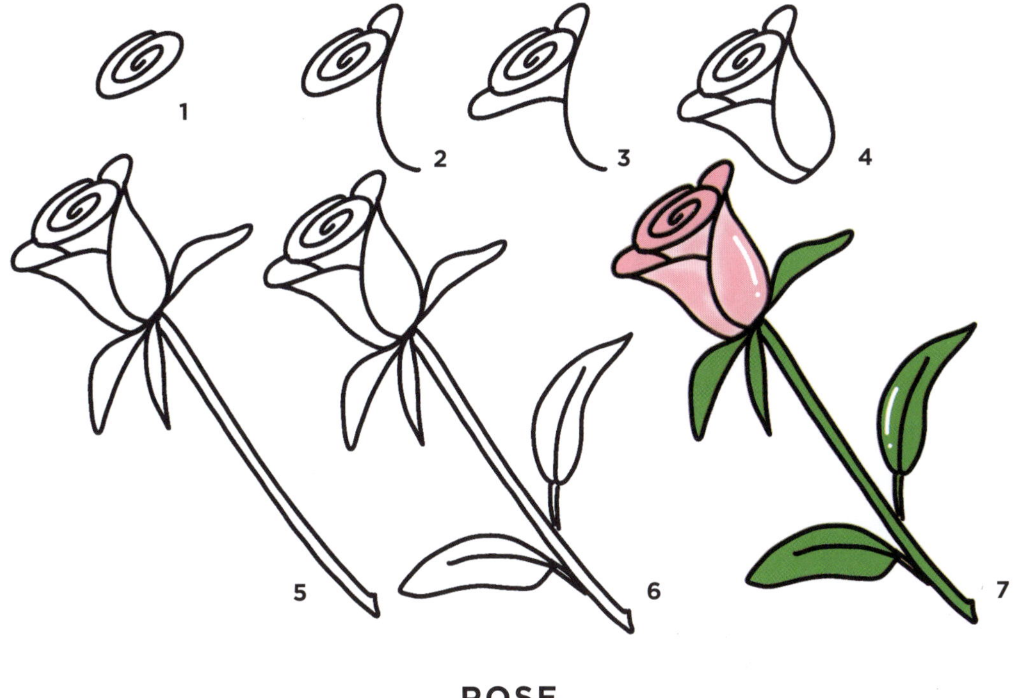

ROSE

We learned that a simple rosebud is just a spiral; now, we're going to build on that to create a budding long-stem rose. Draw your spiral to start, then add curving lines coming down from each side to create petals that are beginning to open. A "U" shape forms the base of the bud, then add a stem and a few leaves.

LILY OF THE VALLEY

Another fun floral element to sketch is a lily of the valley. This type of flower begins with an upside-down "J" shape. Draw several small upside-down "U" shapes for the bell-shaped flowers and finish them off with wavy lines and stamens. A leaf and some colors are all you need to complete this pretty little drawing.

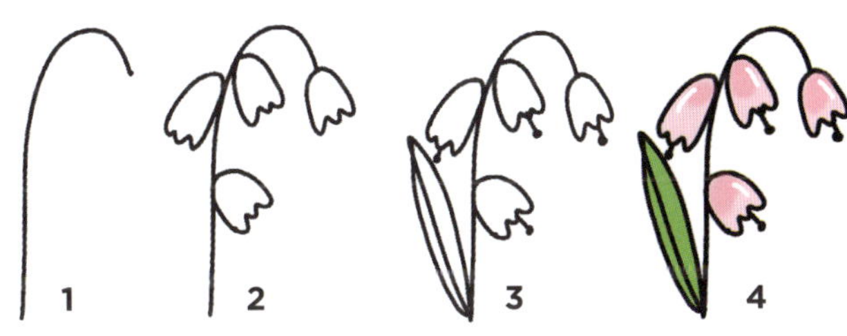

WISHER DANDELION

Who doesn't love making a wish while blowing on one of these fuzzy weeds? Sketching a wisher is easy; just draw a stem, then create an open-circle shape by making a series of short lines all around the outside edge. Draw a few more short lines inside, as well as a leaf and a stem, and you'll be ready to make a wish!

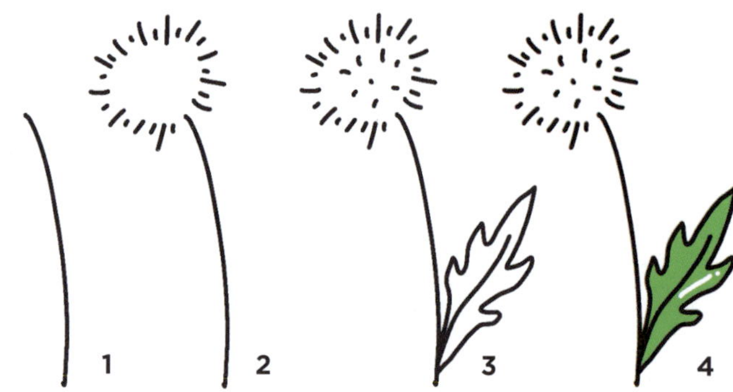

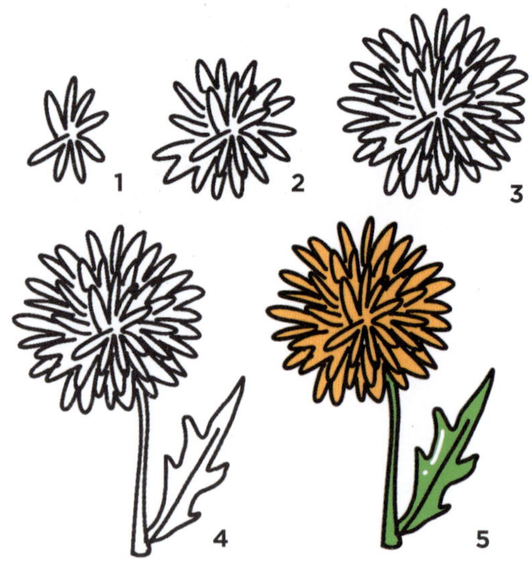

DANDELION

It may be a weed, but a dandelion is such a cheerful little bloom! To draw one, you'll start with a grouping of petals for the center, followed by a second and a third layer. The petals are just continuous lines that form long thin bumps. Add a stem—and a leaf if you like—then give it that bright yellow color!

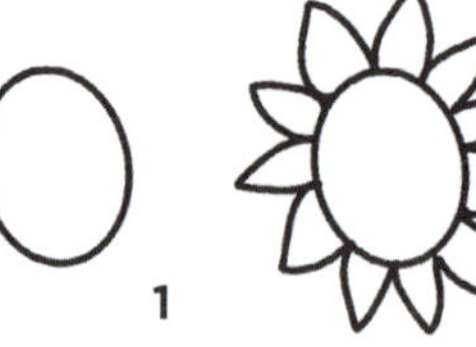

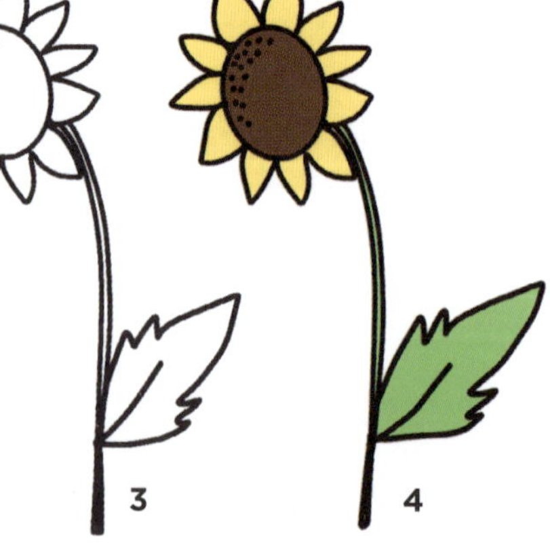

SUNFLOWER

The focal point of a sunflower is its enormous center, so the first thing you'll draw is a large circle/oval shape. Next, sketch a series of petals all around it. Sunflowers also have long stems that curve slightly downward as they reach the head of the flower, so you'll want to make sure yours does too. Finally, add a leaf if you like, then color it in with those iconic sunflower shades.

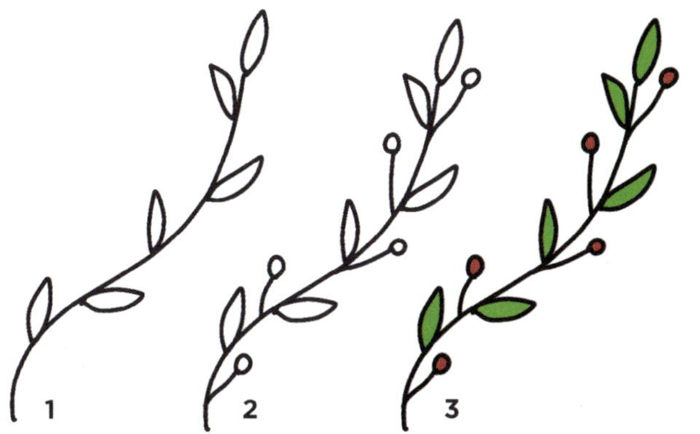

BERRY VINE

Another type of leafy embellishment I often use is a vine with berries. Like other vines, this one starts with a waving or curving line for the stem. Then, you'll draw leaves on each side, as well as short lines with circles on top to represent the berries. Color the leaves green, and the berries any shade you like.

BERRY BRANCH

Berries are a simple, colorful embellishment to draw. First, make a vertical line for the center branch, then draw short lines coming off it in both directions. Add a few more short lines coming off those secondary branches. Finally, draw a circle at the end of each line. It's okay to slightly vary the sizes and colors of the circles because real berries aren't identical. For detail, draw a small filled-in oval near the top of each berry.

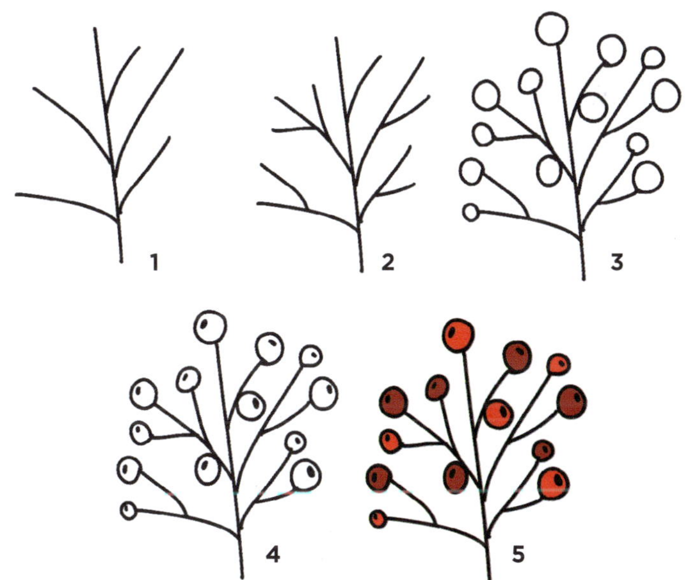

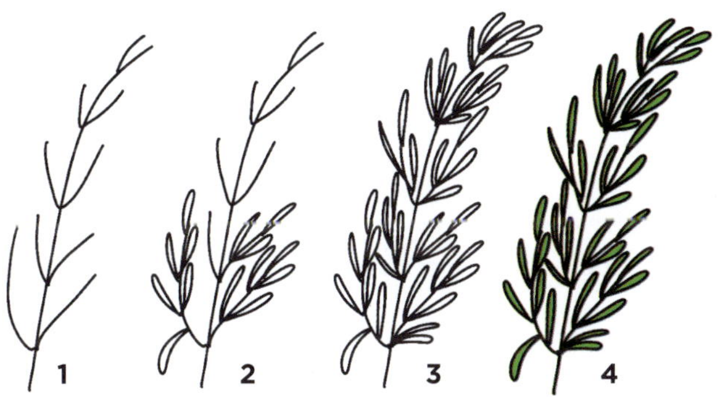

ROSEMARY

I love growing herbs in my garden, and I enjoy drawing them almost as much. Rosemary is such a fragrant plant with a distinctive appearance. Start with a line for the main stem and some "V" shapes along that stem for the branches. Then, add long thin teardrop shapes all over each branch.

BASIL

Drawing basil is mostly overlapping a bunch of leaf shapes. Start with two large fat leaves pointing in opposite directions and connected at the bottoms. Add a third large leaf, then two smaller ones in the center. You can also add another tiny leaf at the bottom. Erase the extra lines where your leaves overlap, then sketch veins inside each leaf. Can't you almost smell the basil?

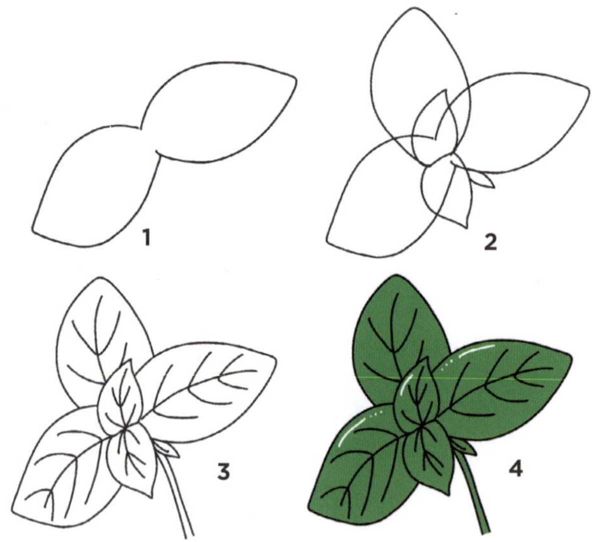

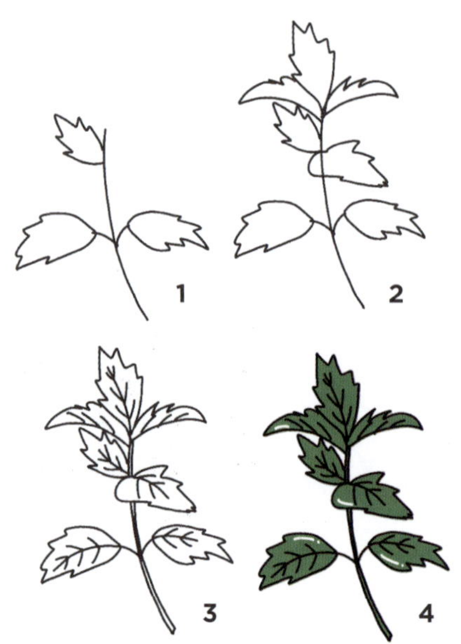

MINT

To sketch a sprig of mint, start with a curving stem and a few leaves. Mint leaves are wider at the bottom than the top and have rough edges. Add a few more leaves going down the stem. The leaves usually appear in groups of two across the stem from each other. Draw veins in the leaves for extra detail, then add color.

SAGE

Sage leaves are large and flat with a slightly rounded point on the end. After sketching a curving stem, draw a series of leaves in this shape, each with one line running through the center. Then, color in the leaves with a light gray-green.

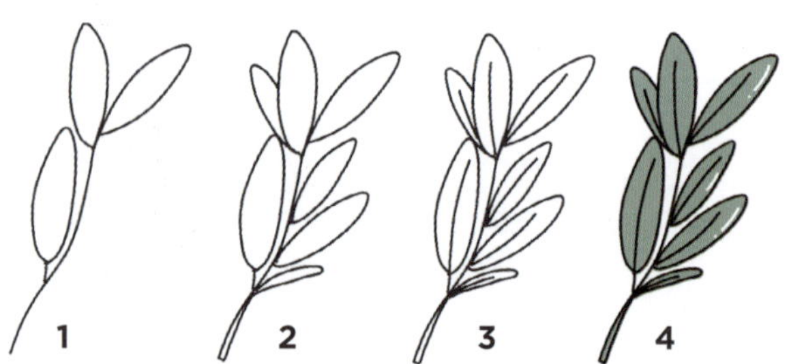

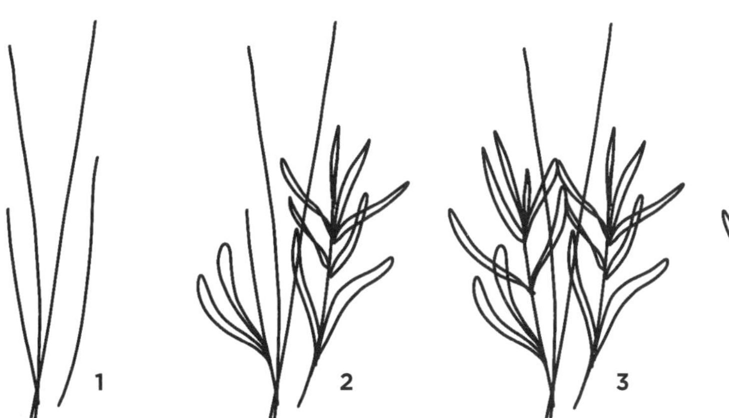

LAVENDER

To sketch lavender, start with four vertical lines; the two center ones should be taller than the others. Starting at the bottom of the two outside lines, work your way up each one, drawing long thin teardrop shapes that curve and wave in different directions. Erase any of the overlapping lines, then add tiny teardrop shapes at the tops of the taller lines for the blooms. Don't forget to color in your design with lavender's namesake shade!

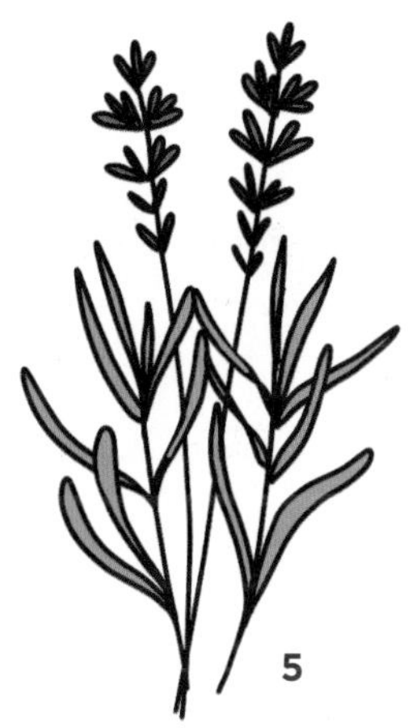

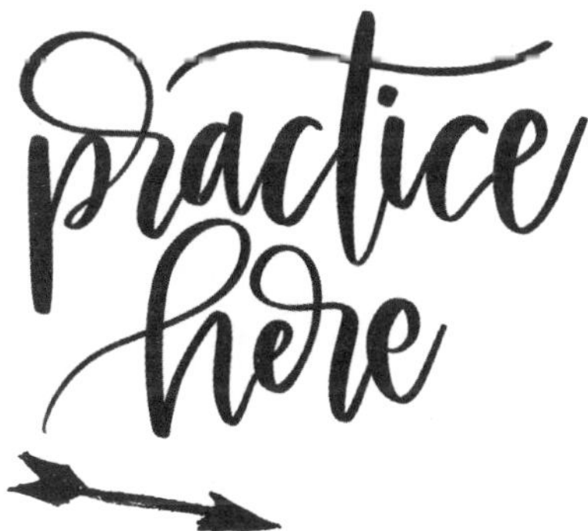

GARDEN TOOLS

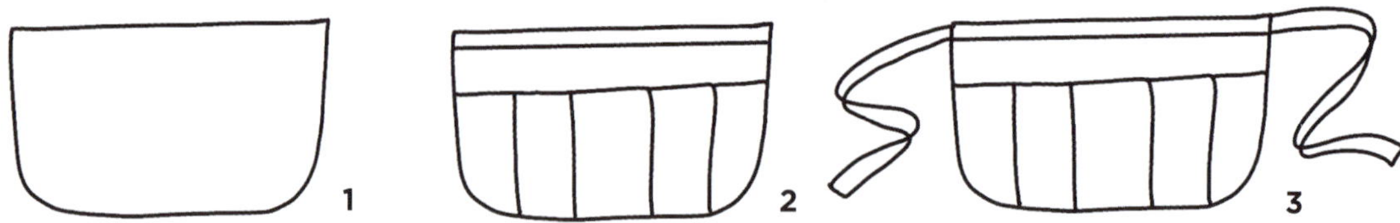

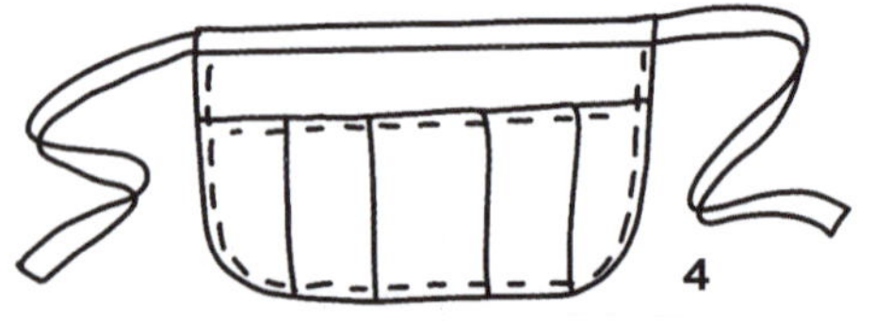

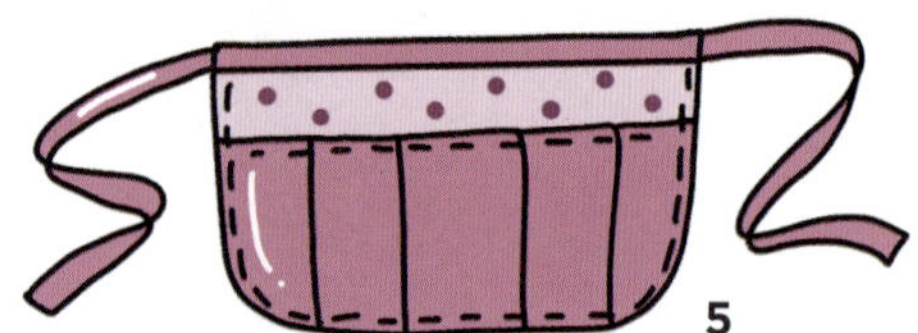

GARDEN APRON

A gardening apron not only protects your clothing, it's a great way to keep your tools within arm's reach. To draw this one, start with a rectangular shape that has rounded edges on the bottom. Then, divide it up with pockets. Add ties on the sides and a dashed line around the basic shape to represent the stitching. After you learn to draw the tools, feel free to add a few inside the pockets!

GARDEN GLOVES

Start by sketching four long thin "U" shapes for the fingers of the left glove. Then, repeat the same shapes for the right glove. I like to put the right one on a diagonal so that it crosses over the left one. Next, add upside-down "U" shapes for the thumbs and a cuff for the glove on the right. Little details like short lines to represent ribbing and stitching add character to the illustration.

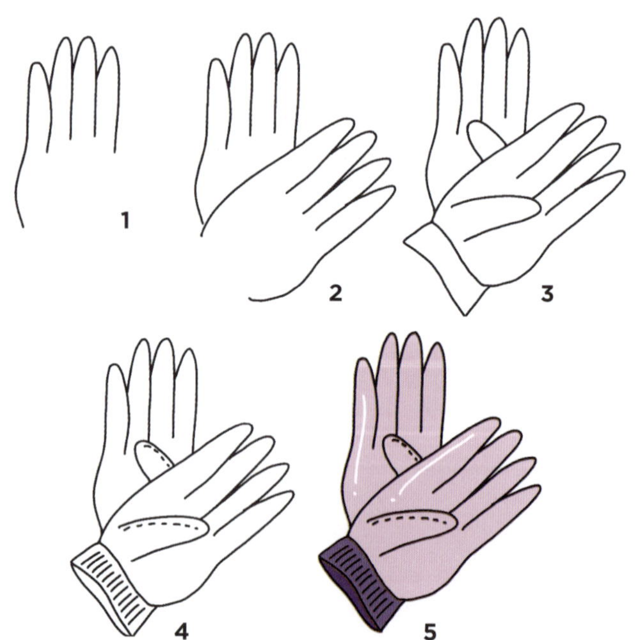

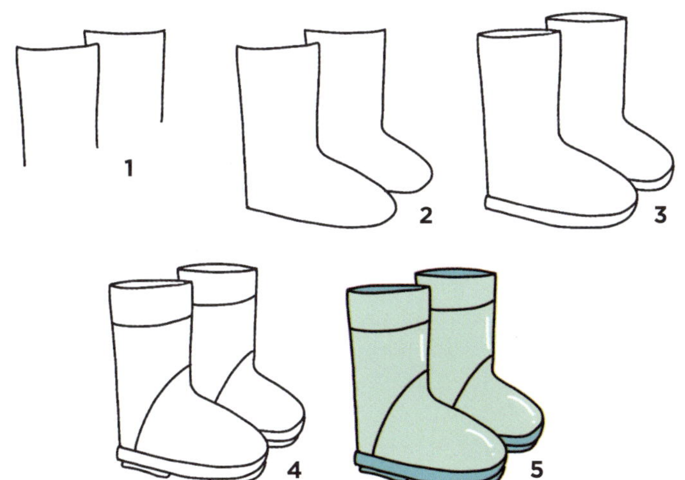

BOOTS

Sketching garden boots is easier than it seems. First, draw two rectangle shapes that are open on the bottom; the left one should be slightly lower and in front of the one on the right. Next, use sideways "U" shapes at the bottom to create the bottom of the boots. Add curving lines at the bottom and the top, as well as inside the boot shapes for depth and detail, and you're done! See? Easy peasy.

WATERING CAN

When drawing a watering can, you'll want to start with the lines for the sides and the bottom. Let the sides come together a little closer at the top than at the bottom. Add an oval with a line through it for the top of the can, then draw the spout: two lines with a semicircle on top. Personalize your drawing by decorating the can any way you like and adding a few drops of water coming from the spout.

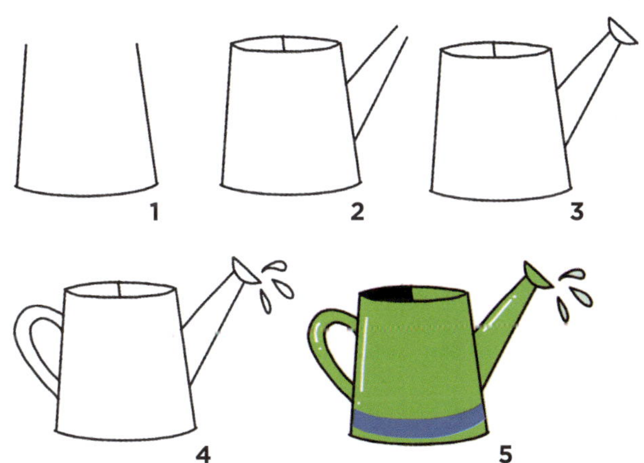

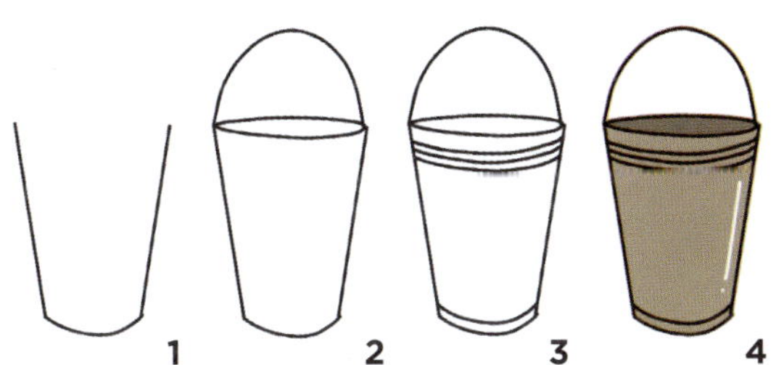

BUCKET

Sketch two vertical lines that are closer together at the bottom than the top. Connect them at the bottom with a slightly curving line, then draw an oval for the top. Add a handle and a few stripes across the surface of the bucket for texture.

FLOWERPOT

The basic flowerpot shape is just like the bucket: two vertical lines joined by a curving line at the bottom. This time, though, you'll add a rim to the pot—a slightly curved rectangle. Finish the drawing with a semicircle on top to add depth to the opening of the pot.

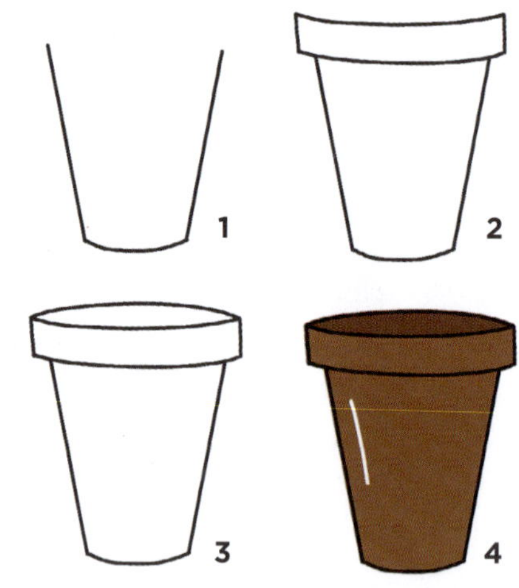

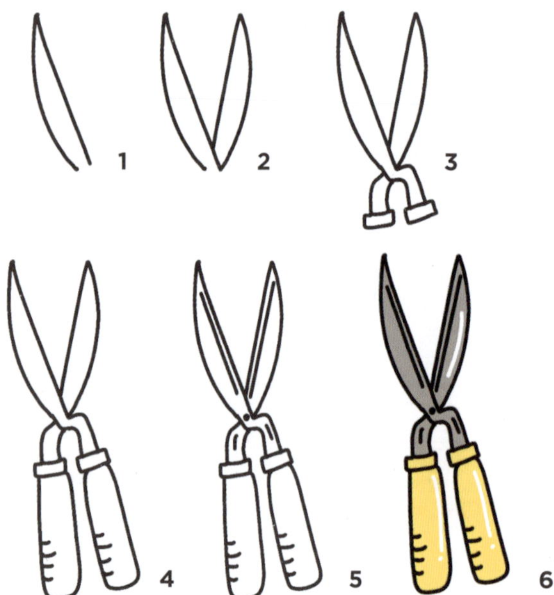

GARDEN CLIPPERS

The best way to begin drawing clippers is with the blades. I like to start with the left side, then draw the one on the right slightly behind it. Where the blade bases meet, form an upside-down "U" shape to finish off the metal section. Then, add a handle below each blade by drawing a small rectangle with a larger rounded rectangle attached.

TROWEL

A trowel is just a combination of some basic shapes: a slightly rounded triangle for the blade, then two rectangular shapes for the handle. Add a few detail lines and some color, and you have a cute little trowel to plant your doodle garden!

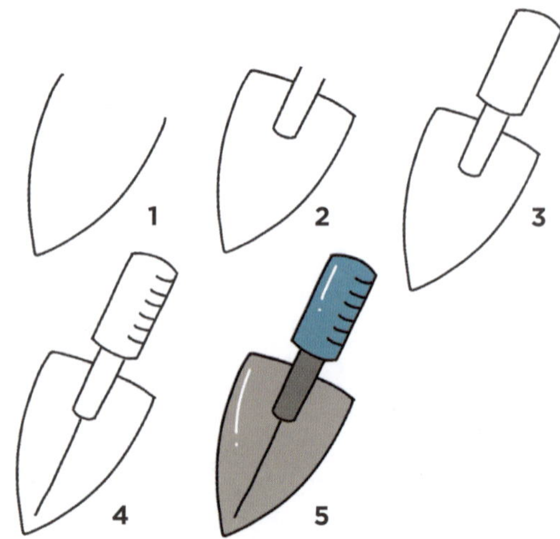

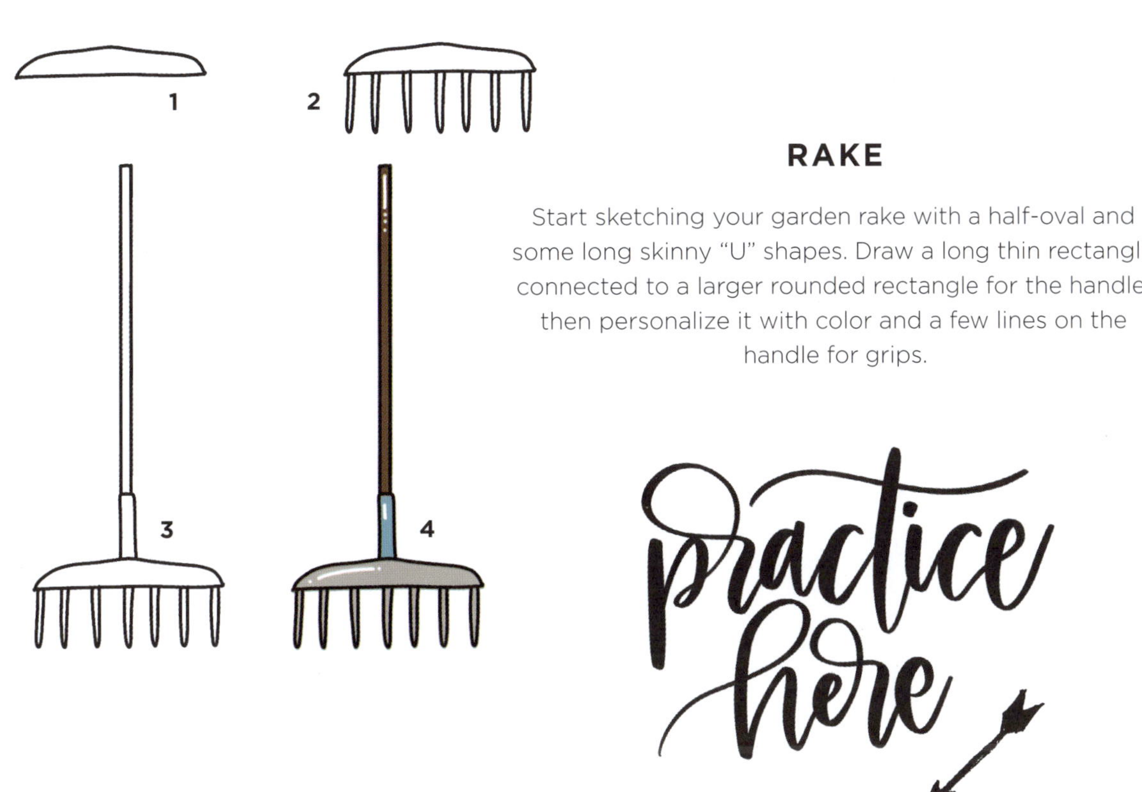

RAKE

Start sketching your garden rake with a half-oval and some long skinny "U" shapes. Draw a long thin rectangle connected to a larger rounded rectangle for the handle, then personalize it with color and a few lines on the handle for grips.

HOE

The blade of a hoe is a basic trapezoid, so we'll start with that! Next, draw a few curving lines—one that's just above the blade and then one that's shaped a lot like a question mark. Add a long rectangle for the handle. Finally, add some detail lines and a small round hole to the handle to finish off this garden tool.

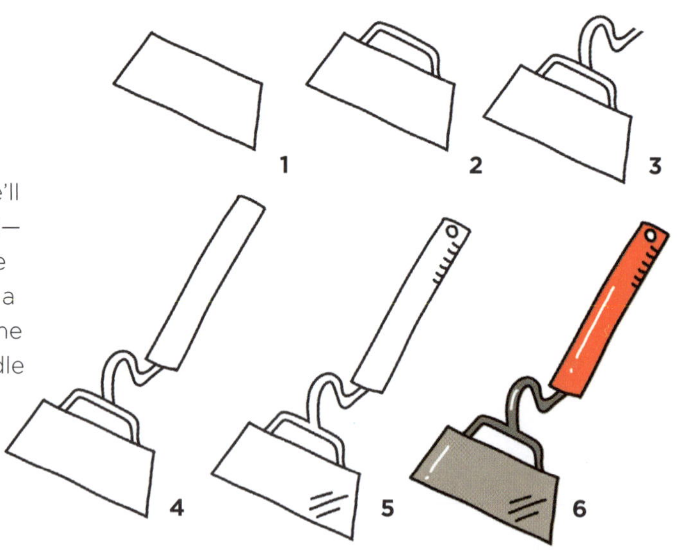

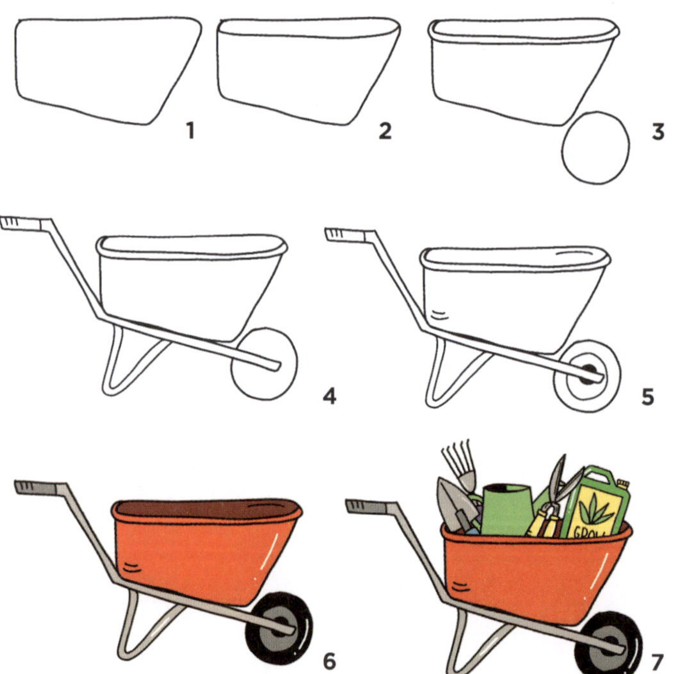

WHEELBARROW

The first step is creating the shape of the bed. Then, add some curving lines to create the rim and show depth. Next, draw a wheel in front, then connect it to the bed by sketching the frame and handle. Feel free to fill your wheelbarrow with other drawings, like tools, leaves or anything else you like.

FERTILIZER

Fertilizer containers are really simple to draw, so the details are what will help your sketch stand out. Start with a rectangular "U" shape, then add a line across the top for the top of the container and the handle. Sketch a cap, a label and a small shape to show where the opening of the handle is. Finish your sketch by decorating the label with any type of plant and/or words that you like!

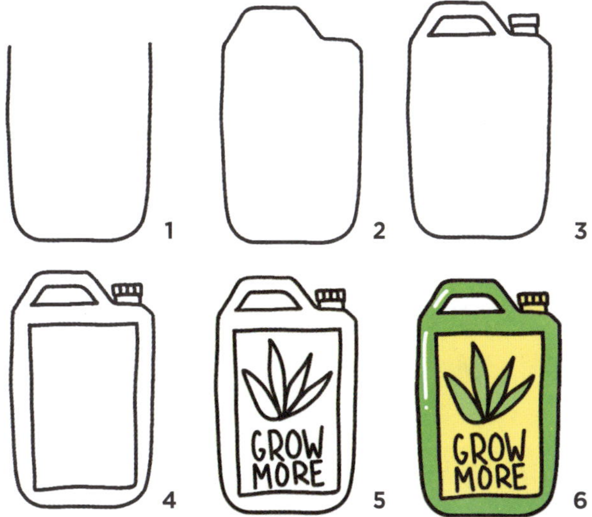

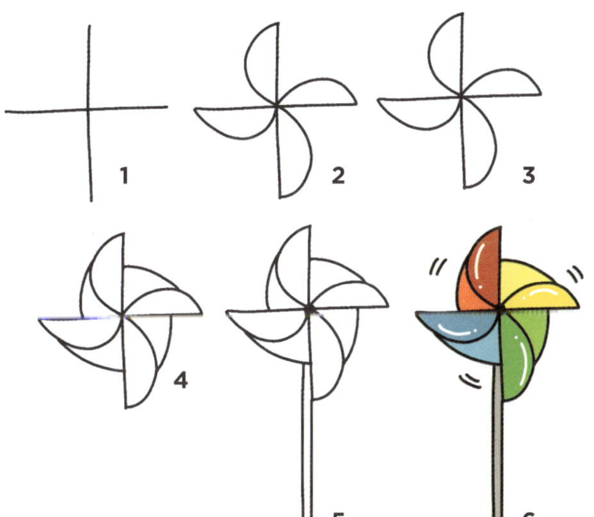

PINWHEEL

This pinwheel begins as four semicircles, each facing a different direction and with the ends meeting in the middle. Draw curving lines to connect each semicircle to the one next to it, then add a stick. To show that your pinwheel is rotating, just sketch a few sets of short curving lines around the outside.

BUGS & GARDEN CRITTERS

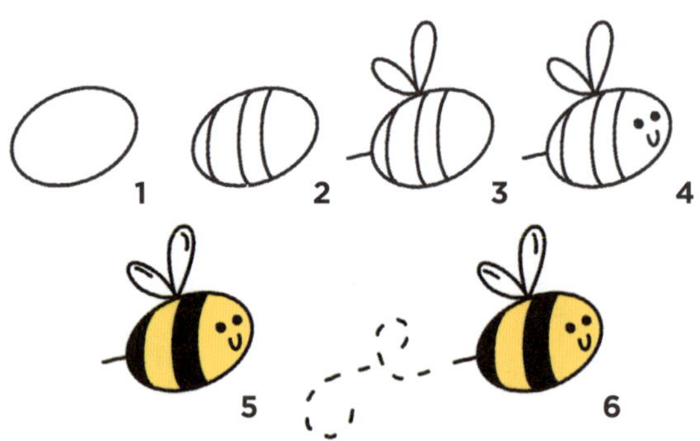

CUTE BEE

Drawing a bee begins with an oval for the body, then some curving lines inside for the stripes. Next, add two teardrop-shaped wings and a short line to represent a stinger. Eyes and a smile, along with that classic black-and-yellow color scheme, finish off the illustration. To make it look like your bee is in flight, draw a dashed line from behind the stinger to anywhere on the page.

WORM

Yes, earthworms can actually be cute! Draw this one by making a squiggly line, then sketching a second matching squiggle below it to form the body. Divide the body into sections with short lines. Don't forget to give your worm some personality by adding a happy little face! A few small lines give the idea that your earthworm is wiggling!

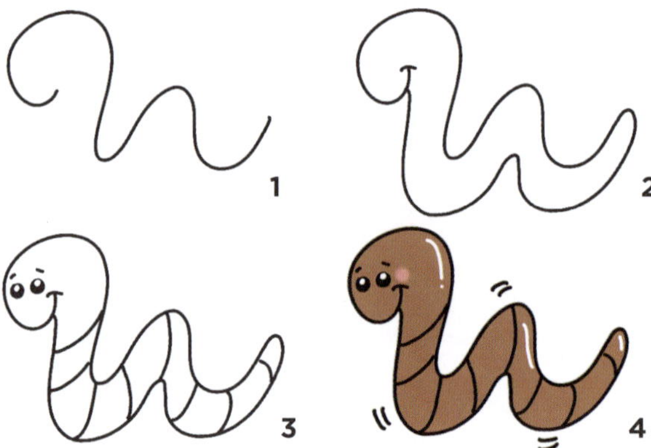

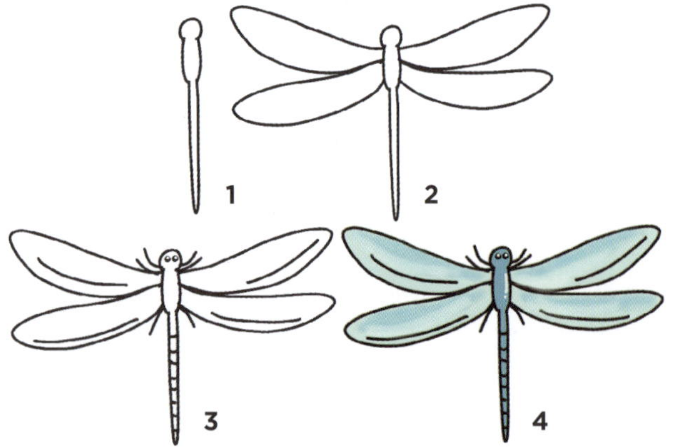

DRAGONFLY

Start with the dragonfly's long thin body in the center. Then, draw two wings on each side of the upper section of the body. Add details—like legs, eyes and lines—on the wings and the lower body, then use any colors you like to bring your drawing to life.

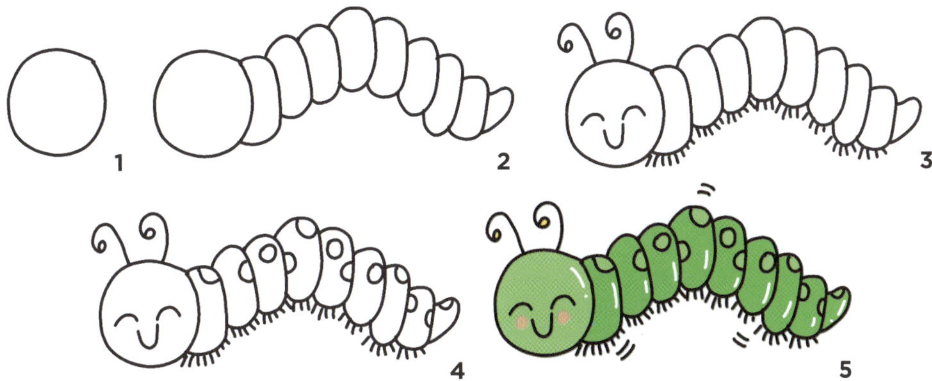

CATERPILLAR

A caterpillar is really fun to draw! We'll start with its big round head. Then, draw a series of oval shapes, each connecting to the one before it to form the body. Let your shapes drift higher and then lower to give the appearance that the caterpillar is in motion. Finally, add legs, a face and antennae. You can also add fun details like polka dots on the body to give your caterpillar some pizzazz, then color the caterpillar in. If you like, add in a few short lines to show your caterpillar in motion.

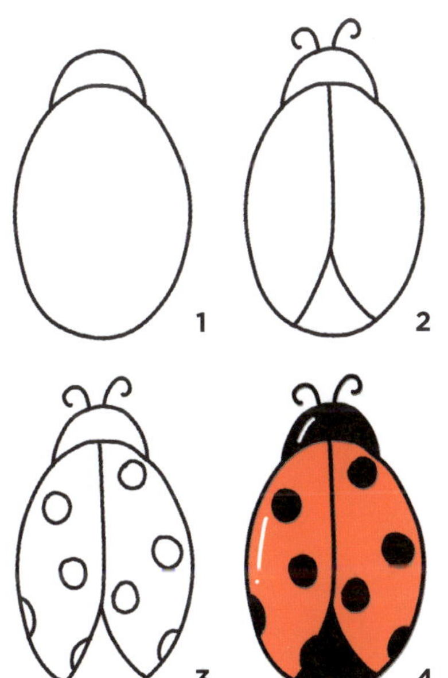

LADYBUG

Ladybugs are close to my heart, as they're a symbol used in the adoption community. The year we were in the process of adopting our son, Nathan, I had countless ladybugs land on me and appear in our garden. To draw this special insect, sketch an oval for the body and a semicircle for the head. Divide the body in half using long, curved lines to show the wings, add the distinctive spots and, of course, color it red and black.

BUTTERFLY

There are many ways to draw a butterfly and many types of butterflies in nature. For this one, we'll start by drawing two sideways heart shapes for the upper wings, then add two teardrop shapes for the lower wings. Add a body with antennae in between the wings, then play around with drawing a variety of shapes inside each wing. There's no wrong way to decorate the wings! Try lots of different designs and you'll create a bunch of beautiful and unique butterflies.

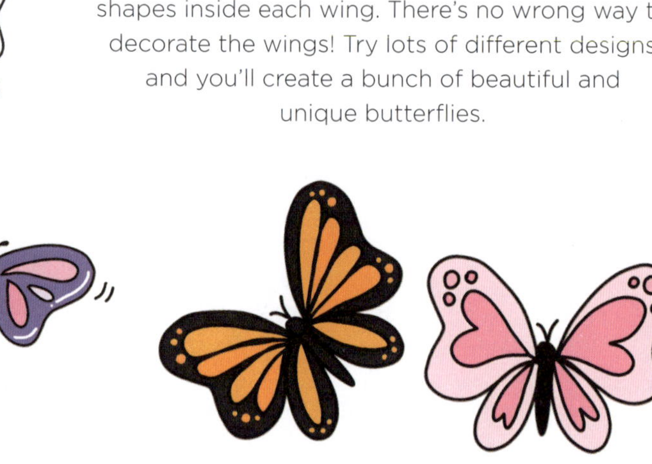

SNAIL

It's quite easy to doodle a snail; the body is a curving teardrop shape and the shell is a simple spiral. The fun comes when you add a cute face to give it some character. And don't forget those classic "V"-shaped antennae! There are lots of different shapes and colors of snail shells, as well as patterns on the shell itself, so feel free to get creative.

NOTE: If you're looking for a spider and web, which often appear in gardens, check out page 87 in the Halloween section of the At the Holidays chapter!

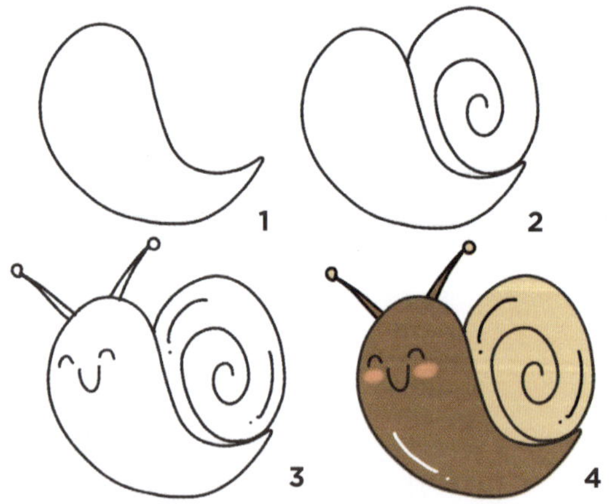

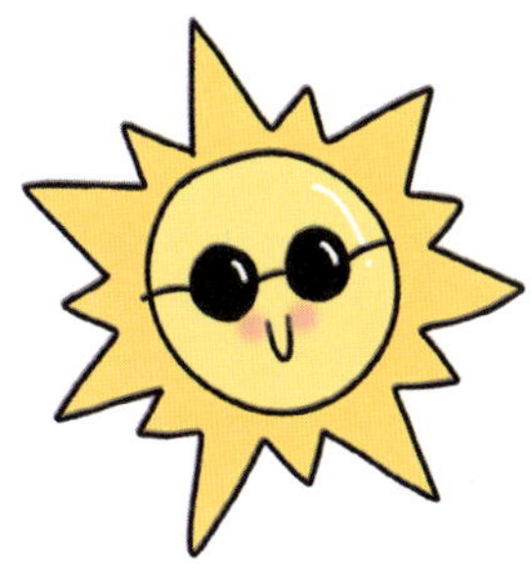

AT THE *Beach*

For many of us, summer means a vacation to the beach. Not only can we doodle the basics, like waves and palm trees, we can also draw summertime essentials like flip-flops, beach towels, sand buckets and even some treats like lemonade and ice cream. We'll also go over how to draw some of the cutest sea creatures you can imagine! These whimsical doodles are perfect for all kinds of summer-themed projects and will be a hit with anyone who enjoys spending time with their toes in the sand.

IN THE SAND

SANDCASTLE

One of the best things about sand is using it to create a castle! Draw your own by sketching a center section with a scalloped top, a door and rounded bottoms on either side of the door to give the building dimension. Then, add a tower on each side slightly behind the main building. Finish up by drawing one more tall tower in the back, then adding details like windows and a flag on top. Add some tiny dots all around to give the illusion of little grains of sand.

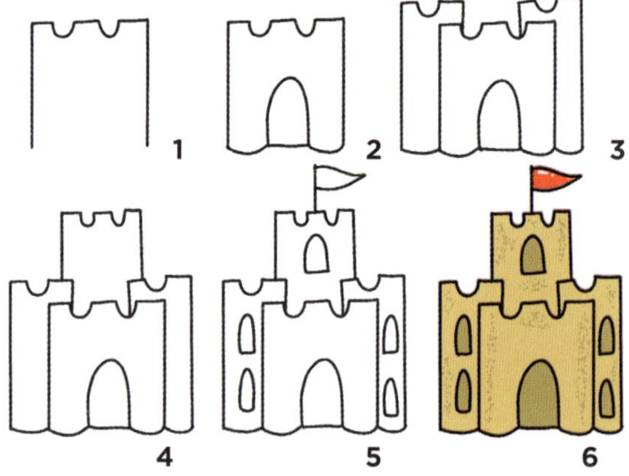

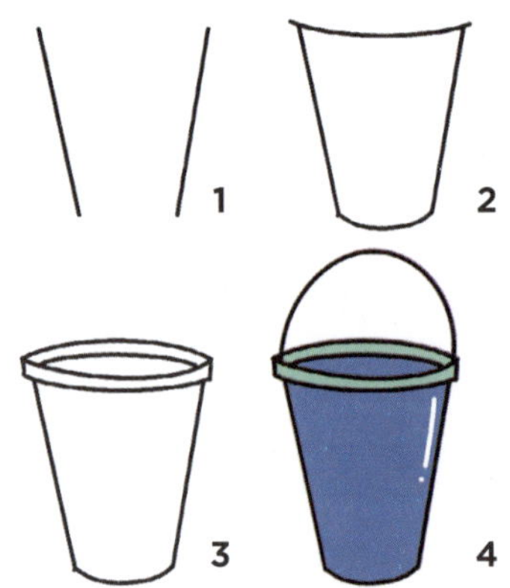

SIMPLE SAND BUCKET

Every child at the beach needs a sand bucket, so it's a perfect summer drawing. This one is made up of just two diagonal lines connected by curving lines at the top and bottom. Add a rim, a handle and some color and your doodle is complete.

SHOVEL

A sand bucket isn't much use without a shovel, so let's doodle one of those too! Start with a boxy upside-down "U" shape. Add a handle on top and a horizontal line on the bottom. Draw some detail lines, then use your favorite markers, colored pencils or crayons to make it a fun bright color.

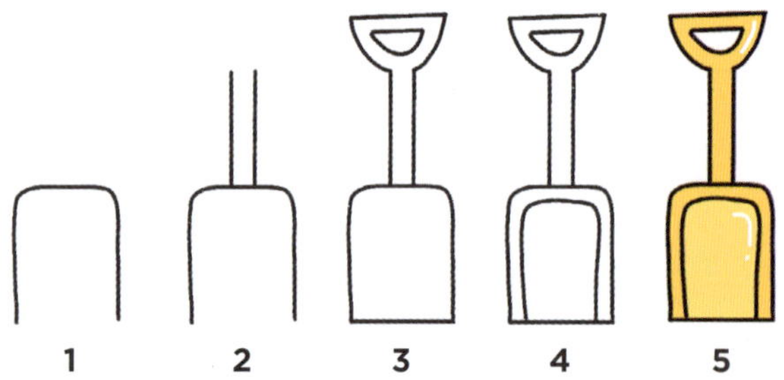

TOWEL

Draw a simple beach towel with two parallel waving lines connected at each end. Add stripes, polka dots or any other design to customize it however you like. Of course, adding color will really make the doodle pop.

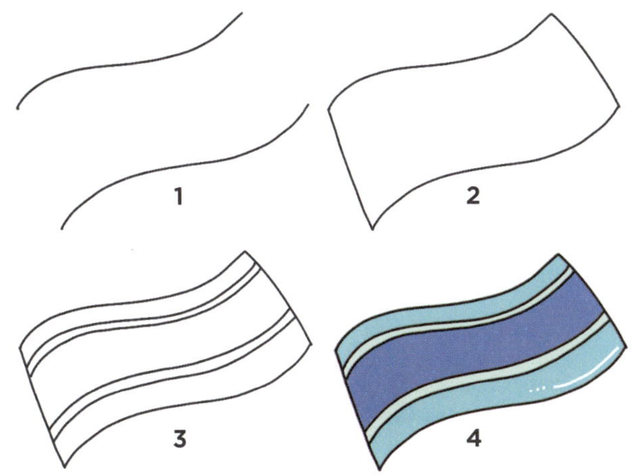

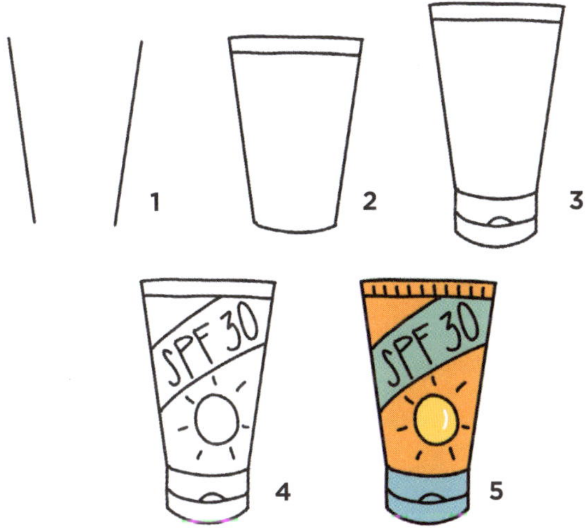

SUNSCREEN

Start with two diagonal lines that are closer at the bottom than the top. As you connect them, the top line should stay straight, while the bottom one is rounded. This forms the shape of the tube. Add a cap, then any kind of design or words. The letters "SPF" and a small sun will make it obvious what's in the tube.

BEACH BAG

The first step in drawing a beach bag is sketching the shape of the bag itself. I like to make it wider at the top than at the bottom. Add a handle, then have fun creating a design or a pattern to decorate it. Try stripes, polka dots, a checkerboard pattern, basket weave or waves.

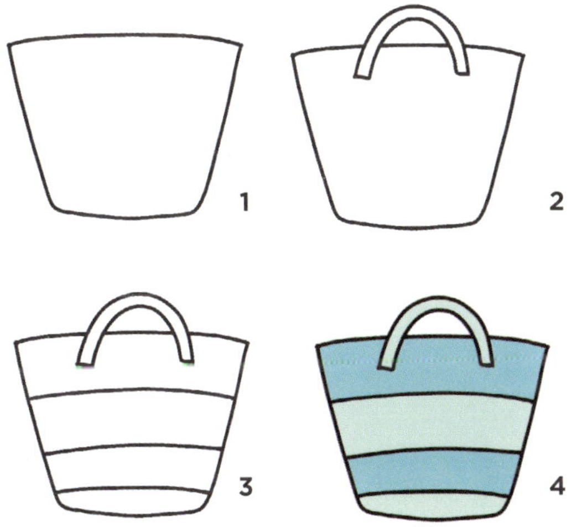

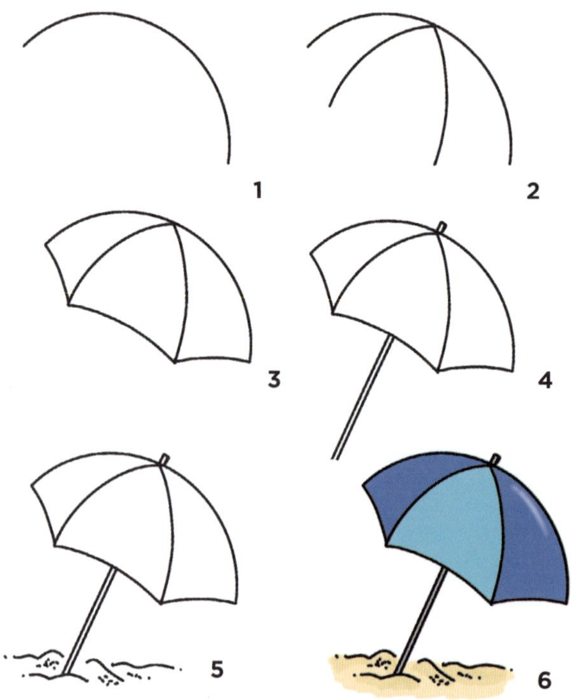

BEACH UMBRELLA

Start with an arch, then use curving lines to divide it into three sections. Connect the bottom of each line to the next one with three more curved lines, forming the umbrella shape. Draw a long thin rectangle for the pole, then add some short wavy lines and dots at the bottom to represent the sand.

BEACH BALL

A beach ball starts off with a simple circle. Give it a distinct beach ball look by sketching a small semicircle at the top, then add curving lines inside to divide it into three sections. Make each section of the ball a different bright color while leaving the semicircle white.

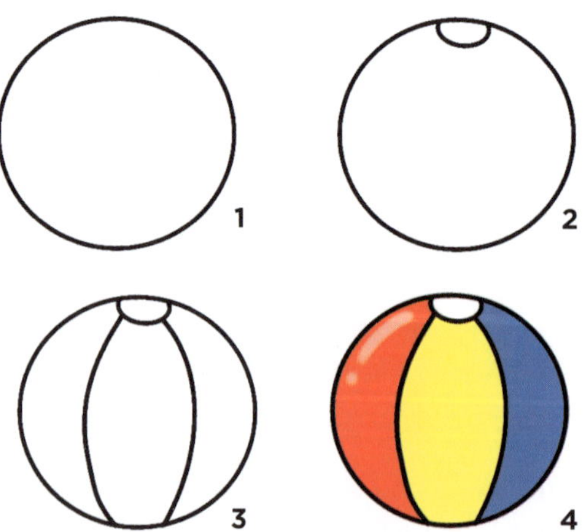

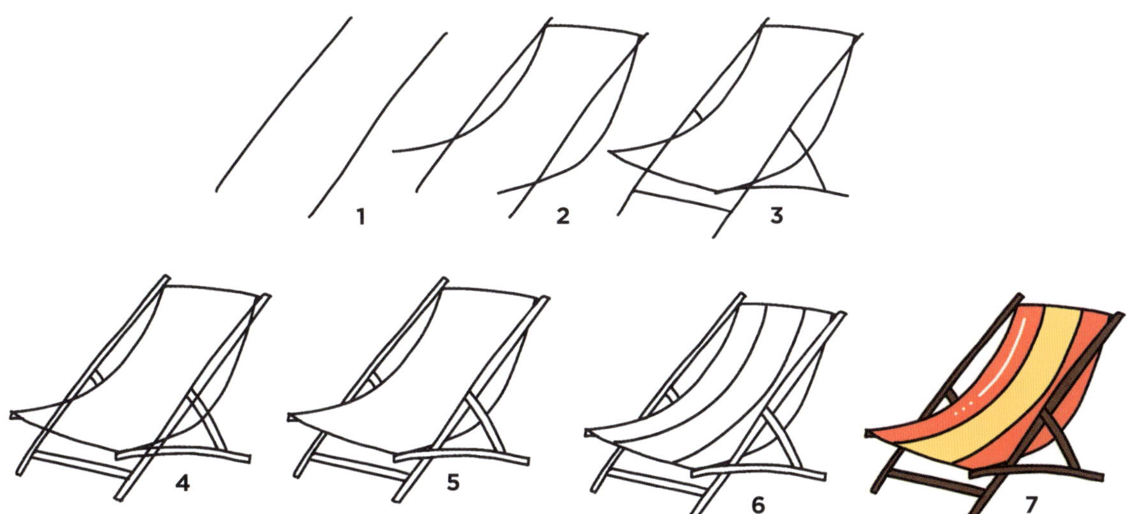

BEACH CHAIR

A beach chair starts with a frame, so draw two parallel diagonal lines. Next, add curving lines to show where the fabric seat will be. Continue to sketch the rest of the frame, first with single lines, then go back and make them into rectangles for dimension. Then, add a design to the seat. This doodle has a lot of overlapping lines, so make sure that you erase the pencil lines you don't want to trace over before adding color.

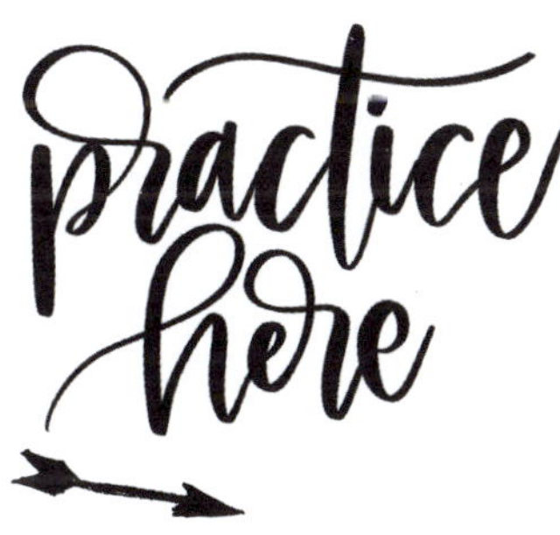

FLIP-FLOPS

Flip-flops are so much fun to wear and doodle! Start by sketching the base shapes, which are simply ovals with a slight indent on one side. Then, add straps in the upper half of the ovals. Draw a second line along the outside edge of each flip-flop to make them look more three-dimensional. Then, have fun adding color.

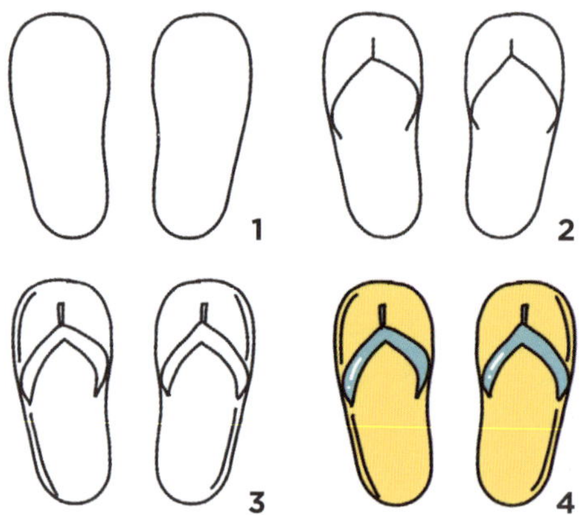

BEACH HAT

An upside-down "U" shape with a curving line at the bottom makes the crown of this fun beach hat. Add a brim and some detail lines, and before you know it, your hat will take shape. Feel free to include any words or other decorations; I added a stripe where the brim meets the rest of the hat. You can also make the brim of your hat wider for a different style!

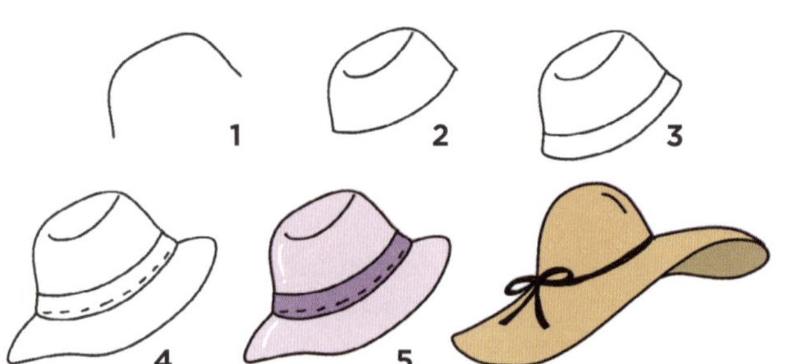

SUNGLASSES

Sunglasses are a necessity for a bright day at the beach! To draw these, start with two semicircles and join them together near the top to form the frames. Add lenses by drawing two more semicircles inside the frames. Sketch a short rectangle on each side of the frames, then add "J"-shaped earpieces. Finally, color your sunglasses. Of course, this same doodle can be used for regular glasses too if you choose not to color the lenses black or gray!

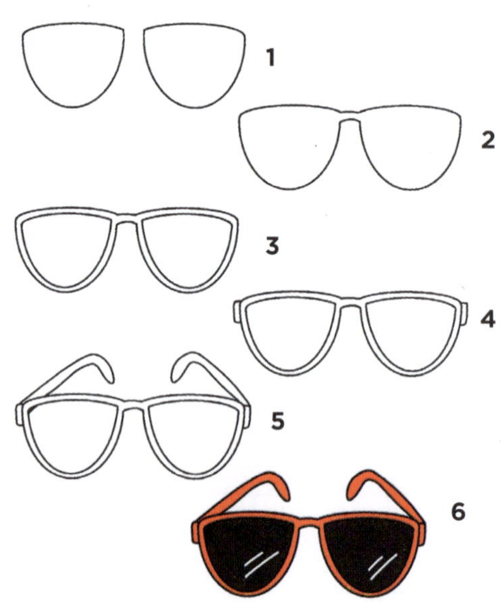

SPIRAL SHELL

This simple round shell is a fun find on any beach and it's basically just a spiral. Draw a short line connecting the end of the spiral to the next layer. Then, all that's left to do is add color.

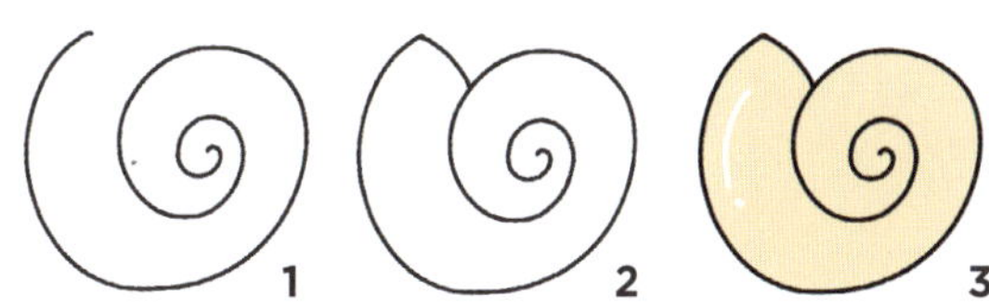

CONCH SHELL

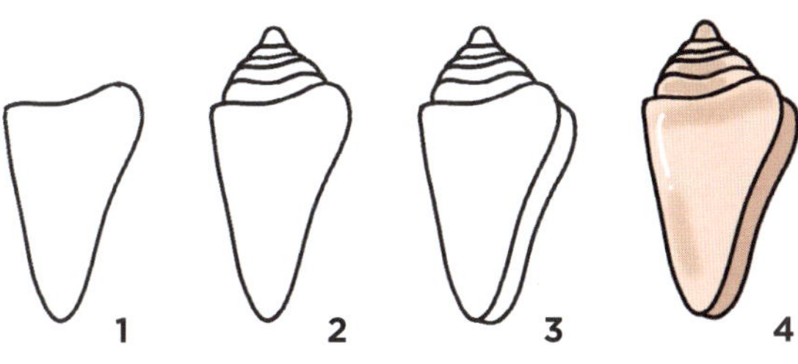

To draw this type of shell, start with a rounded upside-down triangle. Then, use short waving lines to create a series of layers on top, making each layer slightly smaller as you go. Finally, on the right of the shell, draw a curving line. Pinks, grays and light browns are good colors to fill in this shell.

SCALLOP SHELL

The first step in doodling a scallop shell is to sketch the outline: two sides and a series of bumps across the top. Add the bottom of the shell, then draw lines extending down in between each of the bumps. Using different shades of the same color to make darker and lighter areas can add visual interest to your shell.

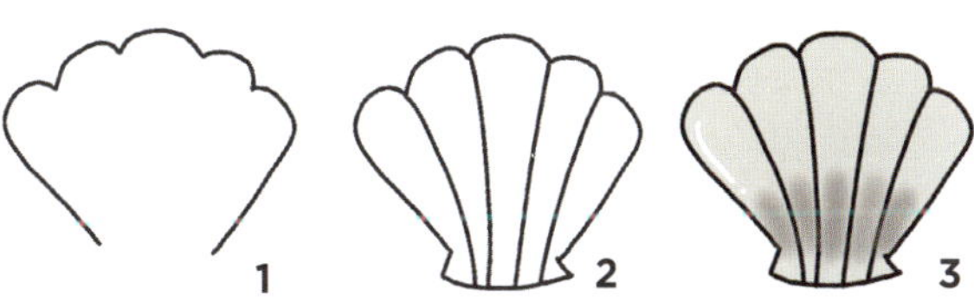

TULIP SHELL

1 2 3 4

To make a tulip shell, first sketch a teardrop shape, then draw the body of the shell extending off to the upper right. Add a series of short curving lines on top, each one smaller than the previous one. Then, your shell is ready to color in.

STARFISH

To doodle a starfish, start by forming one of the arms, then continue around drawing the other four extending in all directions to create the basic star shape. As you color it in, add some tiny dots in the center and extending down onto the base of each arm to show the unique bumpy texture that a starfish has on its back.

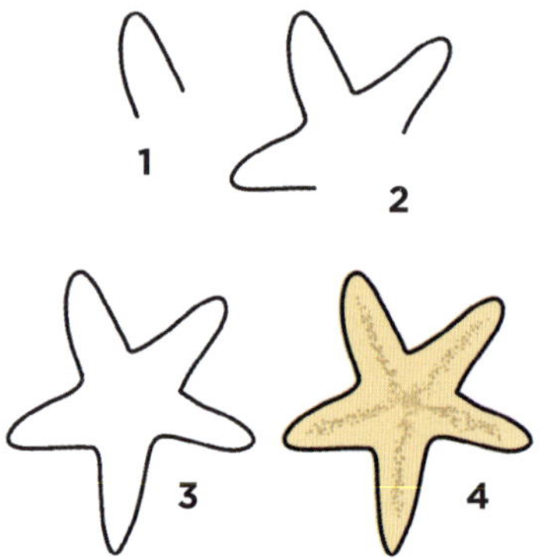

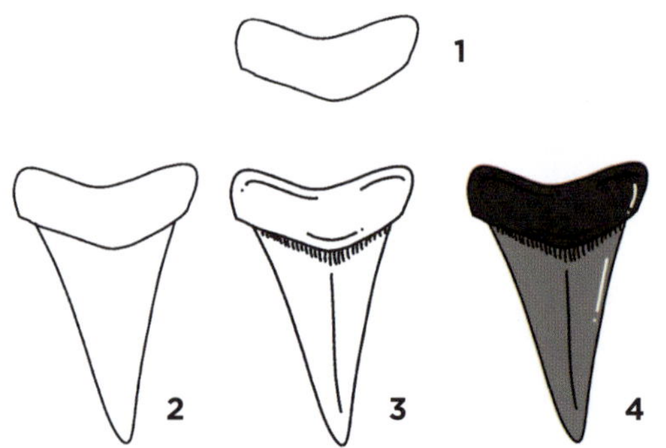

SHARK TOOTH

Finding a shark tooth on the beach can feel like a treasure hunt. Often, instead of being white or light gray, the teeth that wash up are fossils that have turned black and very shiny. To draw one, start with the top part, which is a rounded "V" shape. Add a narrow pointy triangle underneath and some detail lines for dimension.

SUN

The beach just isn't the same without the sun! Draw this one by forming a circle, then adding a zigzag border around it. I like to alternate between lower and higher points to make it more interesting. You can leave your sun just like this and color it in—or you can add a fun face with sunglasses and a smile.

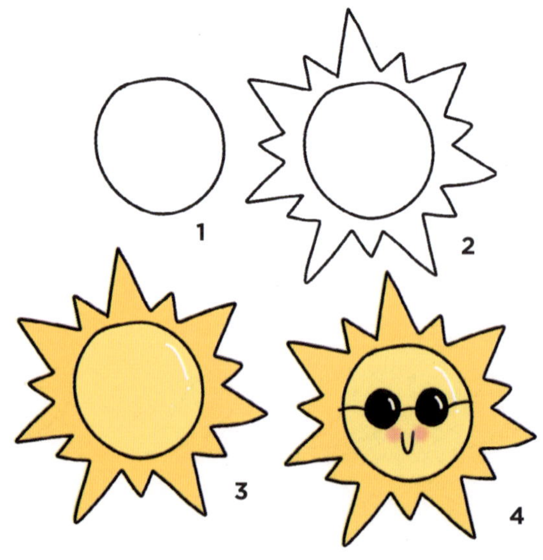

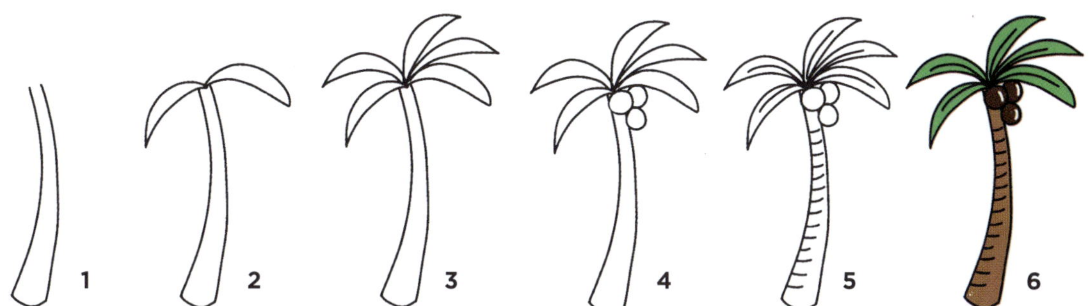

PALM TREE

Palm trees swaying in the breeze are one of the first things I think of when I imagine the beach. Start this doodle by sketching the trunk, then the leafy branches. I usually draw five of these. You can add more if you like, but I recommend sticking with an odd number. A few round coconuts are a fun addition to your tree or you can leave it as is. Make a little beach scene by drawing two palm trees and a hammock hanging between them for the perfect relaxation retreat!

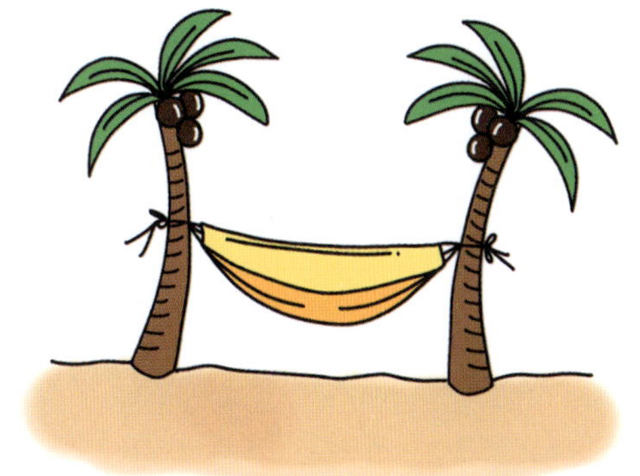

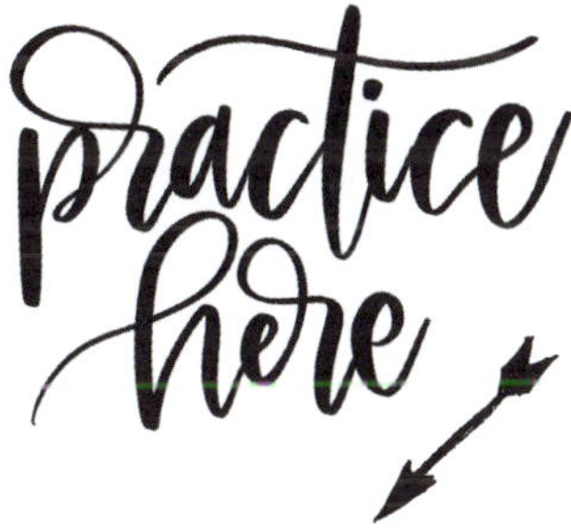

SEAGULL

Whether they are hopping along the sand or trying to steal your lunch, seagulls are part of any beach vacation. To sketch one, start with a curving line for the head and back, then add a long thin feathered tail. Next, draw a curving bill and a rounded tummy that connects to the tail. Add a wing, a stripe on the tail and some color to bring this little guy to life.

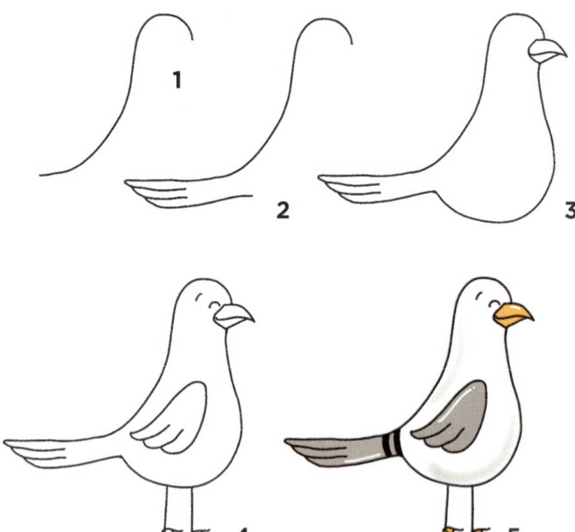

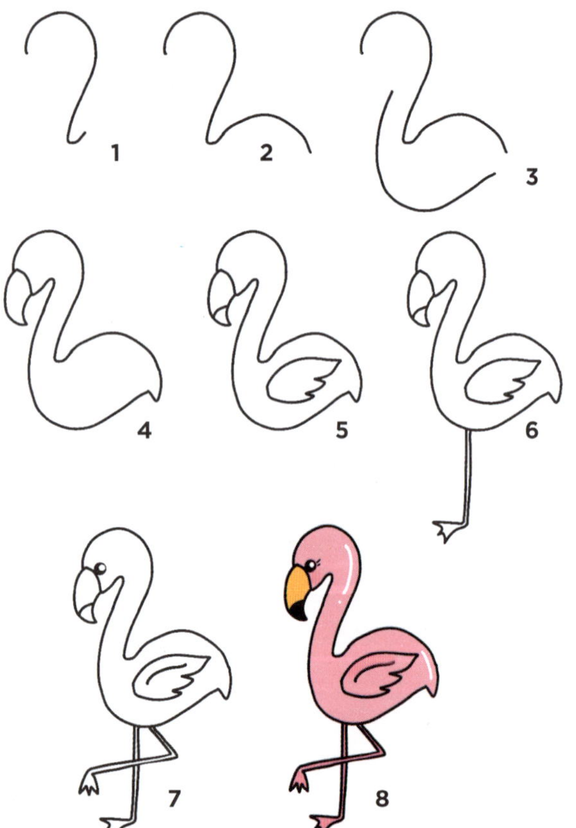

FLAMINGO

What's more fun than a bright pink bird that likes to stand on one incredibly long leg? Everyone loves a flamingo, and this one starts with a curving line for the head and neck. Add an arch for the back and a second arch underneath for the neck and belly. Next, draw a beak and connect the belly to the tail. Sketch a wing, an eye and those long legs, then add the colors that make a flamingo so easy to recognize.

IN & ON THE WATER

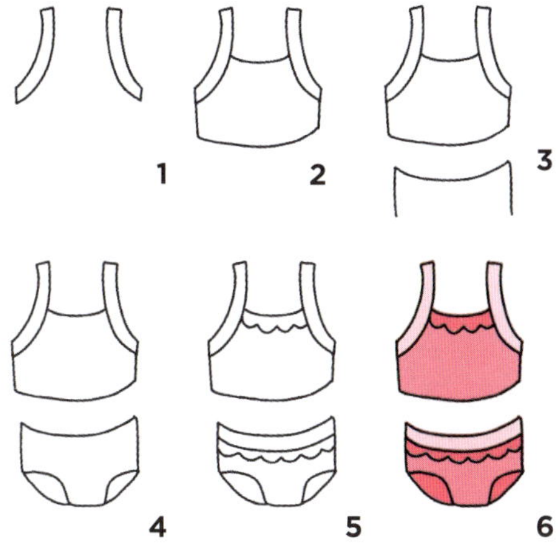

CLASSIC BATHING SUIT

Bathing suits are a must-have for a day in the pool or ocean, so let's draw this easy two-piece version. Start with the straps, then connect them to form the shape of the top. Next, sketch the shape of the bottoms and add semicircles for the leg holes. Have fun adding details like ruffles or a pattern and, of course, color.

ONE-PIECE BATHING SUIT

Start a simple one-piece by drawing the straps and neckline, then add curving lines on each side of the body. Finish off the shape with the leg cutouts at the bottom, and you have a completed suit. Personalize it by adding a pattern, like stripes or polka dots, and of course add your favorite colors.

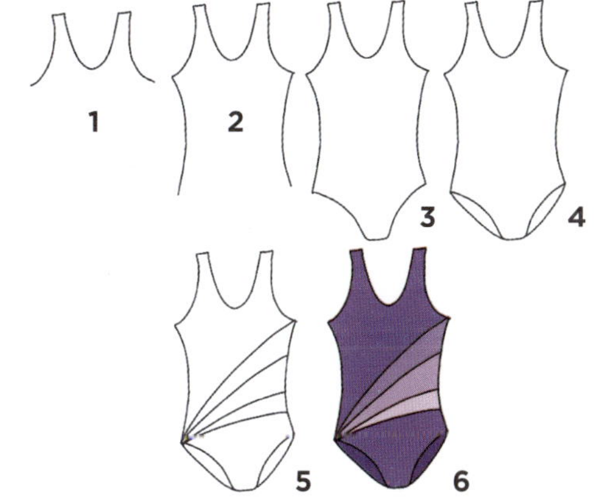

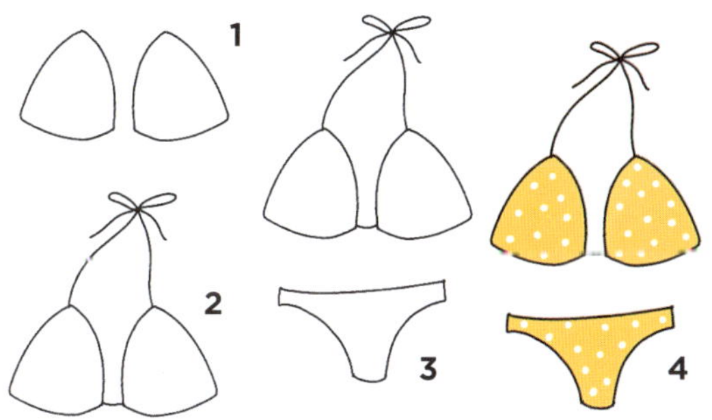

STRING BIKINI

Bikinis are the swimsuit of choice for many beachgoers. To draw them, sketch two rounded triangles and connect them with a line. Then, draw a line coming from the top of each triangle. These two lines should meet above the bikini top and tie together in a little bow. For the bikini bottom, sketch a "T" shape with rounded areas for the leg openings. Finally, add color to your itsy-bitsy bikini.

SWIM TRUNKS

To doodle a pair of swim trunks, start with a rectangle for the waistband, then draw another rectangle for the main part. Divide the trunks into two legs, then add details like pockets, a tie string and short vertical lines to show that the waistband is elastic. Feel free to keep customizing your trunks with stripes, words or other designs to make them your own.

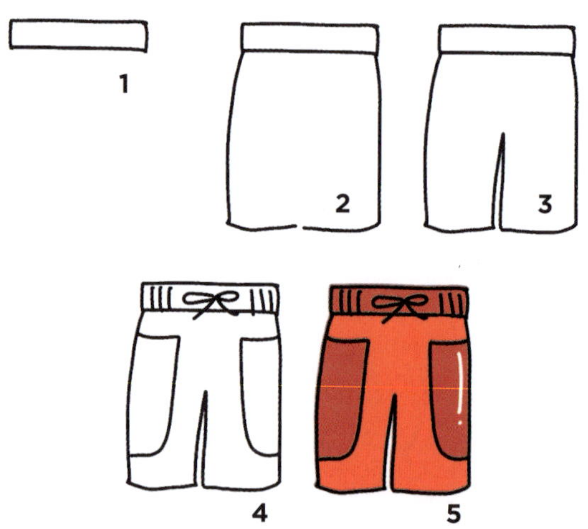

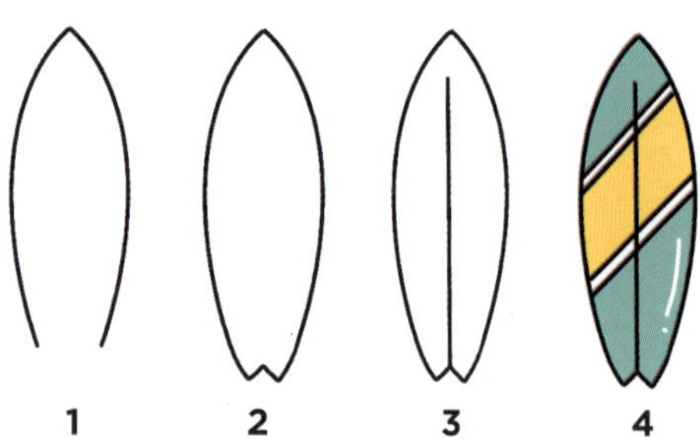

SURFBOARD

A surfboard is made of a simple shape: a long, curved upside-down "V." At the bottom, connect the lines with a small upside-down "V" shape, then draw a line coming up from the point almost to the tip of the board. All that's left to do is add any design you want, along with color. Play around with different kinds of patterns to create a bunch of unique and fun boards!

INNER TUBE

Hit the water with a colorful inner tube! Start with an oval, then add an arch for the flamingo's head. Draw a line around the oval that connects to the head at the top, then forms the flamingo's neck and beak at the bottom. Add details and color to finish your drawing. Instead of a flamingo, you can also turn this into any other kind of tube you like. Try a different animal head or even a simple version, like this gold-and-teal one, using your favorite colors and patterns.

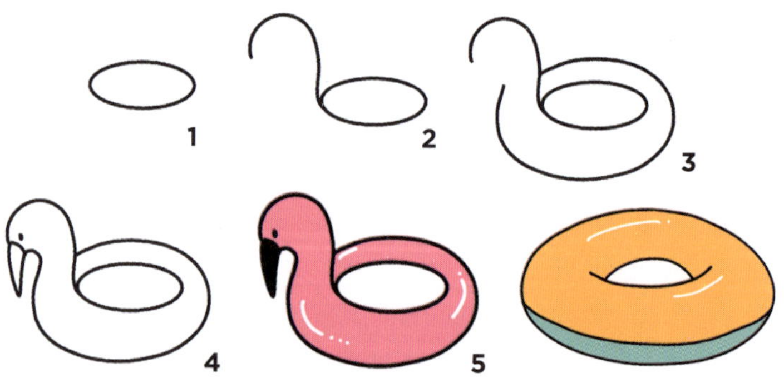

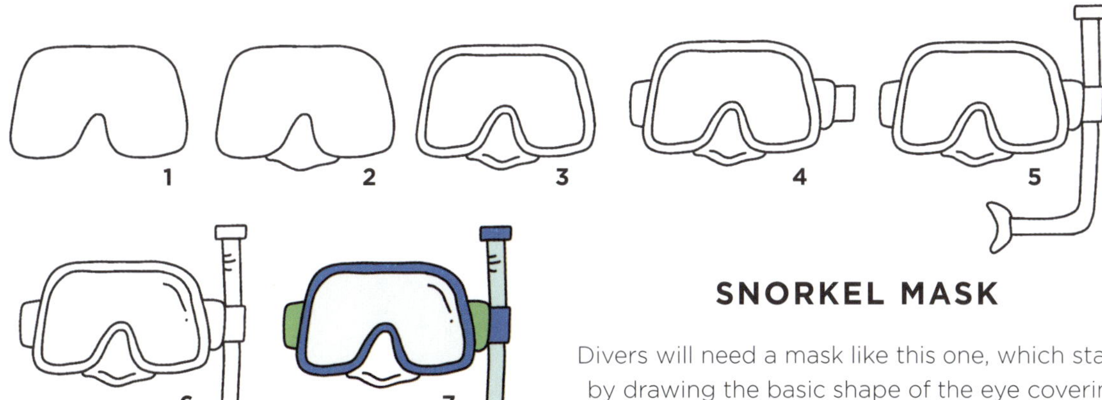

SNORKEL MASK

Divers will need a mask like this one, which starts by drawing the basic shape of the eye covering and adding a nosepiece. Next, add round rectangles to show where the strap connects and a tube shaped like a backward "L." Detail lines and color will make this doodle pop off the page.

LIFE PRESERVER

Safety comes first in the pool and ocean, so let's doodle a life preserver. Simply draw a large circle with a smaller one inside, then use short lines to divide it into sections. Add curving lines around the outside edges for the ropes, along with a few detail lines on the inside edge, then color the four divider areas red.

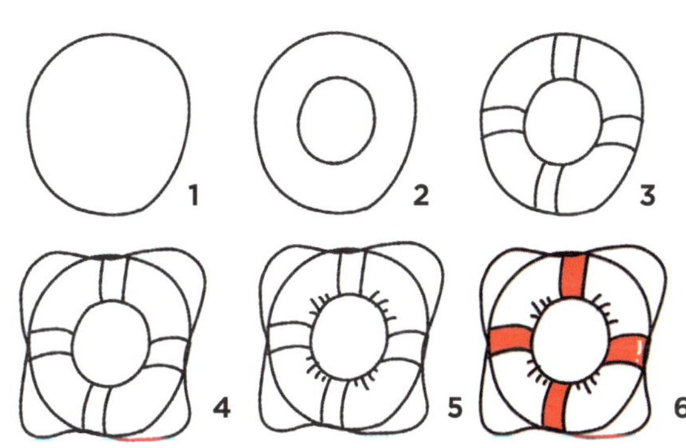

LIFEGUARD RESCUE TUBE

A lifeguard's rescue tube is also an important piece of beach safety equipment. To draw one, sketch a long thin teardrop shape. Then, add the three shapes inside that make it easy for someone to carry or hold on to the tube. Color in the tube red, leaving those shapes white, and add details like a cross and/or the word "LIFEGUARD" or simply "GUARD."

ANCHOR

Drop this anchor by drawing a cross shape with a curving moon shape at the bottom. Add a round top with a hole for the rope, as well as rounded shapes on the ends of the crossbar. Finish the shape at the bottom by drawing a small triangle on each end. Since this drawing has a lot of overlapping lines, make sure that you erase the extra pencil lines before outlining and adding color.

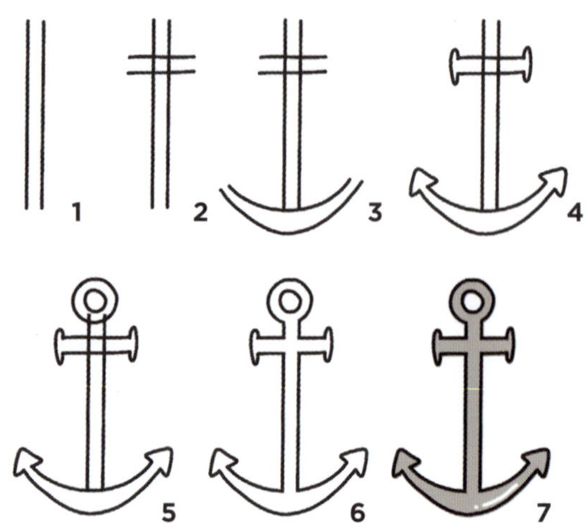

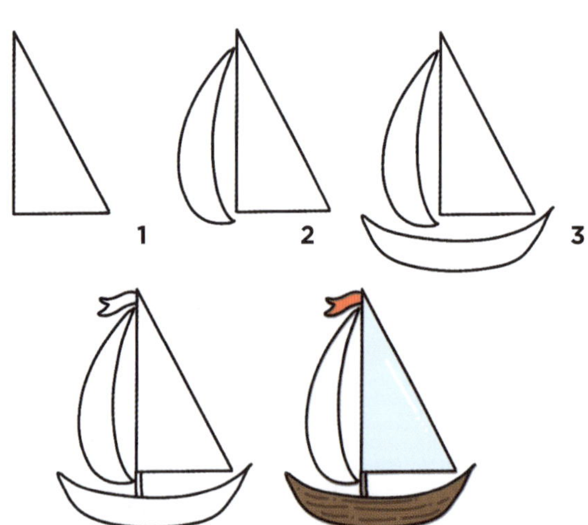

SAILBOAT

Start this little sailboat by drawing a right triangle, then add a curving moon shape on its left. Draw another moon shape at the bottom for the boat itself, then add lines to connect the sails to it. Finally, sketch a little flag at the highest point to make this drawing complete.

OCEAN WAVE

One of my favorite things about the ocean is watching the waves crest and crash onto the shore. It can be tricky to capture that motion, but this is an easy way to approach it. Start with a basic wave shape, then draw a wiggly line inside near the top. Next, add some detail lines and a few water droplets on each side of the wave. Color the top part of the wave white or a lighter shade of blue than the rest.

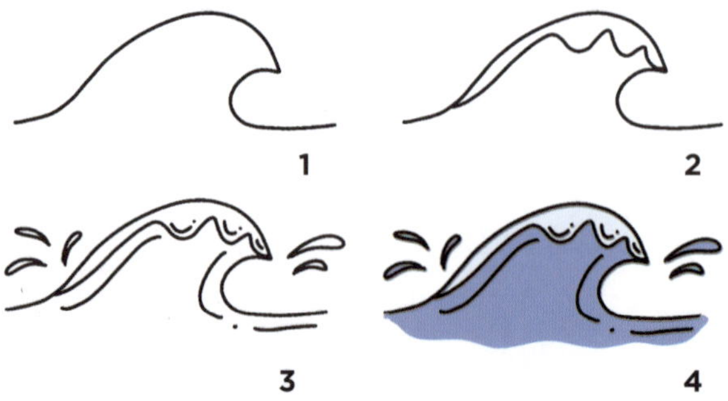

UNDER THE SEA

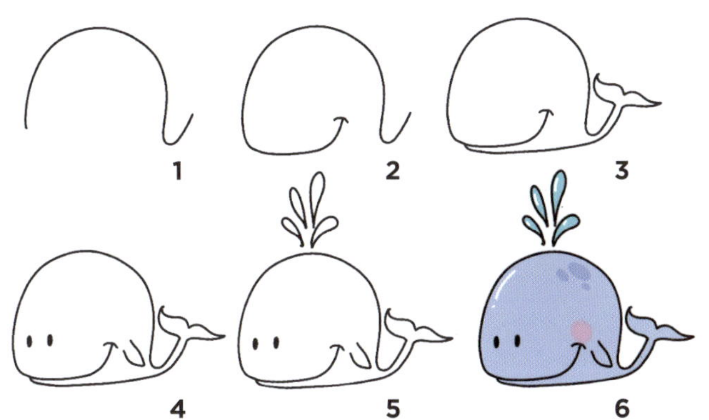

WHALE

Real whales are majestic, enormous and even dangerous. This little doodle shows a more playful side of the king of the ocean. Start with a large arch for the body, then turn the line underneath into a big smile. Next, draw a tail that connects to the rest of the body, then add eyes and a fin. Finally, add some water droplets coming from the blowhole at the top of the whale's head.

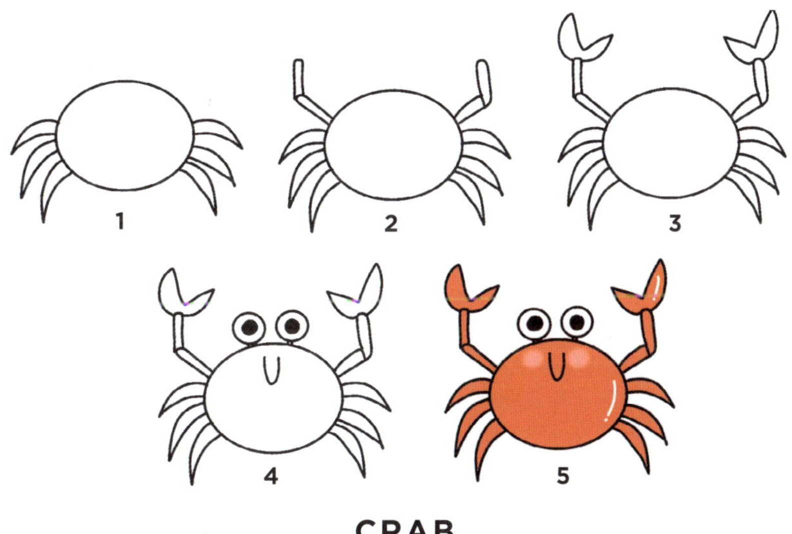

CRAB

Crabs may not be the cutest creatures in the ocean, but this doodle can be! Start by drawing an oval, then add three curving triangles for legs on each side. Next, give your crab arms and claws, then add eyes and a smile to bring out his personality.

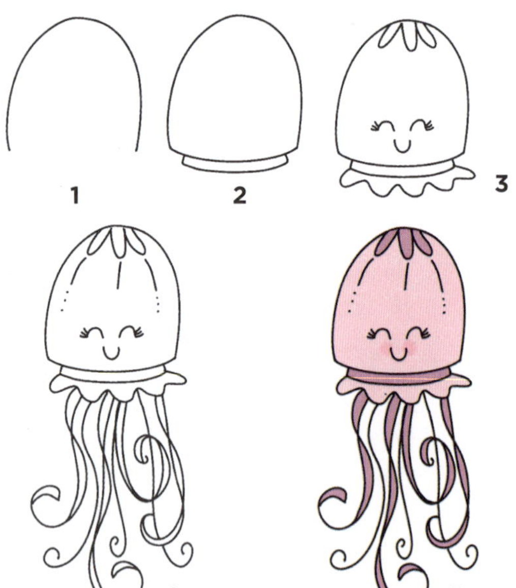

JELLYFISH

The body of a jellyfish is simple to sketch: an upside-down "U" shape with a line across the bottom. It's all the little details that make this doodle so much fun. Add a scalloped ruffle along the bottom of the body and on top of the head as well as an adorable little smiling face—I even added some eyelashes to mine. Then, have fun drawing bunches of curls and swirls for the tentacles that go in all different directions.

SIMPLE FISH

There are plenty of fish in the sea, and no two are exactly alike. That means there are also infinite ways to draw one. For this particular fish, draw a teardrop-shaped body and add fins to the top and bottom. Then, sketch a tail, a face and one more fin inside the body. Add details like scalloped lines to represent scales, then color your fish. Want to try drawing a different kind? Go for it! Build on these basic steps and try your own variations.

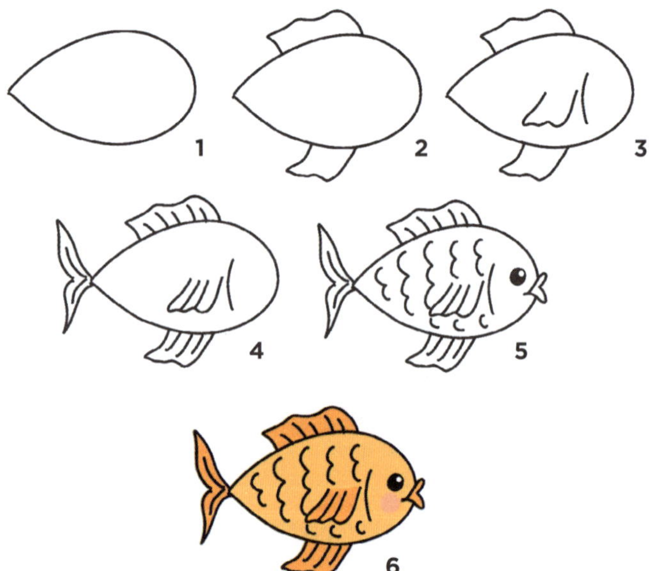

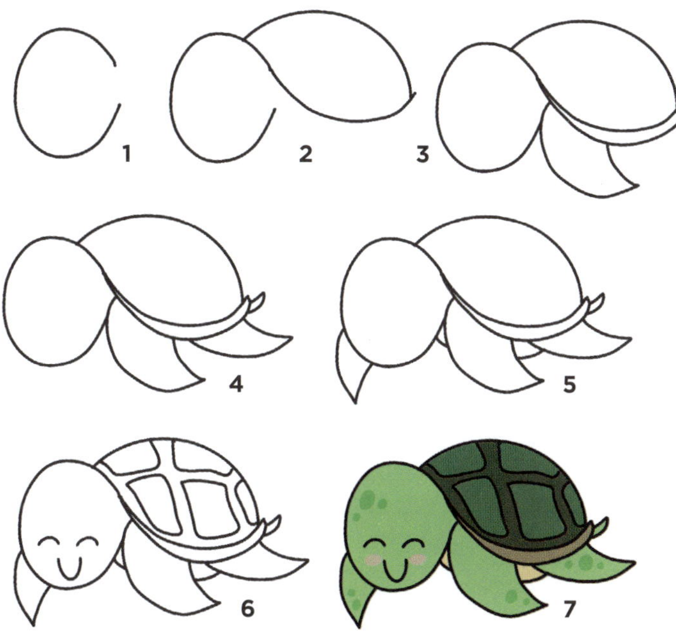

SEA TURTLE

A few years ago, I had the opportunity to see a bunch of baby sea turtles hatching from the nest and making their way to the ocean. It was incredible! When you can't see them in person, though, this cute sea turtle doodle is the next best thing. Start by drawing the head shape and a shell. This will look a lot like a sideways "8." Then, add a tiny tail and three flippers using rounded "V" shapes. Sketch a pattern of rectangle shapes on the shell and add lots of color to bring your turtle to life.

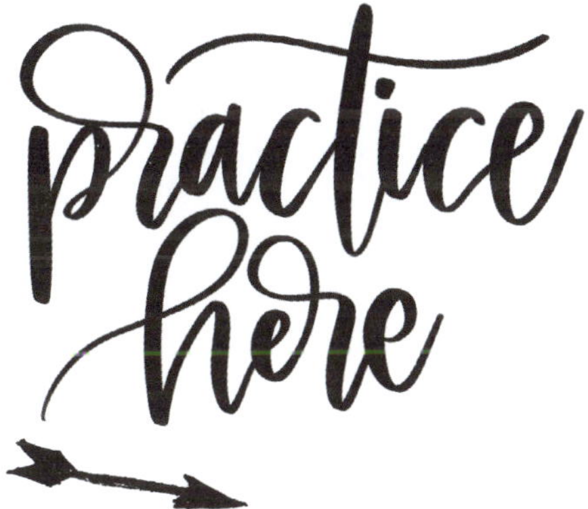

BLOWFISH

Blowfish are certainly one of the more interesting sea creatures, especially when they're all puffed up! To doodle one, start by sketching a basic circle shape and adding a jagged tail and fins. Then, to give it that puffy, spiked appearance, draw a series of small "V" shapes all over the body. You'll want to go back and erase your pencil lines where these overlap your original circle. Finally, draw a face with eyes, a mouth and, most importantly, two curving lines for the puffy cheeks.

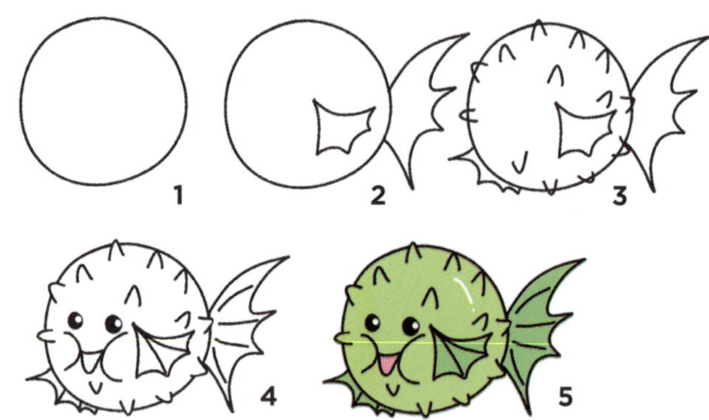

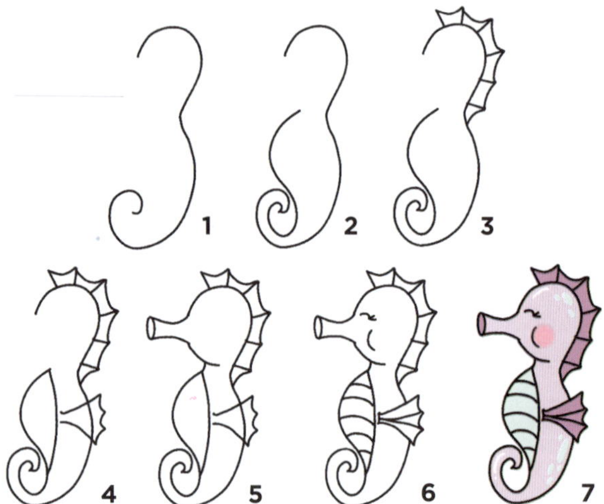

SEAHORSE

Seahorses are fascinating creatures, and they're also a lot of fun to doodle. Start by sketching the basic head and body shape with that characteristic spiral tail. Then, add detailing on the head by drawing a series of short lines and connecting them with curving lines in between. Draw a section for the belly and a little fin next to it. Next, draw the seahorse's long tubelike snout, some horizontal lines across the belly and some lines inside the fin. Finally, add a face, color and any other small details to make your seahorse unique.

STINGRAY

Stingrays are incredibly graceful as they glide through the water, which we can try to capture in this cute drawing. First, draw a waving line, then connect the ends with a curving line across the bottom. Add an upside-down teardrop shape on the right side, which makes it look like the stingray is in motion. Finally, add details like the tail and a happy face, then color your new friend.

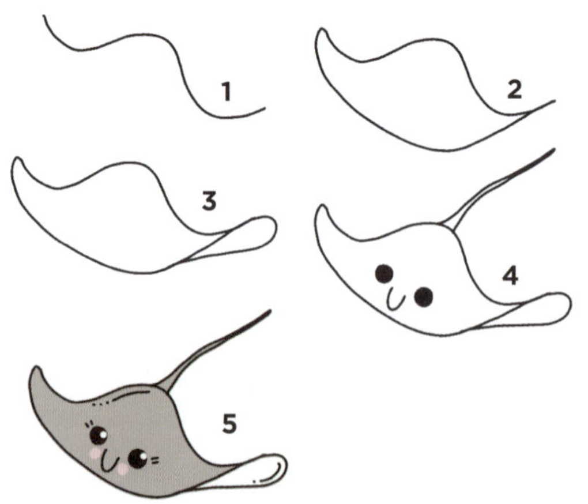

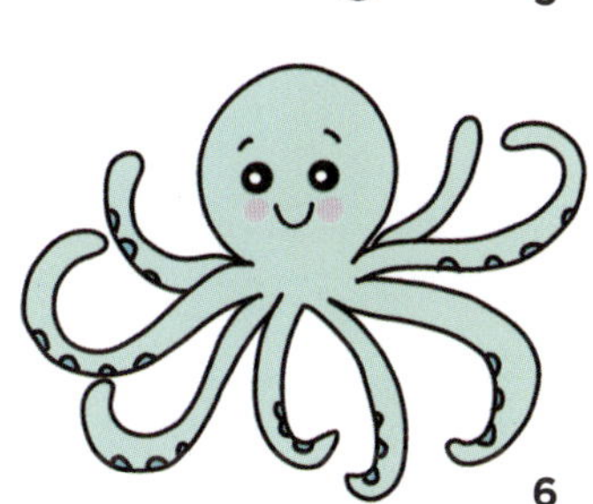

OCTOPUS

To make a cute octopus, first draw a rounded shape for the head. Then, add two long curving arms going out from both sides of the head, then add two more shorter arms above/behind those. Draw four more arms, curving slightly in different directions. Sketch a face, along with some semicircles on some of the arms. The final step is to color your octopus in any way you like.

SHARK

Although I never want to run into a real shark at the beach, we can doodle a friendly one. First, draw a curving line for the belly, then a slightly less curved one for the back, leaving a slight space at the tail end. Next, add fins and a tail, then a line dividing the belly area from the rest of the body. Give your shark gills, an eye and a little smile to make him happy and not so scary.

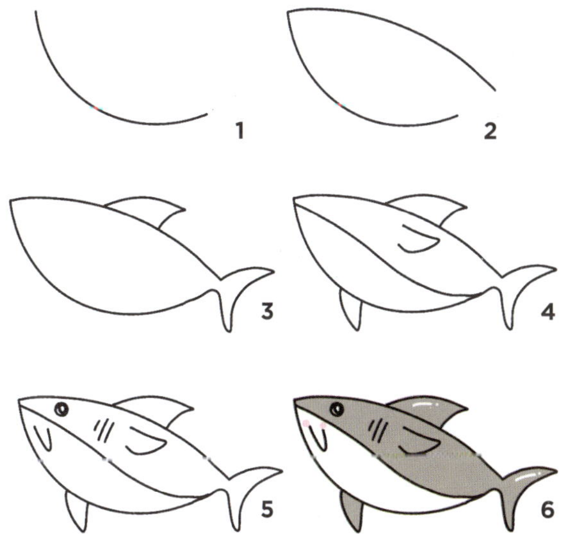

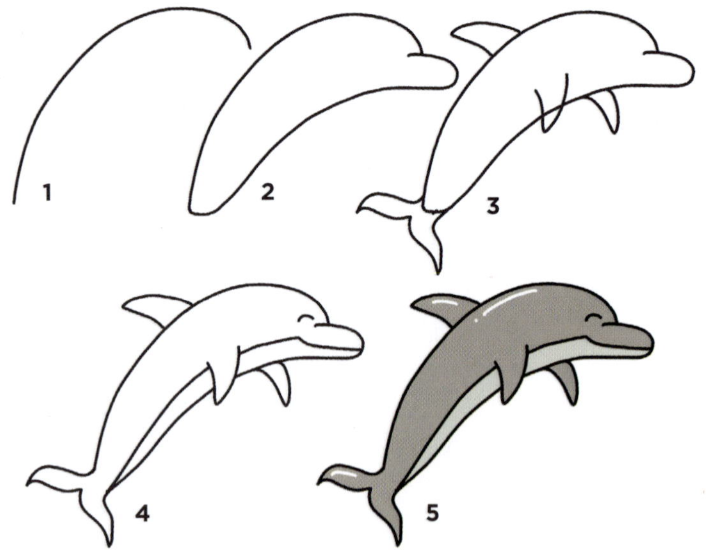

DOLPHIN

Dolphins are intelligent, friendly and just plain adorable! Start your dolphin doodle by drawing a curving line for its back, then add a curving line for its belly and nose. Next, add three fins and a tail. Finally, add an eye and a long line dividing the dolphin's belly from the rest of the body. Erase any of the overlapping pencil lines, color your doodle and your dolphin will be ready to play.

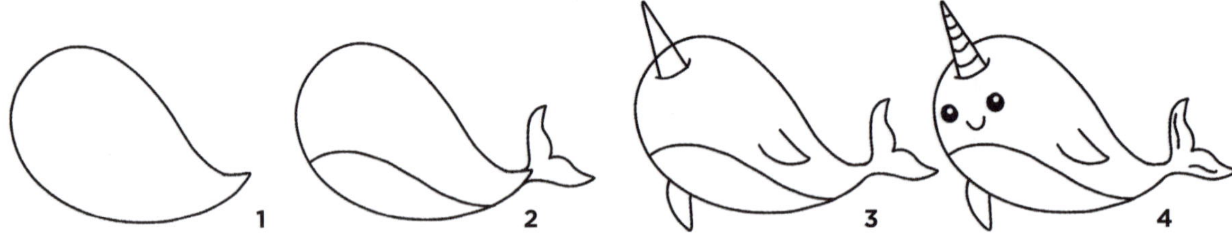

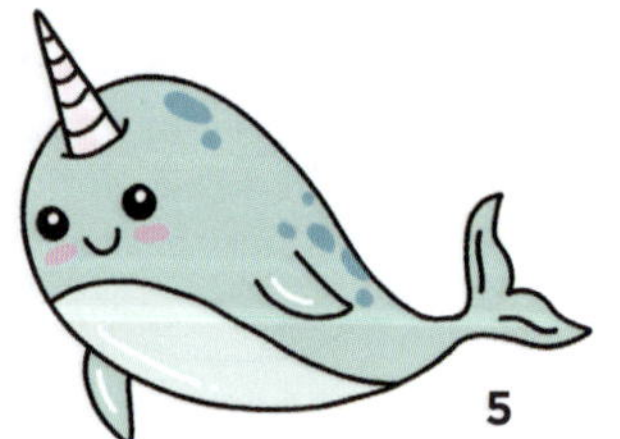

NARWHAL

While they're not typically beachgoers, narwhals are definitely worth a doodle. To draw one, simply sketch a wide teardrop shape, then add a tail and divide off a section for the belly. Next, add fins and that all-important horn in the center of the head. Draw a happy face and some detail lines on the horn and tail, then color your unicorn of the sea.

CLAM

Drawing a clamshell isn't as complicated as it might seem. Start by sketching the top part of the shell, which is an arch with a scalloped line across the bottom. Then, add another scalloped line coming down from the top left corner to add dimension. Next, sketch the bottom of the shell, which is a wide curving scalloped line. This should connect with the top part of the shell on both sides. Go back and double all of the scalloped lines. Add an inside area where the round pearl treasure sits, as well as some detail lines and color.

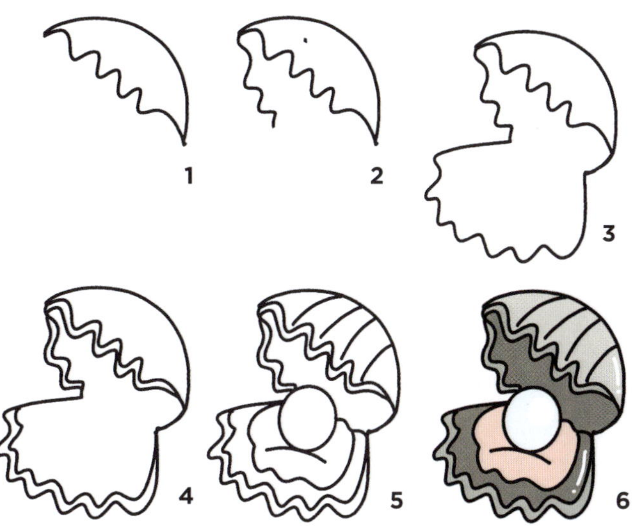

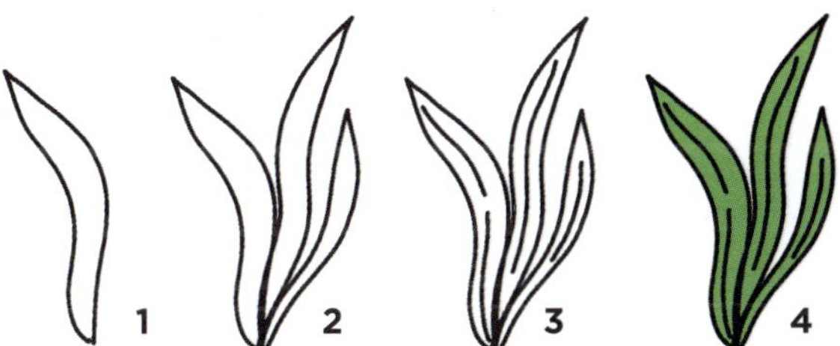

SEAWEED

To sketch seaweed, make a grouping of long thin leaf shapes that are connected at the bottom and curve in different directions. My example has three, but you can draw as many as you like. Draw lines through the center of each leaf shape, then add color. This doodle combines well with bubbles!

BUBBLES

Bubbles are some of the easiest doodles to draw because they're nothing more than circles! I like to vary the size, making some larger and others smaller, since no two bubbles are the same. To color them in, I recommend using very light shades of blue and adding a bit of shading and a highlight to help show that they're bubbles rather than just balls.

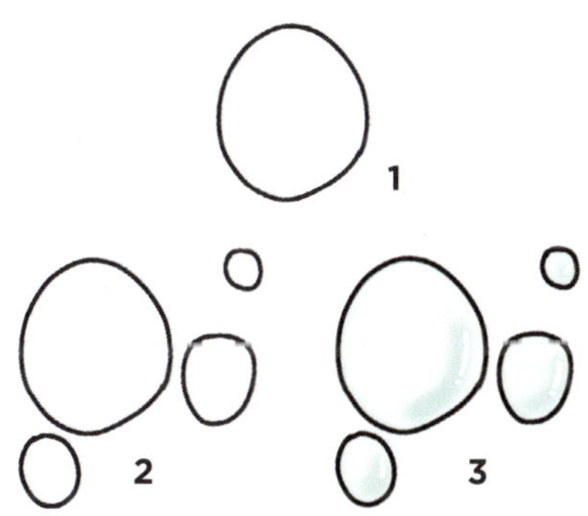

SUMMER TREATS

POPSICLES

Popsicles are as easy to draw as they are to eat! Just make an upside-down "U" shape and close it off at the bottom with a horizontal line. Add a stick on the bottom and a few arches inside to give some dimension to your tasty treat!

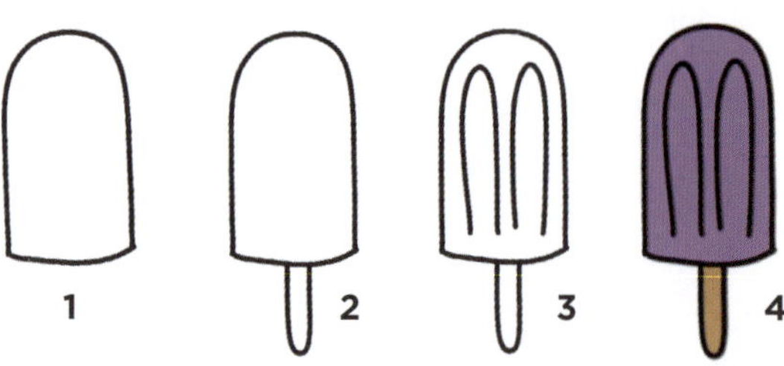

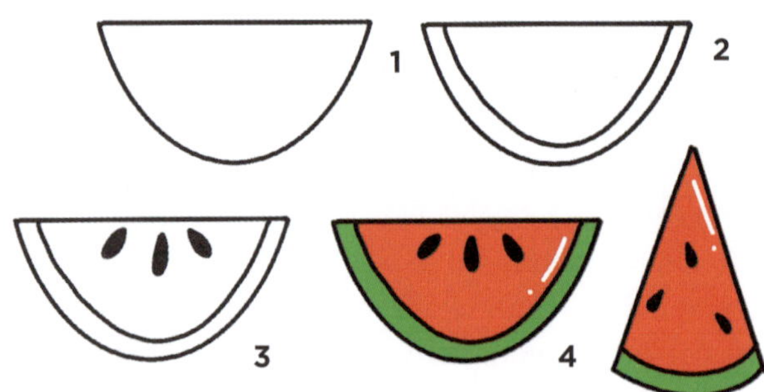

WATERMELON

Watermelon is such a perfect summer snack, and it's incredibly simple to sketch. Draw a wide "U" shape with a horizontal line across the top, then add a curving line inside to show where the rind is. Add a few teardrop-shaped seeds and, of course, those classic watermelon colors. You can also adapt the watermelon drawing to show a triangle slice instead of the rounded "U" shape.

PINEAPPLE

Drawing a pineapple starts with the basic oval-like shape and a group of spiky leaves on top. Then, add tiny "V" shapes all over to represent the points on the outside of the fruit. Color it in and you've got yourself a tasty summer treat.

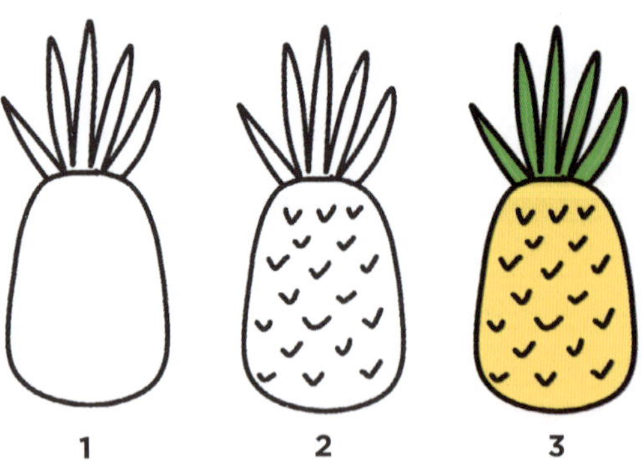

ICE CREAM

An ice-cream cone is the perfect treat on a hot day. Draw this one by sketching a large "V" shape for the cone and a rounded scoop with a scalloped bottom. You can make some slight swirls within the scallop line for even more texture. Add a checkered pattern to the cone and details to make the ice cream your favorite flavor—such as chocolate chips or sprinkles—and don't forget the cherry on top!

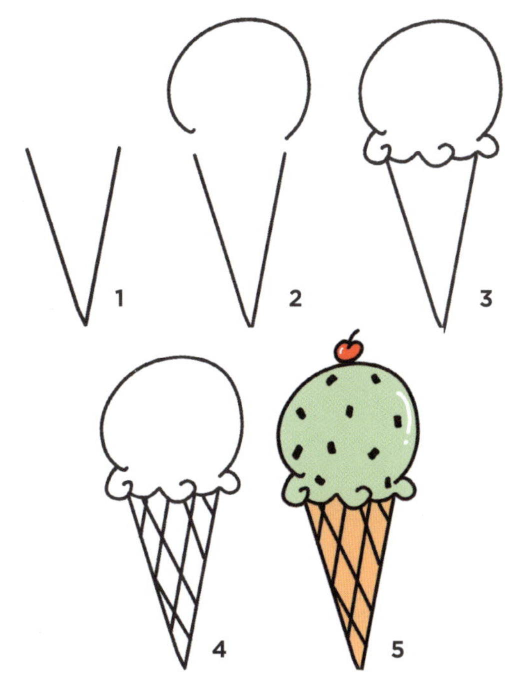

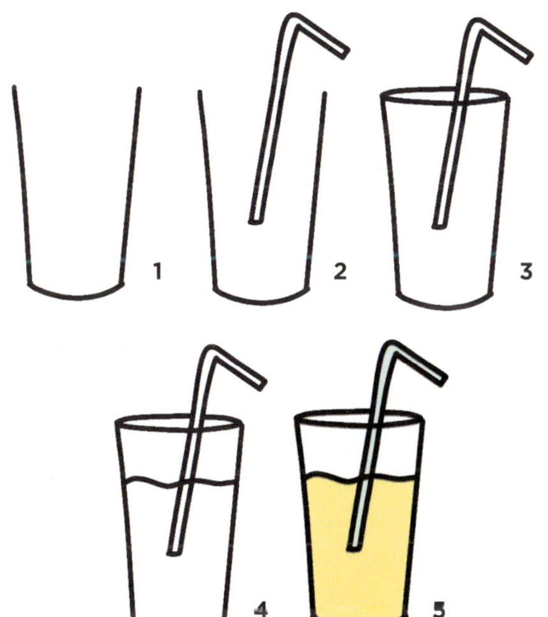

LEMONADE

There's nothing like a cold drink on a summer day. Start this doodle by drawing the sides and the bottom of the glass, then add a straw. Next, draw an oval at the top of the glass and a waving line where you want the top of the liquid to be. I colored mine yellow to represent lemonade, but you can turn yours into whatever cold drink you like best.

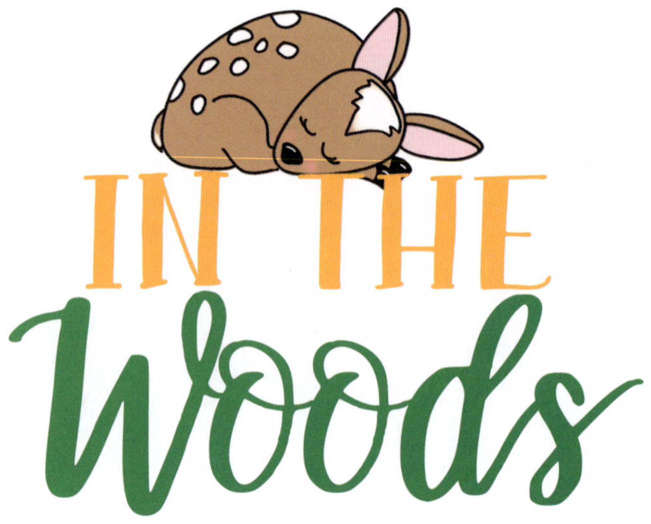

IN THE Woods

While my personal idea of an agreeable vacation is a trip to a four-star hotel, many folks enjoy camping and exploring the great outdoors. There are plenty of beautiful things to see in nature, as well as supplies associated with a camping trip that we can learn to draw. And, of course, don't forget the many adorable woodland animals we can find in the forest. These doodles make great embellishments for all kinds of projects, whether you're in the woods, planning a trip or just thinking about nature from the comfort of your favorite chair.

WOODLAND ANIMALS

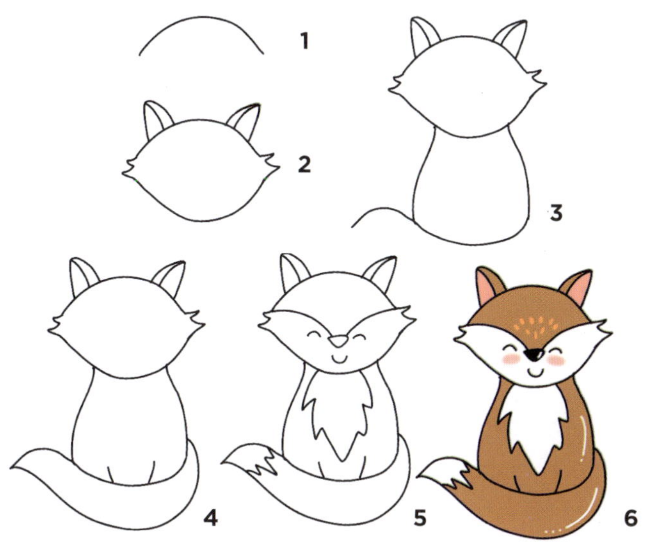

FOX

To draw this friendly little fox, make a football shape for the head and add ears. Next, draw the basic body shape and wrap the tail around in front of the fox's feet. Make a wide "V" shape on the head, with a triangle nose in the middle, and add a cheerful face, then add jagged lines to draw the white patches on his tummy and tail. Finally, add color and details like little spots to let your fox's personality shine.

OWL

Owls come in many shapes and sizes, so there are plenty of ways to draw them. To doodle this one, start with parentheses and connect them at the top to form a head. Add feathered tufts on each side, an arching "V" shape on the head and another set of parentheses for the body. Give your owl a rounded wing on each side, then add eyes, a beak and feet. As you color, you can add additional details like eyelashes or tiny "V" shapes on the head to show the texture of the feathers.

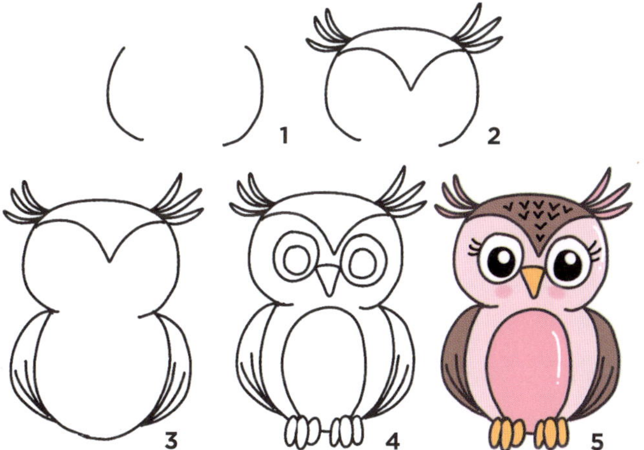

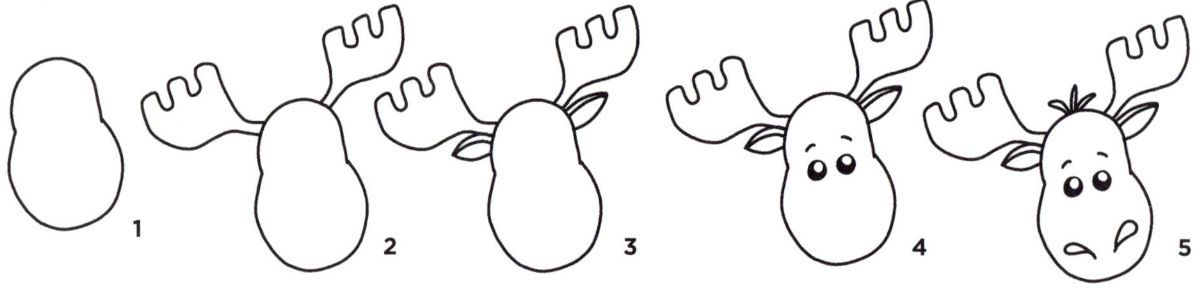

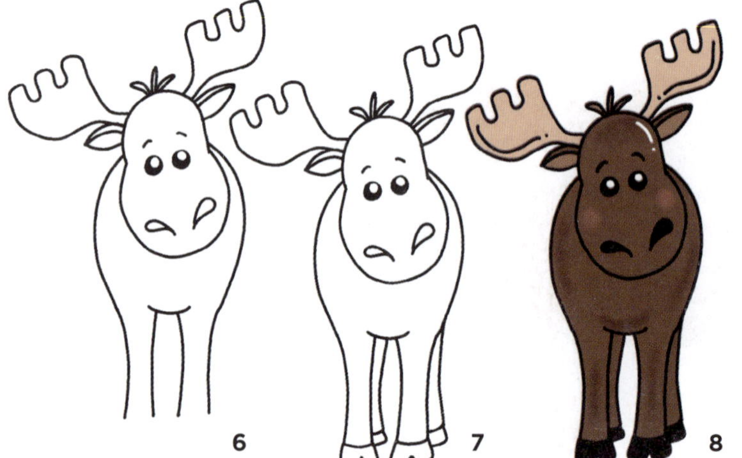

MOOSE

Start this moose sketch by drawing a potato-shaped head and adding antlers and ears. Next, finish the face by adding eyes, nostrils and a tuft of hair. Draw a body coming down from the head into two front legs, then sketch the other two legs and hooves. Color your moose and add highlights and detail lines to complete the doodle.

HEDGEHOG

Despite its prickles, a hedgehog is one of the cutest woodland animals to doodle. To draw yours, start with the head and belly. Then, add a series of zigzags for the pointy needles on the top of the head and the back. Draw some short lines dividing the belly area from the needled area, and add a face, hands and feet. Fill in the back area with more short-line needles. The last step is to add color to your hedgehog and admire how adorable it is.

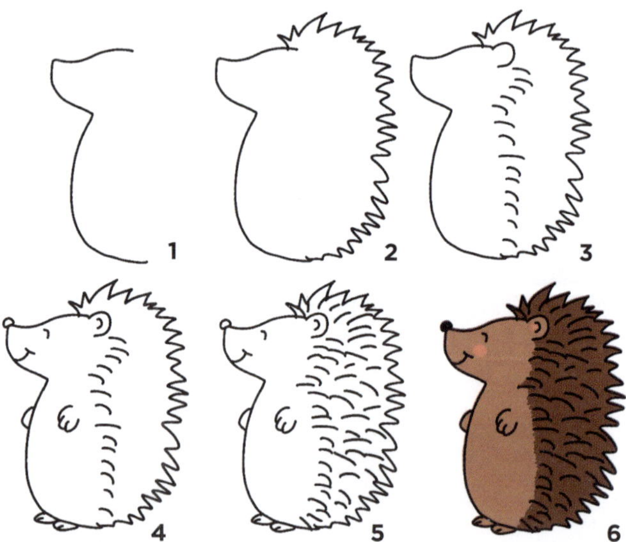

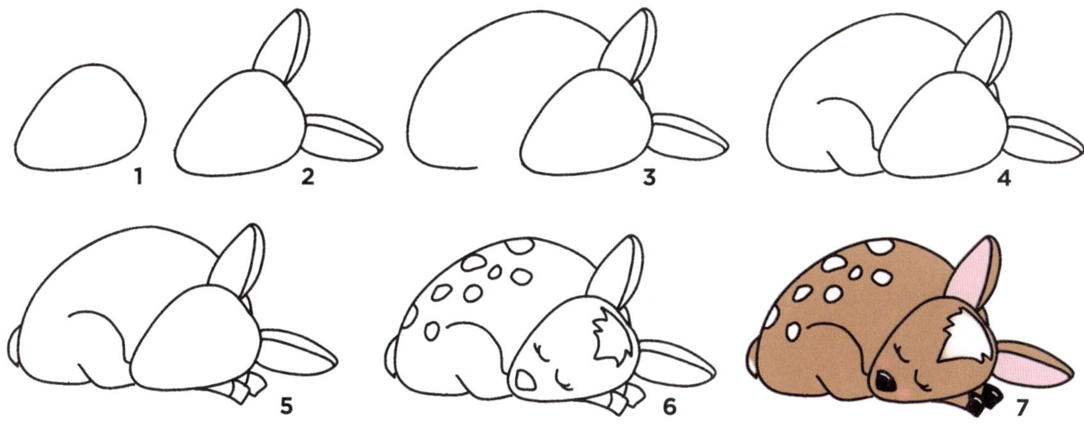

DEER

Let's doodle a cute little sleeping fawn! First, sketch a rounded triangle shape for the head, then add large ears and a curving line for the fawn's body. Draw the top of the back leg and the tail, then sketch the bottoms of two legs to the right of the head. Add spots to the fawn's back and a patch of fur on top of the head. Finally, draw a face and color your doodle.

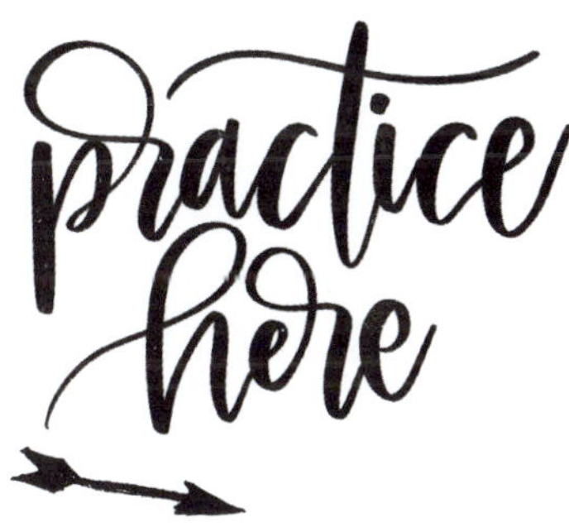

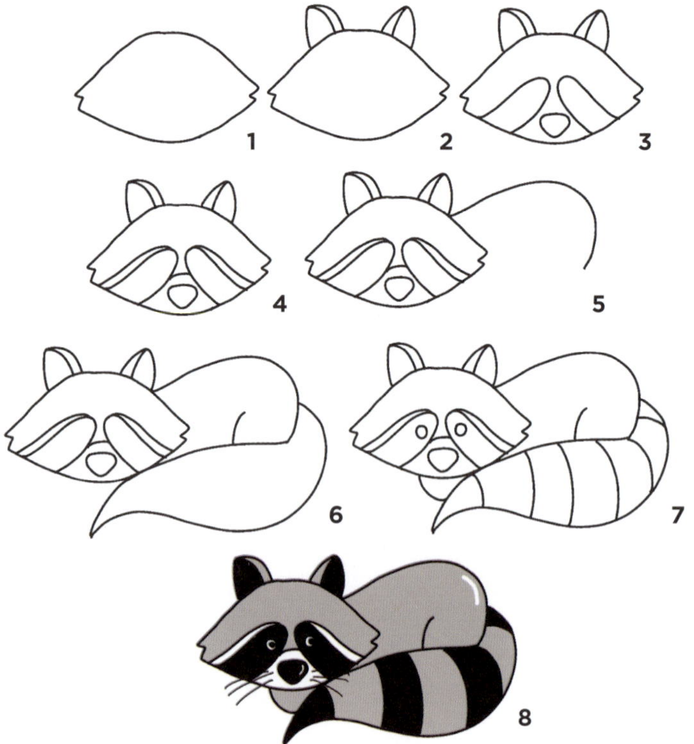

RACCOON

This little raccoon is just patiently waiting at your campsite to steal your leftovers! Draw a football shape for his face, add ears and a nose, then draw long curving "U" shapes for the dark patches around the eyes. Make a curving line for his back and bottom, then sketch a big fluffy tail that comes around the front of the body to the face. Add a curving line for the front of the body and divide the tail into stripes. As you color your raccoon, give him eyes, whiskers and any other tiny details you like.

BEEHIVE

Beehives are fun doodles to create, and they pair perfectly with the little bee on page 28. A beehive is a series of bumps divided into layers, each one slightly wider than the one above it. Once you have the basic shape of the hive, add a tiny archway at the bottom for the bees to enter and some detail lines for texture. Don't forget to add a few buzzy bees around the outside protecting their honey! If you'd like to doodle a honey-loving bear for your woods, simply color in the polar bear doodle on page 71 brown or black!

NOTE: To find doodles for a squirrel and bird, check out pages 131 and 130 in the Around Town chapter!

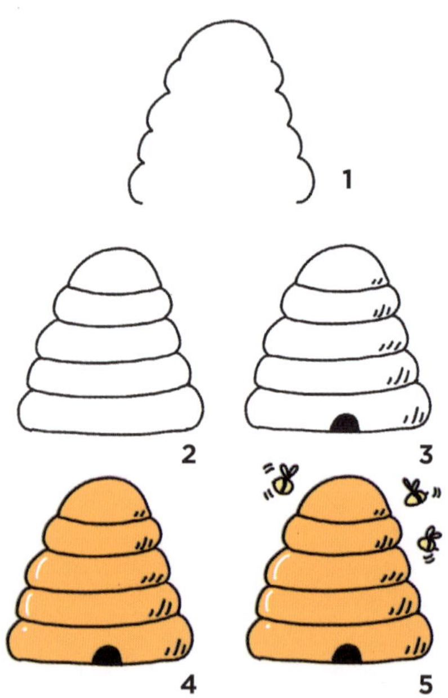

NATURE & CAMPING

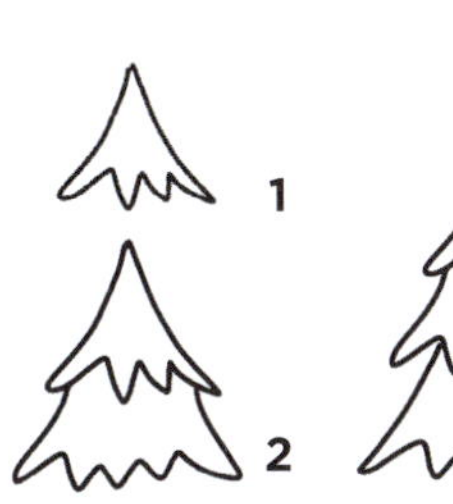

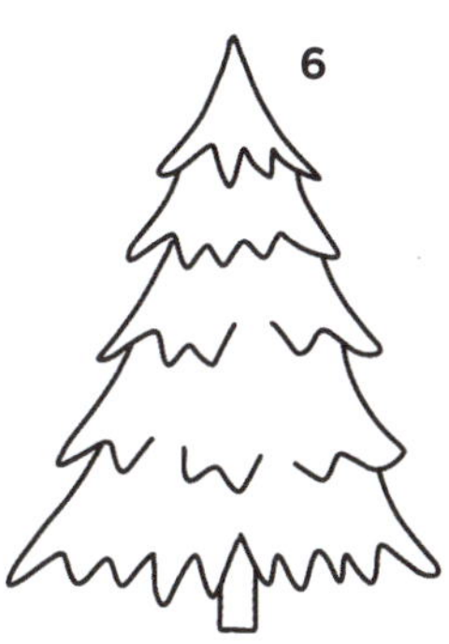

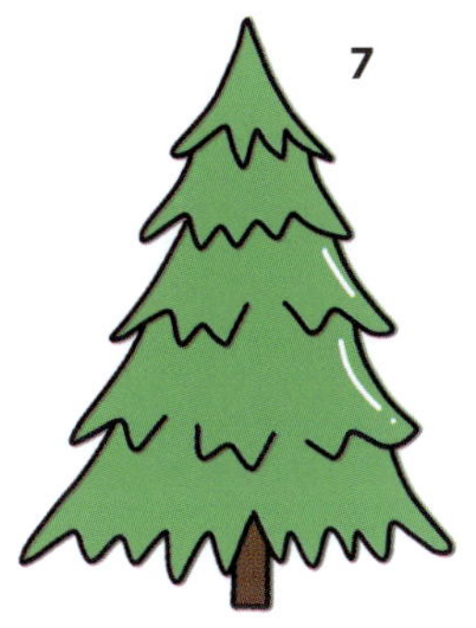

SIMPLE EVERGREEN TREE

The woods are full of evergreens, and this type of tree makes a fun addition to cards, calendars, journals and all kinds of art projects. It's also very useful around the holidays! Start by sketching a triangle shape with a zigzag line across the bottom. Repeat this basic idea, letting your shapes get larger as you move down toward the base of the tree. Add a rectangle for a trunk, then color in the tree with your favorite shade of green. A wintry variation is to give your tree the appearance of being snow-covered by leaving the zigzag tips of each layer white.

SLEEPING BAG

Sleeping bags are a must-have when camping in the woods. Start this one by drawing a large spiral, then draw two lines coming out from it for the rolled-up bag. Add a band for the tie, then continue sketching the main part of the bag. The basic shape should be wider on the ends and thinner in the center. Draw a circle for a knot and short strings coming off it to complete the tie.

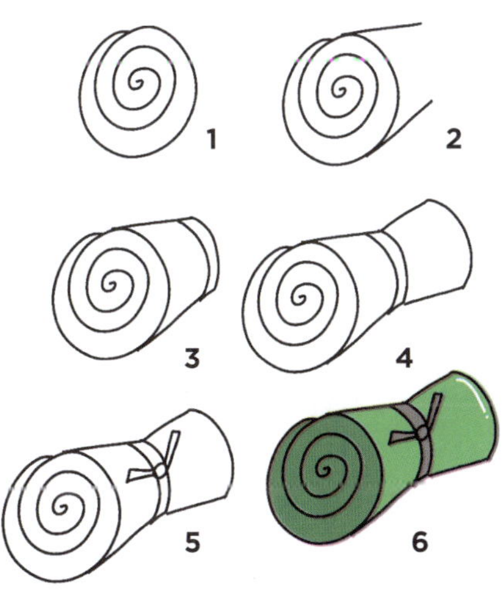

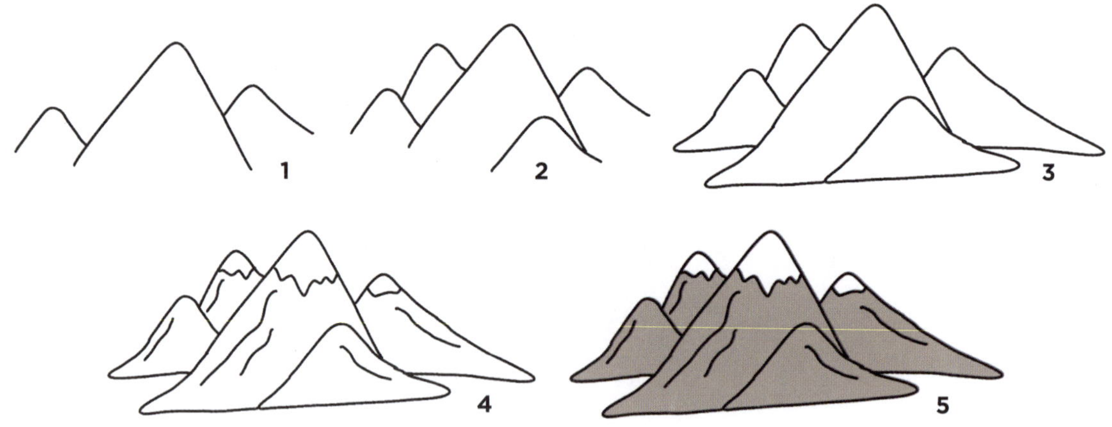

MOUNTAINS

Mountains are some of the most majestic things in nature, so it's hard to do them justice in a doodle. To draw them, create a series of peaks by making rounded "V" shapes at different heights. It's great to have them overlap one another. Draw horizontal lines as the base of your mountains, then add detail lines to show a jagged rocky texture. For snow-capped mountains, create a small section at the peak to leave white while you color in the rest brown or gray.

CAMPFIRE

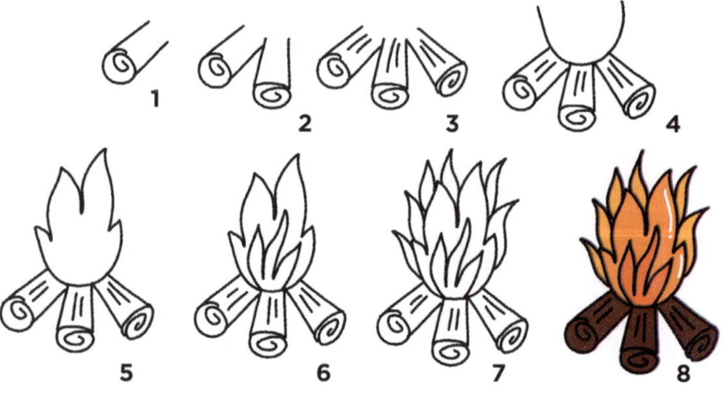

This campfire doodle begins much like the sleeping bag. Each log is a spiral with lines extending out from the sides. Draw three (or more) logs, then a "U"-shaped base for the fire. Sketch a few flames at varying heights, then add more flame shapes inside and on the outsides of your fire. As you add color, remember that fire appears the darkest in the center, where there's the most heat, and gets lighter as it goes out toward the ends of the flames.

ACORN

Acorns are a common find in the forest, and they're a great embellishment to draw, especially when fall rolls around. They're also a great companion for the cheerful little squirrel on page 131 in the Around Town chapter. First, draw a "U" shape, then add a cap, a stem and a leaf. Give the cap a checkered pattern and add a tiny semicircle to the bottom of the nut to complete the drawing.

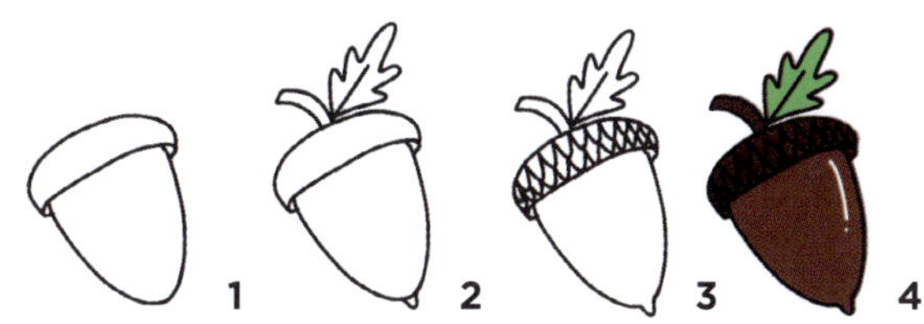

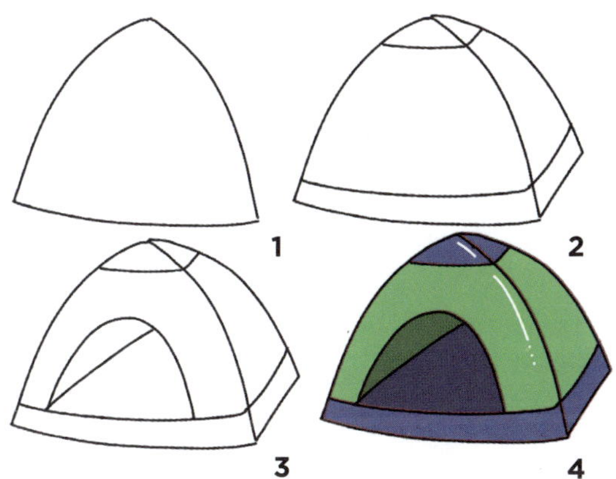

TENT

Sketch a large rounded triangle with a smaller one off to the side. Add an arched doorway, as well as any stripes or other designs you'd like on the outside of the tent. As you add color, think about making the areas inside the tent darker shades of the colors on the outside to show shadows and depth.

CAMPER/RV

If I were to camp, something like this doodle would be much more my style than a tent. To draw this happy little camper, make a rounded rectangle that's slightly taller on one side than the other. Next, sketch a tire on the left and a hitch on the right. Give your camper a door and a window, then have fun adding other decorative touches, like curtains, a festive banner, hearts, stripes or anything else you want to add to make it look like a home away from home.

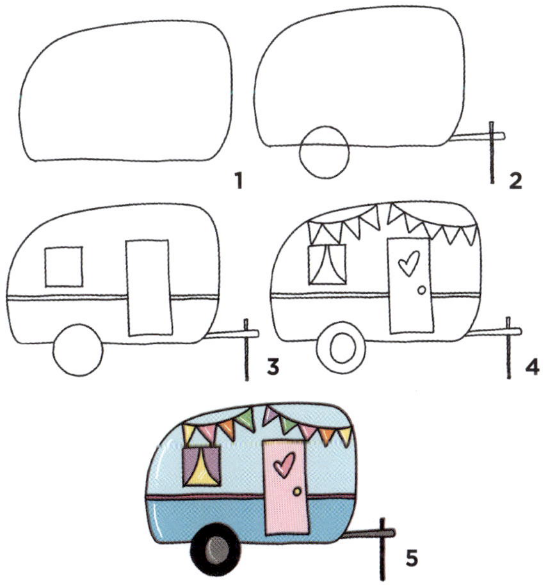

LANTERN

The first step in drawing a lantern is to make a set of parentheses for the sides of the globe. Connect them at the top and the bottom, then add some rounded rectangles for the lid and the base. Draw a double circle on top and an arm on each side, then finish your doodle with a little flame inside. Add color, detail lines and highlights to complete your drawing.

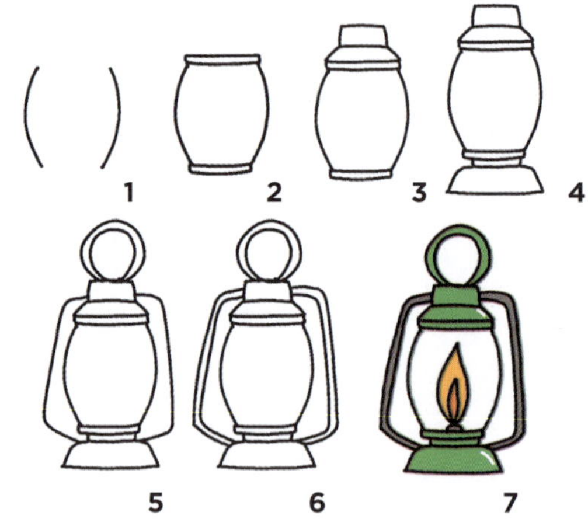

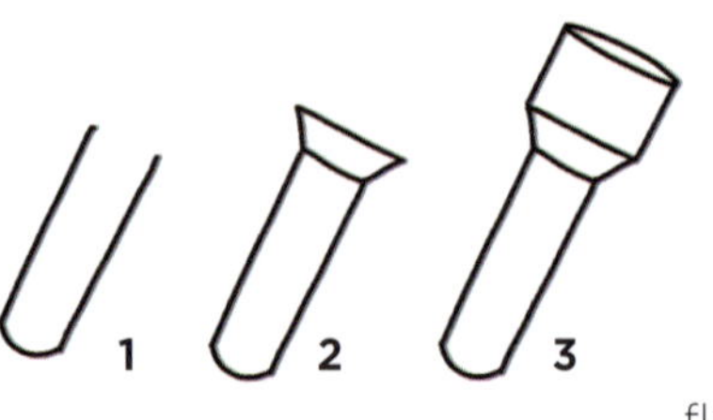

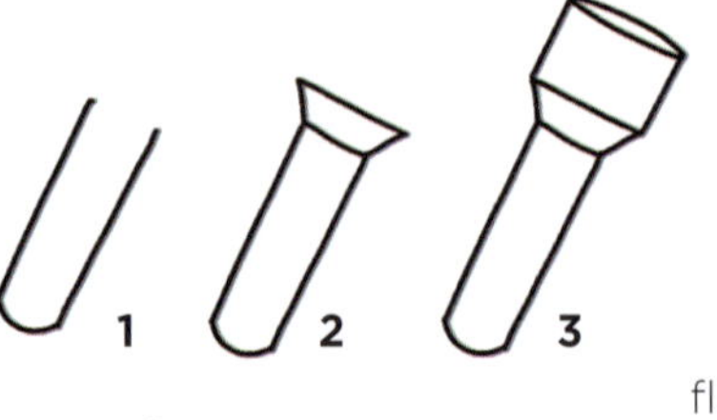

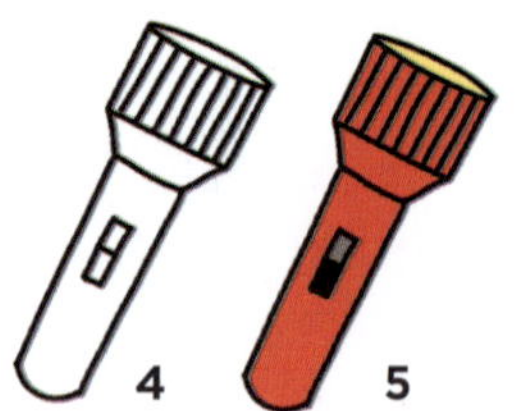

FLASHLIGHT

No one wants to be in the woods after dark without a flashlight! Draw this one by sketching the long handle, then a trapezoid, a rectangle and an oval to finish off the basic flashlight shape. To make your flashlight more realistic, add details like a switch and vertical lines to show texture. When coloring in your flashlight, color the oval part yellow to give the appearance that it's turned on.

COMPASS

A compass can be an incredibly helpful tool, pointing you in the right direction as you hike. To doodle it, draw a circle with a slightly smaller circle inside labeled "N," "S," "E" and "W." You get to choose where the needle of this compass is pointing as you sketch it in place, then add a ring at the top to finish the doodle.

You could also doodle a hiking map using the same basic shape as the subway map on page 124 in the Around Town chapter. Simply adapt it by coloring it in green to indicate a forest, with brown hiking paths and blue lakes.

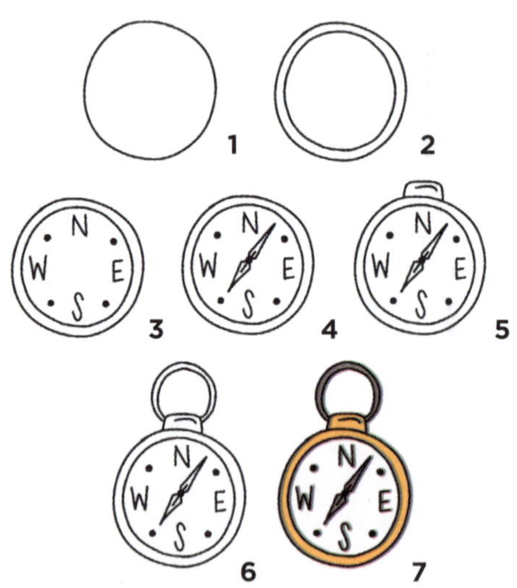

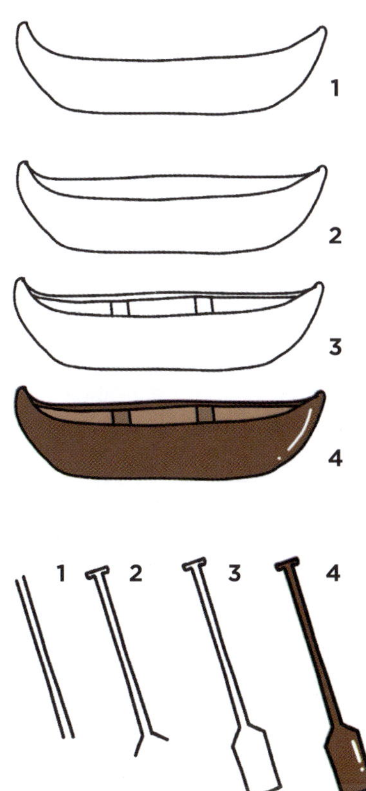

CANOE & PADDLE

To draw a canoe, start with the basic shape: a crescent that resembles a slightly squished banana. Add a horizontal line across the top to create the other side of the canoe and make it appear three-dimensional. Finally, divide the inside of the canoe into several sections, then color it in.

A canoe isn't much good without the ability to make it move across the water. To draw a paddle or an oar, start with a long thin rectangle for the shaft. Then, add a short rectangle on the top for the grip and a house shape (a rectangle with a triangle on top) on the bottom end for the blade.

KAYAK & PADDLE

This doodle of a kayak gives an overhead view to help differentiate it from a canoe. To draw it, make a long thin shape with a point on each end, then draw a curving line on one side to add dimension. Sketch an oval and a semicircle inside the main shape, then your drawing is ready to be colored in.

Unlike a canoe paddle, a kayak paddle has a blade on each end of the shaft. Draw a long thin rectangle with pointed ends, then sketch a rounded rectangle on either side. Add color and highlights to take your doodle to the next level.

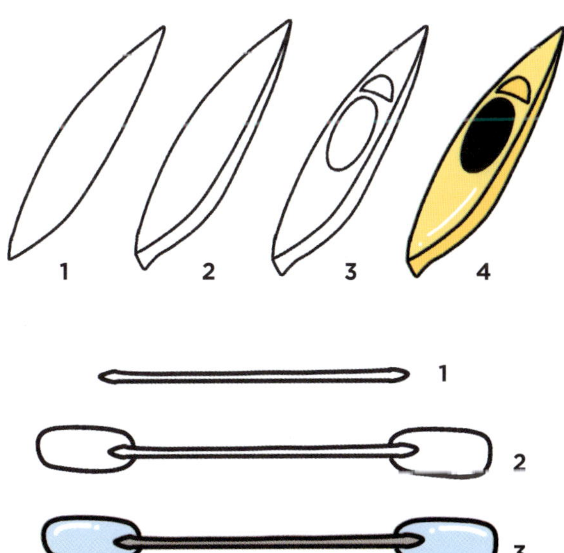

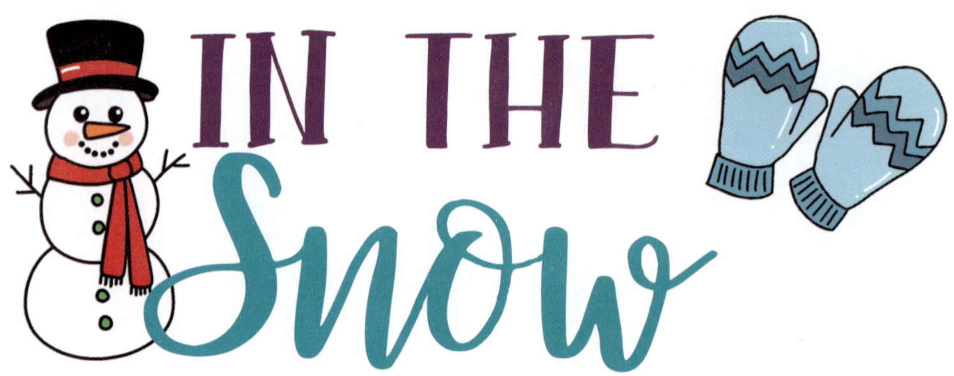

There's something magical about the time of year when snow starts to fall and there's a chill in the air. Like every season, winter has special qualities, and there are lots of cold-weather doodles we can create. Snowflakes, warm winter accessories and animals that live in polar regions are just a few of the drawings this chilly season has to offer. Let's grab a pair of mittens and learn to doodle our favorite things in the snow.

SNOW & ICE

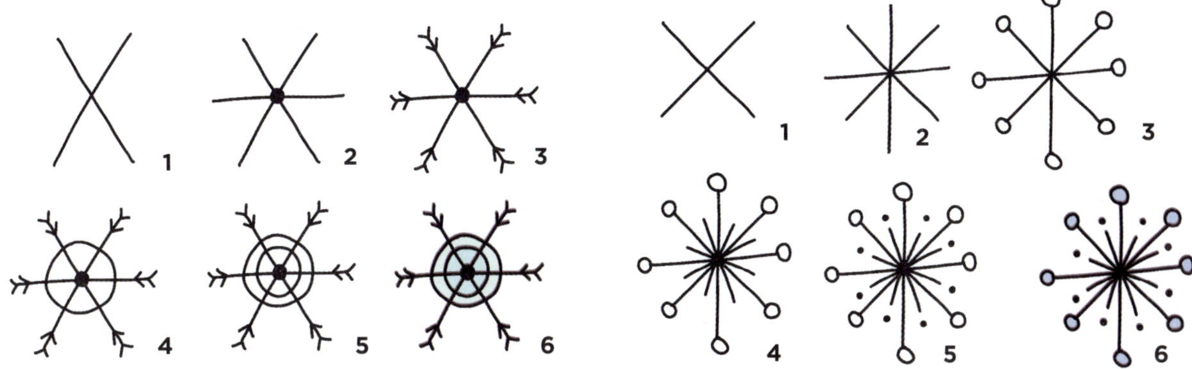

SNOWFLAKES

No two snowflakes are alike, so there are infinite ways to draw them. One way is to draw three intersecting lines, each with two small "V" shapes on the ends. Draw a series of circles inside and color the round part. You can draw this snowflake alone or mixed with other styles for a big snowfall.

For this variation of a snowflake (above right), draw four intersecting lines, then add a tiny circle on the ends of each one. Draw a series of shorter lines in between the existing ones, then add a dot just above each one. To add color, fill in the circles with shades of white, silver, gray or blue.

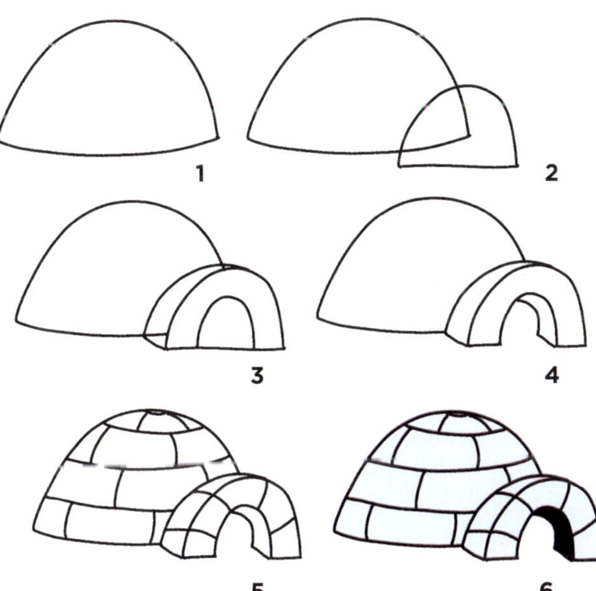

IGLOO

To sketch an igloo, draw a large semicircle with a smaller one overlapping it on the right. Add an arched entryway and a line for dimension, then, using horizontal and vertical lines, divide the entire doodle into a pattern of ice blocks. Leave your igloo white or color it a light shade of blue to show how cold it is.

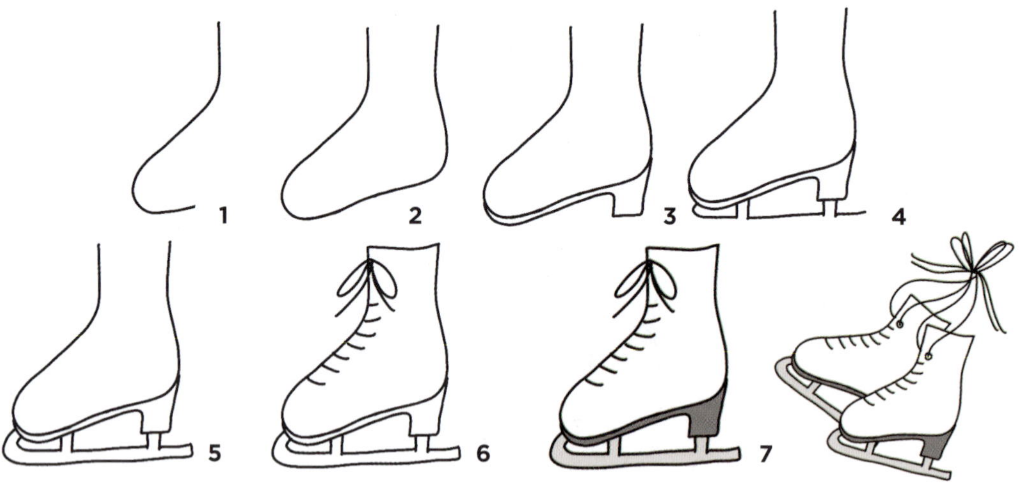

ICE SKATE

Ice-skating is a favorite winter sport for all ages. To sketch a skate, draw a basic boot shape and add a heel. Then, draw a blade underneath, attached to the boot in two spots. Give the boot laces and a tie, then color in your skate to complete the picture. You can draw just one skate or put two together to form a pair.

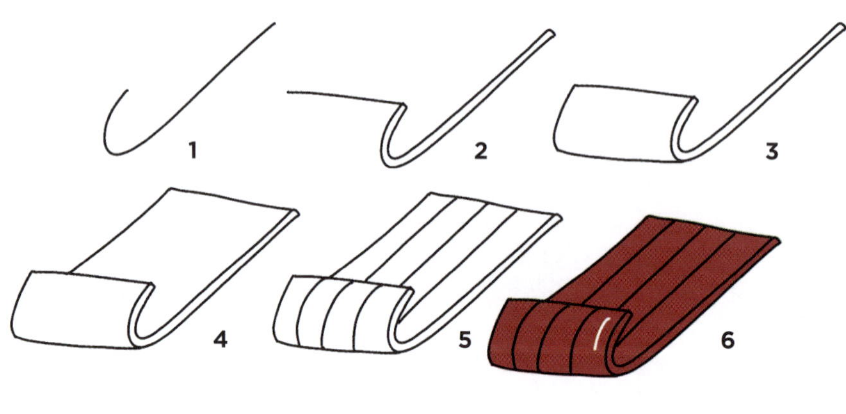

SLED

Who wouldn't want a ride down the hill on this old-fashioned sled? Draw a "J" shape with a horizontal line extending out to the left, then form the front part of the sled. Finish sketching the rectangular shape of the back section and add a series of lines to the entire doodle to show that the sled is made of wood.

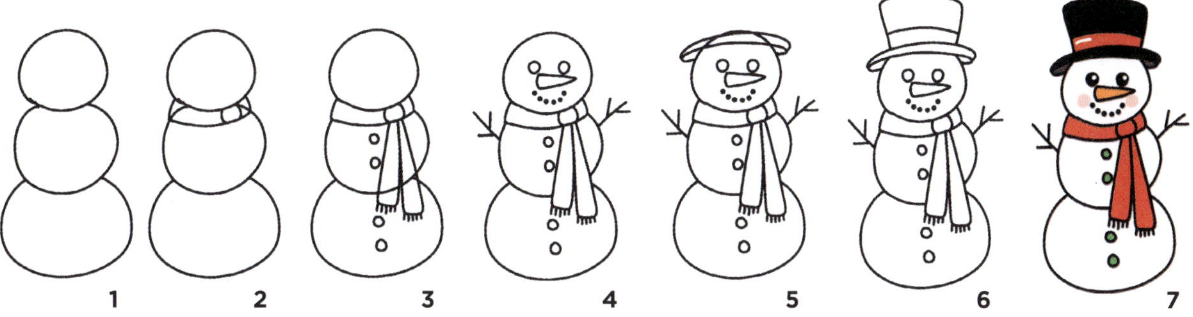

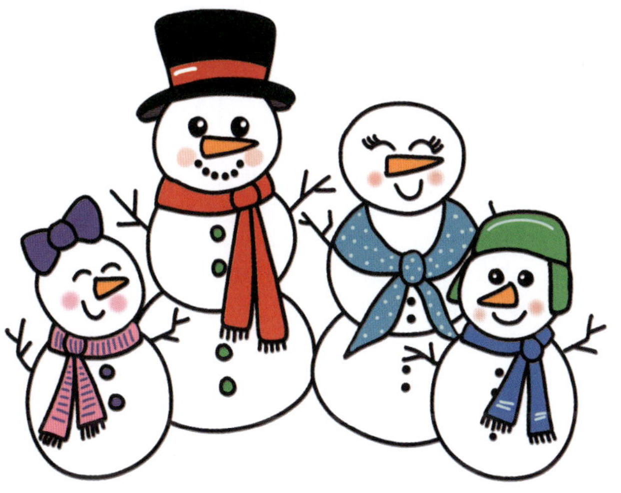

SNOWMAN

Drawing a snowman is warmer than building one, so let's doodle three stacked circles for a body. Next, add a scarf and buttons, as well as two stick arms. And, of course, he'll need a face with two eyes, a carrot nose and a smile. You can stop here or give your snowman a top hat like Frosty. This one has a lot of overlapping lines, so be sure to erase them before outlining and coloring in. You can draw this snowman on his own or create a whole family of snow people in various sizes, each with their own style of hat and accessories.

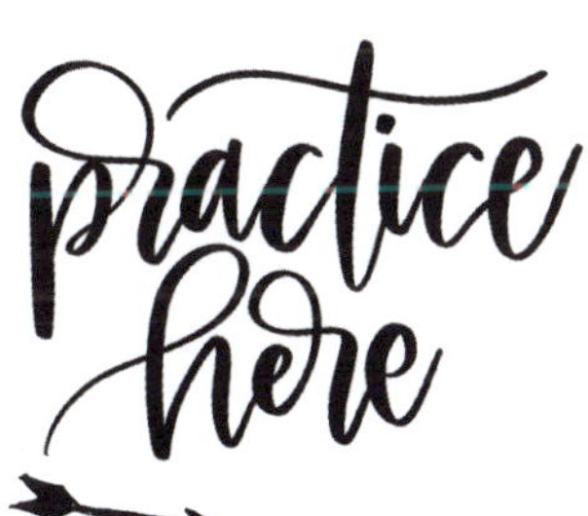

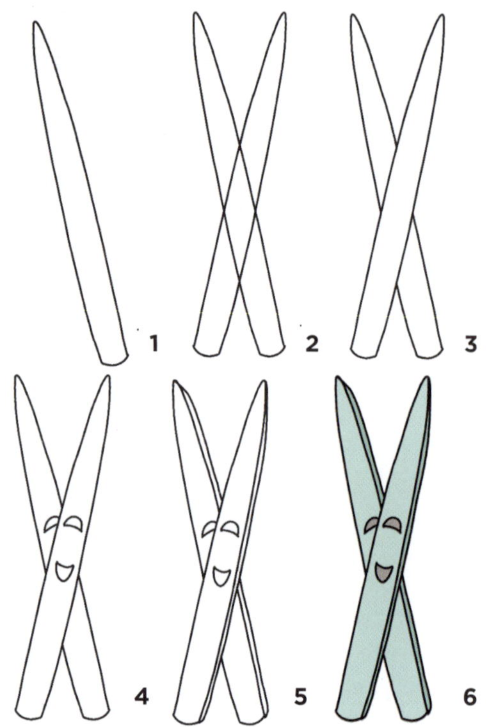

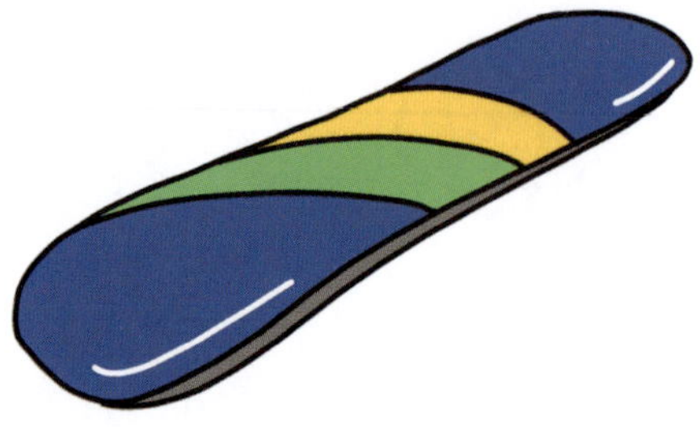

SKIS & SNOWBOARD

To doodle a pair of skis, draw two long thin, rounded triangle shapes crossing one over another in an "X" pattern. Erase the overlapping lines, then add small semicircles where the ski boots attach and a line just to the outside of each ski to show dimension. A simple snowboard is easy to draw too; it's just a wide curved rectangle with rounded edges. Use any colors you like to personalize your skis and snowboard.

SNOW GLOBE

To draw a snow globe, sketch a circle shape on top of a base, then add whatever winter scene you like on the inside. I drew a simple pine tree shape in mine and added a wavy line to represent the snow at the bottom. Draw a highlight area where the light hits the glass of the globe, then add color to your doodle. I used a very light blue for the glass and a white gel pen is perfect for adding tiny dots of swirling snow.

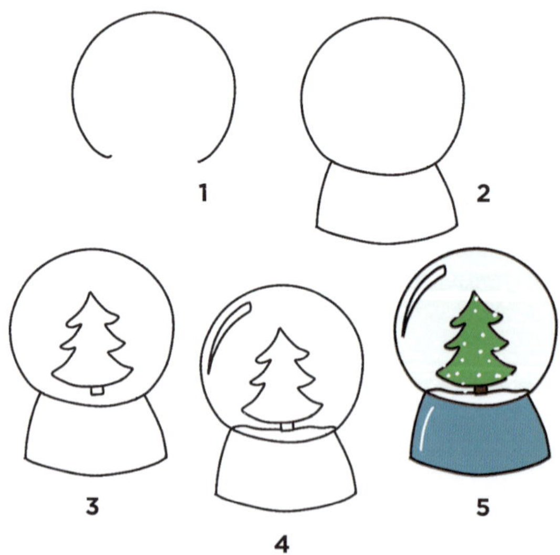

WINTER WEAR

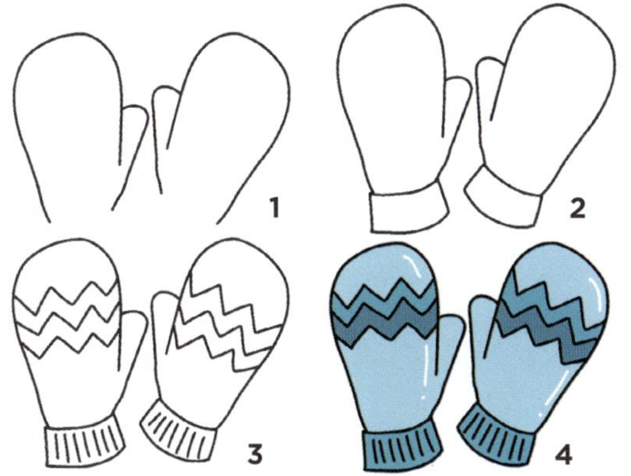

MITTENS

This winter mitten doodle starts with two upside-down "U" shapes with thumbs on opposite sides. Add a band at the bottom of each mitten, then draw detail lines on the bands and on the mittens themselves. Use whatever patterns and colors you like to customize this winter accessory.

WINTER HAT

Draw an upside-down "U" shape with a rectangle band for the main shape. Add a fluffy pom-pom on top and details like lines along the band. I gave my hat a zigzag pattern; you can do the same or use any other decorative pattern to make your hat unique.

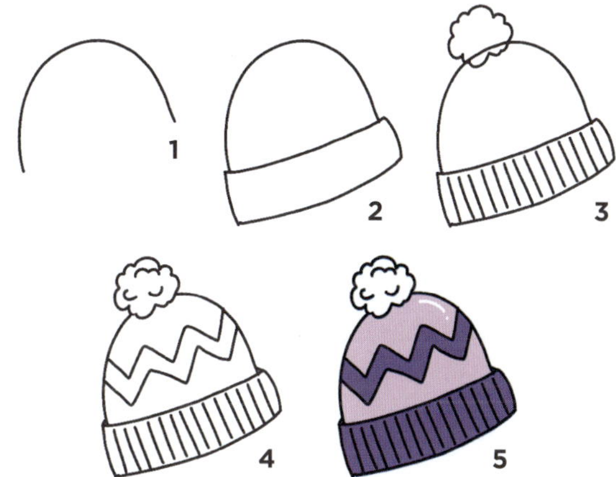

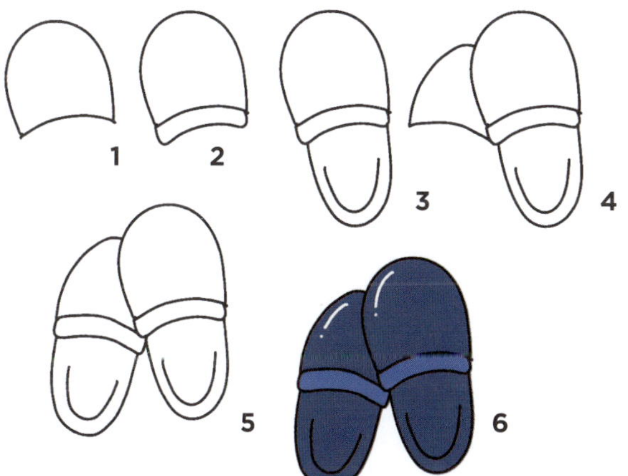

SLIPPERS

There's nothing like curling up in your slippers after a long winter's day. To draw a pair, make a semicircle with a band for the top part of one slipper and add a "U" shape for the sole. Then, draw a second slipper slightly underneath the top of the first one. Color in your slippers with solid shades or add a decorative pattern.

ARCTIC ANIMALS

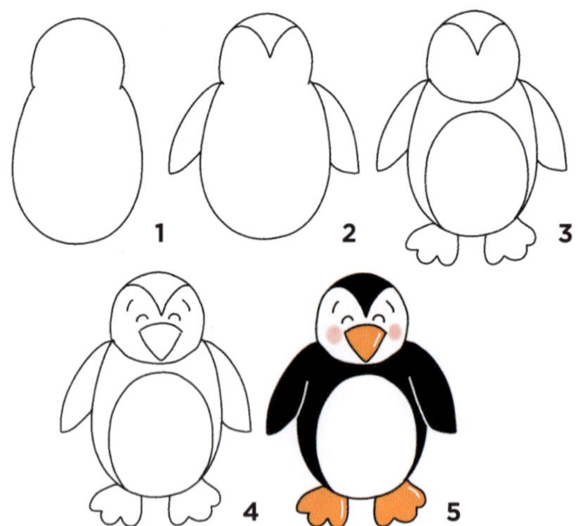

PENGUIN

This cheerful penguin has a body shaped like a wide "8" with a wing on each side. Once you've drawn the base, add a point on the top of the head and a rounded line separating the belly from the rest of the body. Draw two webbed feet and a happy face, then use color to finish your penguin. You can use a white gel pen to indicate where the wings overlap the body.

SEAL

Start by sketching the seal's head and a downward-curving line for the back. Add another shorter curving line on the bottom and a flipper. Finish the seal's body with a "V" shaped tail and a second front flipper, drawing detail lines on those areas. Give your seal a face, then color in your little wintery friend light gray or leave it white.

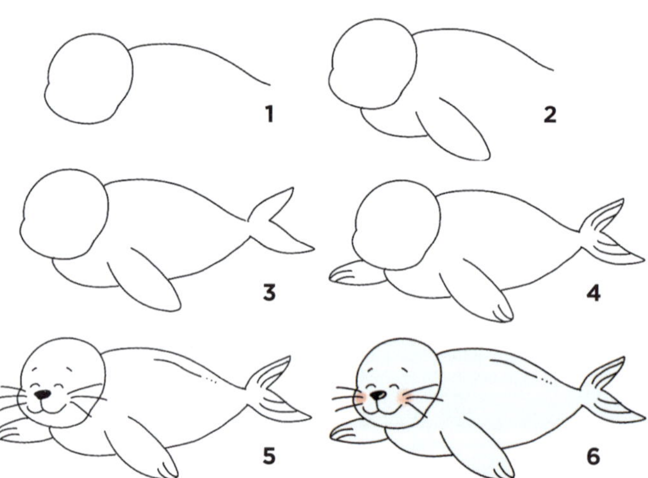

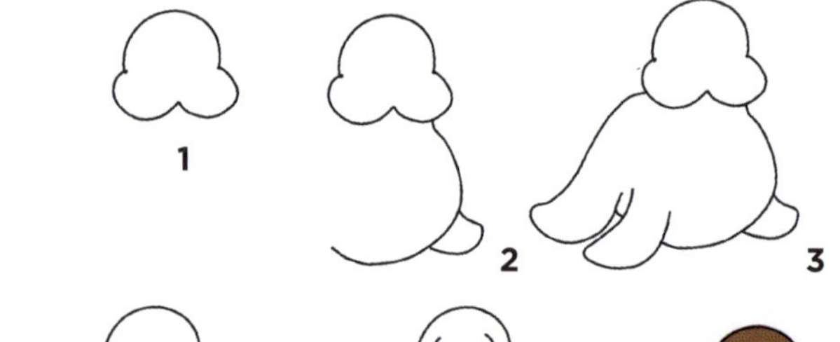

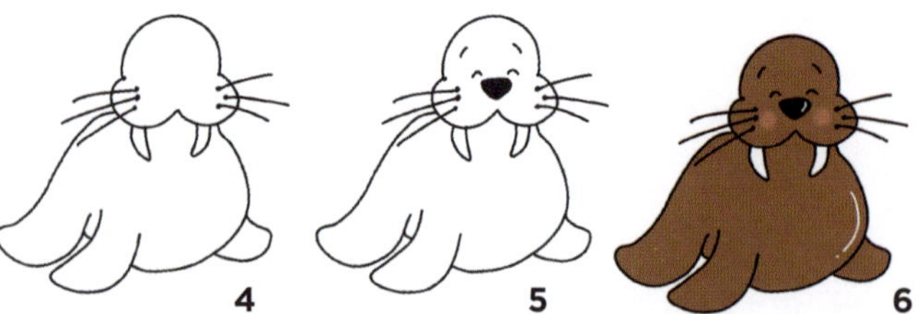

WALRUS

The first step in drawing a walrus is to sketch a semicircle with a sideways "3" shape at the bottom for the head. Next, add a large curved line for a rounded belly, two front flippers and a tail. Finally, give your walrus tusks and whiskers, along with eyes and a big triangle-shaped nose to finish off that happy face.

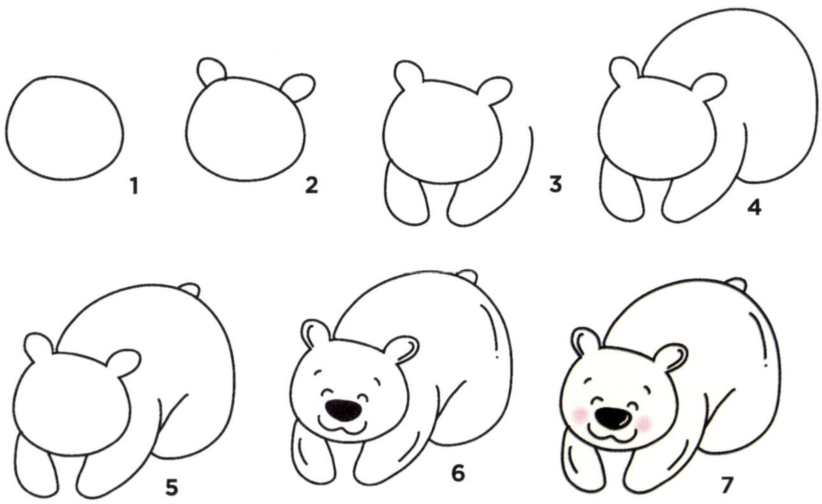

POLAR BEAR

A polar bear doodle starts with an oval head and two tiny ears on top. Next, add short rounded arms in front and a large curving line to form the body. Give your bear a hind leg and a little tail, along with eyes, a nose and a smile shaped like a sideways "3." You can leave your bear white or use a very light brown or gray to add just a hint of color, plus those rosy cheeks!

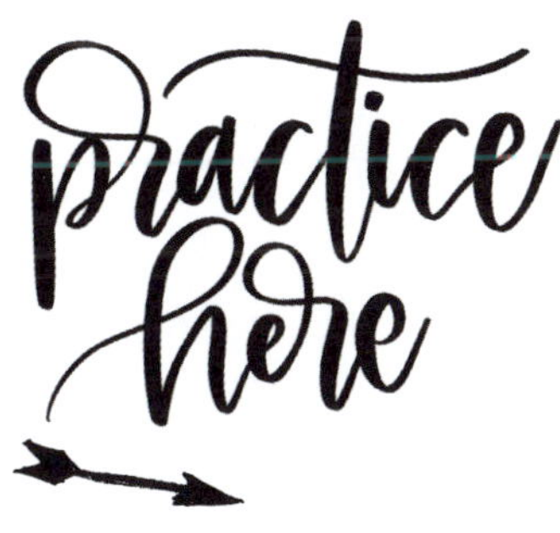

AT THE Holidays

Every year is filled with celebrations and holidays, and there may be no doodles more fun to draw than those associated with these special days. From New Year's Eve to Thanksgiving, Hanukkah and Christmas, every holiday has its own special symbols we can incorporate into our hand-drawn cards, gift tags, calendars, planners and more. This is by no means an exhaustive list of holiday symbols, but hopefully it will get you started with some festive illustrations. I've also included some banners, balloons and other party décor and food that you can use when celebrating any special occasion!

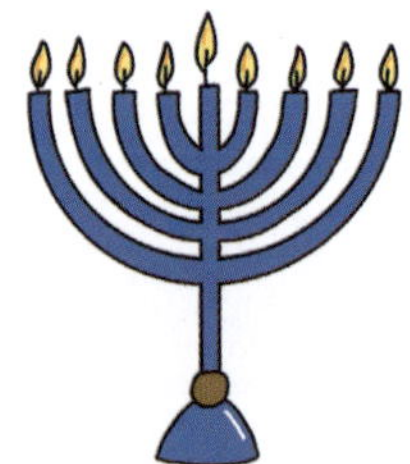

CHRISTMAS

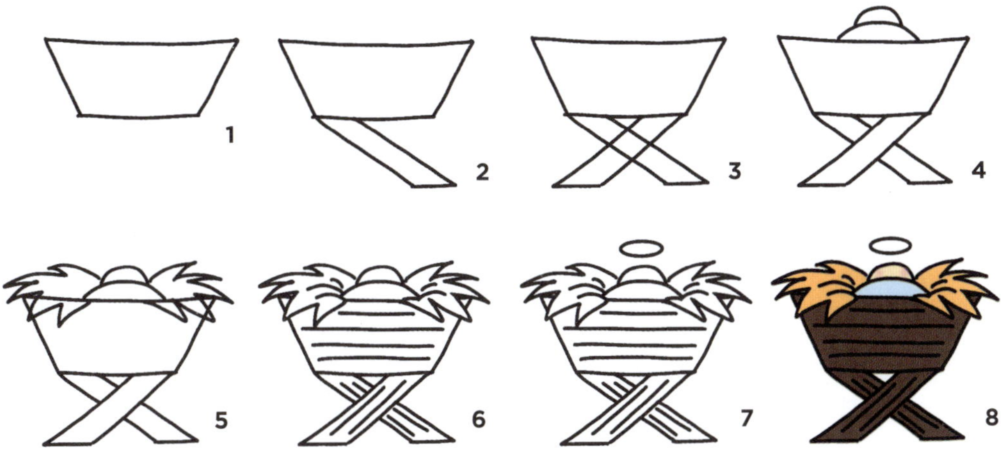

MANGER

Baby Jesus is the most important part of Christmas, so it's only fitting that we learn to draw Him first. Start by sketching the manger, which is a trapezoid shape with legs that cross over each other to form an "X" shape. Next, draw two semicircles for the baby's head and body and add tufts of hay on both sides. Add detail lines in the hay and all over the manger to show texture and draw a tiny halo above the baby's head.

STAR

The Christmas star led the Magi to baby Jesus and shone more brightly than any other star in the sky. To draw it, form four points, with the one on the bottom being larger/longer than the other three. Then, add a smaller point in the space between each of the larger ones, so that you have an eight-pointed shape. Erase the overlapping lines and add short detail lines coming out from the star to show how brightly it shines.

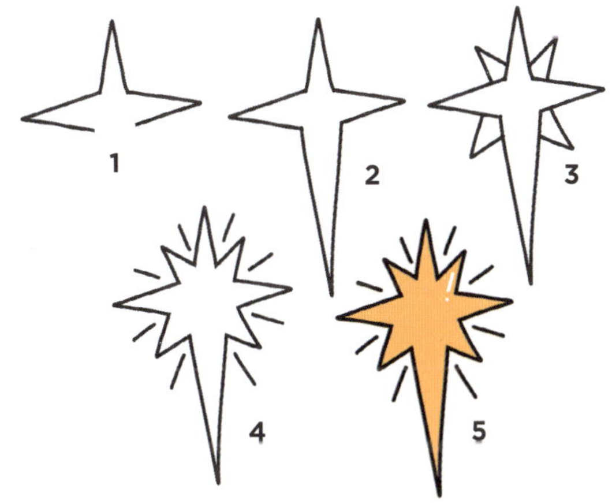

HOLLY

To draw holly leaves, make two multi-pointed lines that connect at the top and bottom. I like to draw these leaves in sets of two or three, then add a few berries where they join. Finally, draw a line through the center of each leaf. For realistic holly, color in your leaves a dark green and the berries a bright red.

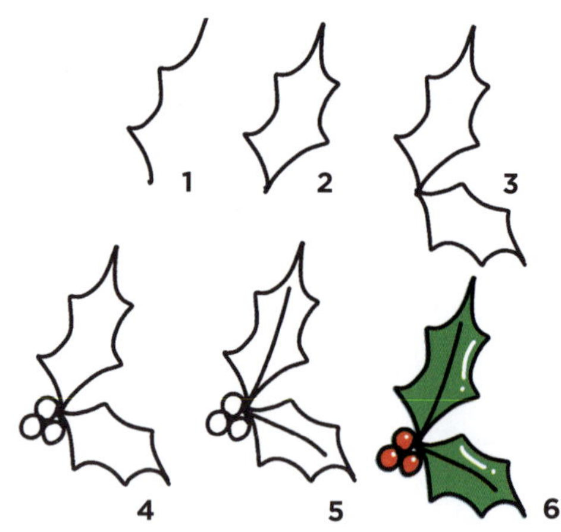

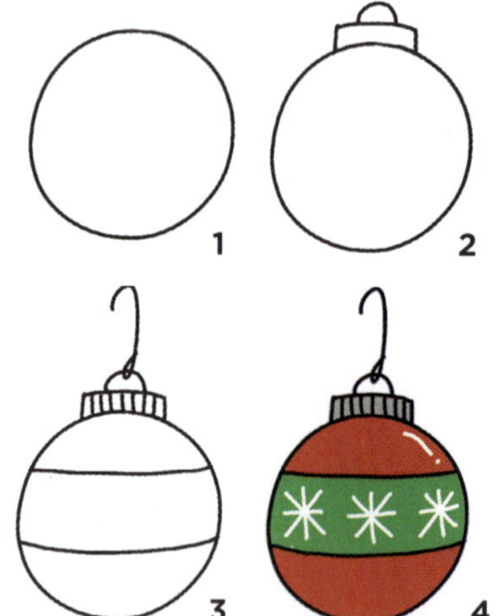

ORNAMENT

A simple ornament is just a circle with a rectangle on top and a "J"-shaped hook. Of course, you can add variety to your ornament doodles by playing around with different shapes and sizes, as well as ways to decorate them. I added a stripe with snowflakes across the center of this one and colored it in traditional red and green.

GIFT

Doodle this wrapped gift by making a square with an angled rectangle on the side and the top to form a cube. Next, draw lines to divide the cube so that it looks like a box with a lid. Add a bow on top and a ribbon coming down the front of the box. Color in the box and the ribbon and, if you like, you can even doodle it under a tree!

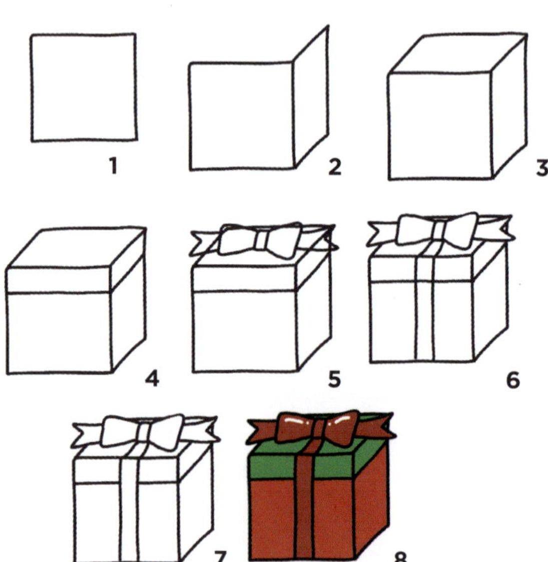

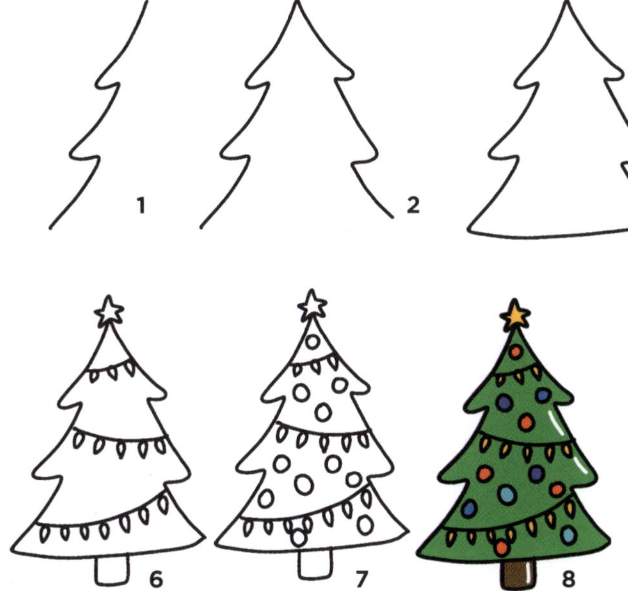

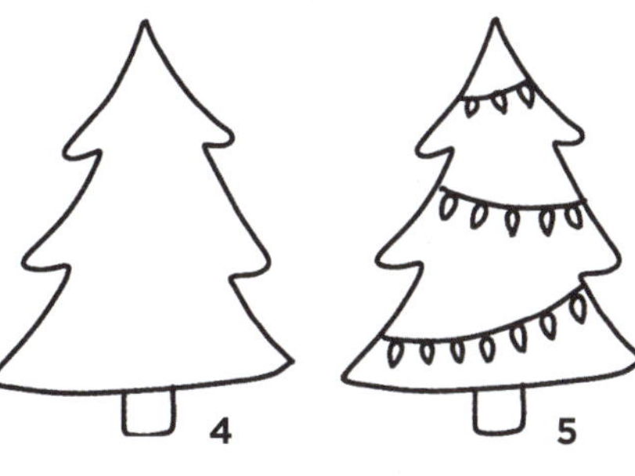

CHRISTMAS TREE

Christmas trees are perfect for embellishing cards, gift tags and more. Draw the sides of the tree first, then connect them with a curving line at the bottom. Add a trunk, then decorate your tree with tiny lights, ornaments and a star on top.

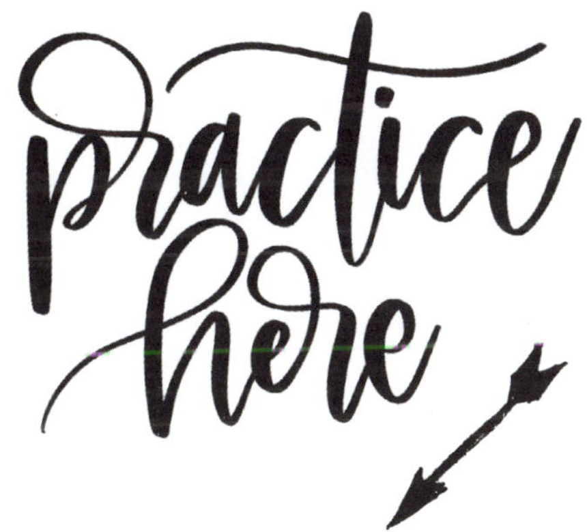

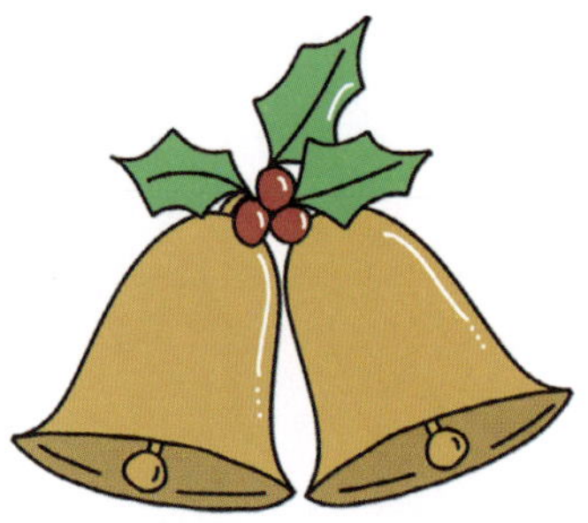

BELLS

Will you hear the bells on Christmas day? You can draw them, starting with a curving arch and an oval at the bottom. Sketch a round clapper inside the oval, then add a bow on top of the bell. Erase the overlapping lines before outlining and coloring in the ribbon and bell. You can draw one bell by itself or put two together, attached with a bow or some festive holly.

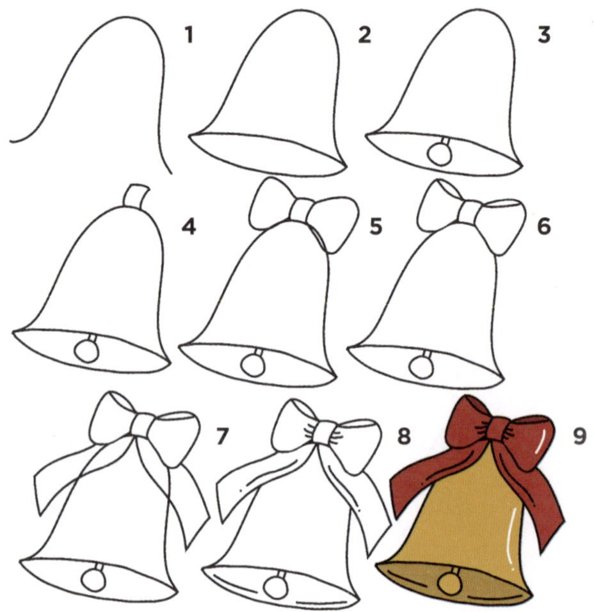

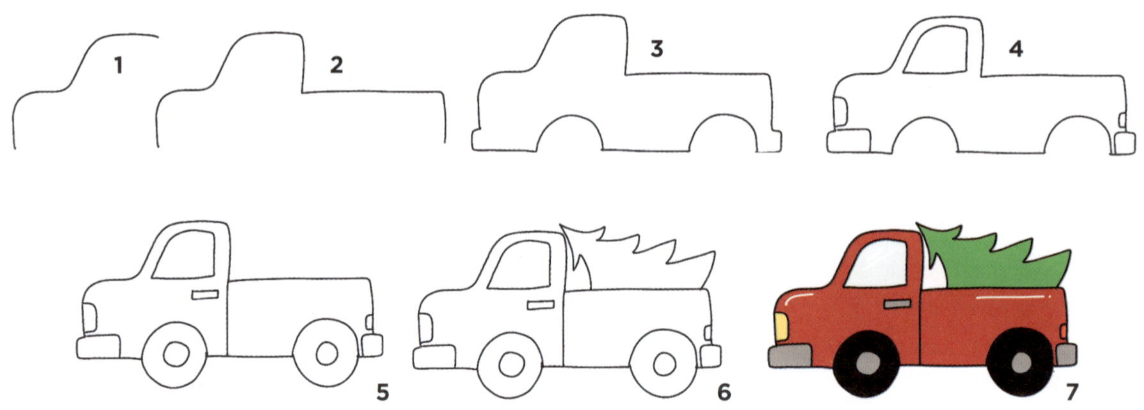

PICKUP TRUCK

The classic red pickup truck with a tree in the back is becoming a very popular holiday image. Doodle this one by sketching a curving line for the roof and hood, then form the bed of the truck. Add a bumper, headlights, a window and spots for the tires, then draw the tires themselves along with a door handle. Finally, sketch a freshly cut tree in the truck's bed.

STRING LIGHTS

Doodle a strand of Christmas lights by drawing a curving line with tiny rectangles going across it on both sides. Add a teardrop-shaped lightbulb to each rectangle. Then, color your bulbs and add highlights, as well as little detail lines, to show that they are shining. These lights make a really fun border for an envelope or a drawing, and you can also use them to decorate a drawing of a tree or a house.

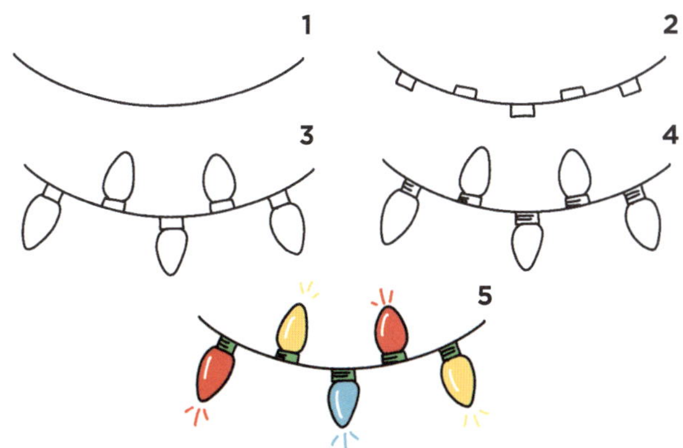

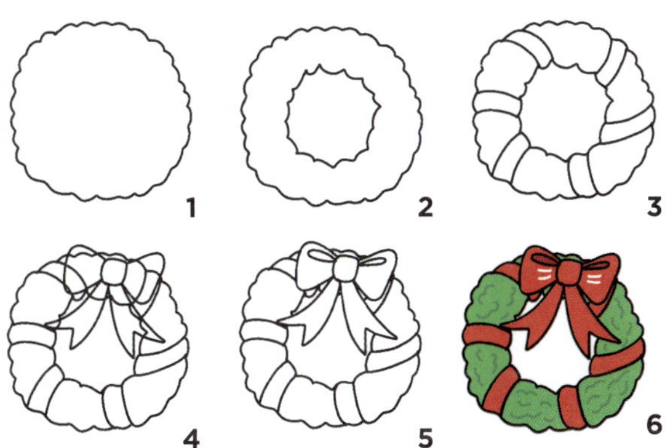

WREATH

Christmas wreaths are festive on the front door or inside the house; draw this one by creating a large bumpy circle with a smaller one inside. Add lines around the circle to represent the ribbon, then draw a bow at the top. Color your wreath, adding little bumpy lines throughout to suggest the fluffy texture of greenery.

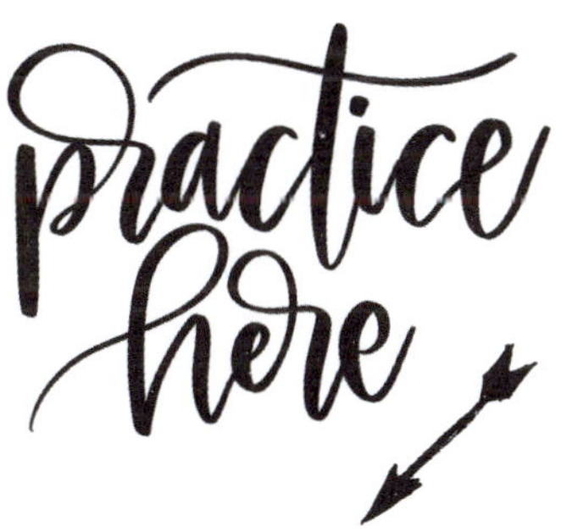

CANDY CANE

Candy canes are a favorite Christmas treat and they're simple to doodle. Draw an upside-down "J" shape, then add a series of stripes. Traditional candy canes are white with red stripes, but now they are available in so many different flavors that there's no wrong way to color in yours.

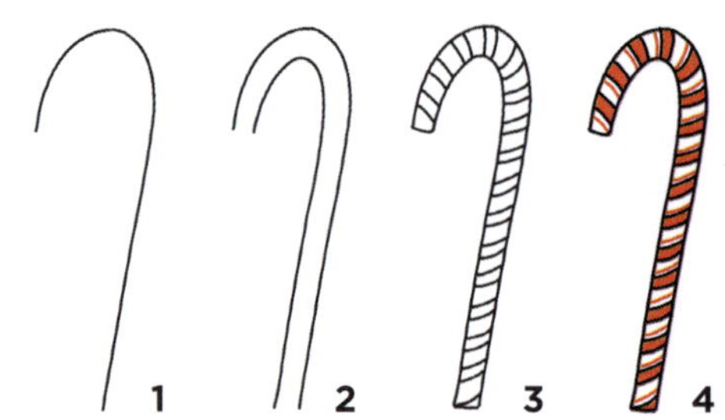

CANDLE

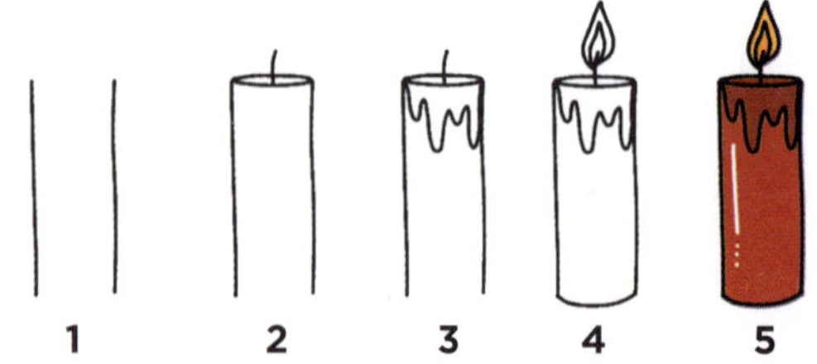

Draw a pillar candle by sketching two parallel lines with an oval connecting them on top. It can be as tall, short, wide or thin as you want it to be. Next, add a short line for the wick and a wavy line to indicate where the wax has melted. Finally, add a teardrop-shaped flame around the wick.

STOCKING

A stocking is very much like a sock, starting with a basic boot shape. Add a wide brim across the top with a loop in the corner for hanging the stocking on the mantel. For more detail, mark off the toe and the heel areas with short curving lines and add a series of dashes around the band to look like stitches.

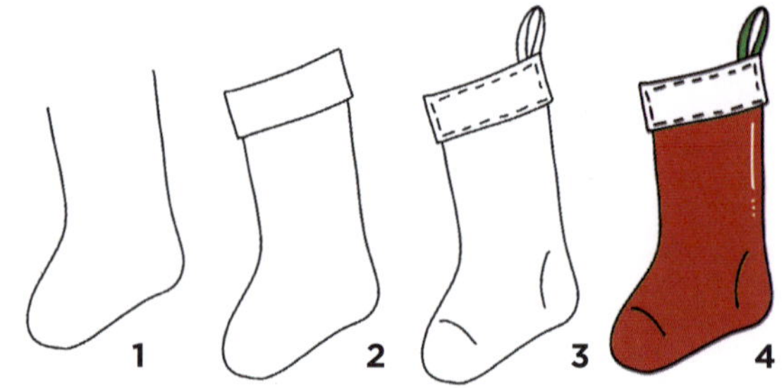

SANTA HAT

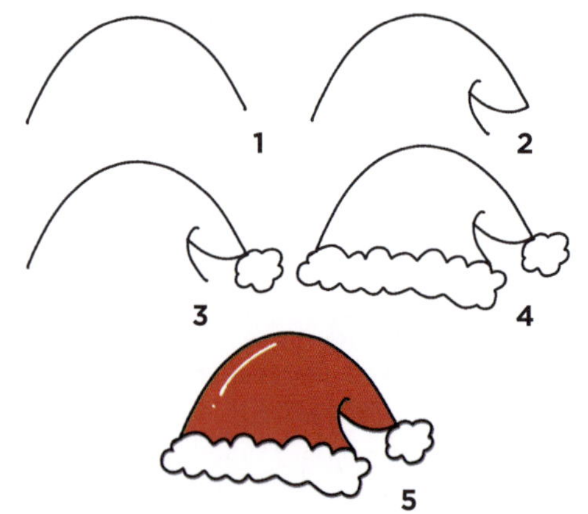

Ho, ho, ho! Draw Santa's hat by making an arch and sketching a point at the end. Give it a fluffy brim and a pom-pom at the end and color it in bright red so everyone knows it belongs to Father Christmas!

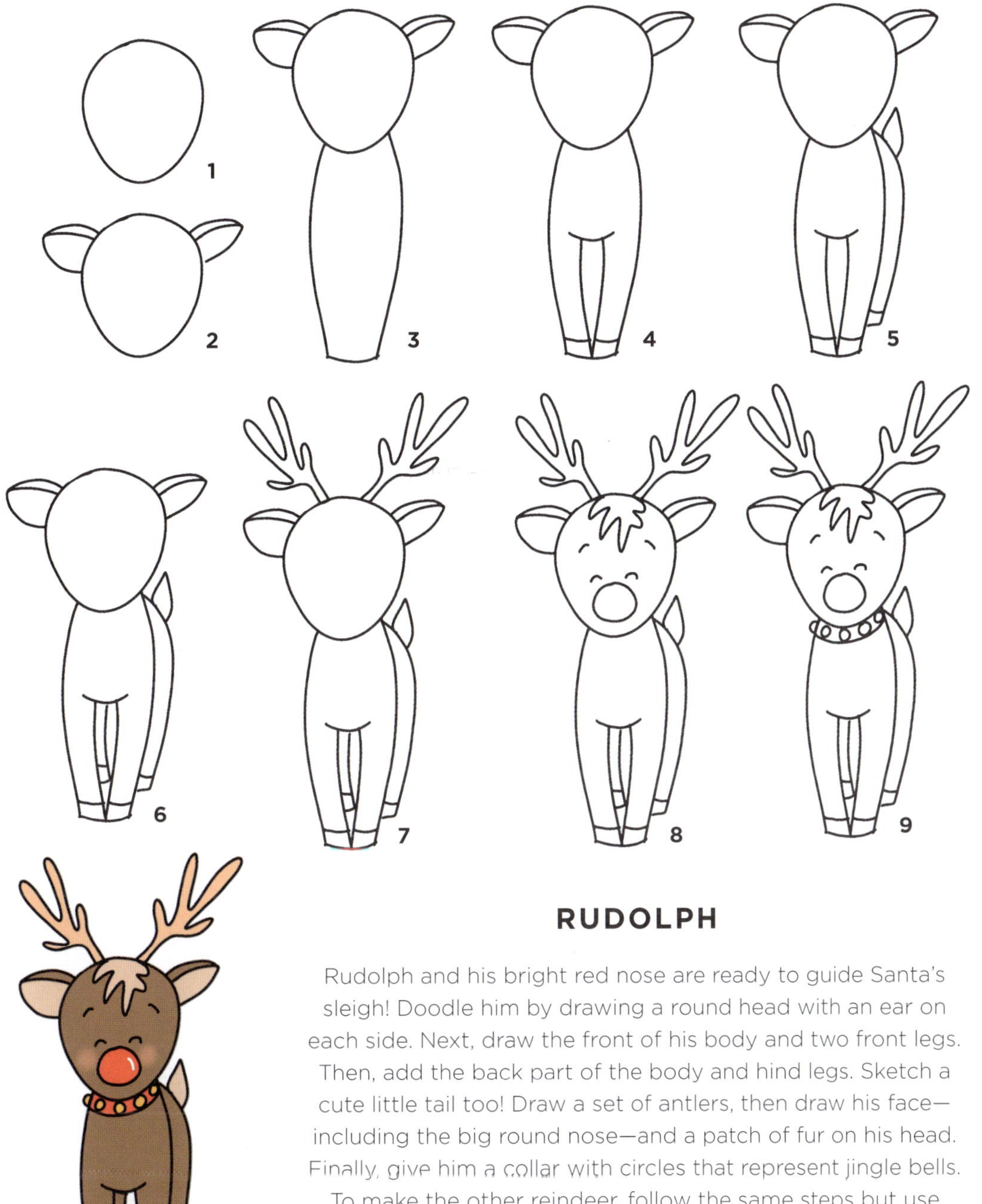

RUDOLPH

Rudolph and his bright red nose are ready to guide Santa's sleigh! Doodle him by drawing a round head with an ear on each side. Next, draw the front of his body and two front legs. Then, add the back part of the body and hind legs. Sketch a cute little tail too! Draw a set of antlers, then draw his face—including the big round nose—and a patch of fur on his head. Finally, give him a collar with circles that represent jingle bells. To make the other reindeer, follow the same steps but use smaller noses that don't glow.

NEW YEAR'S

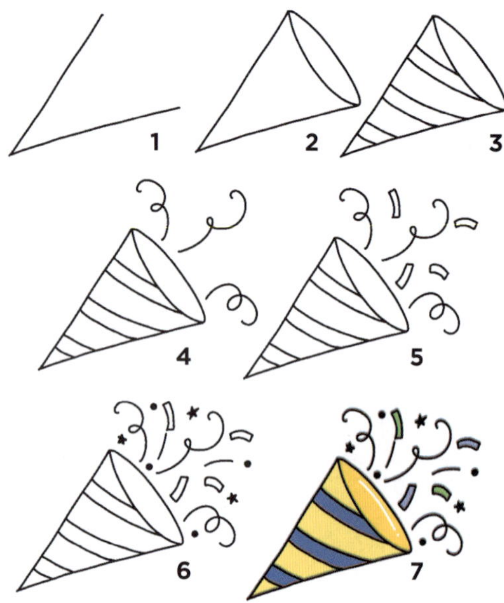

CONFETTI POPPER

The base of a confetti popper is simply a triangle with an oval at the base. The fun part comes when you decorate and color it in! Add stripes, dots, words or any pattern you like to the triangle, then it's time to make some confetti. Draw a variety of curling lines, tiny dots and stars, and small rectangles to represent the confetti flying out into the air in celebration.

CHAMPAGNE GLASSES

Champagne glasses are a great doodle for ringing in the new year, as well as for all kinds of other celebratory occasions. To draw them, start with two narrow "U" shapes tilting toward each other and add ovals on top. Then, sketch stems and bases below each glass and draw ovals inside to show the champagne. For an extra effect, add a few tiny bubbles rising up in between the glasses.

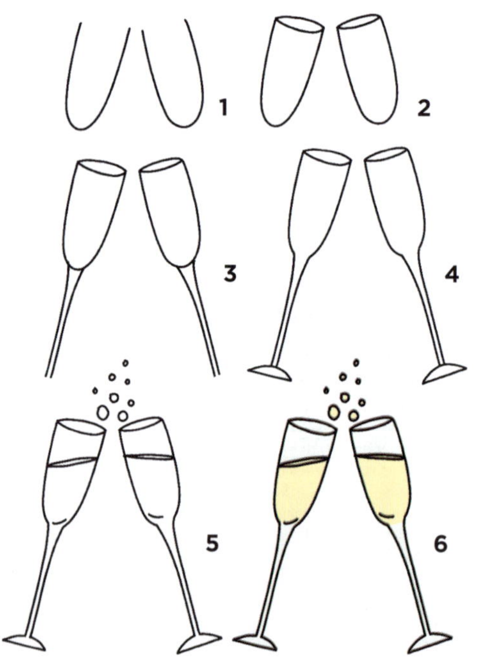

VALENTINE'S DAY

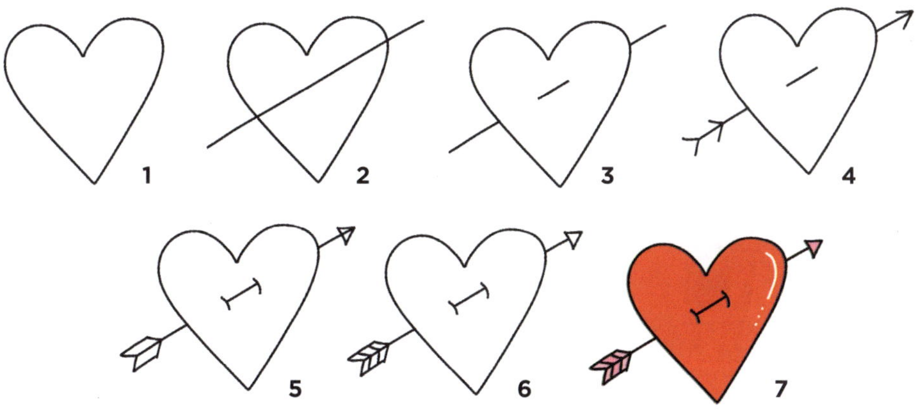

HEART & ARROW

This heart has been hit with Cupid's arrow! Draw it by making a heart shape with a diagonal line going through it. Erase parts of the line on either side of the center section and give the arrow a triangle point. Add details to the other end of the arrow, then color your illustration.

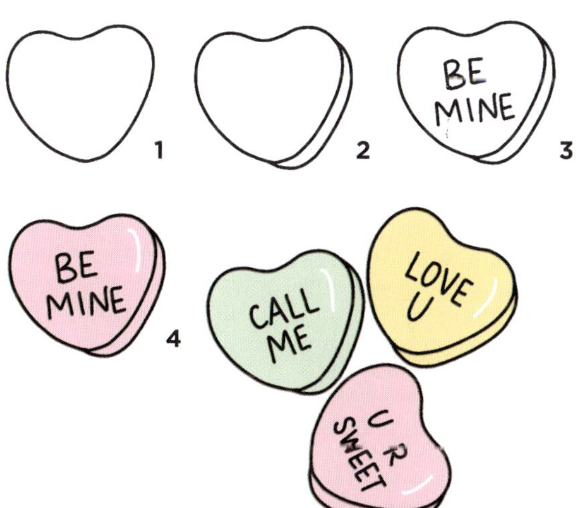

CANDY HEARTS

Sweet candy hearts are synonymous with Valentine's Day, whether you like to eat them or not. To doodle them, start with a rounded heart shape that has a curving line on one side to show dimension. Then, add your favorite phrases, like "BE MINE," "U R SWEET," "CALL ME" or "LOVE U." When you add color, remember that these sweet treats are usually pastel shades.

ST. PATRICK'S DAY

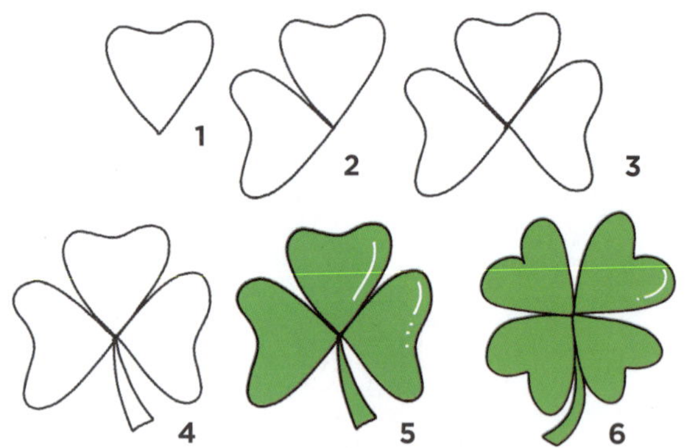

SHAMROCK

Shamrocks were one of the visual aides used by St. Patrick to help explain the concept of the Holy Trinity to the Irish people. They are incredibly simple to draw; just form three rounded heart shapes connected together in the center, then add a stem. To turn this doodle into a lucky four-leaf clover, just add a fourth heart on the bottom and move the stem to a spot in between two of the hearts.

POT OF GOLD

The pot of gold at the end of the rainbow may not really exist, but we can draw one that does. Sketch a rounded shape with an oval at the top for the base of the pot, then add two small circles on the bottom to help it stand. Draw semicircles inside for the golden treasure and sketch a handle on each side. When you color your doodle, add some gold or yellow lines coming out from the treasure to show how brightly it shines!

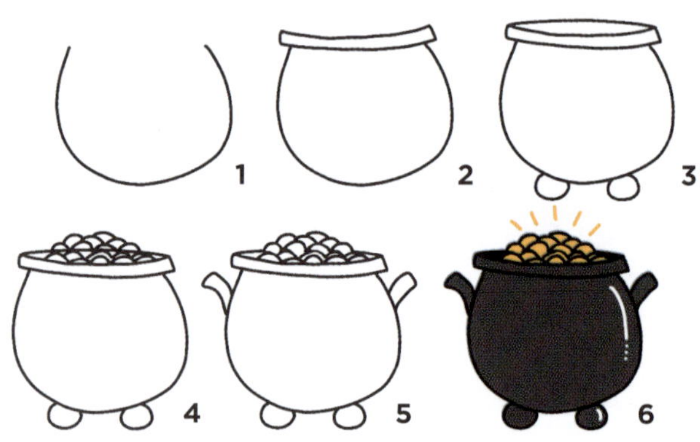

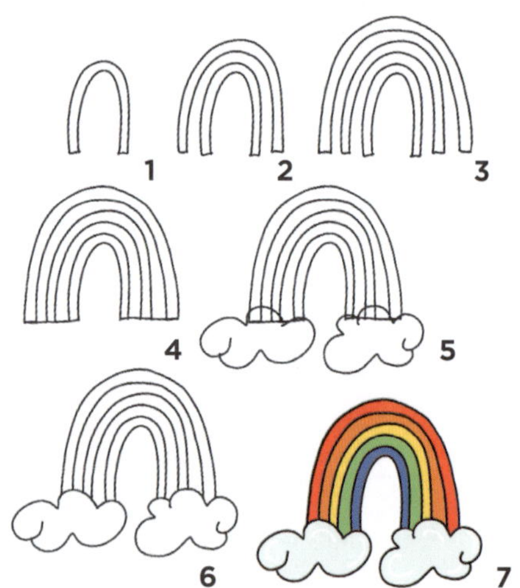

RAINBOW

This colorful rainbow doodle is perfect for St. Patrick's Day, but it's also a fun embellishment all year long. Start with a series of arches, then add a fluffy cloud on each end, erasing any overlapping lines. For a traditional rainbow, follow the "ROY G. BIV" color scheme or play around with different color patterns to make a bohemian-style rainbow instead.

EASTER

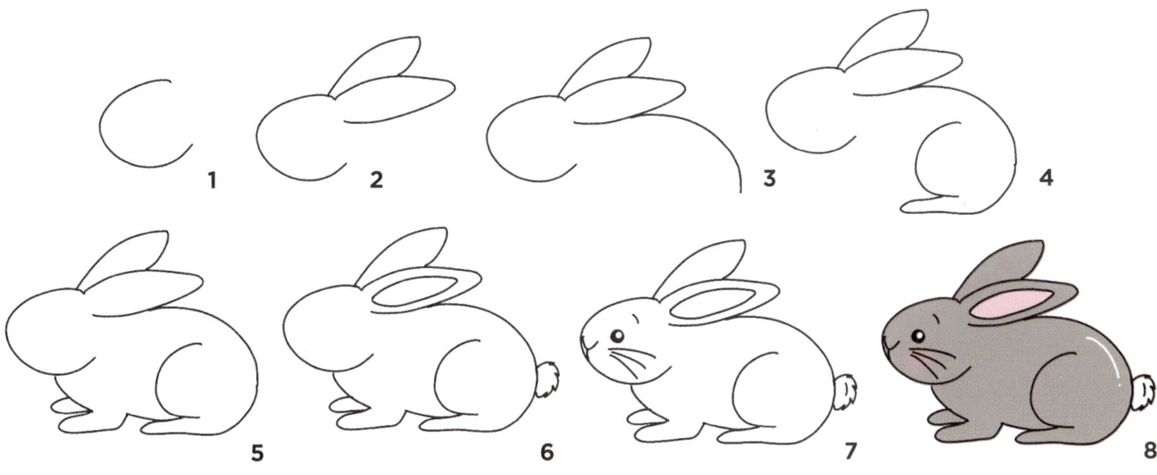

BUNNY

While the Easter Bunny may be the most famous of rabbits, this little bunny drawing can be used at any time and for any kind of project. To draw it, start with a "C"-shaped face and a pair of long ears. Add a curving line for the back and bring it around to form a back leg and a foot. Add front feet and a tummy, along with a fluffy tail. Finally, add details like the face, whiskers and an area to color in inside the front ear.

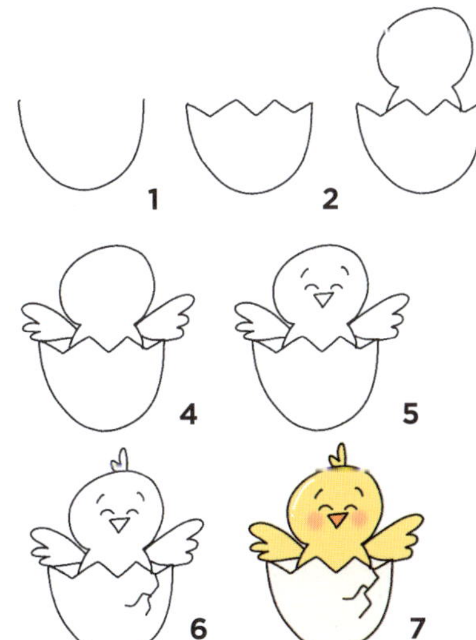

HATCHING CHICK

This baby chick is quite excited to be hatching just in time for spring! Draw his egg first, making a "U" shape with a zigzag top. Then, add the chick inside by drawing a head and a body with a little set of wings. Give him a face and a few feathers on top of his head and add the final detail of a crack in the eggshell.

EASTER BASKET

Sketch the basket's base first and add a band across the top. Next, add a checkerboard pattern to show the basket's weave. Make a large arch for the handle and draw a curving line on top of the base to give the basket dimension. Leave the basket empty or fill it with candy (page 89) and eggs (below).

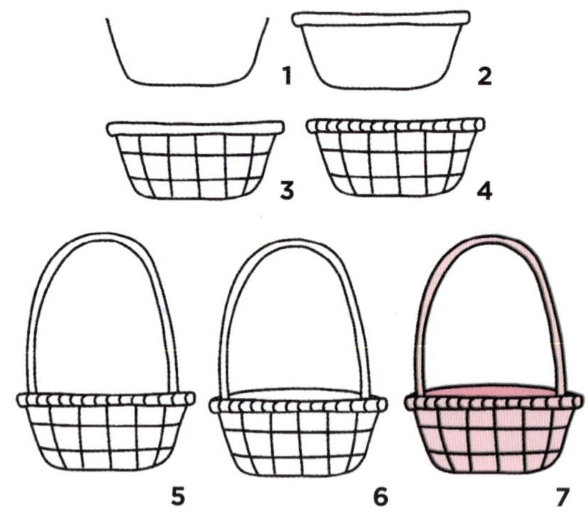

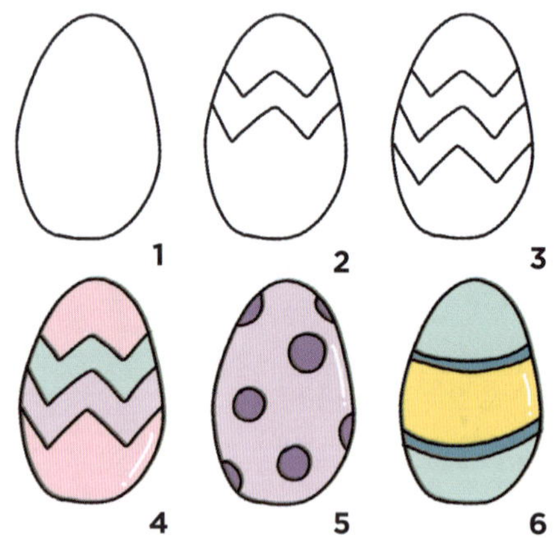

EASTER EGGS

Easter eggs are some of the easiest holiday doodles to draw. Sketch a basic egg shape, then have fun decorating it with all kinds of patterns. I made dots, stripes and zigzags on mine and chose a variety of pastel colors.

LILY

Easter lilies are a beautiful symbol of spring and new life. To draw this one, start with a curved shape with three pointed petals, then add three more until you have a six-petaled shape. Sketch a cluster of curved lines with tiny circles on the end inside the flower. Add a "V" shape for the base of the flower, then draw a stem and long thin leaves.

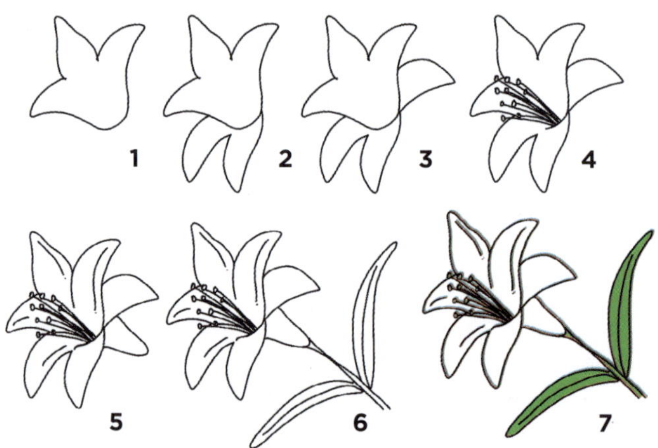

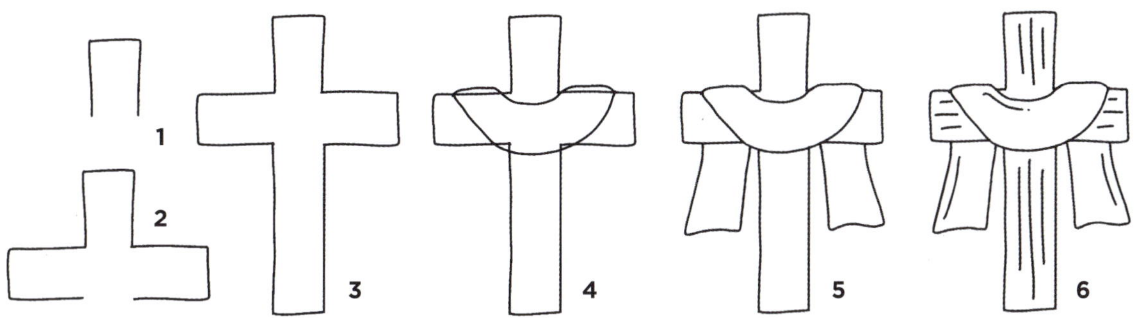

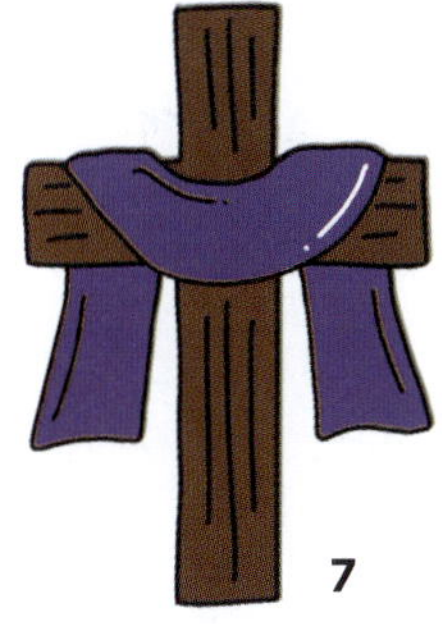

CROSS

A cross is the most significant of all Easter symbols, making a beautiful addition to cards and other Easter projects. To draw the cross itself, sketch a vertical rectangle intersected by a horizontal one. Then, make the fabric drape by drawing a "U" shape across the front and a rounded rectangle shape behind each side of the crossbar. To give the cross a wooden texture, add some detail lines that vary in length. The fabric drape is typically purple during the 40 days leading up to Easter, black on Good Friday and white on Easter Sunday.

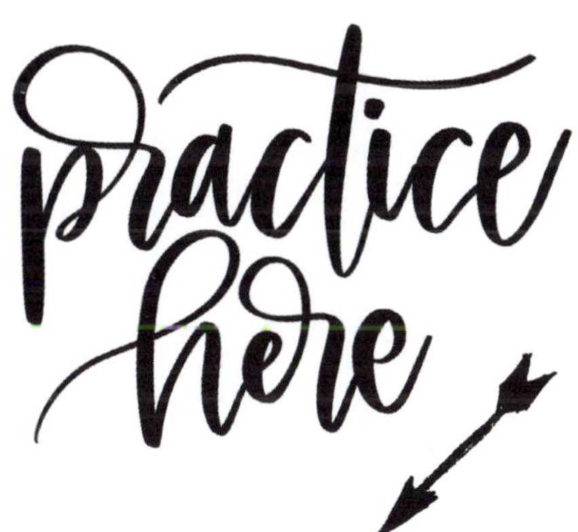

FOURTH OF JULY

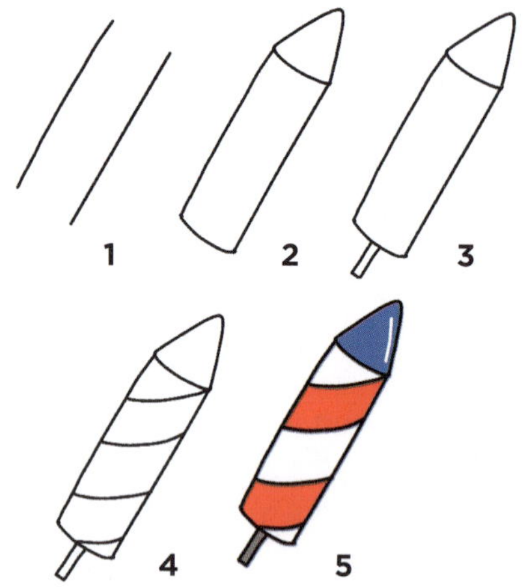

FIREWORK

This festive firework is just a rectangle with a cone shape on top. Add a fuse at the bottom and stripes on the sides, then color it in red, white and blue or whatever colors you like. It's perfect for the Fourth of July, but it also makes a great embellishment for any festive occasion.

TOP HAT

Draw Uncle Sam's top hat by making a tall rectangle with a semicircle on top. Add a band and a long "C"-shaped brim, then draw vertical stripes down the top part of the hat. Color the different sections and, using a white gel pen, add little white stars to the band.

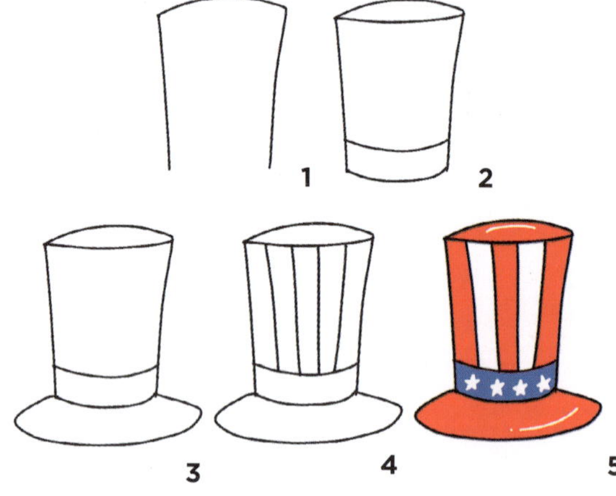

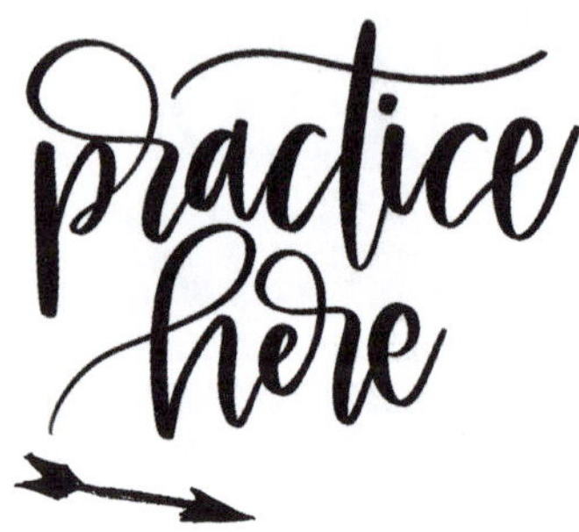

HALLOWEEN

CANDY CORN

Candy corn is a simple, festive doodle made up simply of a triangle divided into three even sections. As you color it in, remember that the tip is white, the middle section is orange and the bottom is either yellow or brown.

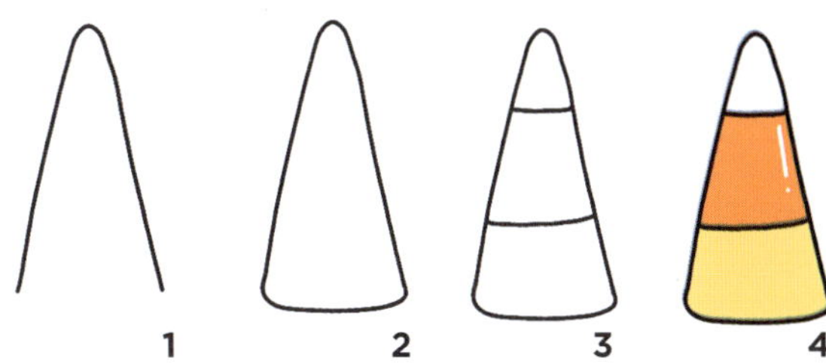

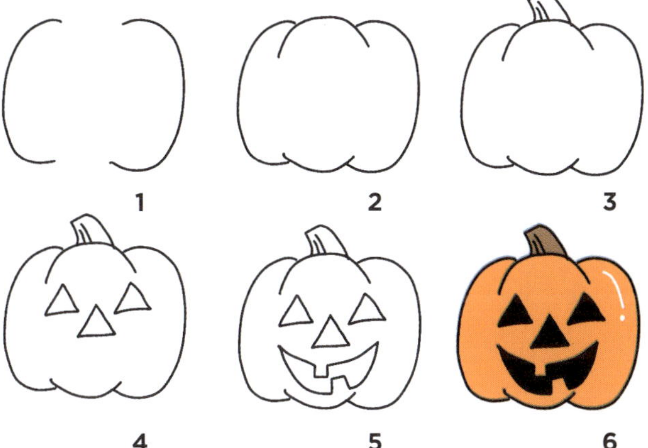

JACK-O'-LANTERN

To start this jack-o'-lantern doodle, draw a pair of parentheses. Connect them with short curving lines to form the basic pumpkin shape, then add a stem and triangles for the eyes and the nose. Finish your jack-o-lantern by sketching a toothy smile and coloring it in.

SPIDER

To doodle a spider, draw an oval with four legs on each side. Add a pair of large round eyes, then color in the body with black, brown or gray. Draw him on his own or include his spiderweb, which you'll learn how to sketch next!

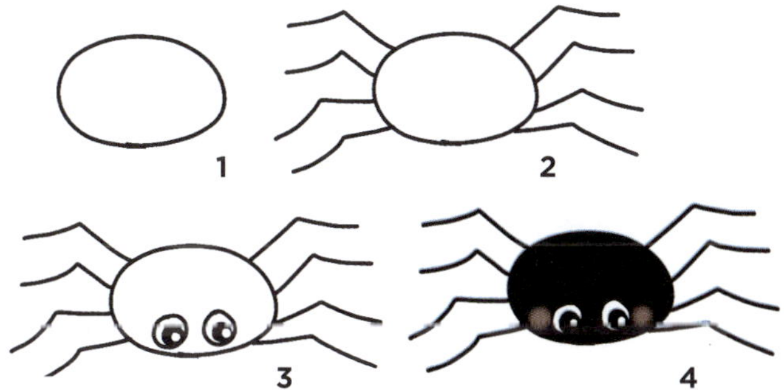

SPIDERWEB

The beginning of a spiderweb is four intersecting lines. Then, start in the center and connect each of the lines to the one beside it with a little curve until you get all the way around. Continue this pattern, making more and more layers until you reach the ends of your lines. You can draw this in any color, but it's especially fun to use a white gel pen on dark paper.

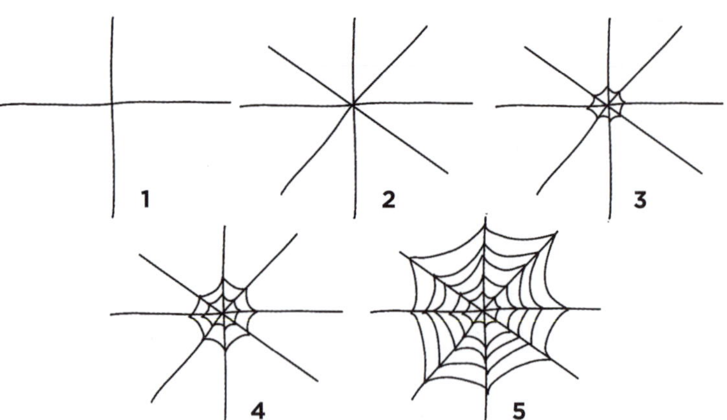

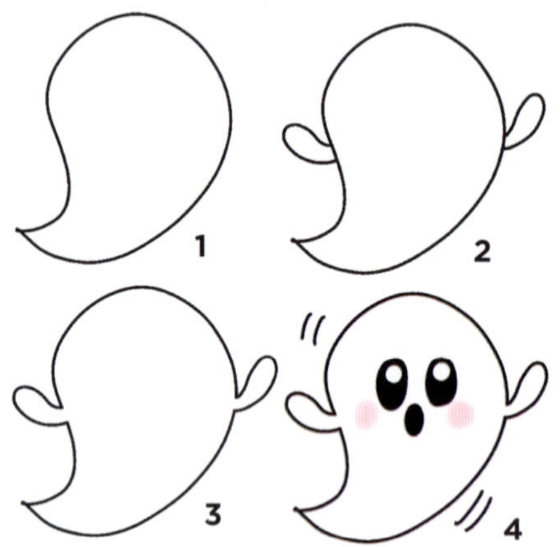

GHOST

To draw this friendly, not-so-spooky ghost, sketch a curved teardrop shape with two tiny teardrop-shaped arms. Add large eyes, an oval mouth and little detail lines to look like the ghost is moving. Although you'll probably leave the body white, you can add a bit of color, like a pair of rosy cheeks.

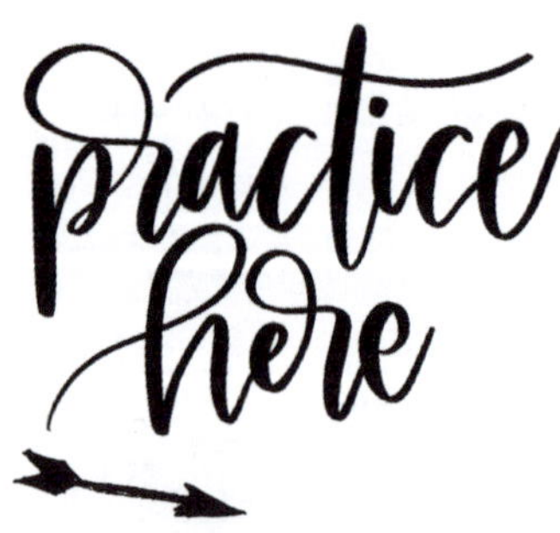

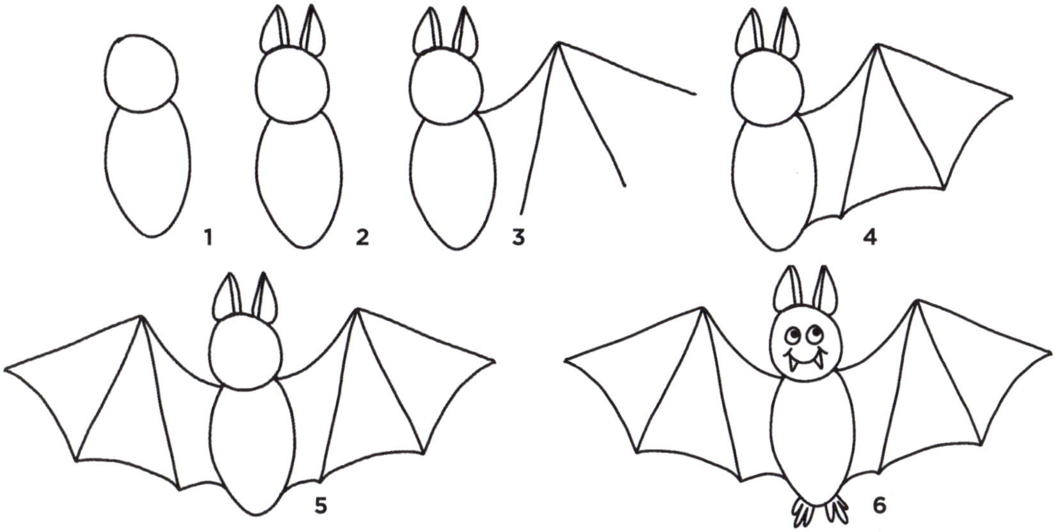

1 2 3 4 5 6 7

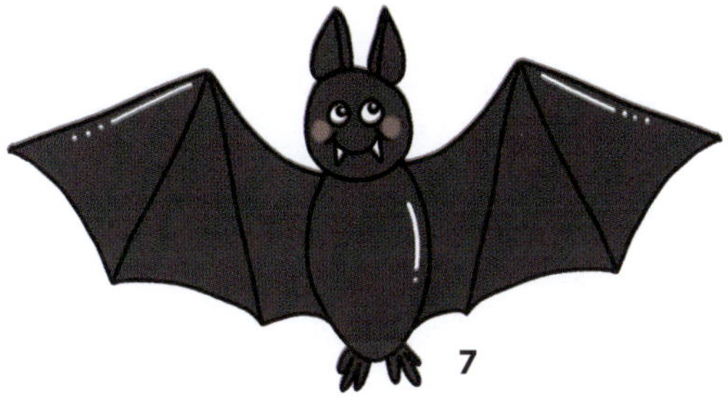

BAT

Drawing a bat starts with a circle head and an oval body with two pointed ears on top. Next, add pointed wings on the sides that are divided into sections with diagonal lines. Give your bat feet and a silly face, then color him in to finish your doodle.

WRAPPED CANDY

The easiest way to draw a piece of candy is to start with its basic shape: a circle, an oval or a rounded rectangle. Then, add a triangle with a zigzag on each side to represent the twisted wrapper. That's all there is to it. Now, color in and label the wrapper to represent your favorite sweet treats.

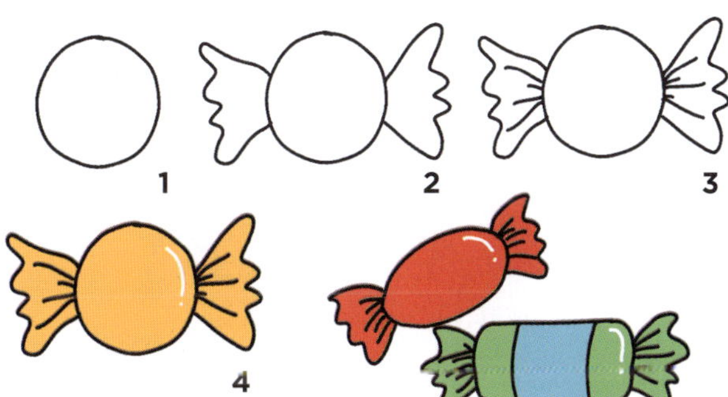

THANKSGIVING

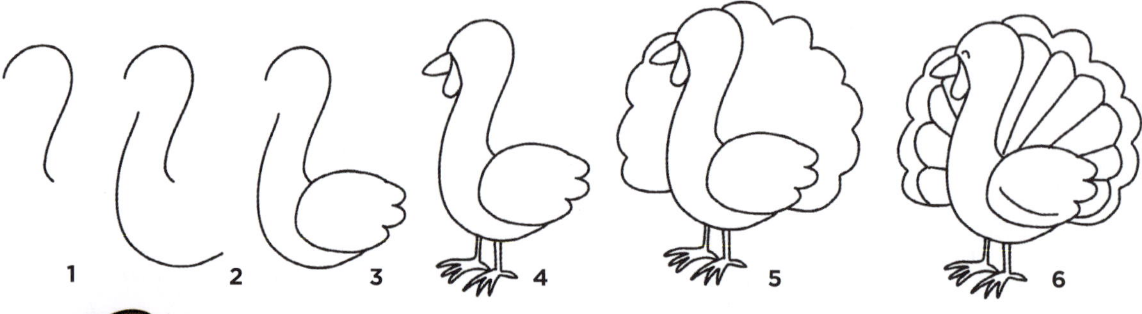

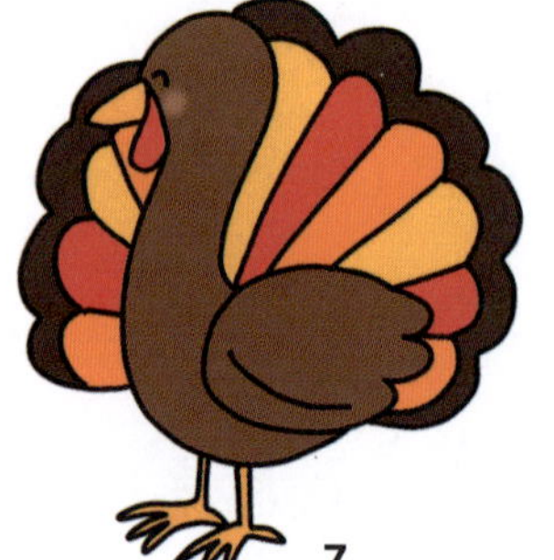

TURKEY

Nothing symbolizes Thanksgiving quite like a turkey! To draw this one, start with curving lines for the head, the neck and the body, then add a large wing. Next, give your turkey a beak, a wattle and feet. Add a bumpy line behind the turkey's body and use lines to divide that area into a bunch of separate feathers. To make your turkey extra festive, use color and details on the face and wing.

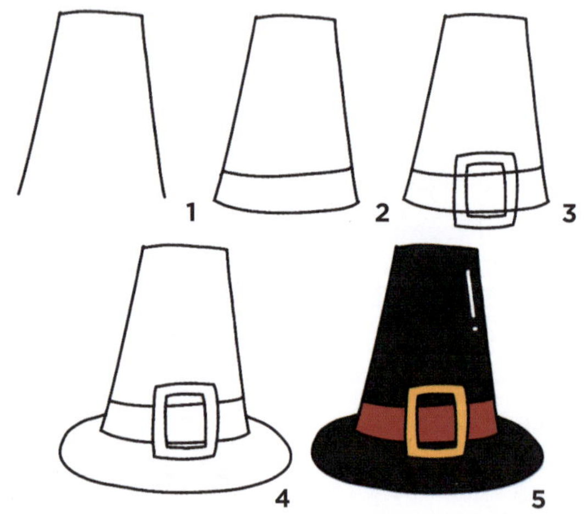

PILGRIM HAT

For the sides of this pilgrim hat, sketch two diagonal lines that are farther apart at the bottom than the top. Connect them at the top and bottom and draw a wide band with a square buckle in the center. Add a long "C"-shaped brim around the bottom and color your hat.

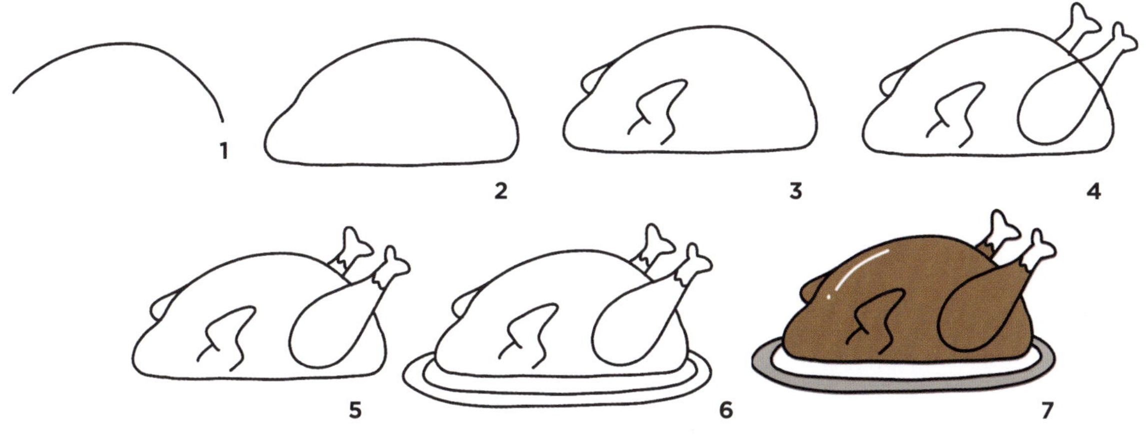

ROAST TURKEY

To draw the turkey after it's on the table, start with a semicircle shape that has a slight bump on one side. Next, add wings on one side and drumsticks on the other. Draw a long "C"-shaped plate under the turkey for serving.

PUMPKIN PIE

The first step in drawing a slice of pumpkin pie is sketching a triangle with a rectangle below it. Next, add a bumpy line for the crust and extend the crust behind and below the pie filling. If you like, add a dollop of whipped cream on top, erasing the line where it overlaps with the pie. The final step is finding the perfect orange-brown color to fill it in.

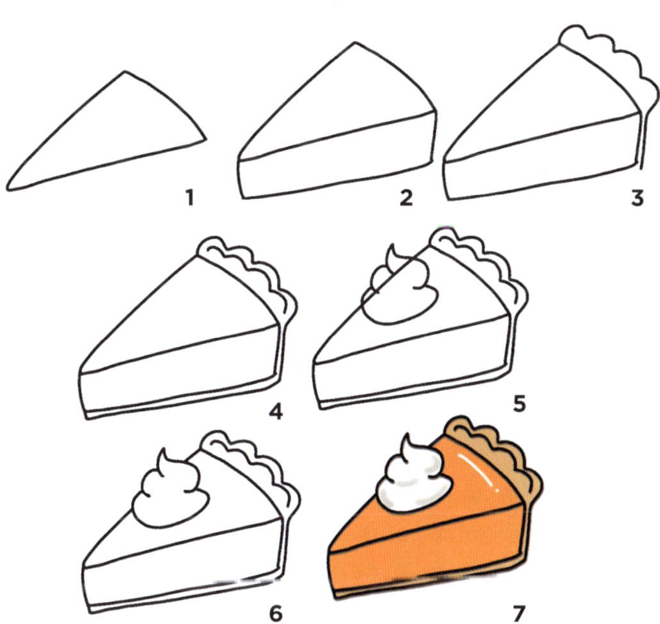

HANUKKAH

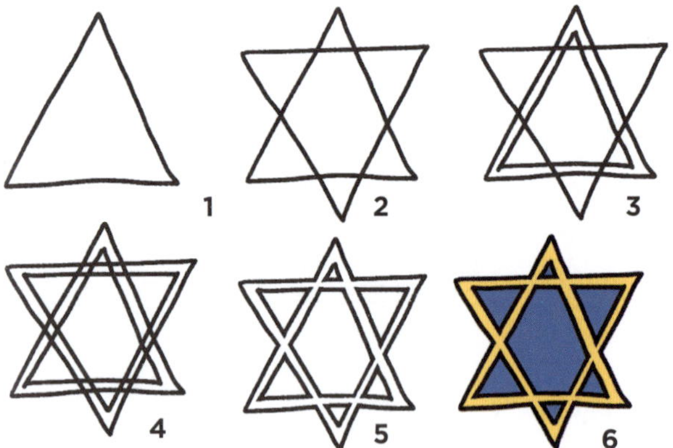

STAR OF DAVID

The central symbol of the Jewish faith is the Star of David, which is formed by two intersecting triangles. You can leave it simple or draw an outline for each triangle, like I did. Erase the overlapping lines before coloring it in. This symbol is not just for Hanukkah, but it can be used year-round or for any Jewish holiday.

DREIDEL

The dreidel game is a lot of fun, whether you're playing for real money or for chocolate. To draw a dreidel, start with three sides of a square and add lines to one side for dimension. Add a rectangular-shaped handle and curving lines at the bottom of each face of the dreidel. Sketch a rounded point for the base, then add a Hebrew letter on each face. If you're not familiar with the language, make sure to consult a real dreidel or another trustworthy source so you write the symbols correctly.

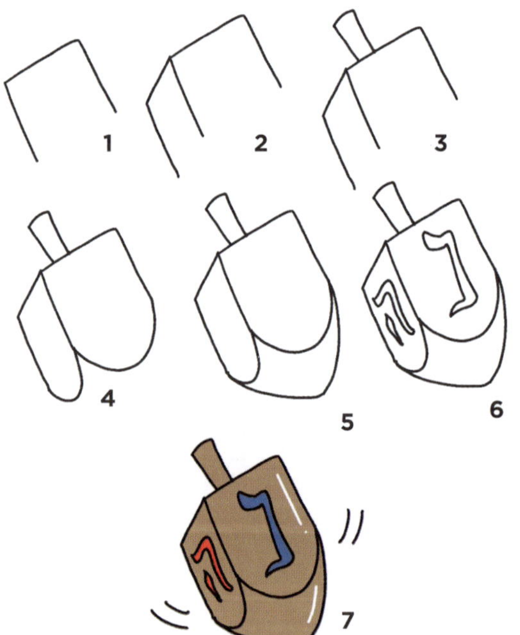

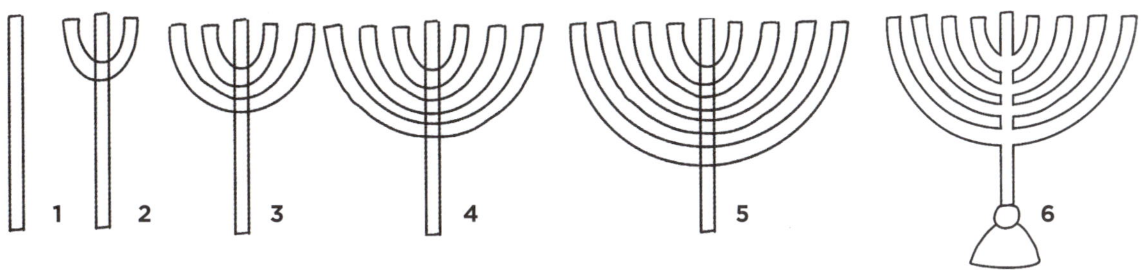

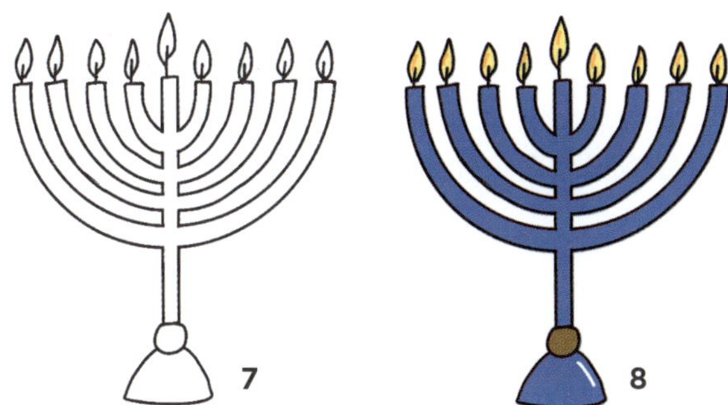

MENORAH

The menorah is an eight-branch candelabra used during the eight days of the Festival of Lights. To draw it, start with a center rectangle, then draw four separate sideways "C" shapes intersecting it, each one larger than the one above. Erase all of the lines that cross over each other, then add a base at the bottom of the center rectangle. Finally, add a little flame on top of each branch.

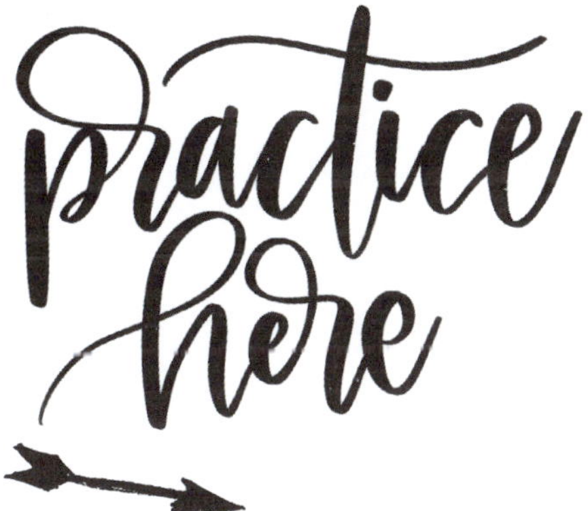

OTHER CELEBRATIONS & PARTY DÉCOR

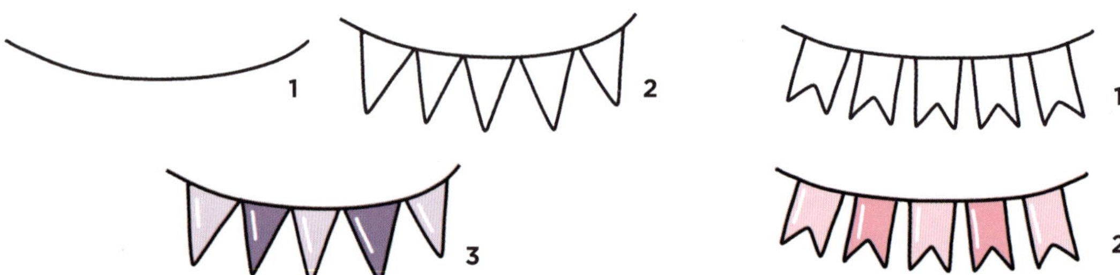

PENNANT BANNERS

A pennant banner is festive for all kinds of parties and celebrations, and it's incredibly simple to draw. Just sketch a wide curving line, then draw a series of upside-down triangles along the bottom of it. To make sure my pennants are properly centered and spaced, I like to start in the center of the line and work my way out to the sides. You can color these in any way you like, and you can even write letters or numbers inside the little flags.

One variation on the pennant banner (above right) is to change the shape of the flags. Instead of triangles, try this shape that's like a rectangle with an upside-down "V" at the bottom. Of course, these aren't the only possibilities; try whatever other shapes you can think of to create your own festive style of banner. This type of banner works well as an embellishment across the top of an envelope or a card.

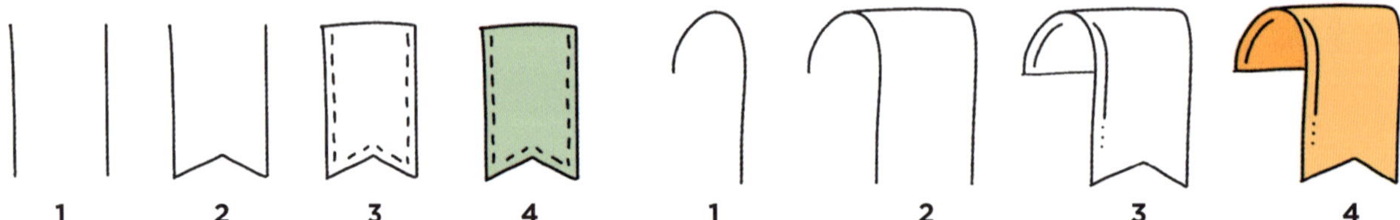

SIMPLE HANGING BANNERS

Sometimes at a party, one large banner does the trick. Draw a rectangle shape with an upside-down "V" at the bottom, then add a series of short dashes around the edges to give the appearance of stitches. Color the banner, then add whatever you want on the inside! This is great for writing a number, like an age or an anniversary, or even for a short message.

If you'd like to give your banner a folded look, start with an upside-down "J," then sketch the basic banner shape to the right. Connect the end of your hook to the side of the banner with a horizontal line to create the illusion of a fold. Then, add detail lines, stitching, numbers, words and/or color to finish your drawing. This type of banner looks great in the corner of a design.

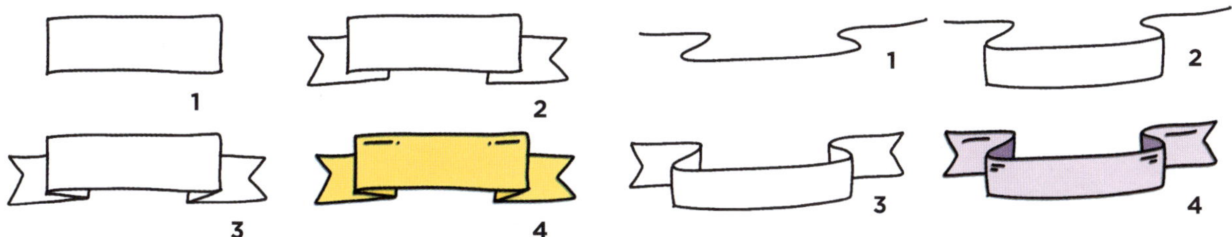

CLASSIC BANNERS

Ribbon banners are the type I use most often when I'm creating a lettered design because they're perfect for writing inside. The simplest version is a horizontal rectangle with a short streamer coming off each side. I like to put "V" shapes on the ends of the streamers for visual interest. Notice that these streamers go lower than the main part of the banner and connect to it with small triangles in the bottom corners to create depth.

Draw this version of a ribbon banner (above right) by making a waving line and dividing off the center area. Next, connect the side streamers to the main part of the banner and add short vertical lines on top to create a dimensional effect. I like to color the folded areas darker than the rest of the banner to enhance the illusion. When you write inside the banner, I suggest using a pencil to position your word first so that you don't run out of space.

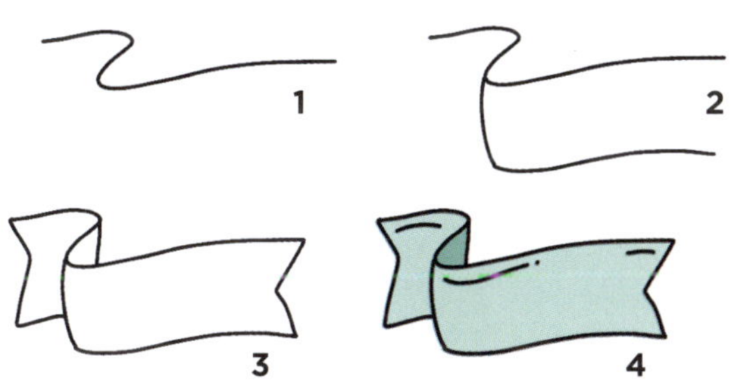

Unlike the previous ribbon banners, this variation to the left has only one fold. Draw a rounded "Z" shape, then form the main part of the banner and add a "V" shape on the side. Next, form the streamer to the left and add a vertical line on top to show the location of the fold. This banner can also be flipped around to come from the opposite direction. Just form an "S" shape to start instead of a "Z" shape and follow the same basic steps!

STREAMER

Streamers can be used in many different ways for party décor. The simplest way to draw one is to make a waving line, then draw a second waving line that crosses over the first in several spots. Connect the two lines at each end and you'll have something that looks like a piece of ribbon that has been twisted. These make a great festive border around a page or an envelope!

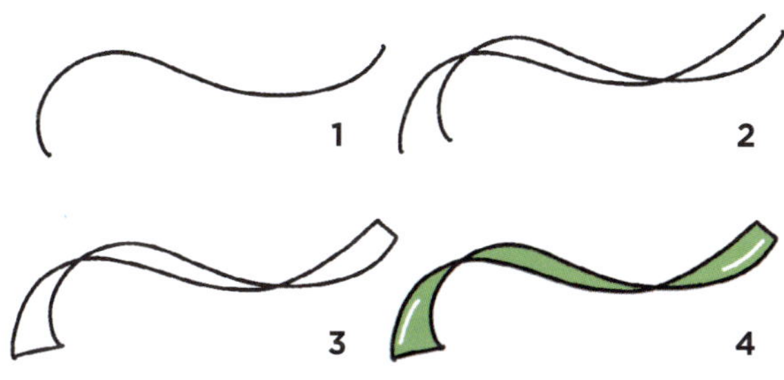

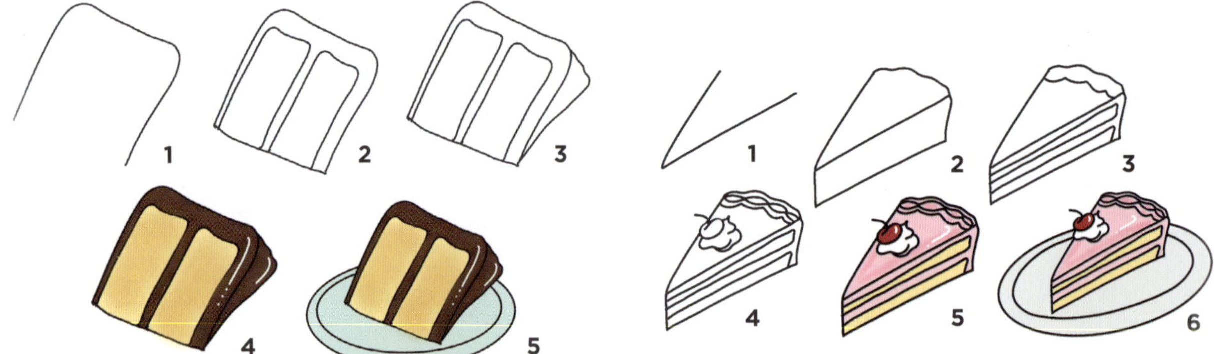

CAKE SLICES

What's a party without cake? Starting with a rounded rectangle on an angle, draw this cake slice. This is a double-layer cake (yes, please!), so add two more rounded rectangle shapes inside the slice with some space in between. These will be the cake areas and the rest will be the frosting. Add a triangle shape to the side to show that the slice is thicker on one side than the other. Finally, add color to transform the cake into your favorite flavor. Add a plate underneath if you like!

Not all cakes are cut the same way, so here's a variation (above right) on our cake slice doodle. This time, start by drawing a triangle for the top of the slice, then add an angled rectangle below it. For a double-layer cake, draw lines to divide the rectangle into sections for cake and frosting. Then, decorate the top of the cake with details like whipped cream and a cherry. You can add a plate underneath or leave the cake on its own. The best part about it is that this doodle cake has zero calories!

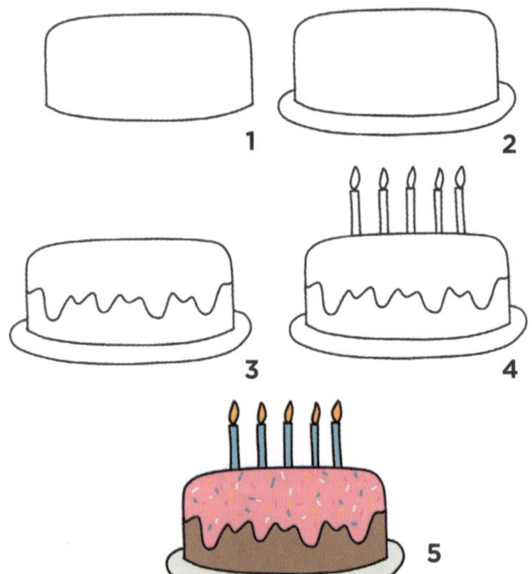

BIRTHDAY CAKE WITH CANDLES

Celebrate festive occasions with this cheerful cake doodle! First, sketch a rounded rectangle for the cake itself, then add a plate below it. Draw a wavy line across the cake for the frosting, then add thin rectangles on top for the candles. Give each candle a teardrop-shaped flame. The final step is to decorate your cake by coloring it and adding any extra details like sprinkles!

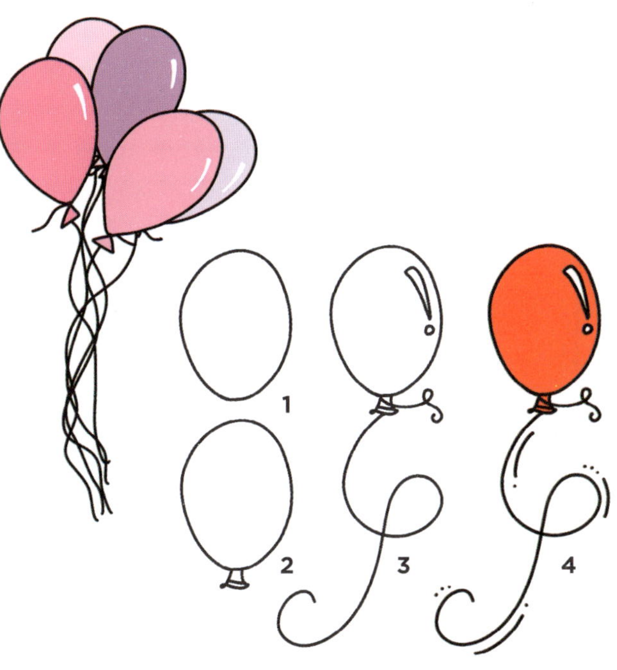

BALLOON

The basic shape of most balloons is an oval that's slightly wider at the top than the bottom. Add a little triangle shape at the bottom for the tie, then draw waving and curling lines for the balloon's string. I also like to add a highlight area on one side where the light would hit the balloon's surface.

Draw one balloon on its own or put several together in a bunch. Feel free to play around with the shape and size—no two balloons are exactly the same in real life either—and to have the strings travel wherever on the paper you want them to go.

practice here

GIFT BAG

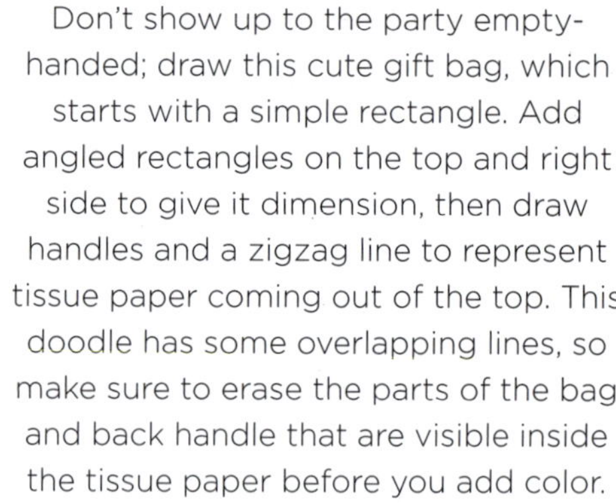

Don't show up to the party empty-handed; draw this cute gift bag, which starts with a simple rectangle. Add angled rectangles on the top and right side to give it dimension, then draw handles and a zigzag line to represent tissue paper coming out of the top. This doodle has some overlapping lines, so make sure to erase the parts of the bag and back handle that are visible inside the tissue paper before you add color.

You can find a gift box doodle on page 74 in the Christmas section! Change up the colors for the box and ribbon however you like; you could even add a cute print like stripes or polka dots.

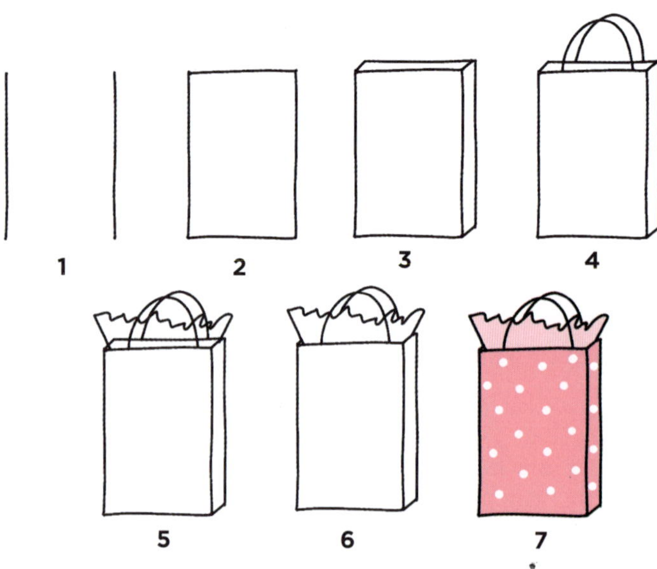

ENVELOPE

Everyone loves getting an invitation to a special event. To draw an invitation envelope, sketch a rectangle, then divide it with two triangles going in opposite directions. Draw a circle where the triangles meet to represent a wax seal or a sticker sealing the envelope. You can also add variety by sealing the envelope with a heart instead.

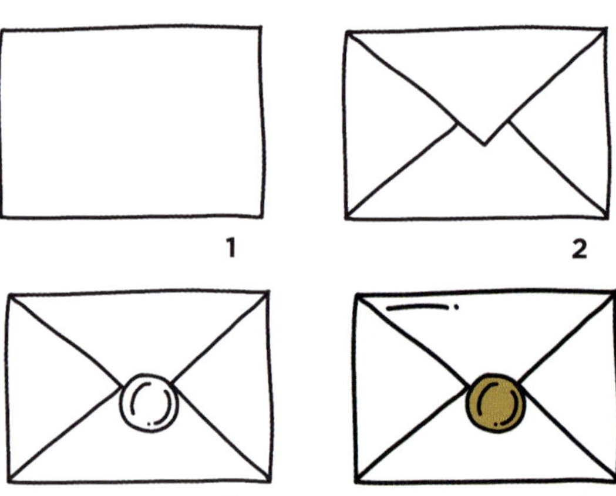

IN YOUR Imagination

There's nothing quite like a fairy tale to transport us from our everyday reality into a fantasy world where our imagination runs wild. Doodles of fictional or extinct creatures, treasures, swords and wands transport us to a place where anything can happen. These drawings are fun escapes for adults and children alike and add whimsy to any project.

FLYING PIG

If you've ever been told something will happen "when pigs fly," you have a good reason to create this doodle. Sketch an oval snout with a circle around it for a head, along with two little pointed ears. Add a curve for the back and four rectangular legs with hooves. Give the pig a belly and a little curling tail, then finally sketch a pair of wings. Short lines on either side of the wings will suggest that your pig is in flight.

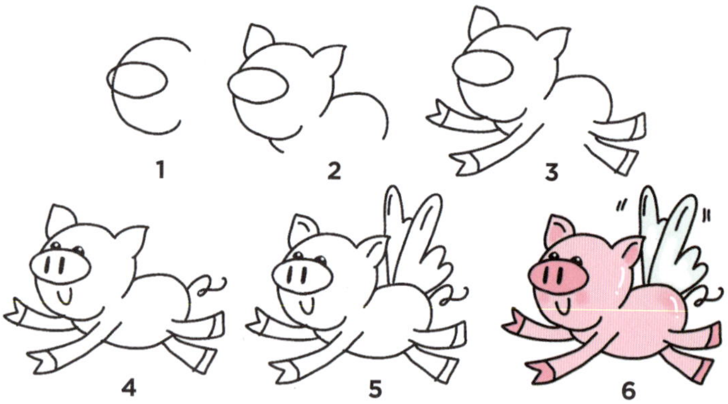

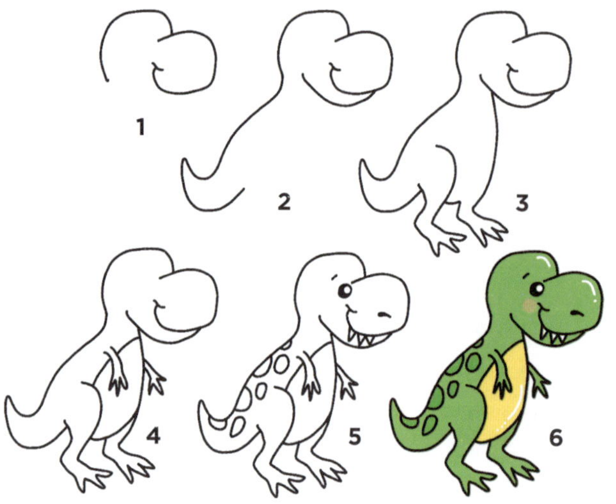

T. REX DINOSAUR

It may have been imposing in real life, but this T. rex is as friendly as they come. Draw a curving line for the head and another for the nose and smile. Next, give the dino a back and tail, as well as a belly and two legs. Draw those infamous tiny arms and a curving line to separate the belly from the rest of the body. Finally, add details like an eye, a nostril, teeth and spots.

BRONTOSAURUS DINOSAUR

To doodle this long-necked dinosaur, start with a curving line for the head and neck, then add the front of the body and two short thick front legs. Sketch a back with a tail and two hind legs, then draw details like eyes, toes and spots on the back.

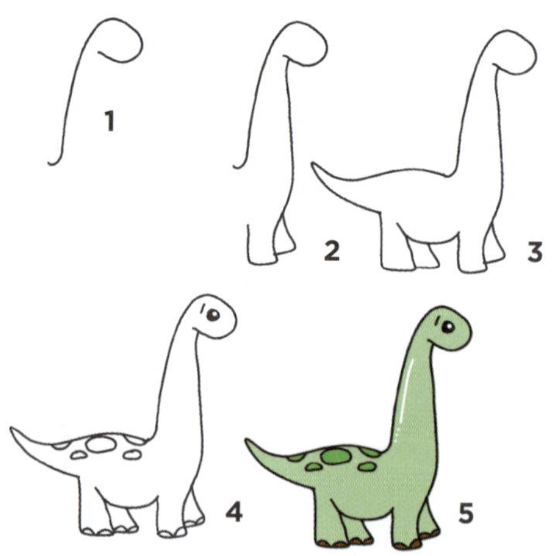

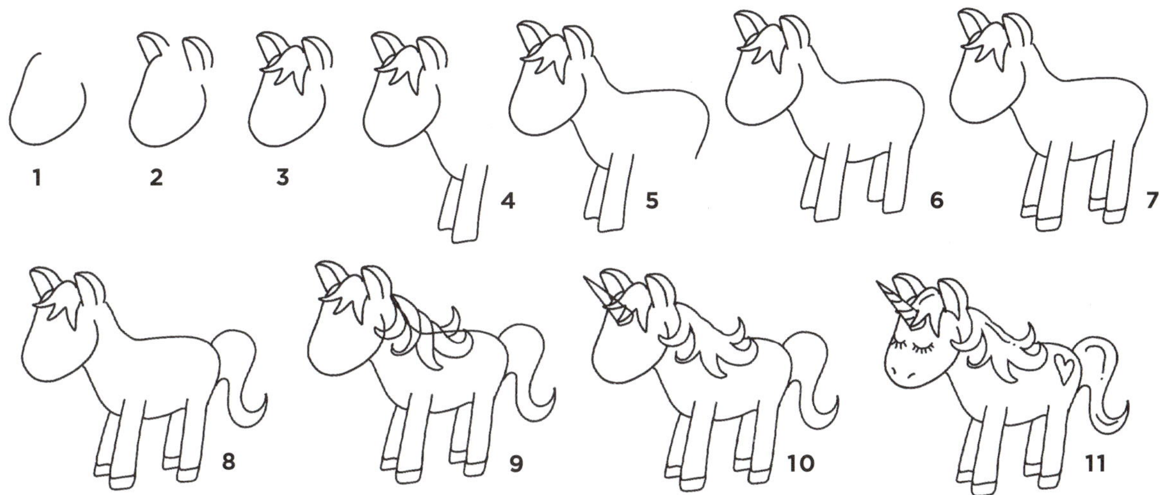

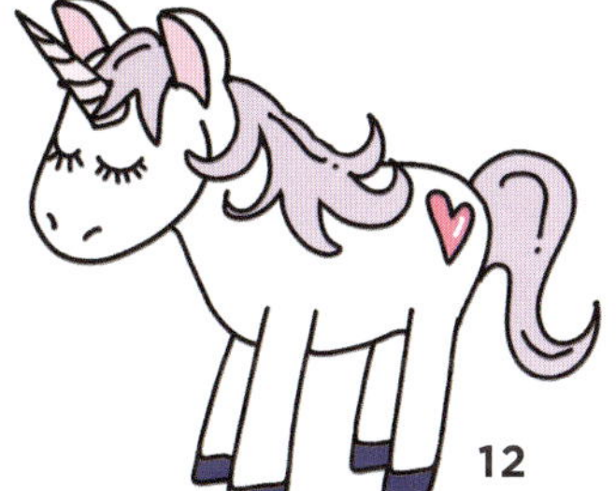

UNICORN

Is there any mythical creature more universally well-loved than the unicorn? To doodle this one, start as if you were drawing a horse with the head, the ears, the body and the legs (just like the horse on page 108). When you get to the tail, make it larger and fluffier than the horse's tail and add a mane that has some curl. Of course, she needs a cone-shaped horn in the center of her forehead and a sweet little face. Add a heart on the back of the body for an extra embellishment, then color your unicorn!

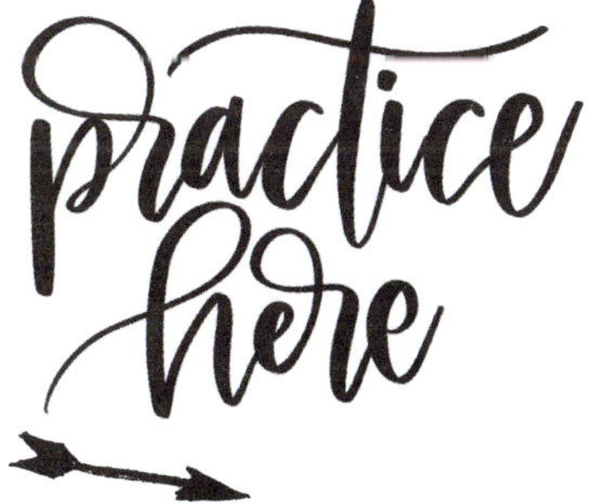

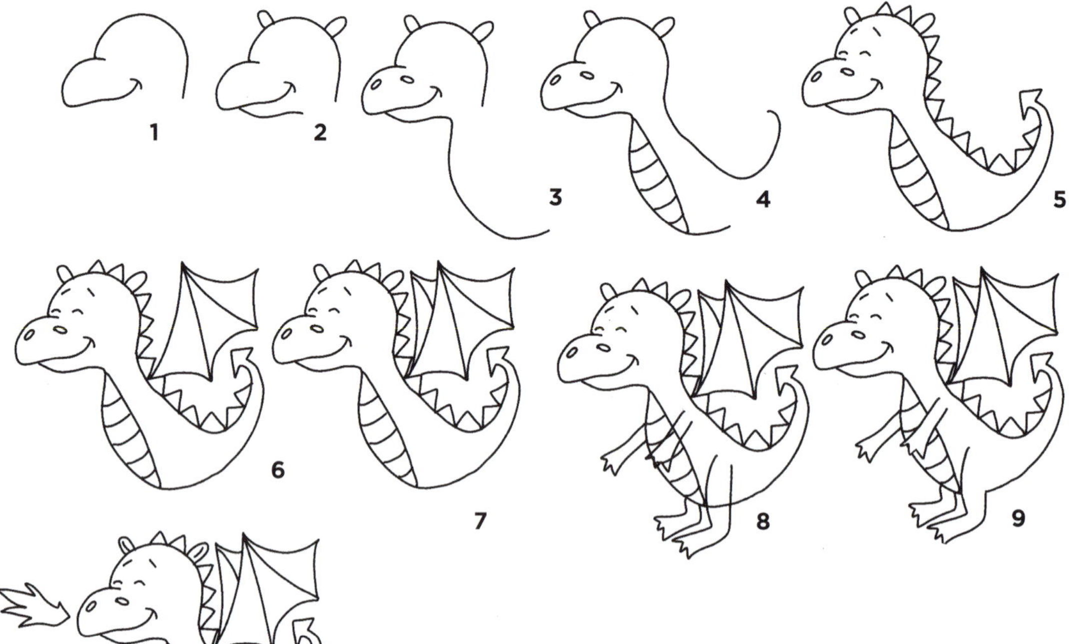

10

11

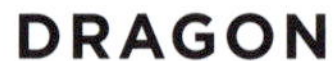

DRAGON

Draw this friendly dragon by making a curve for the head and another for the snout and smile. Add two tiny ears and a belly. Draw the back with a tail that points up. Next, divide the belly from the rest of the body and sketch some horizontal stripes across it. Finish the tail with a pointy tip, then give the dragon a face, some spikes going down its back and a pair of pointed wings. Finally, add arms, legs and a burst of flame. Erase any of the overlapping lines and give your dragon some color to bring it to life.

FAIRY WAND

Fairies and godmothers need their wands, so let's learn to draw one. First, sketch a long thin handle, then draw a five-pointed star on top. Erase the lines in the center of the star. Add curling streamers on each side of the handle, then color your wand. A few short lines coming out from each side of the star will add to the magical effect.

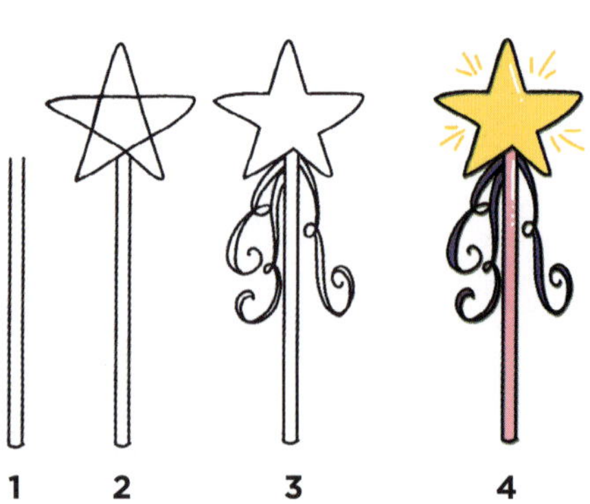

CROWN

This royal crown starts with a zigzag line. Mine has five points, but you can have as many or as few as you like. Draw an oval at the bottom, then add details like diamond- and circle-shaped gemstones. Metallic colors are great for shading in your crown, as well as jewel tones for the gems.

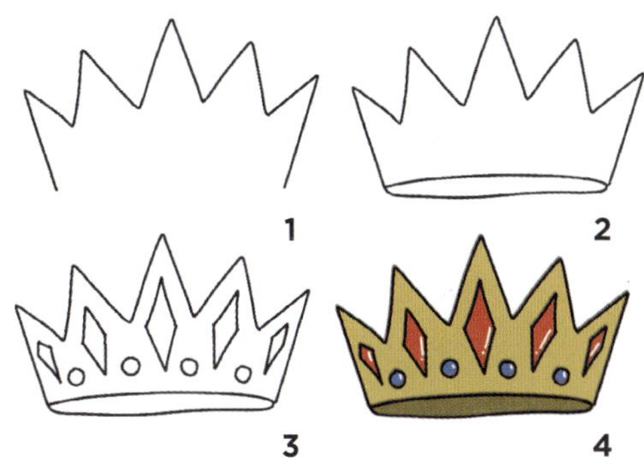

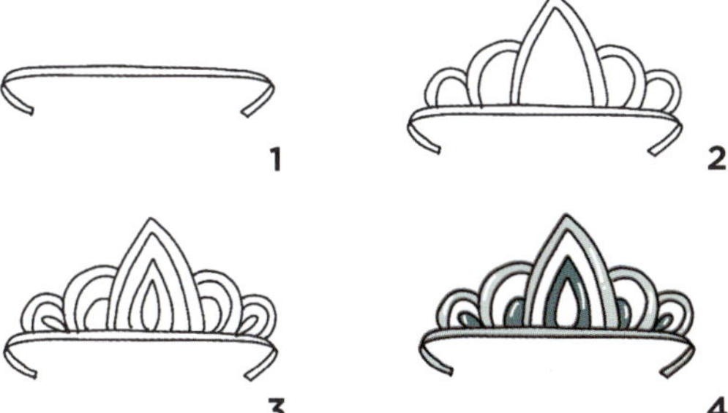

TIARA

The first step in drawing this elegant tiara is making a "C"-shaped band. Next, add a rounded point in the center with several rounded sections on each side. Fill in the sections of the tiara with more lines to show gems and/or other layers, then color the tiara in to finish your doodle.

GLASS SLIPPER

What would have happened to Cinderella if she'd never lost her glass slipper? Doodle this iconic image by forming the toe of the shoe first, then add a high heel. Add a line for dimension to show the other side of the shoe, then color it in. I used a very light shade of blue to show that it is made of glass. You can also use this image to represent any kind of high-heeled shoe.

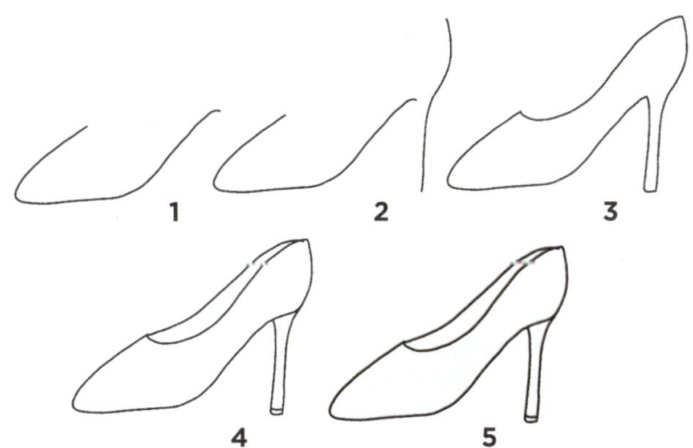

1 2 3

MAGIC WAND

To sketch a magic wand, draw a long thin rectangle with a tiny oval on top. Divide the main part of the wand into three sections and add color. To make it look extra-magical, doodle a little cluster of dots and diamond shapes near one end of the wand.

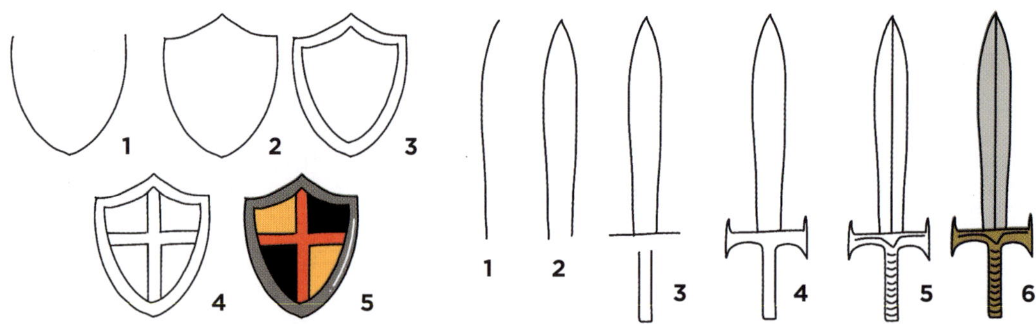

SHIELD & SWORD

Draw a rounded "V" shape with a peaked line across the top. This gives you the shield's basic shape. Then, add whatever pattern, image or coat of arms you want to decorate your shield.

The first step in drawing a sword is to sketch a long thin pointed blade. Next, add a "T"-shaped handle. Draw a vertical line dividing the blade in half, then add detail lines to the handle to make it appear more ornate. Gold, silver and anything metallic are great choices for coloring a sword.

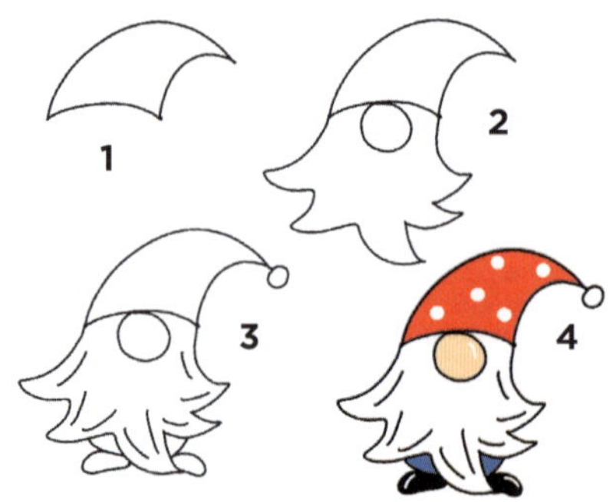

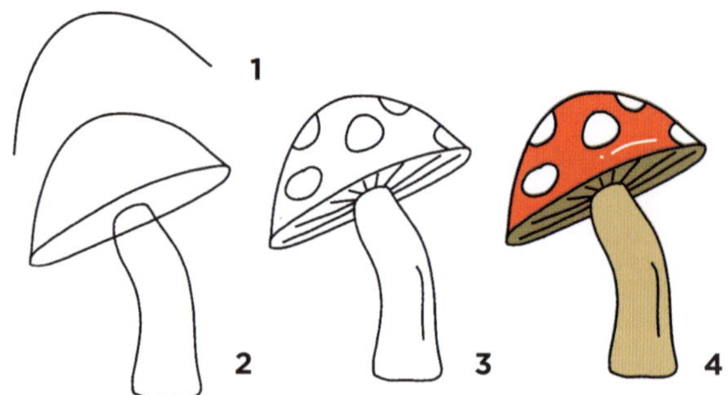

GNOME & TOADSTOOL

Gnomes are incredibly popular doodles for fantasy lovers. Draw this one by making a curving triangle hat with a large round nose just below. Add a pointed beard with just the very bottom of a body and two little feet poking out underneath. Embellish your hat with polka dots or another pattern and add detail lines to show the texture of the beard. This gnome can be customized for any season or occasion.

Doodle this little toadstool for your gnome by sketching an arch with an oval underneath. Next, draw the stem, which isn't completely straight. Decorate the top of the toadstool with circles and the underside with detail lines. Finally, add color to complete your drawing.

TREASURE CHEST

To draw this treasure chest, sketch an angled rectangle with lines coming out from three of the corners. Connect those lines to create the shape of a box. Next, add a rectangle on top and rounded shapes to create the open lid. Add details like a handle and stripes to the chest, then draw the treasure inside! I chose to make little ovals to represent gold, but you could also draw gems or whatever other treasure you think the chest might hold.

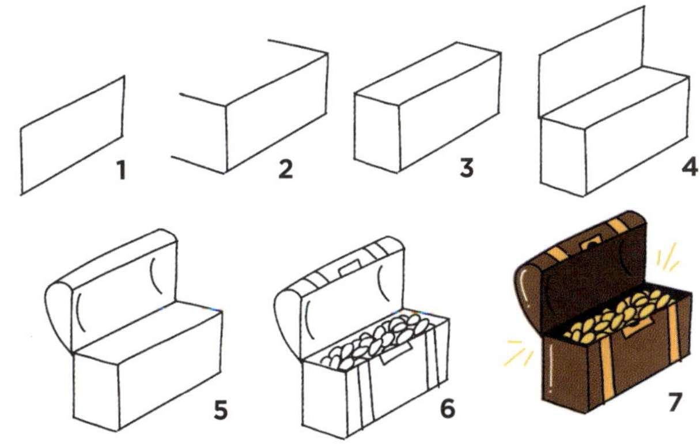

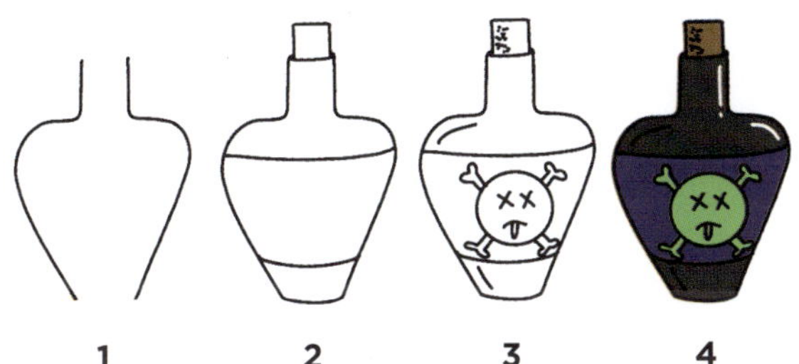

POTION BOTTLE

Watch out for this dangerous potion . . . or is it poison? First, draw your basic bottle shape, then add a long thin neck with a cork at the top. Sketch a label across the bottle, complete with a word or symbol to indicate the danger that lurks inside. The label and bottle colors could easily be adapted to make it a love potion or any other potion you wish for!

PIRATE HAT

To start this pirate hat doodle, draw a wide arch with curving lines coming up from each side. Connect the sides with a line that rises up in the middle to create the basic hat shape. Then, decorate the hat with a skull and crossbones (or a simple "X") in the center and a gold band across the top. If you'd like a boat for your pirate, check out the sailboat on page 44; it would be fun to make it black and draw an extra flag on top with a skull and crossbones!

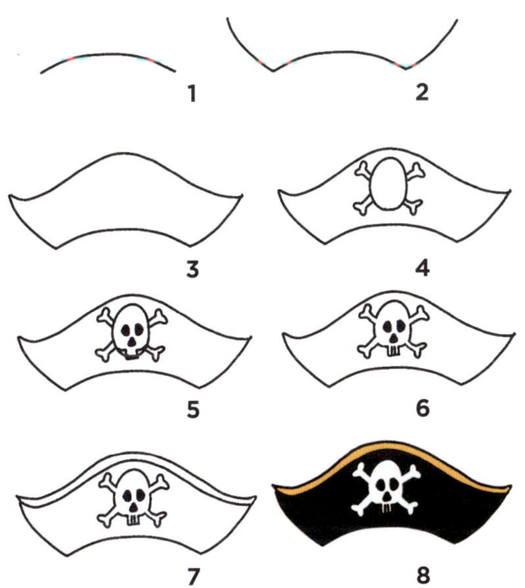

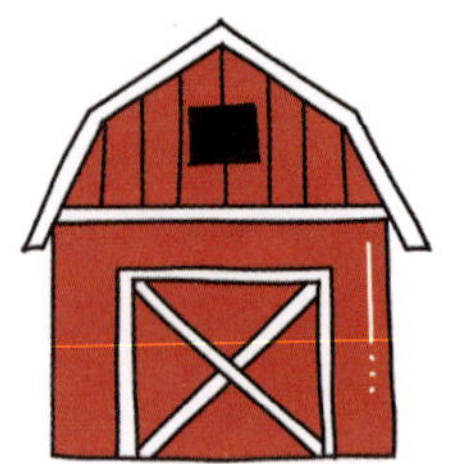

ON THE Farm

There are so many things to see and do on a farm! From the barn and silo themselves to the animals and all the things that grow, there are plenty of adorable doodles we can create. These illustrations can stand alone or you can use lots of them together to create a whole rural scene. Draw them on recipe cards, posters for the county fair and any other projects with country flair.

FARM ANIMALS

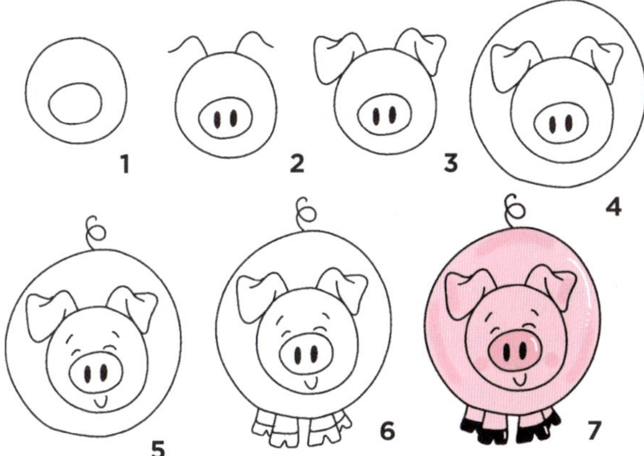

PIG

This playful pig is ready to jump in the mud or eat a big dinner, whichever comes first. Draw a circle for the head with an oval snout inside. Then, add ears on top of the head and nostrils on the snout. Sketch a large circle around the entire head for his plump body and draw a face. Add a curly tail, four short legs and color to finish your pig.

COW

Cows are incredibly important animals, especially on a dairy farm! To sketch this one, start with a semicircle head and an oval snout. Add ears and horns, along with eyes and nostrils to finish the face. Sketch a simple body shape with four rectangular legs and a long thin tail. Finally, add an udder and spots. Many cows are black and white, but they can also be solid black or brown.

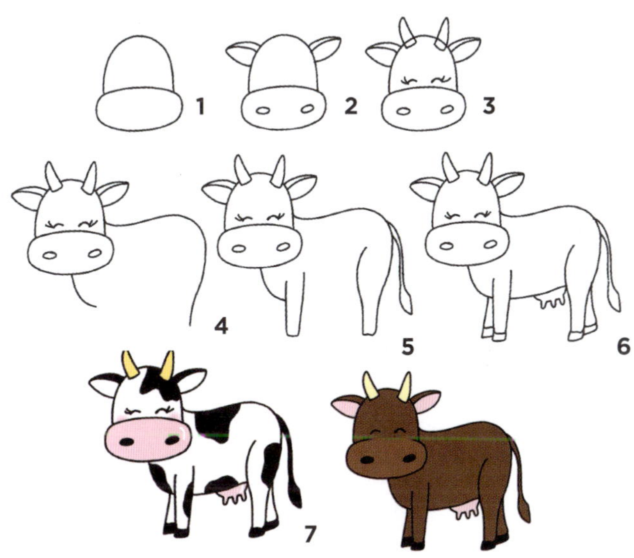

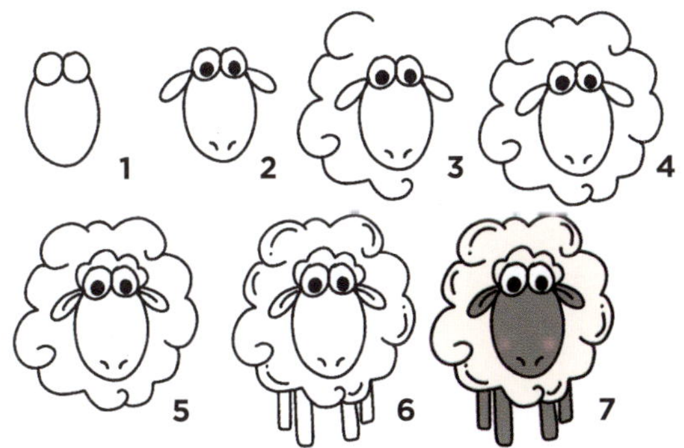

SHEEP

This fluffy sheep has lots of wool for the farmer to shear and is super cute to boot. Draw two round eyes and a "U"-shaped nose to form the face, then add a tiny pair of ears. To create the wool, make a series of curves and bumps all around the head, similar to drawing a cloud. Add a bit of wool just above the eyes and draw four rectangular legs. Draw some small detail lines in the wool to emphasize its fluffy texture.

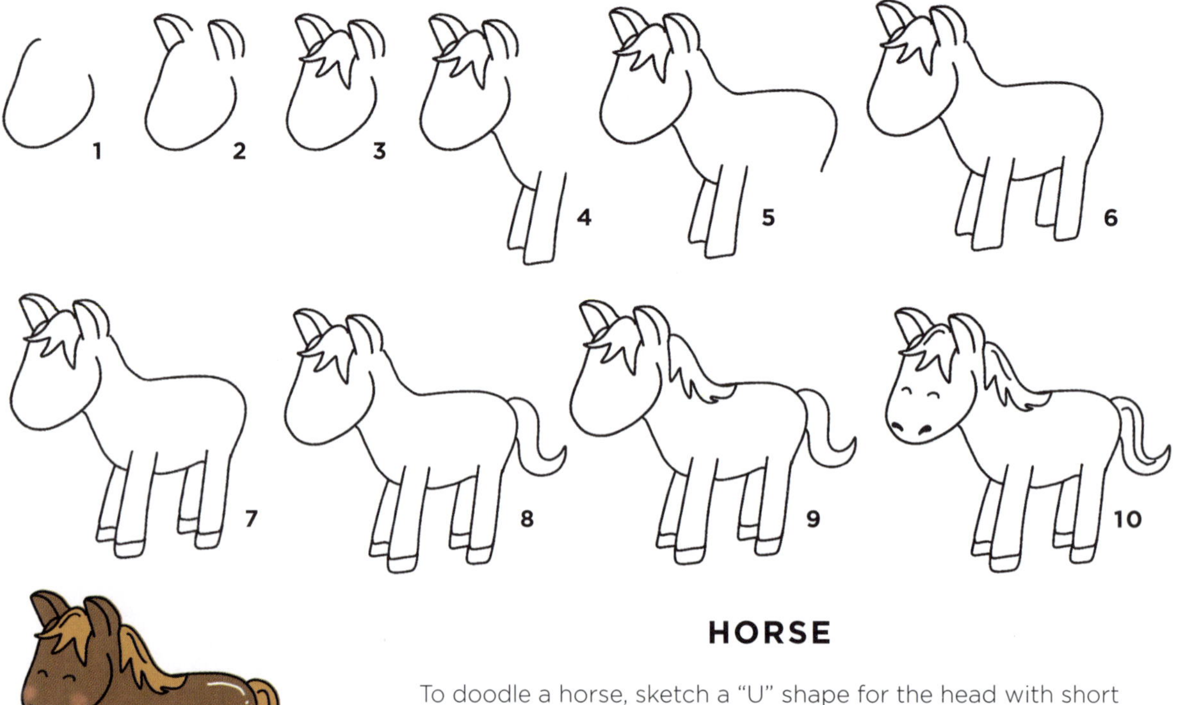

11

HORSE

To doodle a horse, sketch a "U" shape for the head with short forward-facing ears at the top. Add a little tuft of the mane on top of the head, then draw a neck and front legs. Next, sketch the rest of the body and the hind legs and add a tail. Draw the rest of the mane going down the length of the neck and add eyes and nostrils on the horse's face to give him some personality.

LLAMA

Everyone loves a llama, and this adorable doodle can be used for just about any project, not just those on the farm. To draw it, start with a "U" shape for the head, then form the body and legs with bumpy lines to represent the llama's fur. Add ears, a face and a tail, then color in your little llama gray, brown, black or any color of the rainbow.

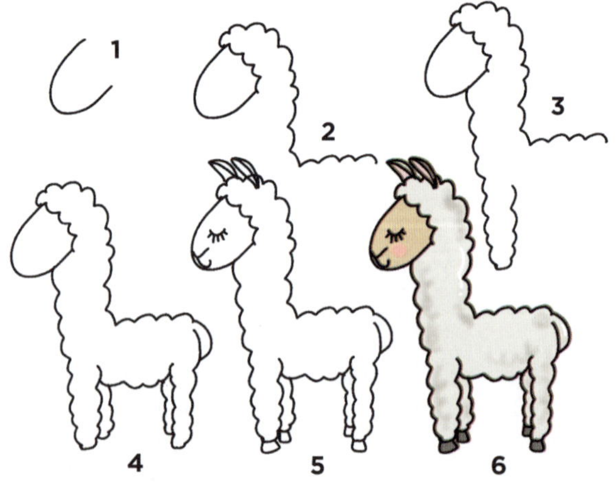

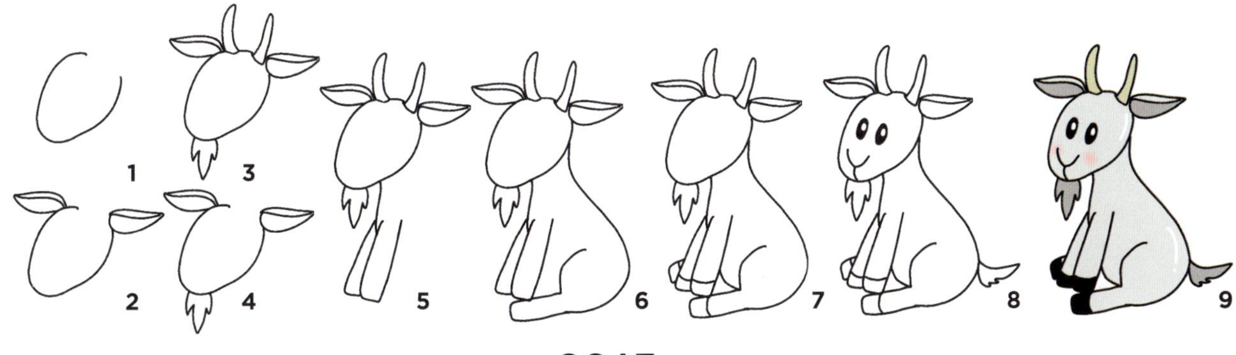

GOAT

This little goat is just sitting and waiting to play. Draw an oval shape for his face with an ear on each side. Add a tuft of hair below his chin and a pair of not-too-pointy horns. Then, sketch his front legs, his back and his hind legs in a seated position. Add a short tail, then color this cheerful little friend.

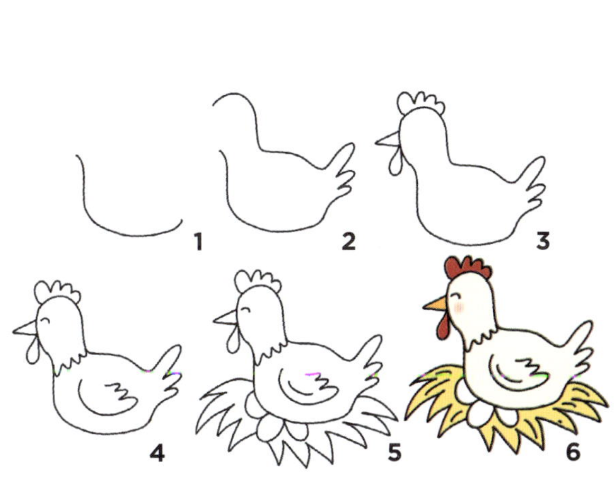

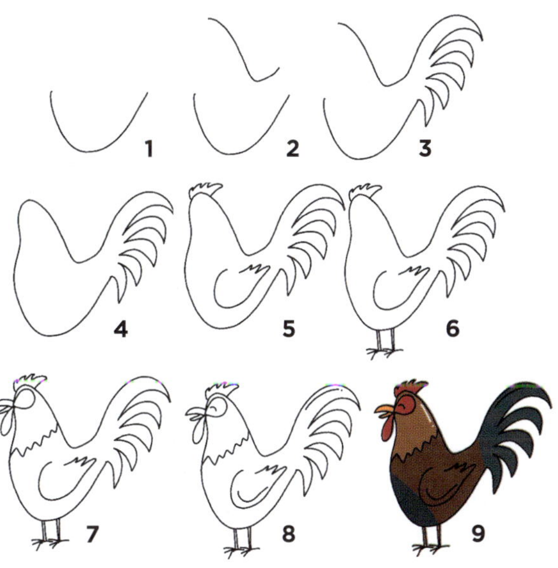

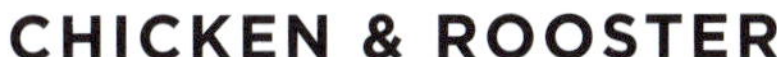

CHICKEN & ROOSTER

This mama chicken is busy sitting on her eggs, waiting for them to hatch. To draw her, make a curved line for the belly, then sketch the head, back and tail. Give her a beak, a wattle and a comb, as well as a wing. Draw a face and a few details on the body and wing, then give the chicken a place to sit by drawing some hay and eggs underneath her body.

There's no sleeping in on a farm, thanks to the resident rooster! Draw this one by sketching the belly and back and connecting them with a large feathered tail. Next, give the rooster a comb on top of his head and a wing, as well as some legs and feet. Add a beak and a wattle, as well as details on the body. Color him in with brown, red and whatever color feathers you'd like.

FARM BUILDINGS & EQUIPMENT

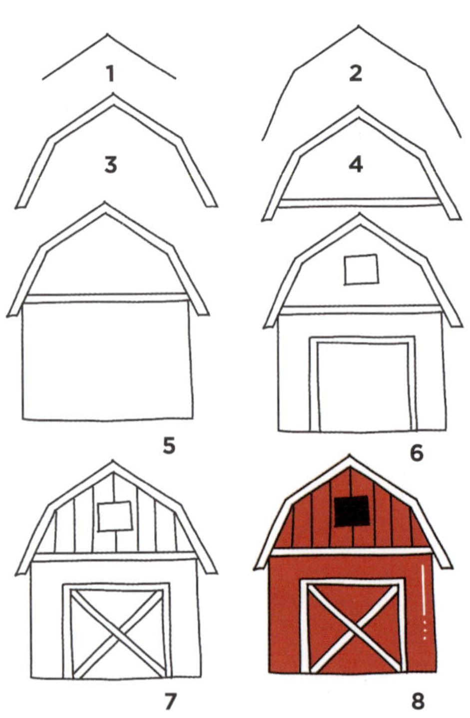

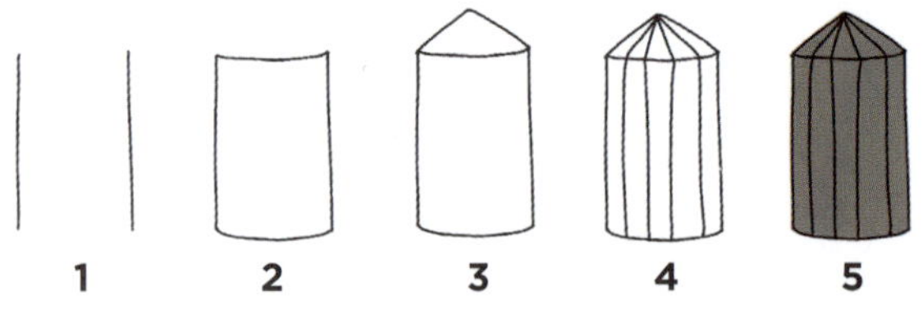

BARN & SILO

Every farm needs a trusty sturdy barn! To draw one, start by drawing an angular peaked roof with a rectangle underneath for the main part of the building. Add a large door, as well as a small opening near the top of the roof. Draw some vertical lines on the roof area for texture and sketch an "X" shape on the barn door. Then, add color, usually a bright shade of red.

Farmers rely on their silos as a place to store the grain they harvest. It's easy to draw one; just sketch a basic rectangle shape with a cone on top. Then, add a series of vertical lines coming from the point of the silo all the way down to the bottom.

HAY

A bale of hay is usually tied together with string, which is the way we're going to draw it. Start by making two bumpy lines connected on the ends with small zigzags to show the hay's poking texture. Add a third bumpy line and connect it to show dimension. Draw strings in between each of the bumps where the hay is tied together and make lots of short little detail lines to show individual pieces of hay inside the bale.

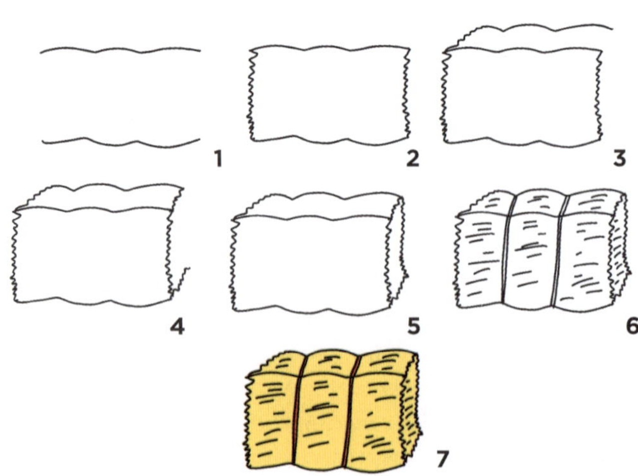

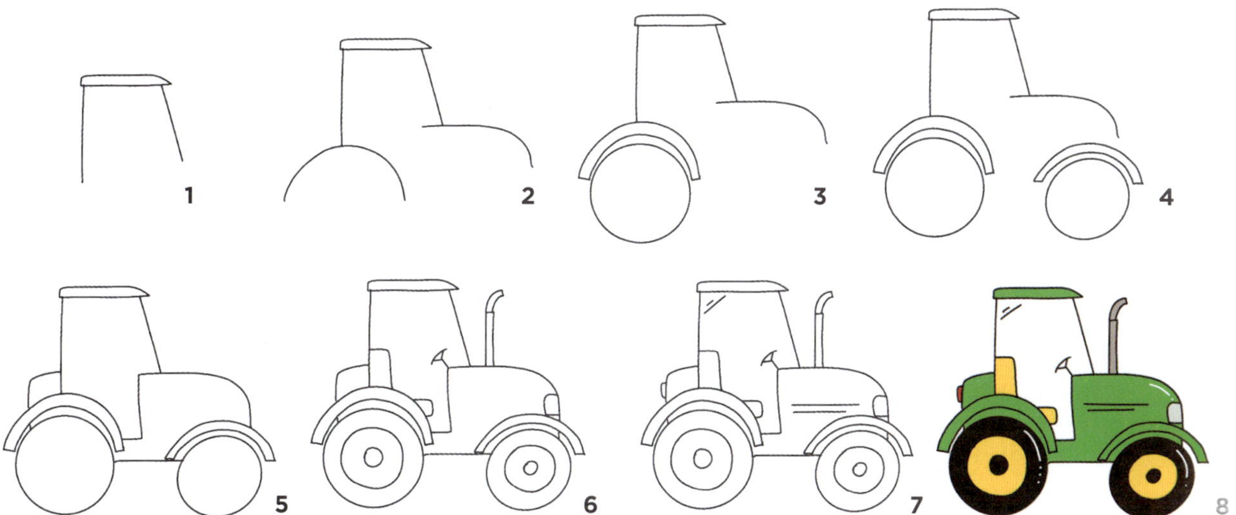

TRACTOR

You won't find a farm without a reliable tractor. To draw this one, make two lines with a little roof on top, then sketch the curve of the hood and the tire. Add a second tire and connect the space in between with a horizontal line. Add details inside the tires, as well as a steering wheel, a seat and an exhaust pipe. Draw detail lines, a headlight and a taillight, then color your tractor so it's ready to head out into the field.

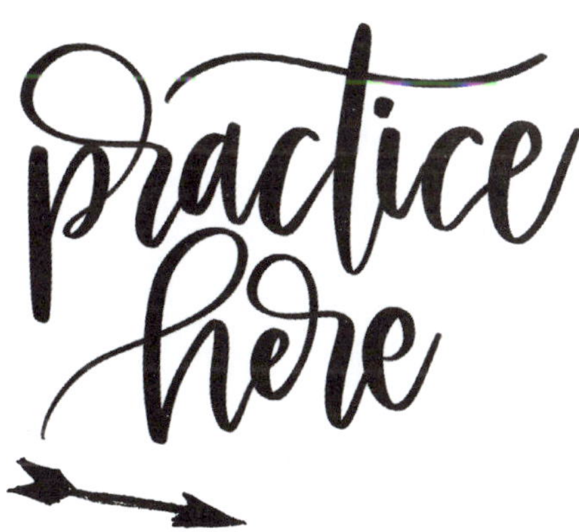

CROPS

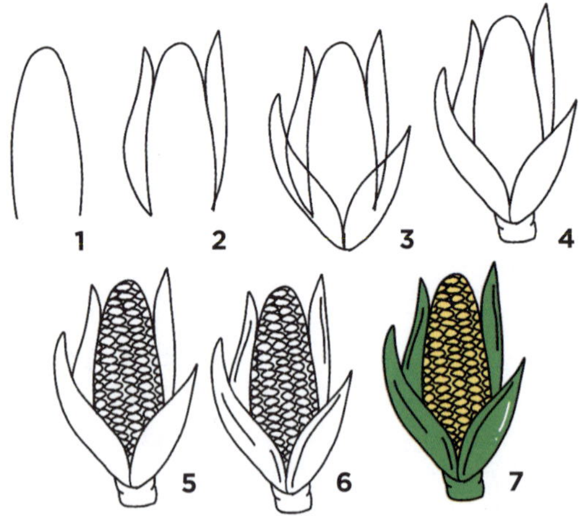

CORN

Start this corn doodle by making a tall thin arch for the ear of corn itself. Next, add pieces of the husk on each side, as well as in front. You'll want to erase the lines where the husk in front overlaps with the corn and the husk in the back. Finally, add a pattern of small oval shapes inside the ear of corn to represent the kernels.

CARROT

To draw a carrot, start with a rounded triangle shape, then add a few leaves on top. Sketch some horizontal detail lines going down the length of the carrot to show its texture. Finally, finish your doodle by coloring it orange and green.

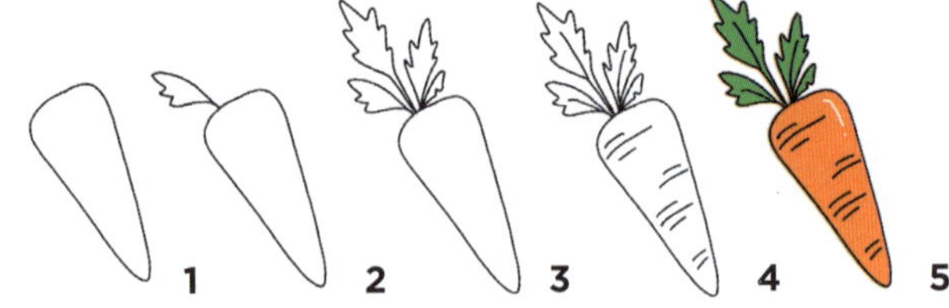

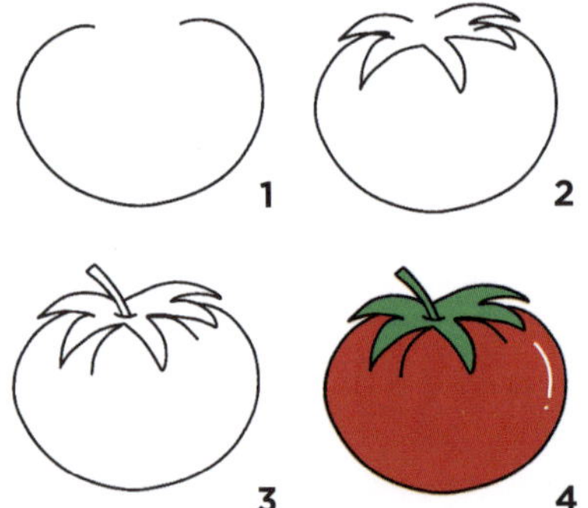

TOMATO

Tomatoes come in different shapes and sizes, so as you draw them, no two will be exactly alike. Make a rounded shape for the tomato's base, then add a series of points and a stem on top. To show that your tomato is ripe and ready to eat, color it a bright shade of red.

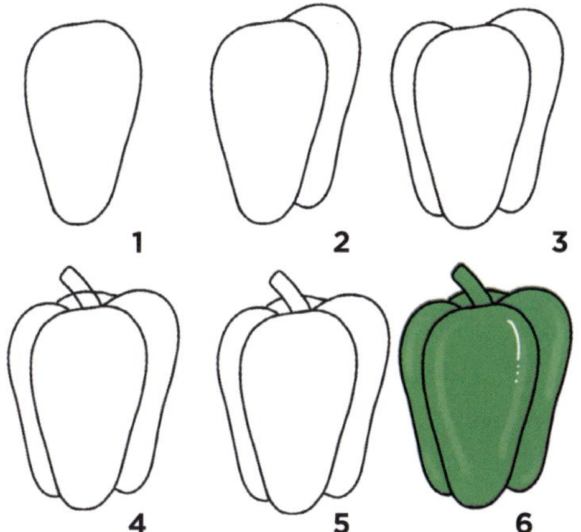

PEPPER

To draw a bell pepper, start with a rounded triangle shape for one of the pepper's lobes. Add curving lines on each side and a semicircle on top to show the other three lobes, as well as a short stem. Bell peppers can be red, orange, yellow or green, depending on which kinds the farmer chooses. Did you know that green bell peppers are just the unripe stage of a red, yellow or orange pepper?

PEAS

This pea doodle shows four peas in a pod, but you can draw as many or as few as you like. Start by drawing a circle for each pea, then add the walls of the pod on each side. Add a stem at the top, a little curling vine and a few detail lines, then, using several shades of green, color the doodle.

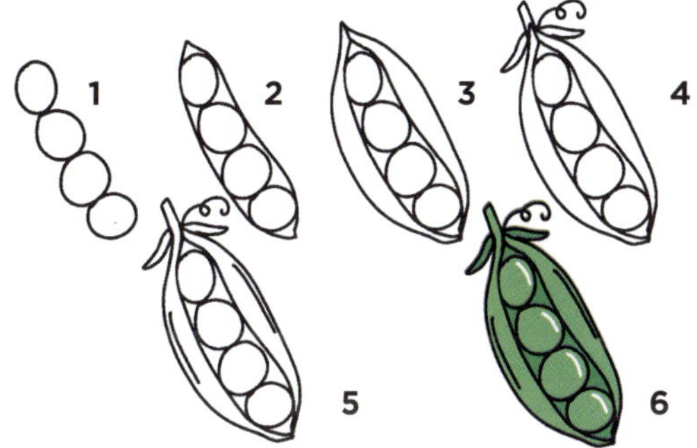

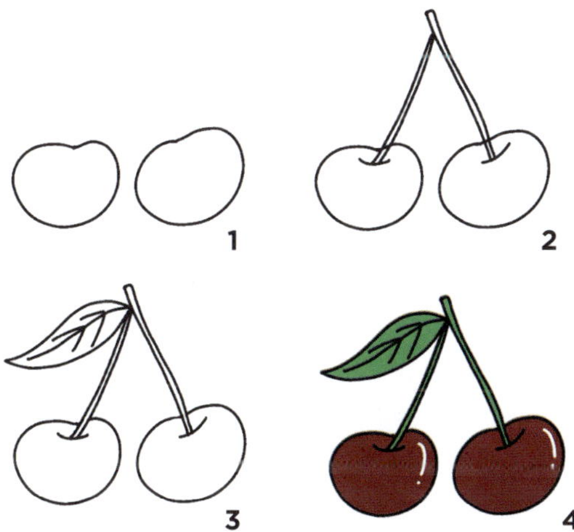

CHERRIES

To draw a pair of cherries, make two rounded shapes that are slightly indented at the top. Next, give each one a stem coming from just inside the shape. The stems should point toward each other and meet at the top. Add a veined leaf, then color your fruit. Real cherries can be bright red, as well as darker shades of red and burgundy, even to the point of looking almost black.

STRAWBERRIES

Strawberries are a favorite fruit for many of us and they're a great addition to summer projects. To doodle them, start by drawing a rounded triangle shape for the fruit itself, then add the leaves and stem on top. For the seeds, draw lots of tiny dots all over the strawberry. Finally, color in the leaves green and add some bright red color to show that the berry is ripe.

Note: If you're looking for an apple doodle to go with your farm harvest, check out page 157 in the At School chapter where we draw an apple for the teacher!

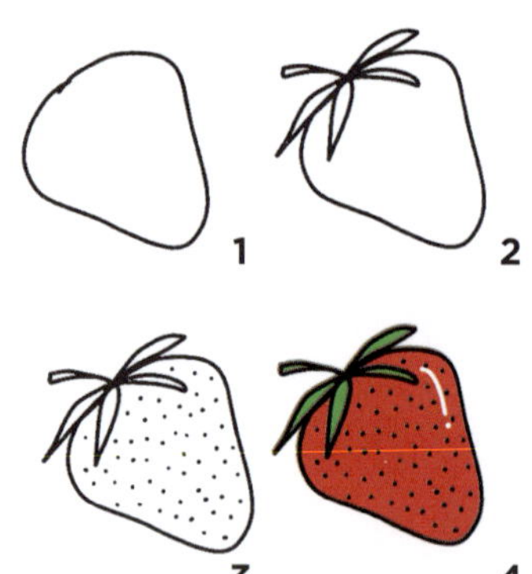

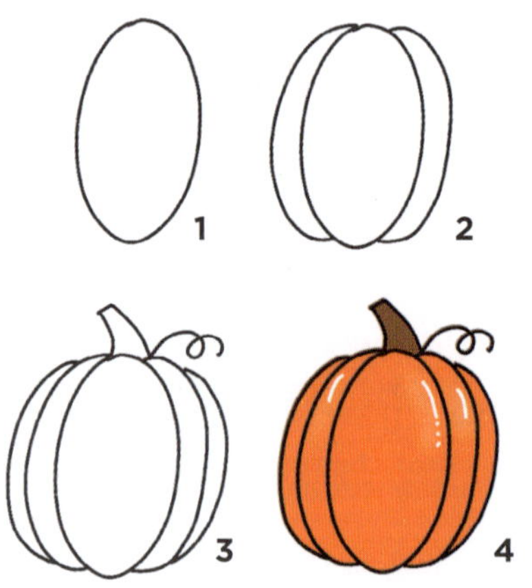

PUMPKIN

Start your pumpkin doodle by drawing an oval, then add two sets of parentheses on each side. Sketch a stem on top, along with a leaf or a little curly vine, then color your pumpkin orange. You can also turn this plain pumpkin into a jack-o'-lantern by adding a festive face (see page 87).

SQUASH

To doodle a squash, sketch a lumpy triangle shape, then add some curving lines inside to show texture. Draw a stem at the top and draw a series of tiny dots in several places throughout the shape. Squash can be yellow, green, orange, white or a combination of those colors.

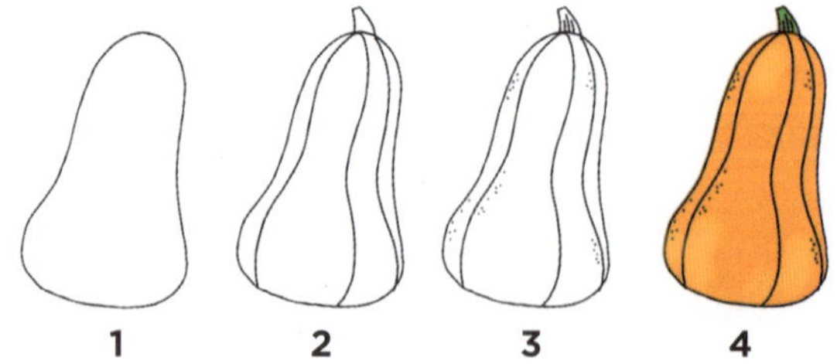

AT THE Zoo

Without a doubt, animals are some of the most fun and most adorable doodles to draw. While some animals can be seen often in our everyday lives, we have to take a trip to the zoo to see those that live in more distant places. This chapter features a collection of animals that make their homes in jungles, rain forests, the savanna and the outback. While those of us who live in North America or Europe may not get to enjoy them very often in real life, we can bring them into our art projects anytime we like.

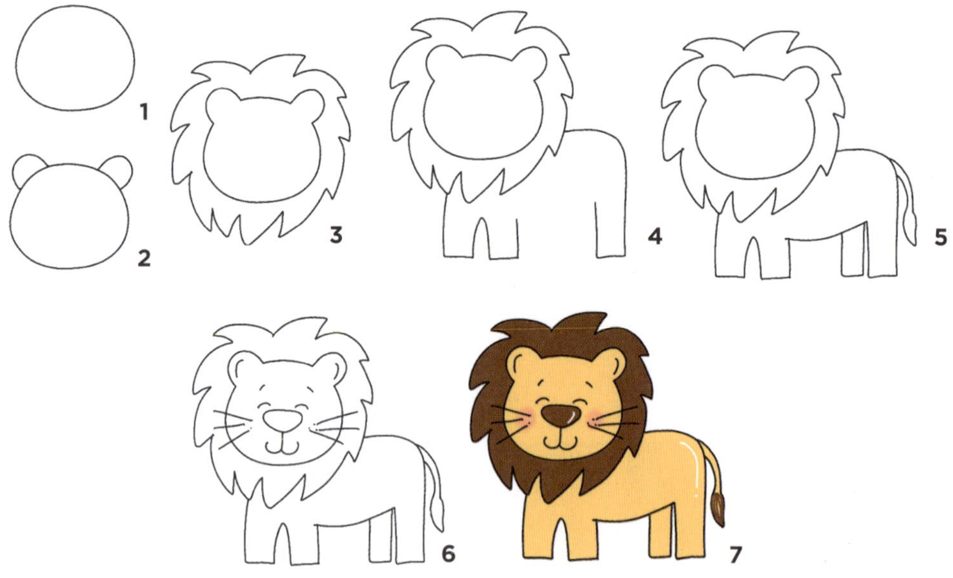

LION

Let's start by drawing the king of the jungle: the lion. Sketch a circular head with rounded ears, then draw a mane all around it. Add a simple body with four rectangular legs and a long thin tail. To bring the face to life, draw eyes, a nose, a smile and whiskers. You can also add detail lines on the ears and to form eyebrows. Color your lion with shades of brown and yellow.

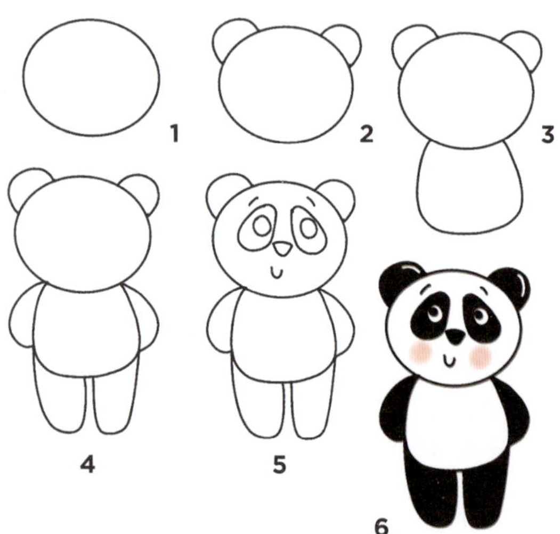

PANDA

I'll never forget the experience of seeing hundreds of pandas in their natural habitat during a trip to Chengdu, China. Their roly-poly bodies, combined with their lazy playfulness, quickly made them one of my favorite animals. To draw one, start with an oval head and rounded ears. Add a rounded rectangle body, then add curving lines for arms and legs. To give the face its characteristic look, draw two large ovals with small circle eyes inside. As you color your panda, keep in mind that the ears, arms, legs and areas around the eyes are black, while the tummy and the rest of the face are white.

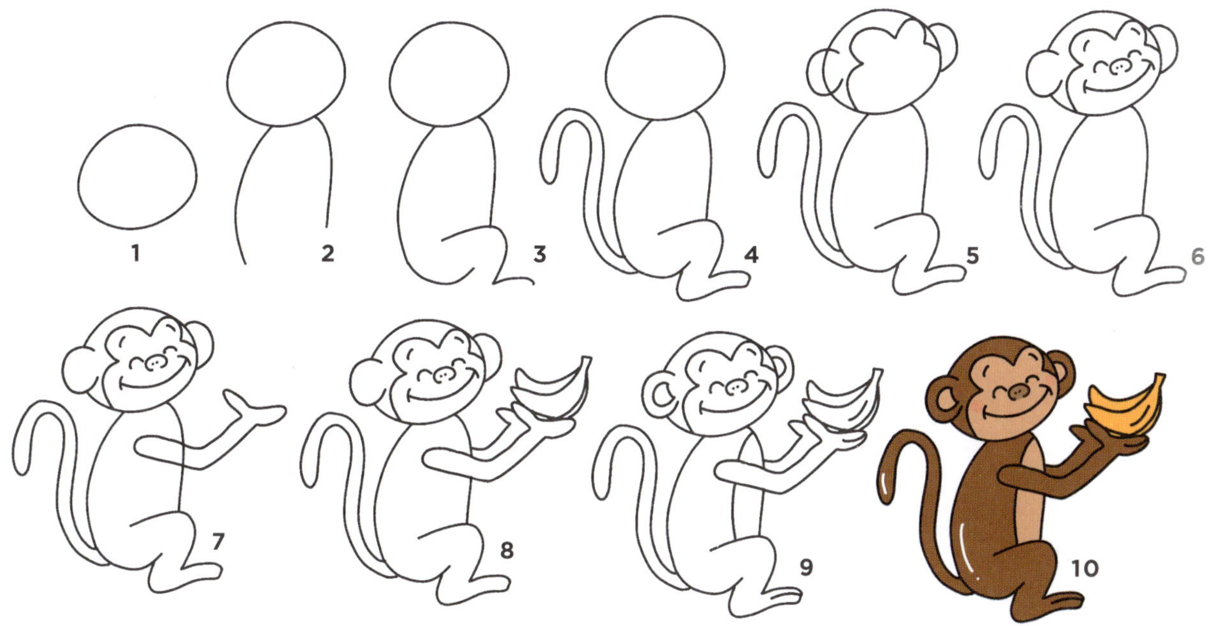

MONKEY

To draw this mischievous little monkey doodle, start with a round head and an oval body. Add a curving tail and a front leg, then draw large "C"-shaped ears and a curving line to divide the face from the rest of the head. Inside the face area, draw eyes, eyebrows, a nose and a giant smile. Next, add arms and give your monkey a handful of bananas. Finally, draw a few details like semicircles inside the ears and lines on the bananas.

ZEBRA

Did you know that no two zebras have the same pattern of stripes? To draw this fascinating animal, make an oval for the head, then add ears, a tuft of hair and a face. Sketch a few triangular shapes on the face to represent stripes. For the body, draw two front legs, then a line coming down from one side for the back of the body and one back leg. Add the final leg, a tail and as many stripes as you'd like. Then, leave the body white and color the stripes black . . . or is it a black body with white stripes? Maybe we'll never know!

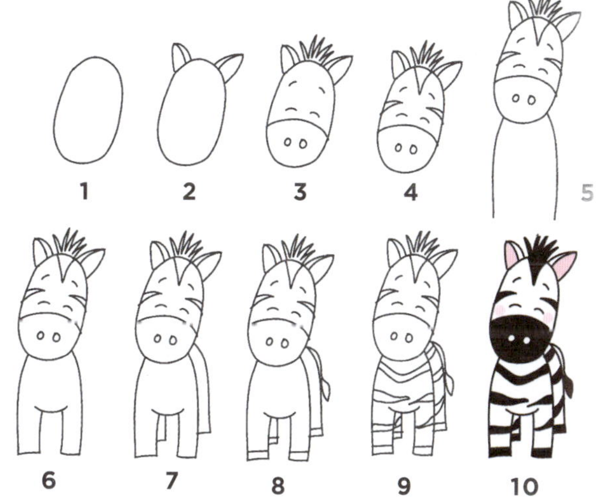

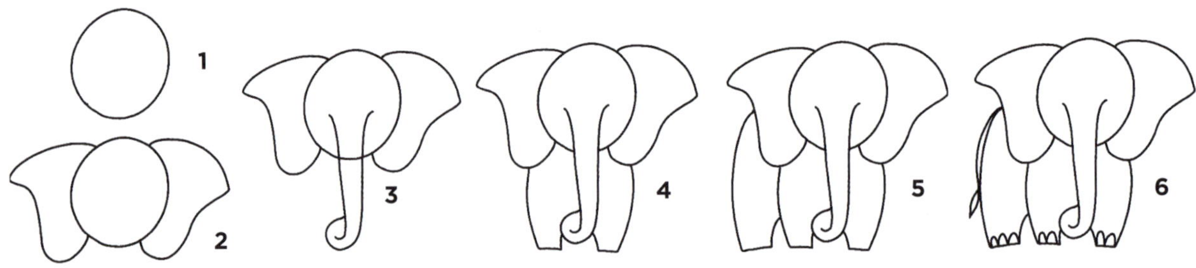

ELEPHANT

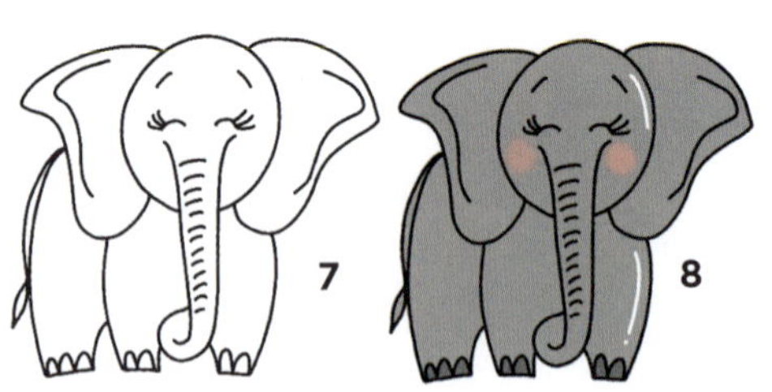

As the largest living land animal, elephants are a special doodle to learn. First, sketch a circle for the head with a big floppy ear on each side. The ear should be larger at the top than at the bottom. Next, add a long thin trunk that curls at the end and two front legs. On one side of the elephant, draw a curving line to represent its back and bottom and bring it up to form a back leg. Add a tail, details on the feet and eyes. Finally, draw small detail lines on the trunk and larger ones inside the ears, then color your elephant.

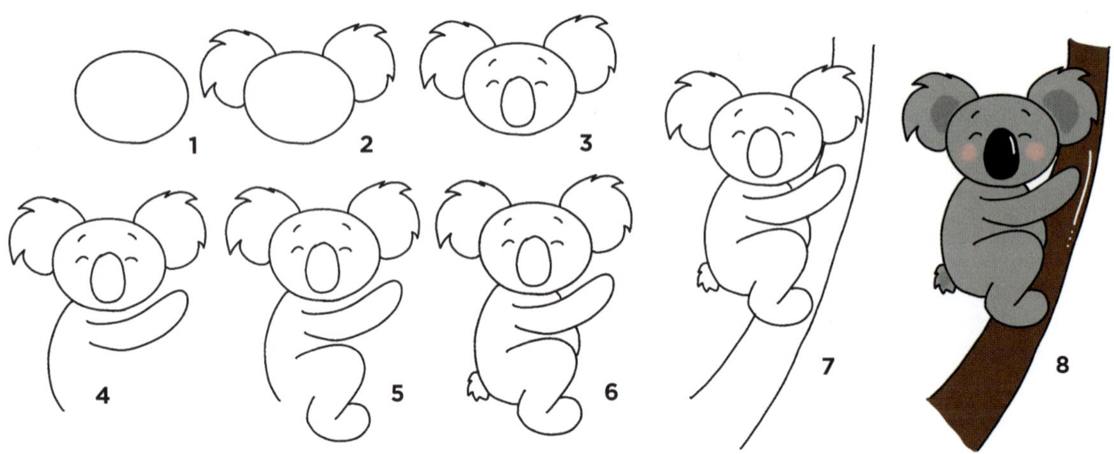

KOALA

You don't have to go to the outback to make friends with this cheerful koala. First, make an oval for the head and add large ears with jagged edges on each side. Draw a big oval nose, along with the rest of the face, then give your koala a simple body with a front arm and a leg. Add a belly and a little round tail, then give your koala a tree to climb by drawing two long curving lines just to his right. Color your drawing and see how happy this koala is to sleep on its branch.

HIPPO

Our hippo is awfully happy to be playing in a big puddle of mud. To create this doodle, start by drawing a sideways "3" shape with a curving line on top for the head. Add a small set of ears and two large teeth, then sketch the rest of the face. Draw curving lines for the back and the belly, then doodle a big mud puddle all around your hippo, with a few stray drops flying out to the sides. Finally, add color to finish off your drawing.

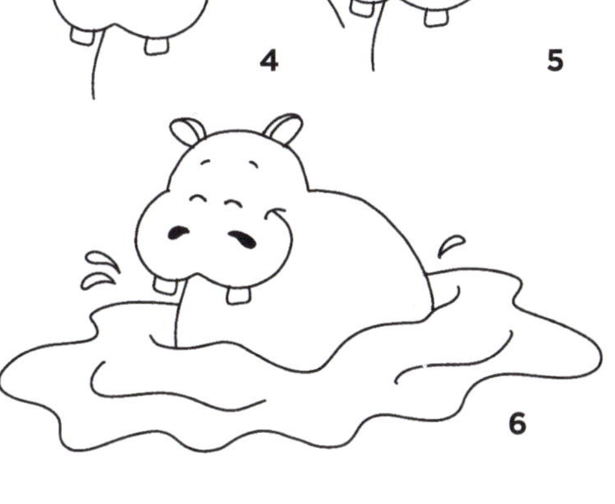

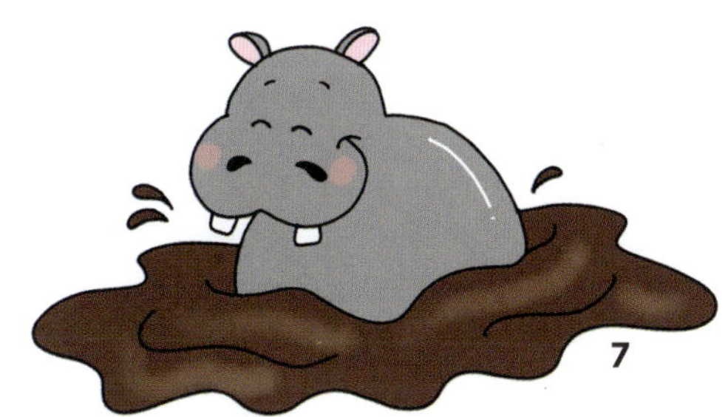

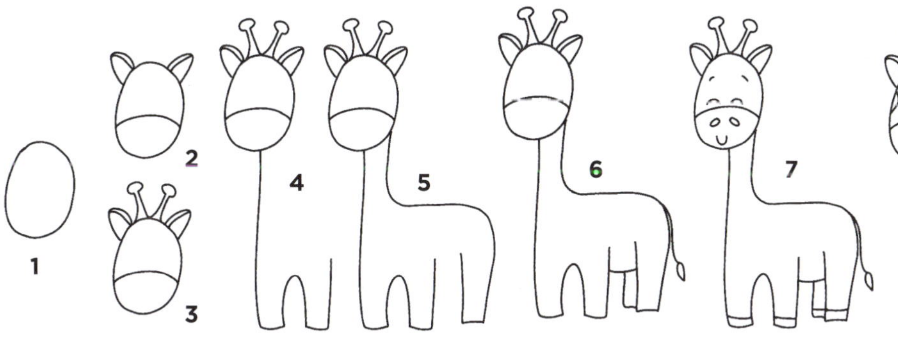

GIRAFFE

While elephants may be the largest, giraffes are definitely the tallest animals, able to reach heights of almost 20 feet! This little giraffe doodle isn't quite that tall, but he makes up for it in cuteness. To draw him, start with an oval-shaped head with a curving line to divide off the nose area. Add two small ears and a pair of ossicones (the hornlike things on top of the head). Give your giraffe a long thin neck, a body and four legs. Next, add a tail, a face, spots and hair on top of the head and going down the neck. Finally, color your giraffe with shades of yellow and brown.

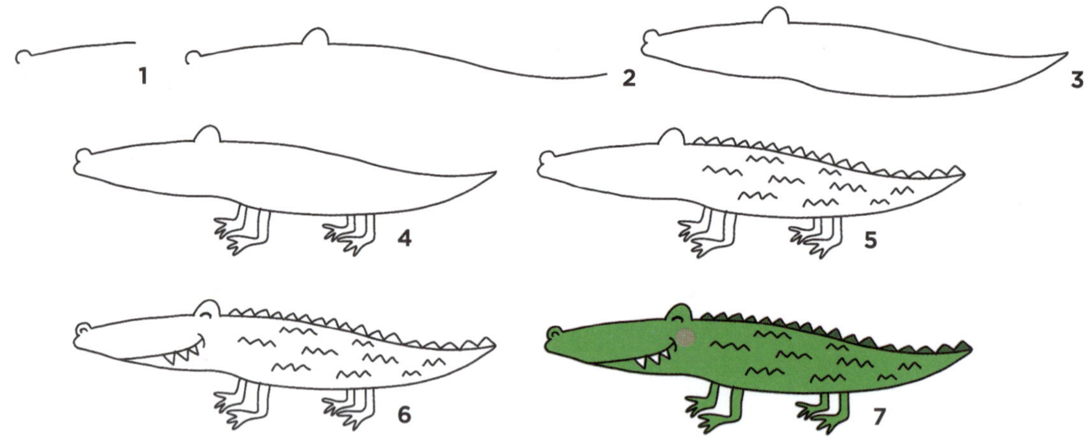

CROCODILE

Crocodiles are known for their "smiles," but you'll be the one smiling when you create this doodle. Start by drawing a curving line with a small bump for the snout and another for the eye. Sketch another curving line below to finish the body and tail and add short legs with feet. Make a series of triangles going down the croc's back and add some zigzags along the inside of the body to represent a scaly texture. Finally, add an eye, a smile with some teeth and color to finish your drawing.

TOUCAN

The first step in drawing a toucan is to sketch its famous beak. Next, add a peanut-shaped body and feet made of three ovals. Sketch a branch below your toucan's feet, then add a three-feathered tail beneath the branch. Finally, divide the body by drawing curving lines to separate the belly and the eye area from the rest. Color your doodle—usually a black body with a white or light yellow belly and a yellow patch around the eye.

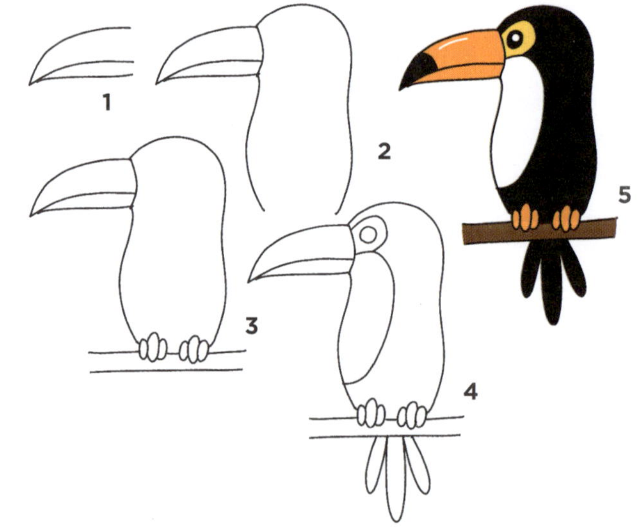

PARROT

To draw this colorful parrot, start with a curving head and a large front wing. Add another curving line to form the belly and draw an open beak. Next, draw a long feathered tail, legs and feet. Give your parrot an eye and a branch to stand on, along with some scallop details along the wing for texture. Finish your doodle by filling in the parts of the bird with an assortment of bright colors.

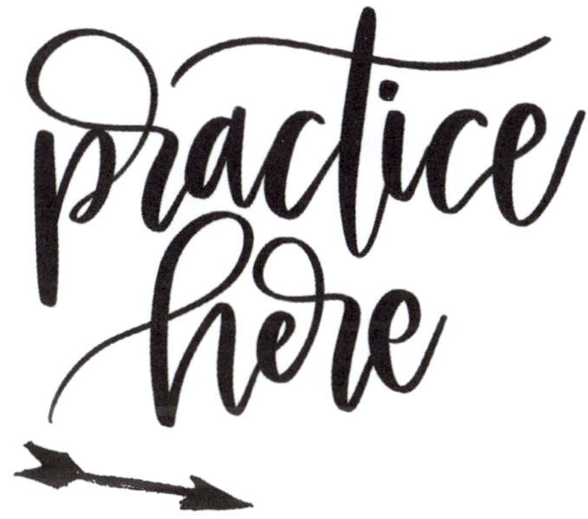

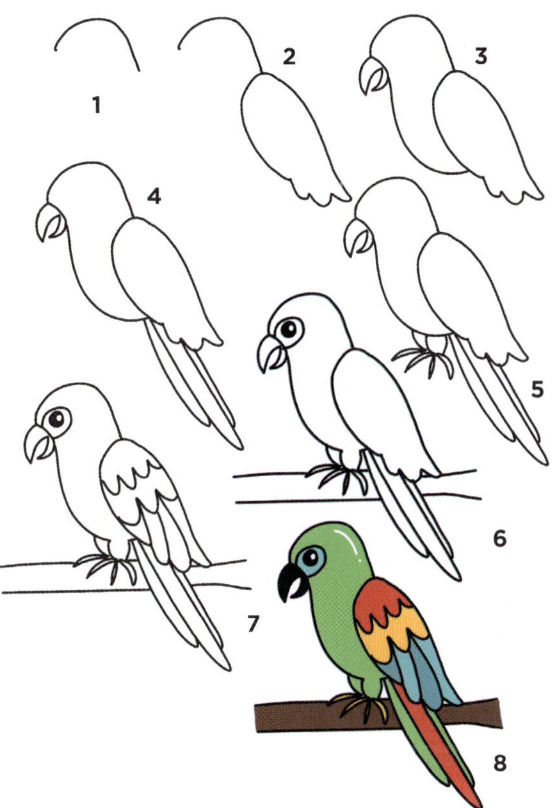

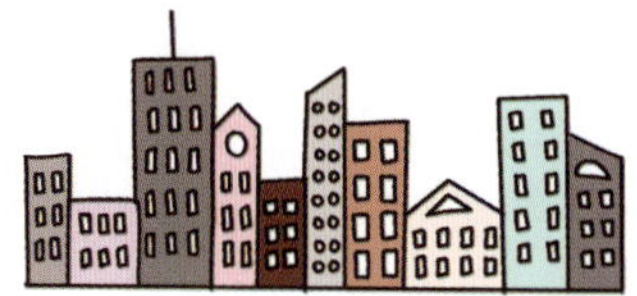

Around Town

Whether you live in a big city or a small town, there are plenty of things to draw all around you. From modes of transportation to the places you go, inspiration can be found in your everyday life. You'll also find some sweet doodles for your local city park with a bench, a tree and cute critters! These city and town doodles are fun to use on all kinds of projects and they're just the beginning. Once you get the hang of how to draw a car or a building, you can adapt these ideas to sketch just about anything you see in your own community.

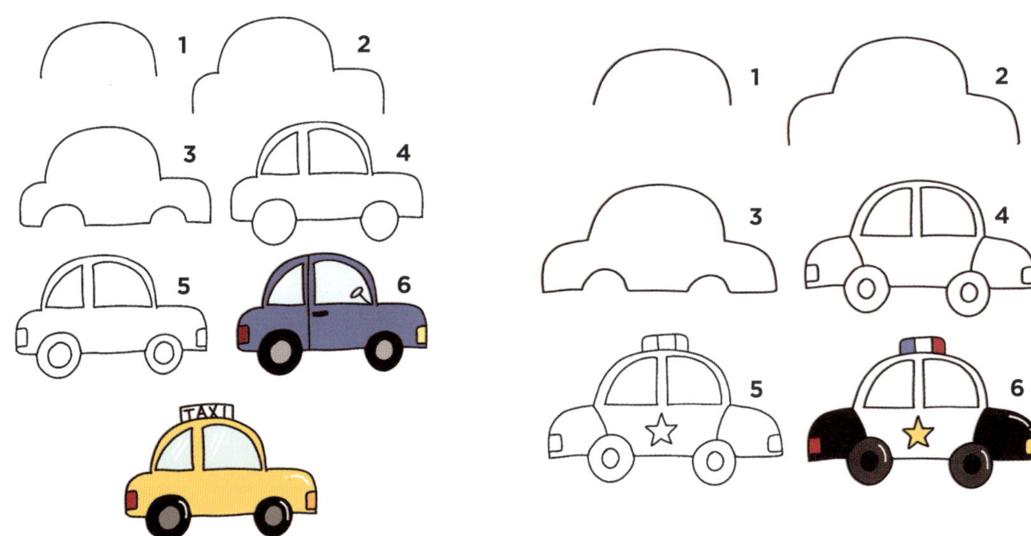

CAR, TAXI & POLICE CAR

Did you know an upside-down "U" shape with a curving line on each side forms the upper part of a car? For this one, I made the front curving line longer for the hood and engine. Next, draw a line across the bottom with two semicircles where the wheels will go. Windows, circles for tires, headlights and taillights will give you a finished car. You could always stop there and color it in for a regular car, or keep going and turn it into a cab by adding a rectangular "TAXI" sign on the top and coloring the car yellow.

Drawing a police car starts with the same basic steps as the taxi. For this one, I made both the front and back equal sizes. To make it look like an old-fashioned police car, draw lines to separate the body of the car into three parts. Then, sketch a rectangle for the lights on top, a star on the side and color in the front and back sections of the car black.

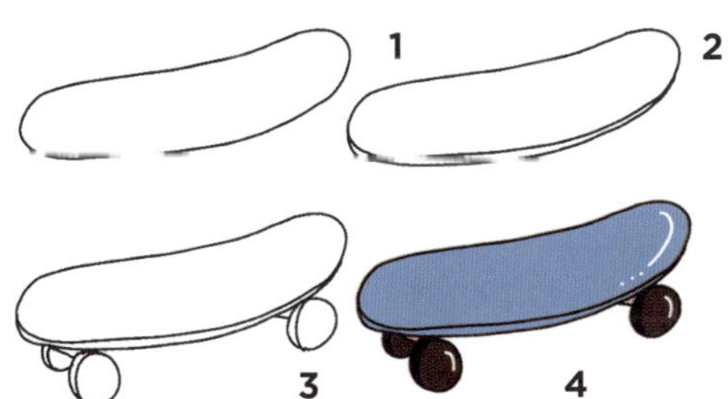

SKATEBOARD

To sketch a skateboard, start with an oval shape that bends slightly upward on one side. Add three visible wheels, then feel free to color or decorate the board itself with any kind of pattern or doodles you like!

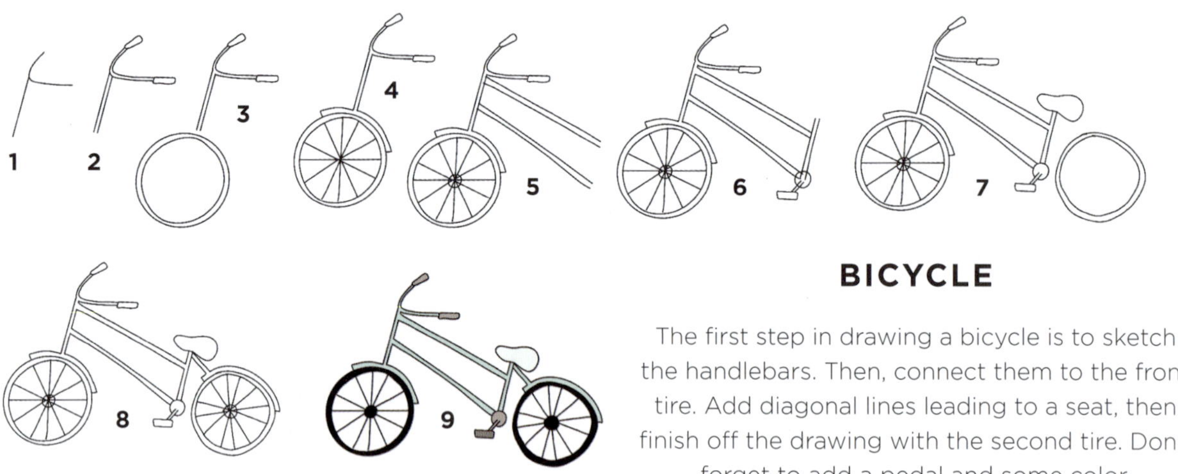

BICYCLE

The first step in drawing a bicycle is to sketch the handlebars. Then, connect them to the front tire. Add diagonal lines leading to a seat, then finish off the drawing with the second tire. Don't forget to add a pedal and some color.

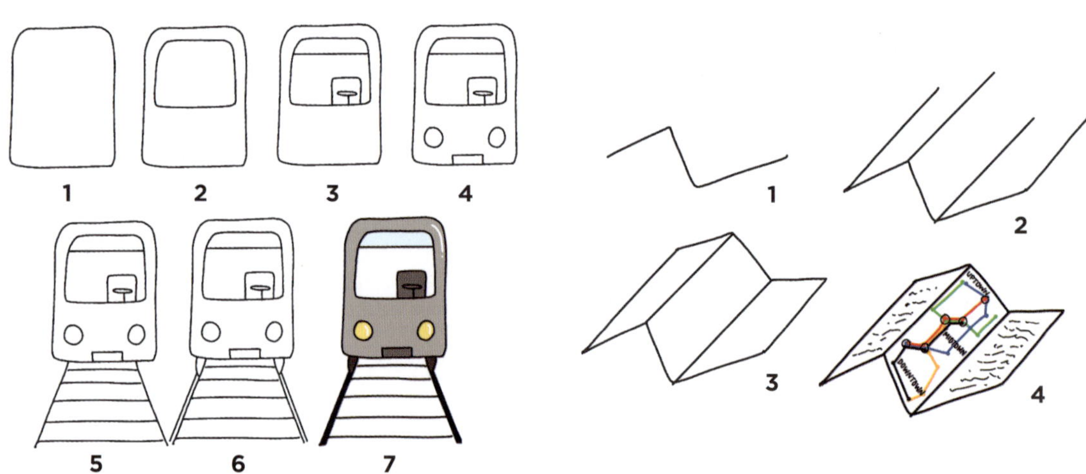

SUBWAY TRAIN & MAP

Drawing a subway train is easiest if we use a front view. Sketch a rounded rectangle for the basic shape and add a front windshield. Next, include details like a steering wheel and seat, headlights, etc. Finally, make sure to give your subway car a track to ride on. Making the track wider at the bottom than the top gives perspective and makes it feel like the train is headed right off the page!

Every subway needs a map! Draw this one by making a zigzag line and extending a diagonal line out from each point. Connect those lines at the top and you'll have the appearance of a paper that folds into thirds. Then, have fun drawing your own little map using different colors to indicate different lines of travel.

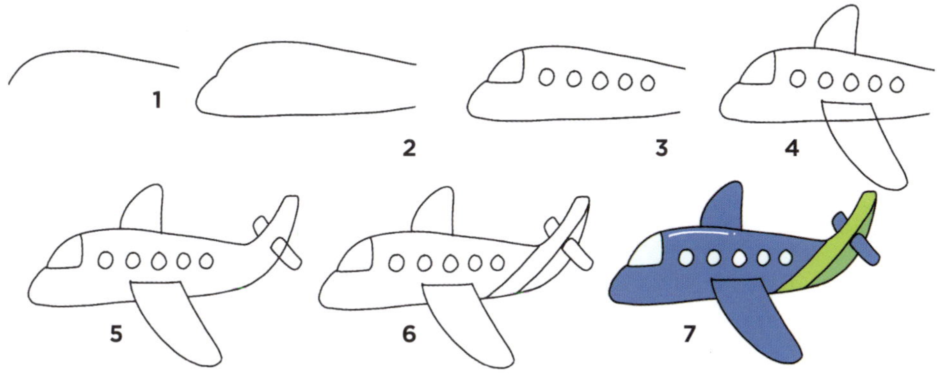

AIRPLANE

To begin your airplane doodle, sketch the basic shape of the main cabin. Add a windshield and a series of windows along the side, then draw in your wings. Finally, add a tail and any other decorative details you like. Color it in to represent your favorite airline or one that's all your own!

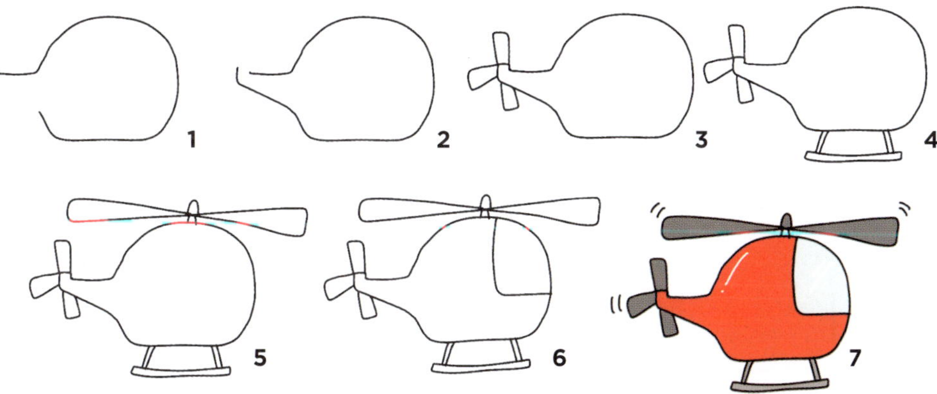

HELICOPTER

Like a plane, a helicopter doodle begins with the body of the aircraft. Next, add the tail. Draw landing skids on the bottom, then the blades on top. Don't forget to give it a window for the cockpit, then color the doodle in. Adding short curving lines near the blades suggests movement and gives the idea that your helicopter is in flight.

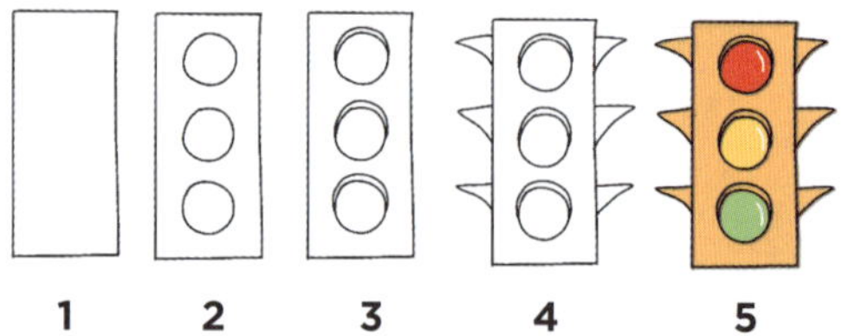

STOPLIGHT

A simple stoplight is nothing more than a rectangle with three circles inside. You can stop there or you can continue and add more detail to show the hoods above the lights. Then, it's time for the most important part: coloring those lights red, yellow and green!

SUITCASE

Pack your suitcase and get ready for a fun doodle trip! If you can draw a rectangle, you can draw a suitcase. Round the corners slightly, then add a little bit of dimension and a handle. Then comes the fun part! You can personalize your suitcase by adding stickers of all shapes and sizes to represent places you've visited or where you'd like to travel someday.

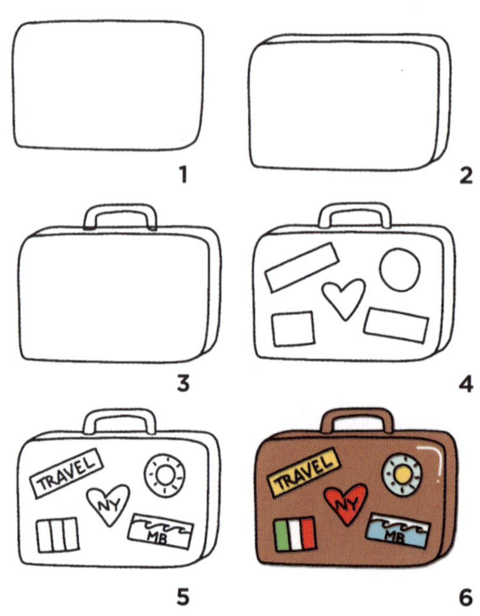

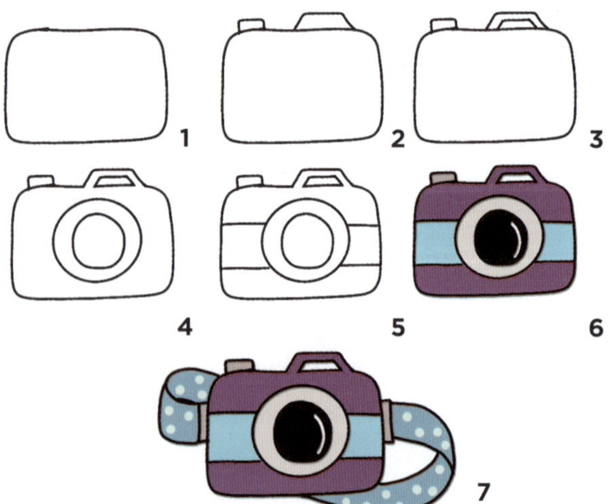

CAMERA

Make sure you have your camera for sightseeing. The basic shape of a camera starts with a rounded rectangle. Add a button for the shutter and a little viewfinder on top, then draw two circles to represent the lens. I added a stripe to mine for visual interest, but you can leave yours plain or decorate your camera body in any way you prefer. Feel free to add a camera strap and decorate it in your own colorful style!

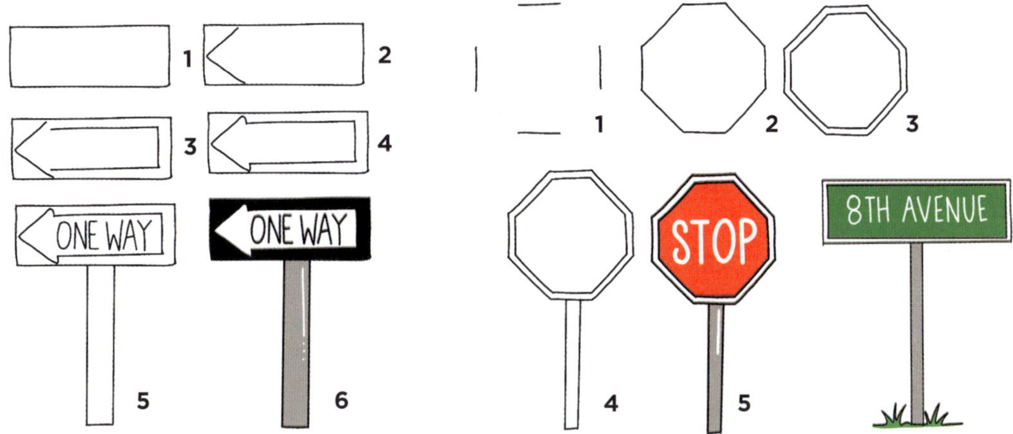

STREET SIGN & STOP SIGN

This common street sign is simply a rectangle with an arrow inside. Print the words "ONE WAY" inside the arrow, then color the outer part of the sign black. This doodle is easy to adapt with the name of the street where you live or from a special memory.

To draw a stop sign, sketch an octagon with a second slightly smaller octagon inside. Color the inner shape red and leave the outer one white. Add the word "STOP" in white, along with a gray or brown pole. White gel pen is a great tool for adding the word on top of the red background.

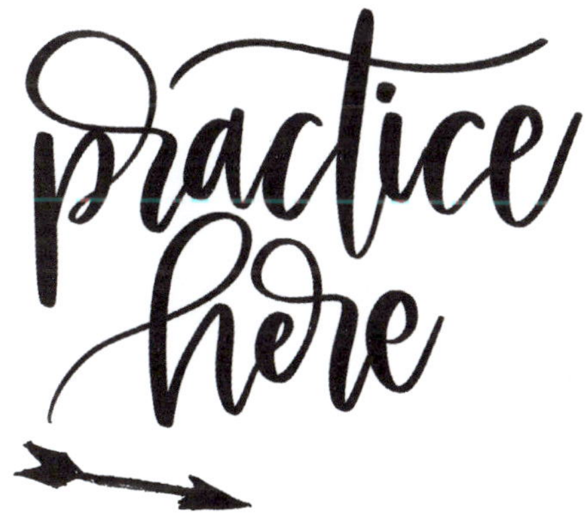

AT THE PARK

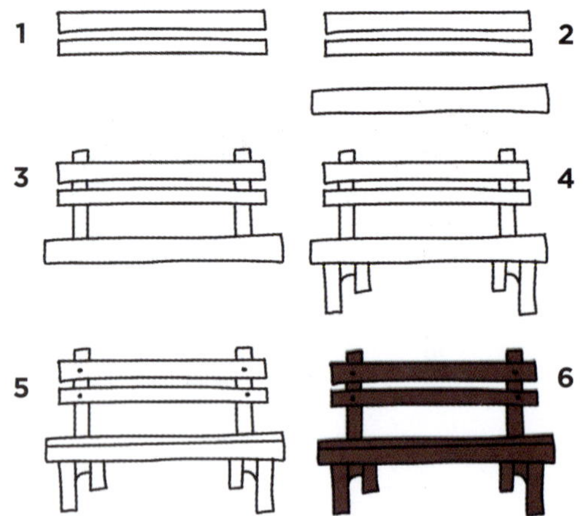

PARK BENCH

What's a city park without a bench to sit on and relax? Draw this one by creating three horizontal rectangles and connecting them with vertical ones for the back and the legs. It's that simple: If you can draw a rectangle, you can draw a bench!

SIMPLE TREE

A park isn't a park without trees, and here's a simple way to draw one. Start with curving vertical lines for the trunk, then give it a fluffy top that's similar to a cloud. Use bumps and swirls to create a mostly round shape, then add color. Your tree can be green or you can color it for spring or fall! Find an evergreen tree on page 59 if you're looking for some more variety.

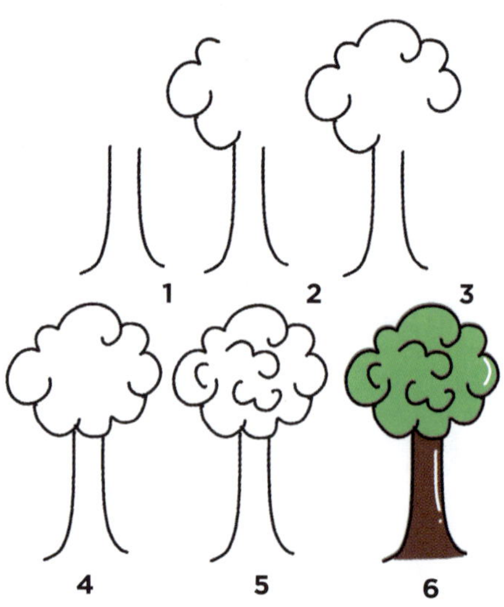

1 2 3 4 5

CLOUD

When I draw a cloud, I begin with one simple swirl. From there, I continue around to the right with a small bump and another swirl, then repeat that on the left side. Keep going with bumps and swirls until they meet at the bottom. Then, you can color your cloud if you like and add embellishments. I typically draw a short line followed by three little dots around every swirl.

KITE

A kite is simply a diamond shape with a cross shape inside. Your kite can go in any direction you choose; I like to draw mine on a bit of a diagonal so it looks like it's in flight. Of course, it needs a tail, so you'll finish it off with a wavy line and tiny bows made of triangles. Then, have fun adding color . . . the more, the better! Feel free to add shapes or designs on your kite as well to make it unique.

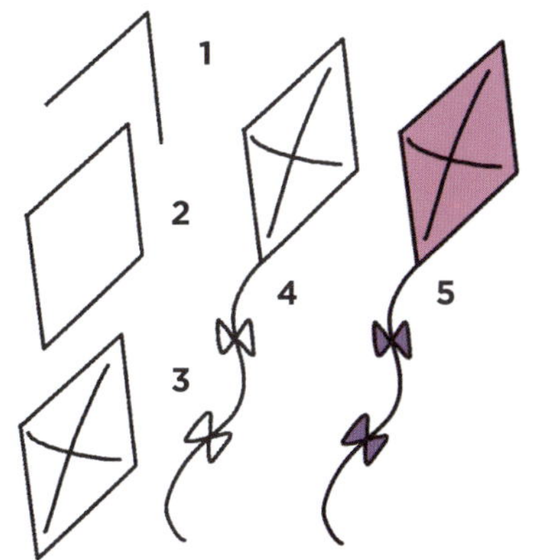

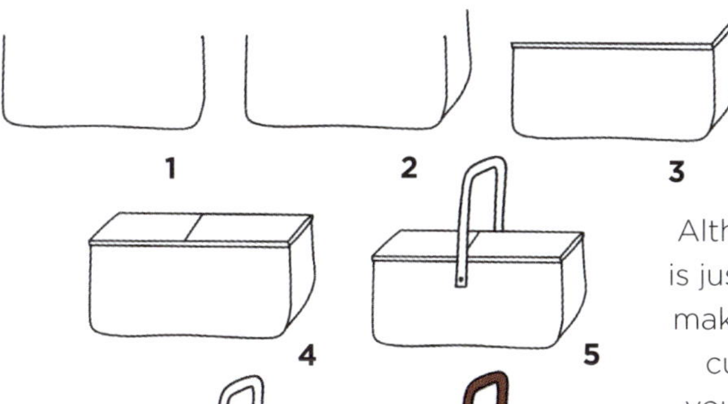

PICNIC BASKET

Although it may look intimidating at first, a picnic basket is just a combination of basic shapes and lines. First, you'll make a line for the base of the basket, then add a shorter curving line to the right to be the basket's side. Next, you'll add the upper edge and the basket's lid. A handle finishes it off, but I also like to add a bit of checkered napkin peeking out. Drawing intersecting lines all over the basket and lid suggests a woven texture.

BIRD'S NEST

To sketch a nest with eggs, start by drawing a wide "U" shape with some curving lines across the top to represent twigs. Fill the shape with more curving lines for the materials the bird used to build its nest. Add several egg shapes on top, then draw a few more short lines beside and behind the eggs to show that the nest is three-dimensional. Finally, add color to complete your drawing. To find a doodle of a baby chick popping out of an egg, check out page 83 in the At the Holidays chapter!

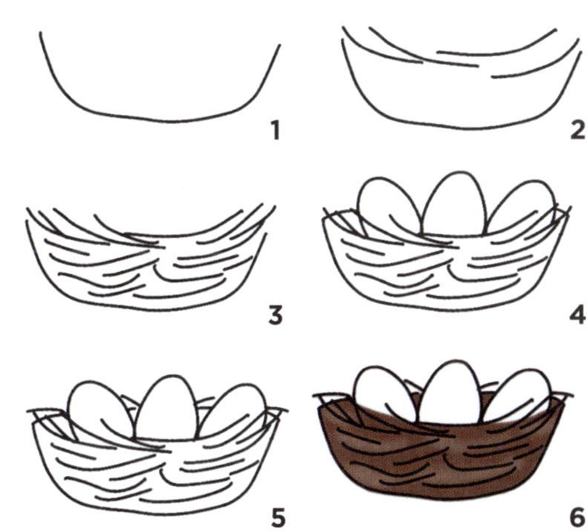

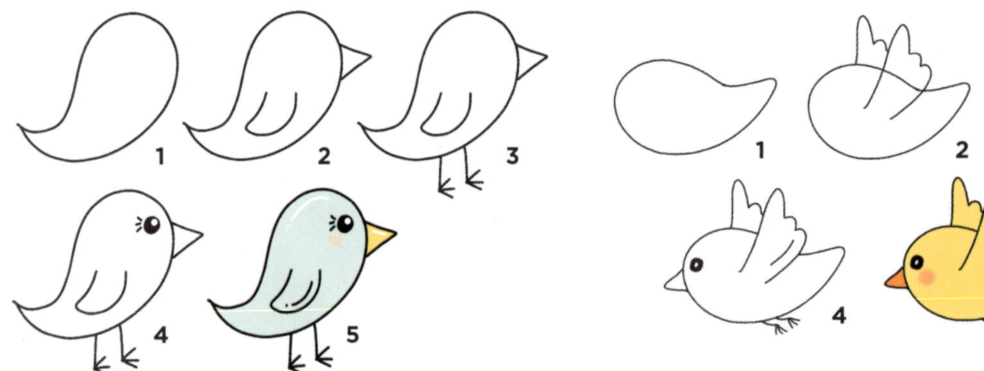

CUTE BIRDS

This simple bird is nothing more than a curving teardrop shape with a triangle beak. Straight lines form its legs and feet, then all that's left is to give it a wing and a face . . . and, of course, some color!

An alternate style of drawing a bird (above right) is one that is in flight! Start by making a sideways teardrop shape for the body. Then, add two wings that angle upward. Give the bird an eye, a beak and feet, then color it any way you like.

PIGEON

If you want to draw a slightly more advanced bird, a pigeon is a great choice for the park. First, draw the shape of the head and wing, then add the tail and belly. Finish off the sketch with a beak and feet! Adding detail lines on the wing and the tail, as well as using a few different grays to color it in, will help to give it that distinctive pigeon identity.

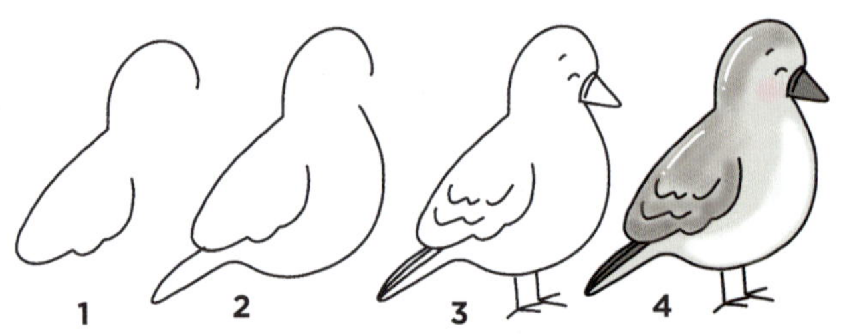

1 2 3 4 5

DUCK

This duck doodle begins with a shape similar to a question mark, then add a triangle beak and a little semicircle cheek. Draw the body shape, add a wing and a face, and your duck is ready to happily swim around in the park.

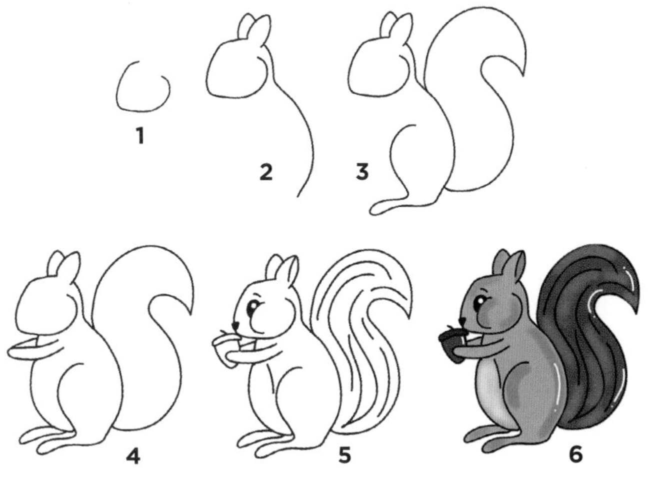

SQUIRREL

What's a park without squirrels to run across the path and try to steal your picnic? The first part of this sketch is forming the face and the ears, then the back portion of the body and the tail. Then, move to the front of the body, drawing the belly and arms, of course holding an acorn (page 61)!

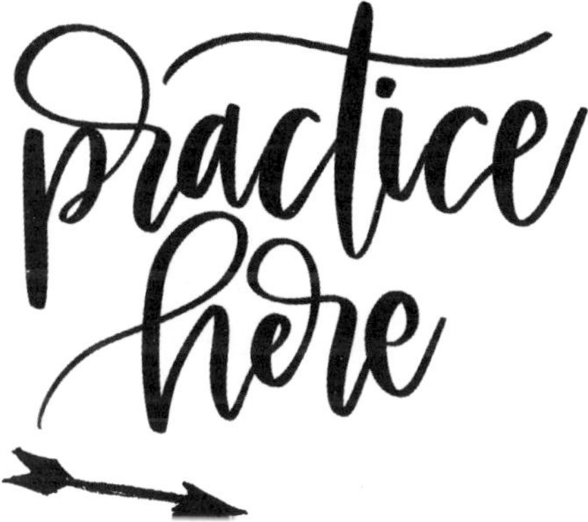

BUILDING & URBAN OBJECTS

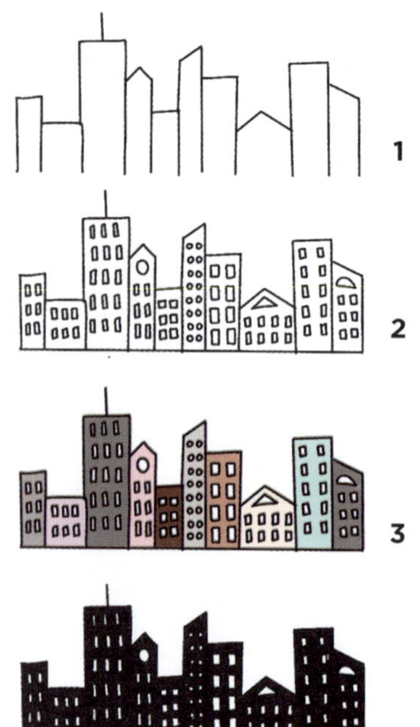

CITY SKYLINE

Every city's skyline is unique! To sketch one, all you have to do is combine a series of simple shapes that represent buildings of various sizes. I typically use rectangles of different heights and widths, and throw in a few peaked and angled roofs for variety. Once you have the shapes sketched, add windows. When you color in your doodle, you get to decide whether it's day or night. For a daytime view, color each building a different shade. For a night view, color everything black except for the windows. You can personalize this doodle for a specific city by adding in a few of its iconic building shapes.

SIMPLE HOUSE

Home is where the heart is, as this sweet little doodle shows. All homes look different, but this one is just two simple shapes: a rectangle with a triangle roof. Add details like a door, windows, a chimney and bushes to make it your own.

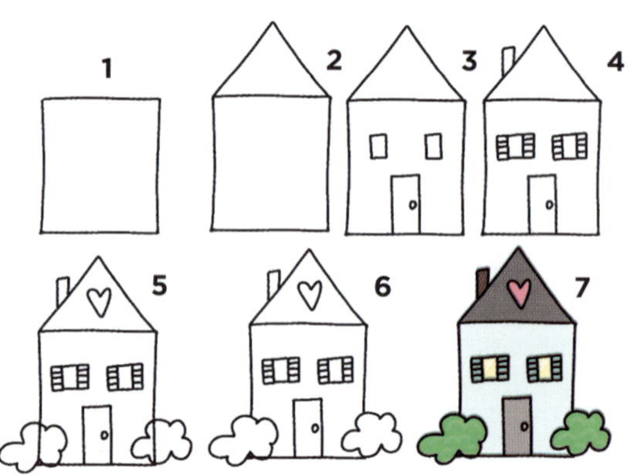

1 2 3 4

SIMPLE BUILDING

This tall building doodle is simply a combination of rectangles and squares, but it can become anything you want it to be. From apartments to an office building, it's the perfect addition to any city. You can even add a Red Cross symbol to the front to transform it into a hospital.

CHURCH

This church building starts like a house, with a square and a triangle for the base. Draw in some windows with arched tops and a set of two doors. Then, add on to each side to expand the building. Details like arched multicolored windows and a cross on the steeple provide the perfect finishing touches. Don't forget the bell tower, which is easy to draw with an arched shape and horizontal lines.

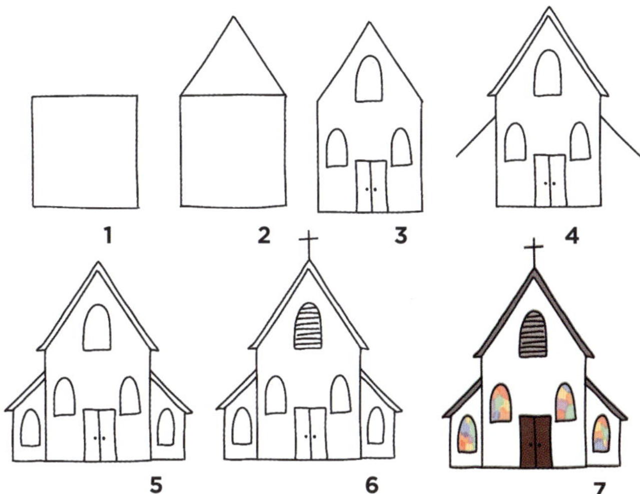

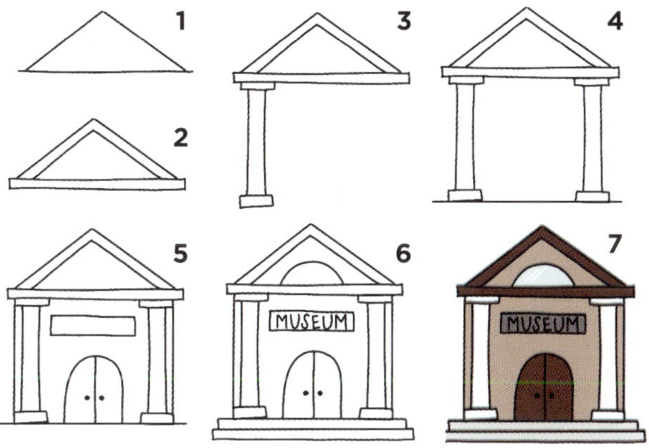

MUSEUM

Like many other buildings, a museum's base is a rectangle with a triangle on top, but it's the vertical columns and wide steps in front that give it a distinct appearance. Add arching doors, an arching window and a sign labeling the building to make it clear what's inside.

FRAMED ARTWORK

Of course, an art museum isn't complete without paintings. Create a fancy frame by drawing a rectangle with a series of bumps all around it. Add a hanger, then sketch in any kind of scene you can imagine. I drew a landscape, but you can also draw a person, an animal, something abstract or whatever kind of artwork you want to display.

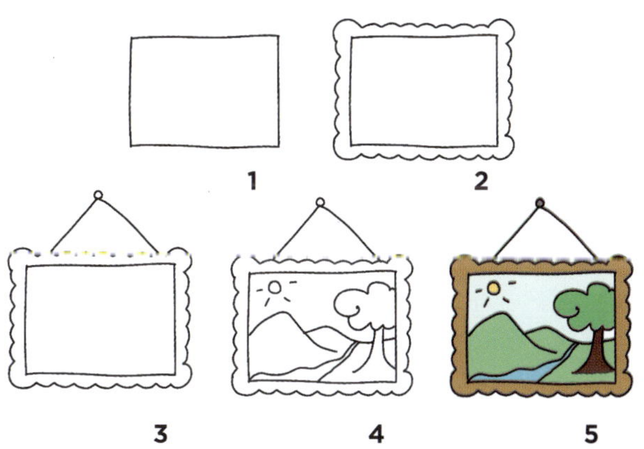

BANDAGE

Unfortunately, sometimes one of the things we need to do around town is visit the doctor for an illness or an injury. To draw this bandage, simply sketch a long rectangle with rounded edges and a small rectangle in the center. Add some dots on either side and color it in to complete the doodle.

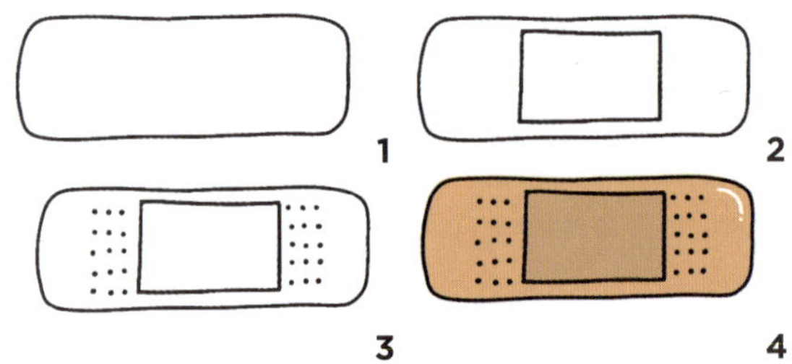

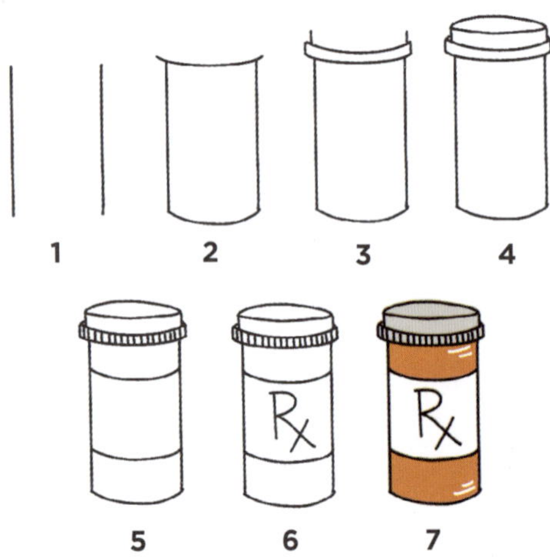

PILL BOTTLE

The base of a pill bottle is made up of two vertical lines connected by a curving line at the bottom to give it a three-dimensional feel. Add a cap with some detail lines and create a label that you can customize with the name of any type of medication.

STETHOSCOPE

Start your drawing of a stethoscope with a rounded "V" shape. Double the shape to form the part that goes around the doctor's neck. Add a rectangle near the base of the "V" shape and detail lines along the sides. Draw small semicircles at the end of each side of the "V" shape for the ear pieces. Sketch a doubled curving line coming from the base of the "V" and add a circle shape at the end for the round metal piece that goes on the patient's chest. Draw a second, smaller circle inside the first one. Color the stethoscope and it's ready for a doctor to use.

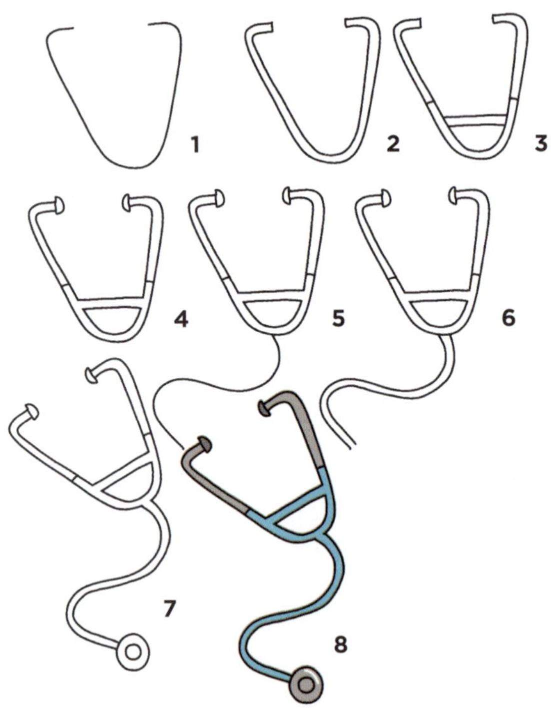

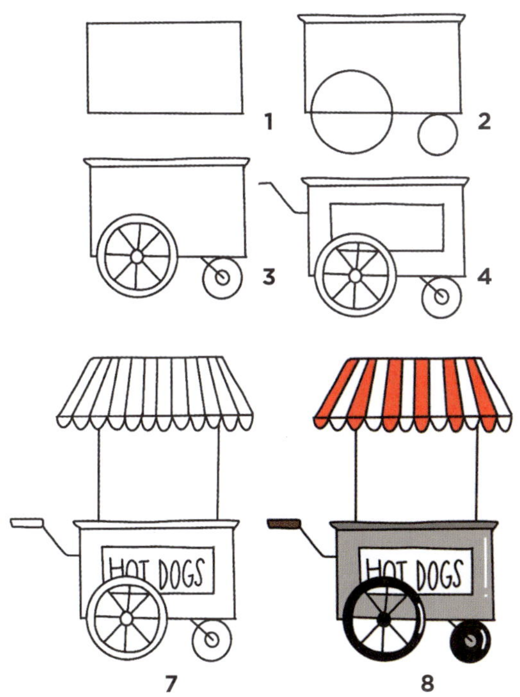

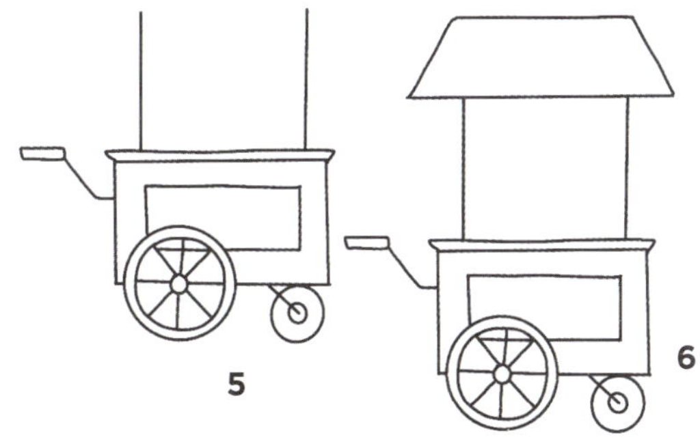

HOT DOG CART

What's a trip to the city without enjoying some street food? To draw a hot dog cart, start with a rectangle that has two circles at the bottom: one large and one small. Add details to the wheels and a handle coming off the side. Sketch two poles and an awning, then personalize the cart with color and anything you'd like to write on the side. This would also make a cute ice cream or lemonade cart!

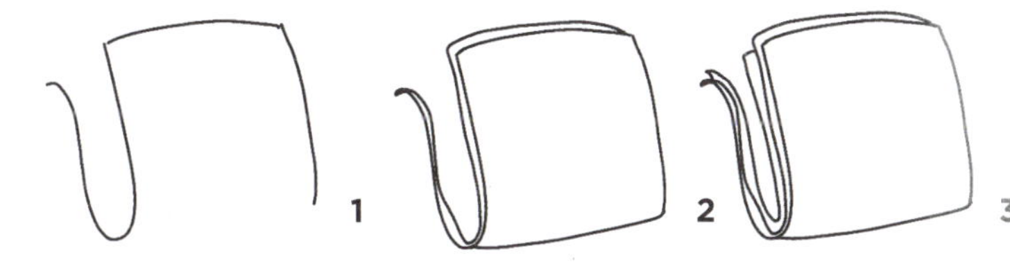

NEWSPAPER

Every town and city needs its daily news. This paper starts with a base shape, then builds on that to add the idea of more and more pages. The most fun part of the doodle is adding whatever little words or illustrations you want to put on the front page.

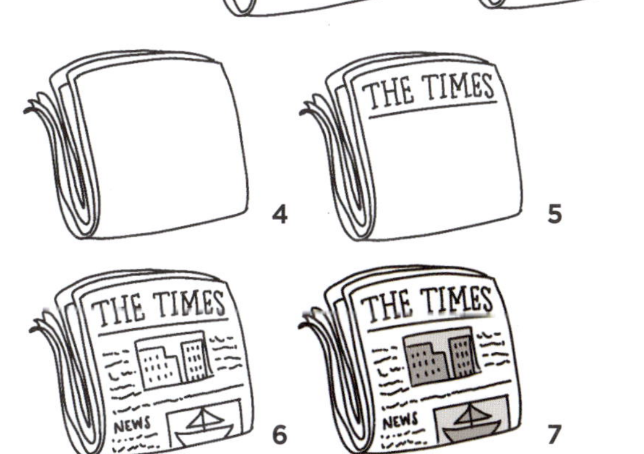

AT THE Stadium

Most of us have favorite sports teams we enjoy watching and the experience is even better when we get the chance to be in the stadium. Surrounded by a crowd, eating the snacks and feeling the excitement in the air, we get to be a part of the event in a special way. The doodles in this chapter will help you capture a little bit of that stadium feeling, as well as help you illustrate symbols for some of the sports you enjoy. Of course, there are a few sports, like tennis and golf, that take place outside of a stadium setting, but we'll still learn to doodle those too!

ON THE FIELD

FOOTBALL & GOAL POST

A football is simply a curving line with a second curving line below it to form the shape of a pointed oval. Once you draw the ball itself, doodling the details is easy: curving lines near each point and a set of laces in the top center. I recommend using a white gel pen to draw the laces so they show up on top of your brown ball.

To draw a goal post, start with a rectangle that's open on the top. Then, draw a second set of lines around it. Add a post connecting it to the ground and a bit of grass to show that it's firmly planted in the field.

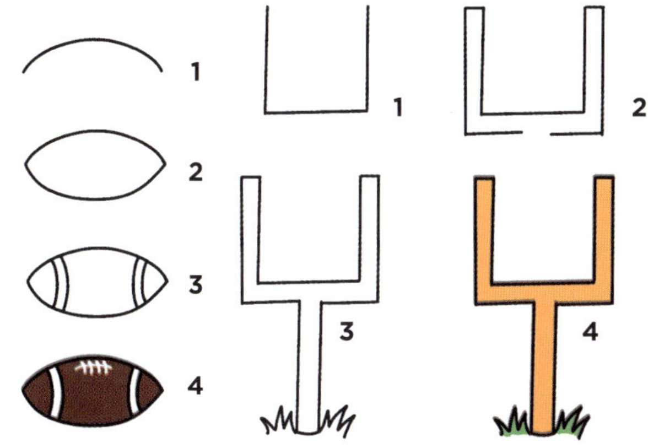

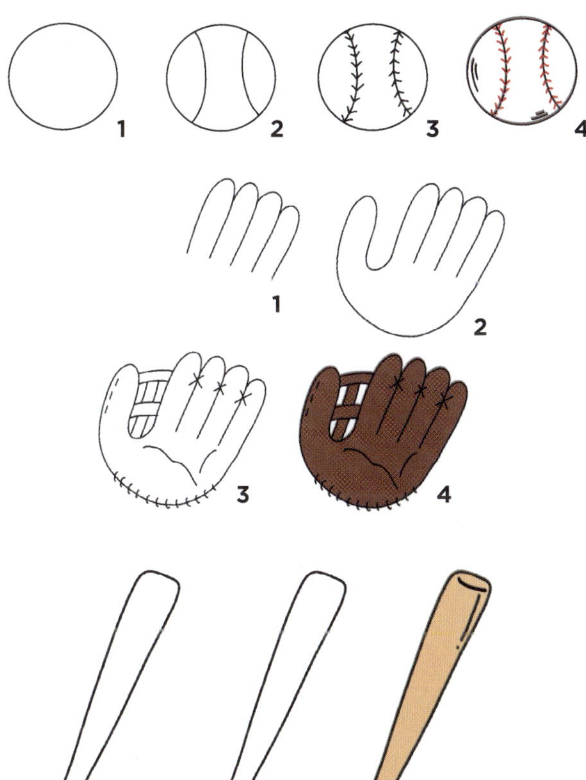

BASEBALL, GLOVE & BAT

Start a baseball doodle with a circle that has a curving line on each side. Then, add that characteristic stitching by drawing "V" shapes up and down each of the curved lines. Make sure that the stitches point in opposite directions just like on a real baseball.

Sketching a baseball glove starts with four upside-down "U" shapes for the fingers. Add the thumb and draw a curving line for the base of the glove. Details like the stitching on the leather and the straps connecting the thumb to the first finger are the most important parts to distinguish this as a baseball glove.

A bat is very simple to draw; just make an upside-down "U" shape and add an oval at the bottom to finish it off. Color your bat and add a few detail lines, then it's ready to hit a home run.

BASEBALL CAP

Begin your hat with an arch that has a wavy line across the bottom. Add the bill and a few curving detail lines to give it that classic cap shape. Feel free to add a logo or any other design to the front of the cap to signify your favorite team.

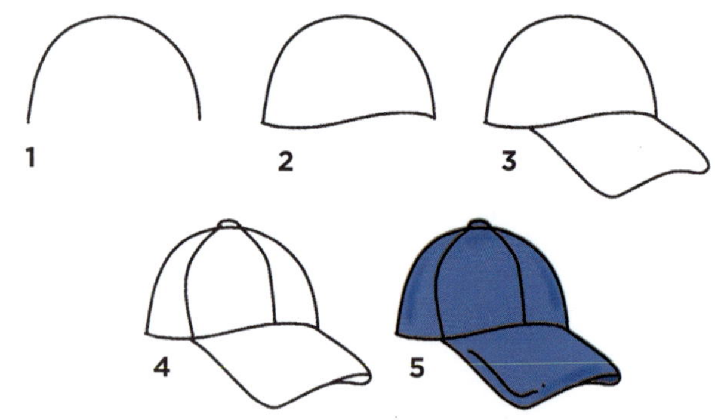

HOME PLATE

Home plate starts with three sides of a rectangle. Then, connect the open section with two lines that form a point at the bottom. Draw a second smaller shape inside the first one and connect it to the corners with short diagonal lines. Color in the outside sections gray for dimension and it's ready for the big game.

TENNIS BALL & RACKET

A tennis ball may be the simplest doodle of all: a circle with two curving lines inside. In fact, it's very similar to drawing a baseball but without the stitching! The key to making it instantly recognizable is by coloring it in that familiar shade of bright green.

Drawing a tennis racket is a bit more complicated than the ball, but it's still just a combination of basic shapes. Start with an oval, then draw a second one just outside it. Add a triangular shape and a rectangle at the bottom for the handle, then fill in the center oval with horizontal and vertical lines crossing over each other. Color and details, like grips on the handle, will make the doodle really pop.

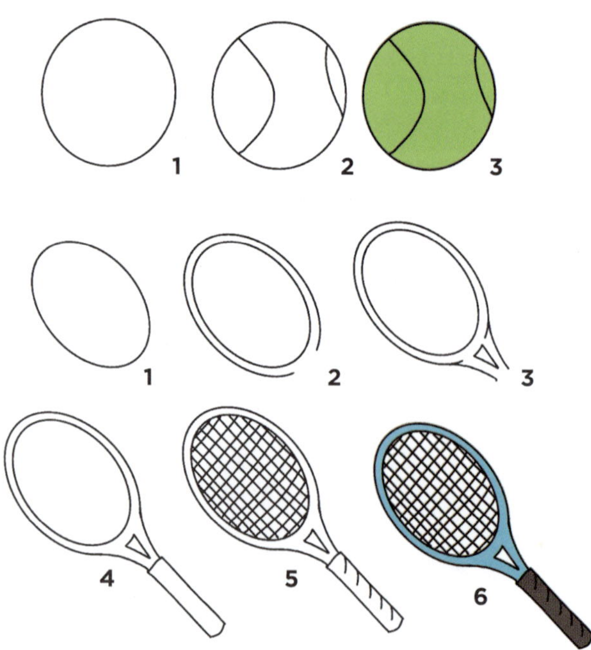

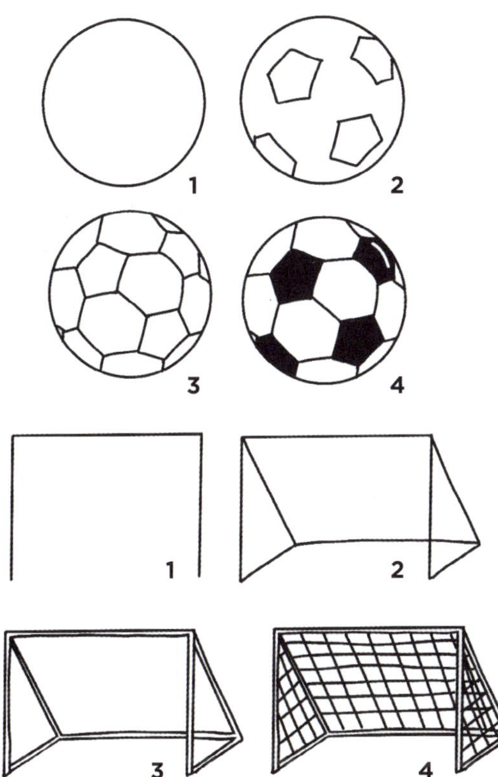

SOCCER BALL & NET

Soccer balls are the trickiest of all sports balls to draw, but they're still totally doable! Start with a circle, then add four hexagon shapes drawn at different angles to indicate a sphere shape. Connect those shapes with short diagonal lines. Color only the original four hexagons and leave the rest of the sections white. Feel free to trace my example until you get a feel for the design.

Drawing a net is simpler than it looks; it's just a matter of perspective and getting your lines in the right places. Start by drawing three sides of a rectangle, leaving the bottom open. Add a diagonal line extending downward from each of the top corners, then draw three lines to form the base. Double the lines so they look thicker than the netting. Finally, add a series of intersecting vertical and horizontal lines for the netting.

WHISTLE

Drawing a whistle starts with a curving line that resembles the number "6." Add a second line to give it dimension, as well as details like an open spot for the sound to come out and a place for it to hook onto a lanyard.

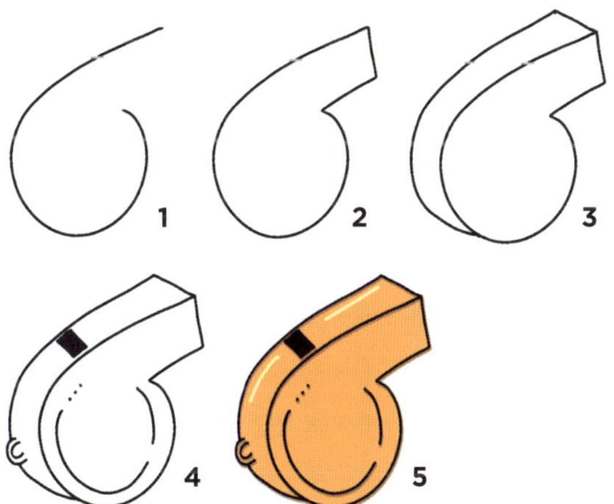

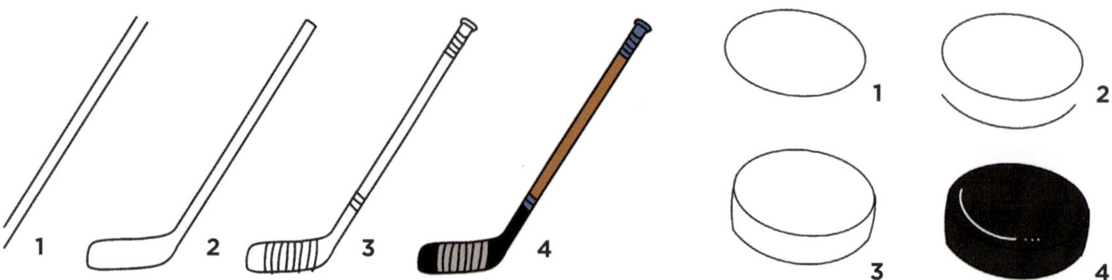

HOCKEY STICK & PUCK

The best place to start drawing a hockey stick is the shaft. Draw two long parallel lines on a diagonal and connect them at the top. At the bottom, sketch the shape of the blade. For ice hockey, this is long and thin and slightly rounded at the toe and heel.

A hockey puck doodle begins with an oval. Then, draw a second curving line below it and attach that line to the oval on each side. This gives your puck a three-dimensional feel. Add color and highlights to finish your illustration.

If you're looking to doodle some ice skates, check out page 66 in the In the Snow chapter! They would be easy to adapt with different colors and lace styles to look like ice hockey skates.

FIELD HOCKEY STICK

A field hockey stick starts off like the ice hockey stick with two long lines that are close together and connected at the top. Add a series of short lines to the handle for detail, then draw the rounded head and toe at the bottom of the stick. Finally, add color to complete your doodle.

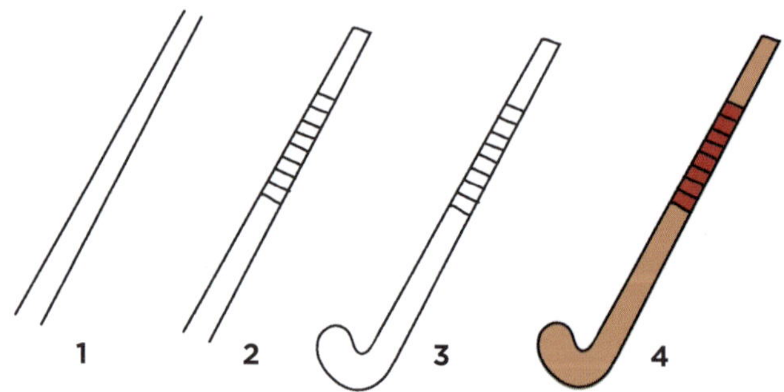

BASKETBALL & HOOP

A basketball is super easy to draw. Start with a circle and add one curving vertical line and one curving horizontal line. Add two more curving lines on either side, coming in toward the middle for that distinctive basketball appearance, then color it in your favorite shade of orange.

The first step in drawing a basketball hoop is to sketch the shape of the backboard. Then, add an oval with two lines for the sides of the net. Details like the square behind the hoop and an outline around the edge of the backboard will take your doodle to the next level. Finally, create a checkered pattern for the net itself!

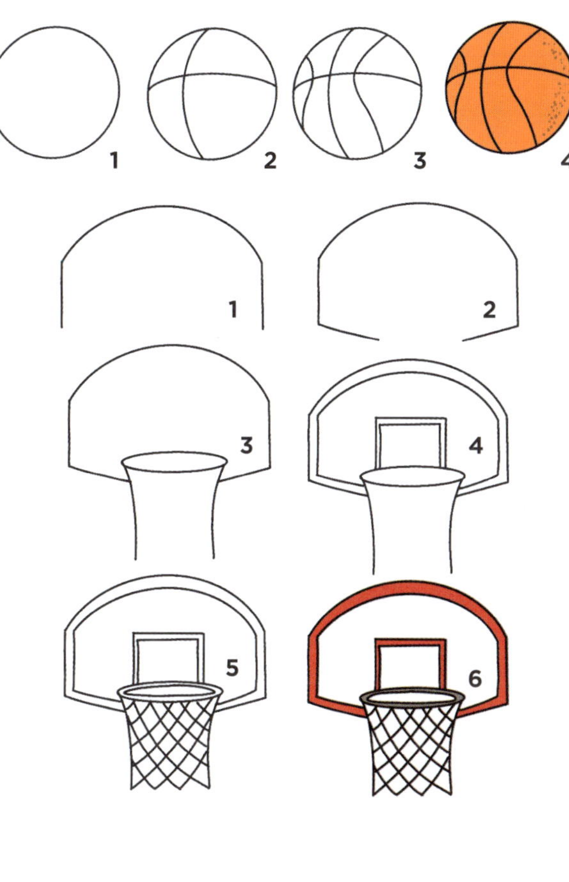

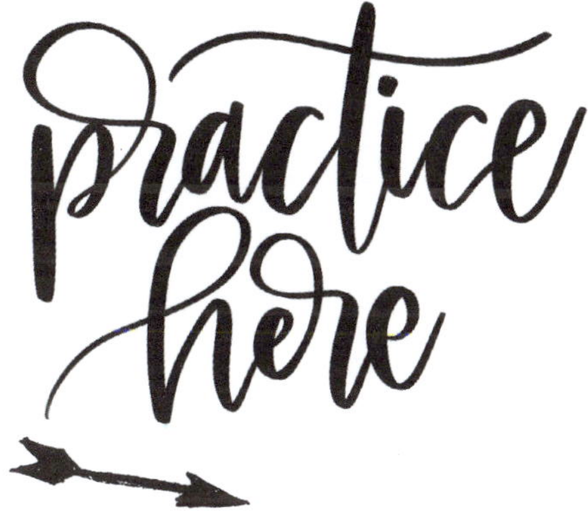

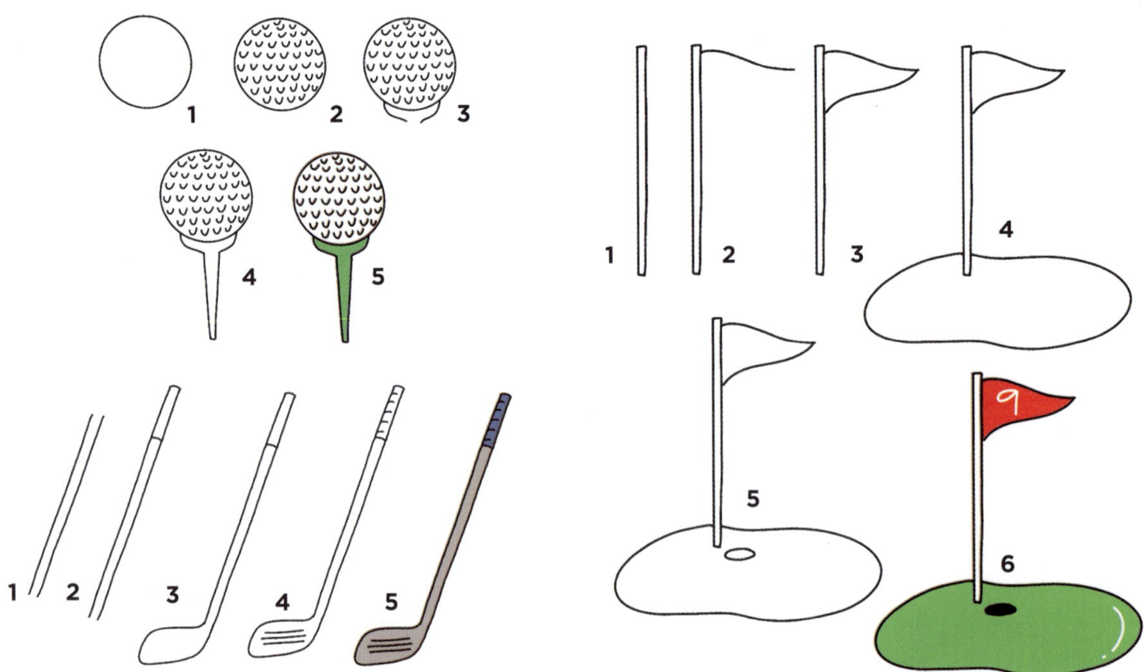

GOLF BALL, CLUB & FLAG

Drawing a golf ball is so simple; just start with a circle and fill it with "U" shapes for the divots all over the surface. To make it even more recognizable, add a "T"-shaped tee underneath.

A golf club starts with a long thin rectangle for the handle, then draw the head of the club itself. If you've ever played or watched the game, you know that clubs come in all shapes and sizes, so feel free to do the same with your sketch. Make an iron, a driver or a putter by changing the shape of the club head.

A long thin rectangle with a triangle makes an excellent flag to mark a golf hole. For the green itself, draw an imperfect oval shape around the bottom of the flag, then add a small circle for the hole. Color your drawing and add a number to the flag (but make sure it's between 1 and 18).

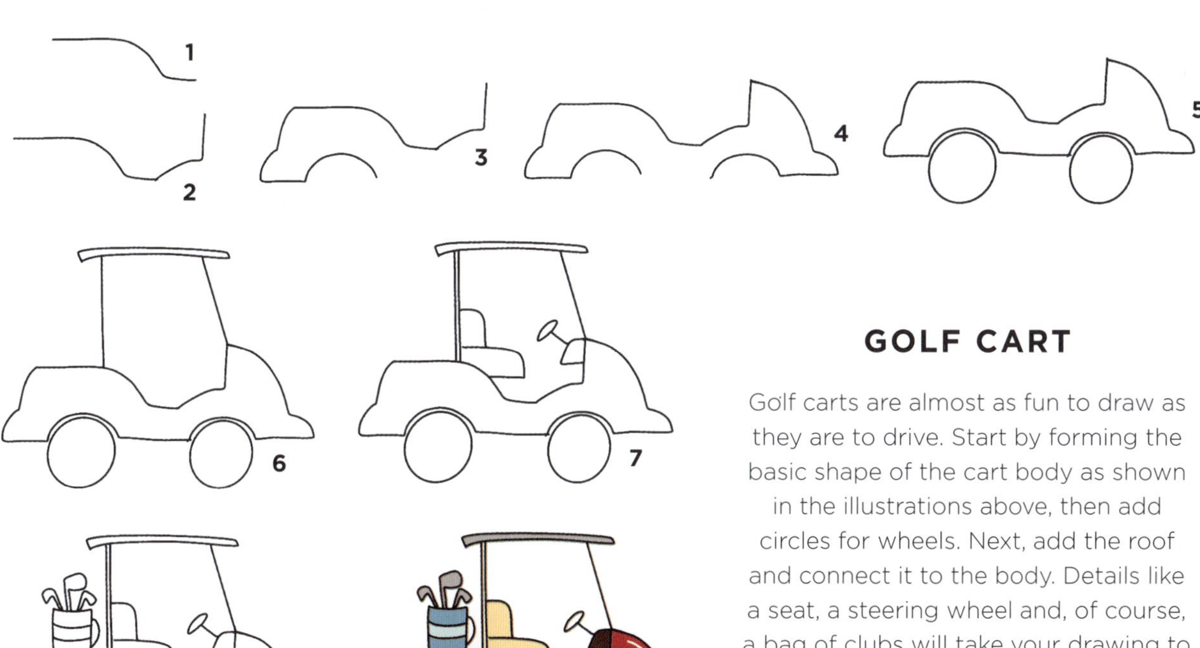

GOLF CART

Golf carts are almost as fun to draw as they are to drive. Start by forming the basic shape of the cart body as shown in the illustrations above, then add circles for wheels. Next, add the roof and connect it to the body. Details like a seat, a steering wheel and, of course, a bag of clubs will take your drawing to the next level. Don't forget to add color and customize your cart just like people do in real life!

SCOREBOARD

To draw a scoreboard, start with a large horizontal rectangle sitting on top of two smaller vertical ones. Add squares inside the large rectangle for each team's score and label them for the home and visiting teams. Detail lines, color and a bit of grass around each post will make this doodle pop off the page.

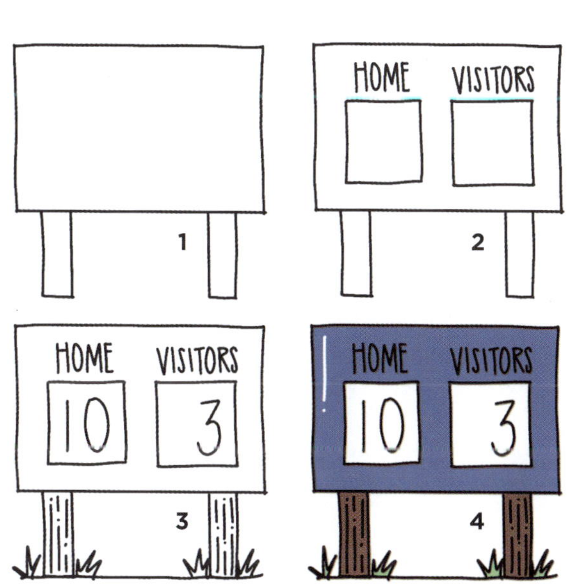

SNACKS IN THE STANDS

POPCORN BOX

What's a sports game without some stadium popcorn? Draw vertical lines that are slightly closer at the bottom than the top, then connect the top with a scalloped line. Add more scallops on a diagonal and give your box a three-dimensional feel by connecting the bottom and sides. Add popcorn, then color in your box. I recommend the classic red and white stripes!

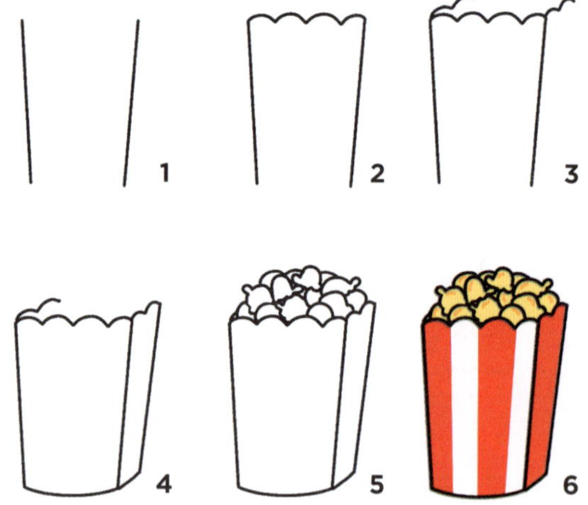

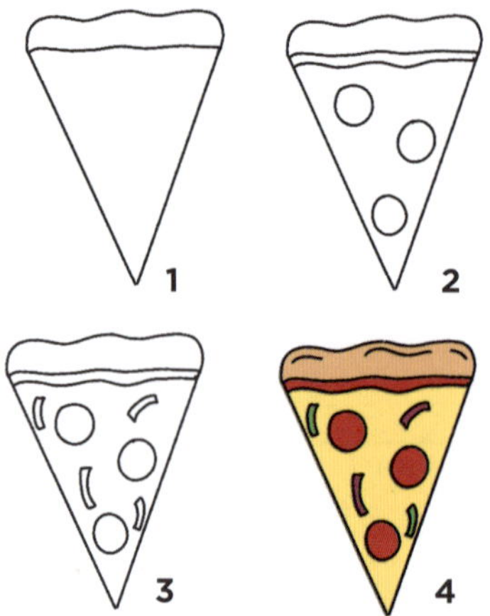

PIZZA SLICE

Pizza is a fun and easy game-day food to draw. Start with a "V" shape that has a waving line on top for the crust. Then, draw a second waving line, slightly below the first one to separate the cheese from the crust. This is where you'll color your sauce. Add circles for pepperoni and/or other basic shapes for onion, olives and other toppings, or keep it simple with just plain cheese.

COTTON CANDY

Cotton candy starts with a "V" shape for the cone. Then, add curving cloud-shaped lines to form the shape of the cotton candy itself; I like to start at the top and work my way down. Don't worry about keeping it neat and even—real cotton candy isn't either of those things! Add some decorations on the cone if you like and some curving detail lines inside the cotton candy to make it look fluffy, then color it in.

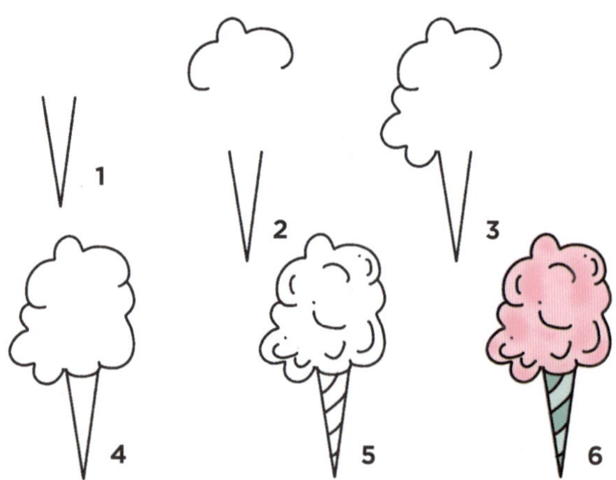

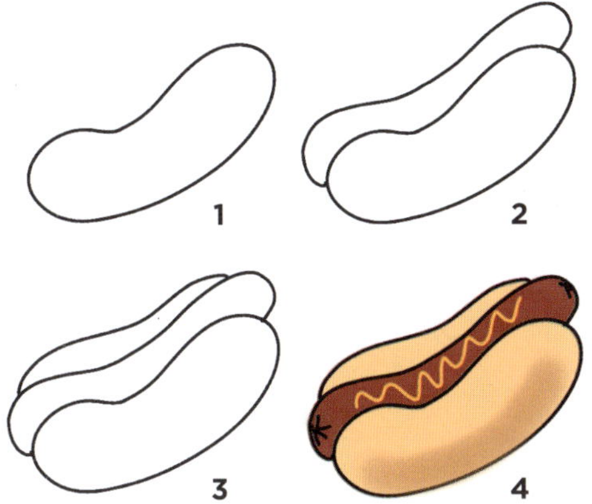

HOT DOG

Sketching a hot dog is easy when you do it in layers. First, draw a slightly curved oval for the bun. Then, add a longer thinner one behind it for the hot dog and one more shorter one behind that for the other side of the bun. Add little sunburst lines on both ends of the hot dog to make it look more realistic. Then, color it in and add your favorite toppings . . . mine is mustard!

PRETZEL

Start your pretzel doodle with a rounded heart shape. Add overlapping ovals for the center twist. Finish by drawing lines for the openings on each side. Color in your pretzel and don't forget to add salt! A white gel pen works great for drawing salt on the brown background.

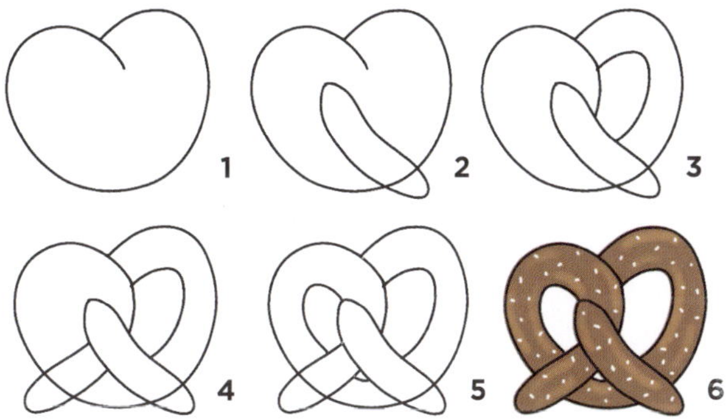

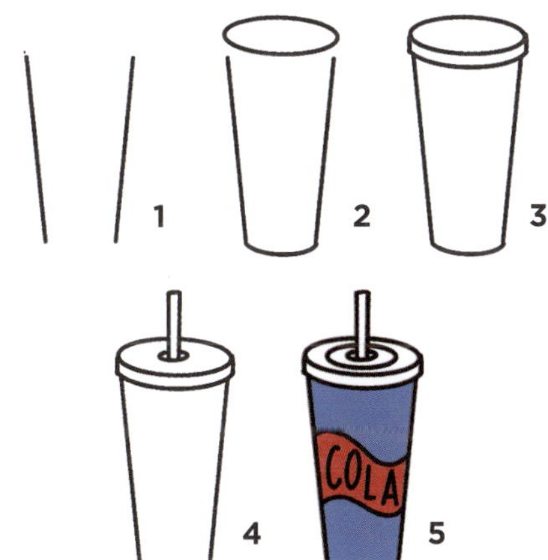

SODA CUP

Start a soda cup doodle by drawing the base of the cup itself, then add an oval lid. A straw and some detail lines will make it feel more three-dimensional. Make your cup one of a kind by adding any kind of pattern, design and colors you like and feel free to write a word like "SODA" or "COLA" to distinguish it from an iced coffee cup (which we'll learn to draw on page 149 in the At the Coffee Shop chapter).

CORN DOG

A corn dog is literally an oval on a stick . . . what could be easier?! Add a little bit of the cornbread coating extending onto the stick to make it look more realistic. The fun comes when you add color and, of course, ketchup and/or mustard. Using your markers to add shading and detail lines helps to make it look three-dimensional.

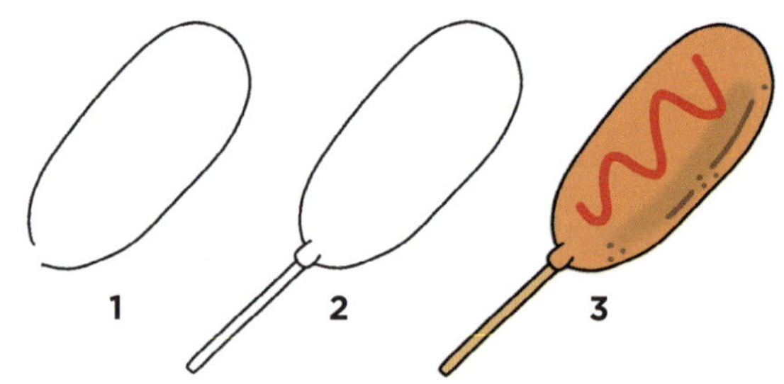

TICKET

Doodling an entrance ticket is all in the details. Start with a rectangle with a semicircle on each side. Add a second rectangle inside, then write "ADMIT ONE" inside for a good general phrase. You can also customize the ticket for a particular sporting event, show or raffle. Color and a series of dots along the top and bottom edges are the perfect finishing touches.

DRINK COOLER

Coolers filled with water and sports drinks are a sideline staple. Draw yours by sketching two vertical lines and connecting them at the top and bottom with slightly rounded lines to give the cooler its cylinder shape. Add a lid, a handle on each side, a spout and decorative lines to give it that distinctive appearance. I colored mine orange, but you can also use red, blue or your favorite team's colors.

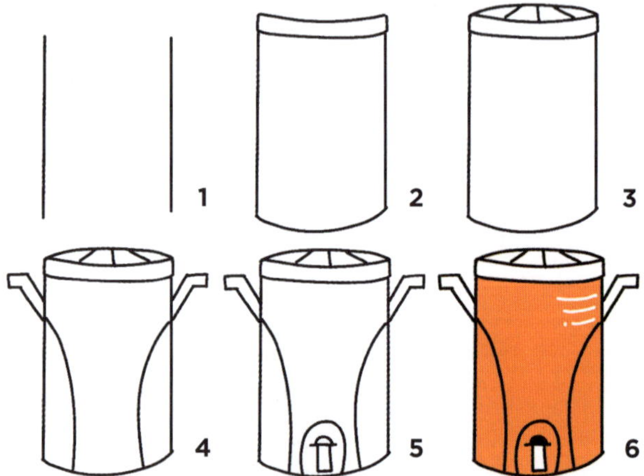

TEAM SPIRIT

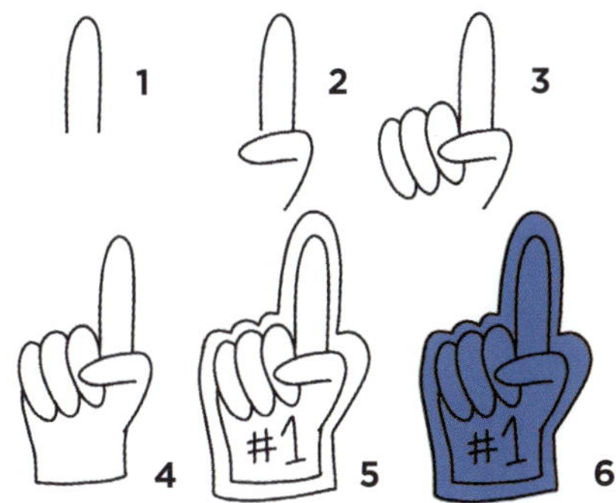

FOAM FINGER

Start a foam finger doodle with a tall, thin upside-down "U" shape for the index finger. Add the thumb and three folded fingers. Outline the entire shape and add "#1" or anything else you like on the palm. Color your foam finger with your favorite team's colors to show that team spirit!

TROPHY

A trophy starts as simply a "U" shape with an oval on top. Add a handle on each side, along with a base formed of a circle, a semicircle and rectangles. Color it in and don't forget to add a plaque with a name, a sport, "1st" or anything else you like to personalize it.

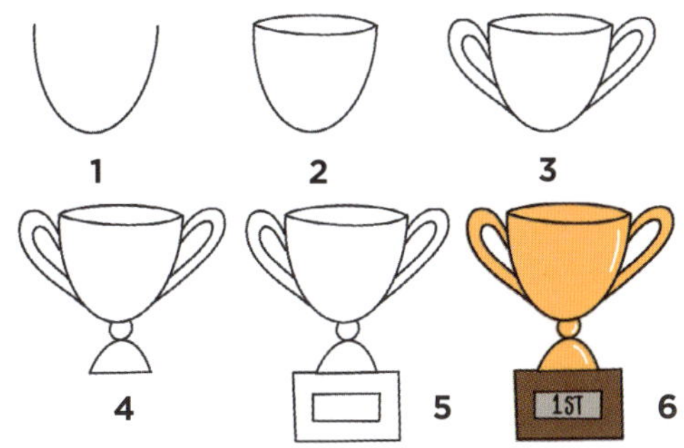

MEDAL

To make an award ribbon, draw a circle with a curving line on top. Add three lines inside the curving one to give shape to the ribbon. If you want your ribbon to be multicolored, you can add more lines inside to divide it into colored sections. Finally, add detail to the medal itself (number "1" of course!) and color in your doodle.

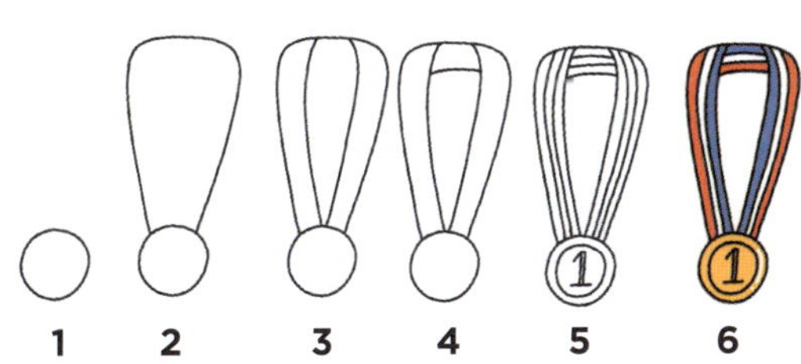

PENNANT FLAG

A pennant is nothing more than a sideways triangle with ties or a stick on one side. Feel free to label it with the name or logo of your favorite team, the number of your favorite player or a more general message, like "GO TEAM." Use your team's colors to finish off the illustration.

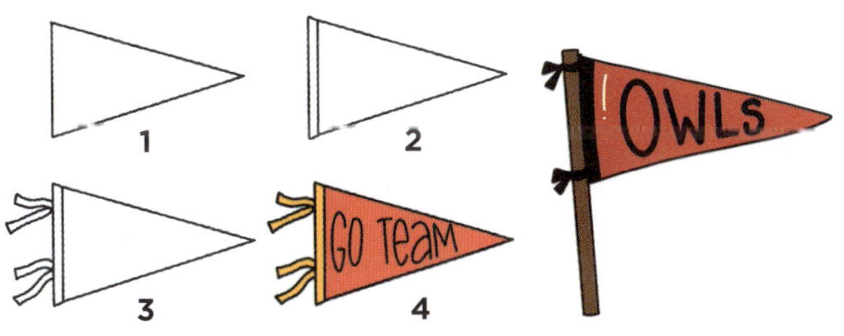

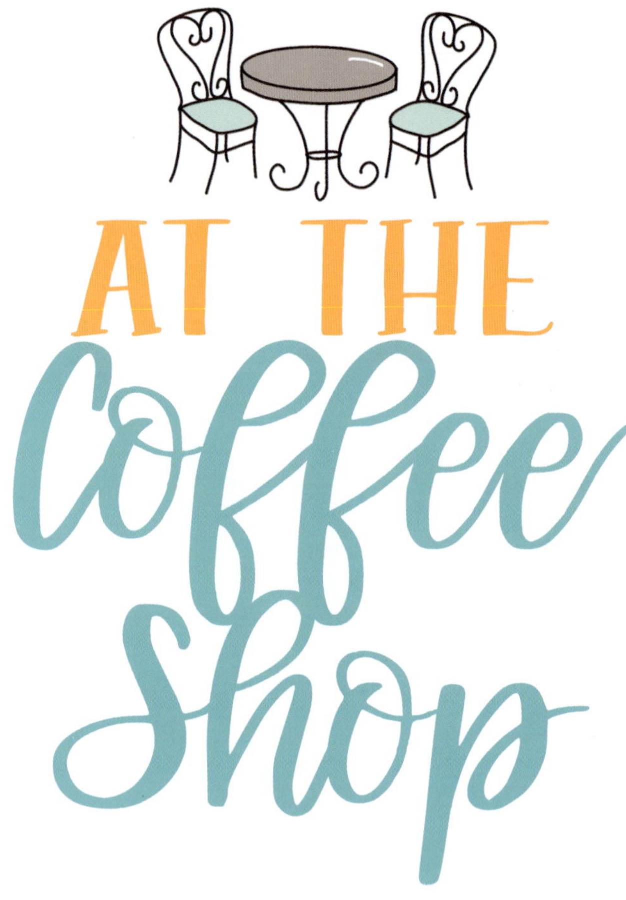

For me, the local coffee shop is at the top of my "favorite places" list. I go there several times a week, usually with my mom or another friend, and I love it for the conversation and the coffee itself. If you're a coffee lover like me, you'll find that this chapter is one of your favorites—filled with all kinds of doodles related to your favorite beverage. If coffee isn't (quite literally) your cup of tea, don't worry, there are drawings for you too. From tea kettles and sugar to sweet treats you'll find at the corner café, there's something here for everyone.

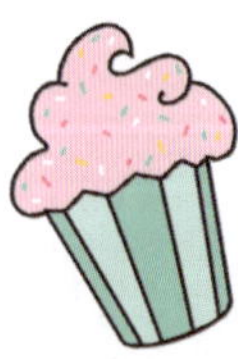

ALL ABOUT COFFEE

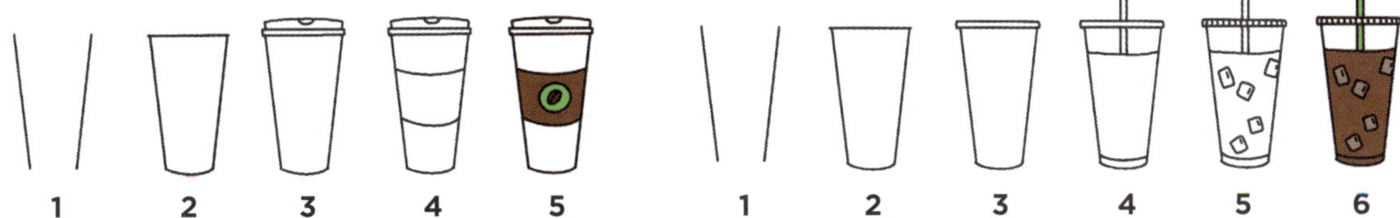

TO-GO COFFEE CUP & ICED COFFEE

To be honest, a to-go coffee cup is probably one of the doodles I use most often. To draw it, start with two diagonal lines connected at the bottom for the cup shape and add a lid on top. Make sure to sketch a little semicircle opening on the lid where you can sip from. Draw a cup sleeve across the center of the cup, which you can decorate with any colors, designs or words you like, including the iconic green circle.

Although the to-go cup is what I doodle most, what I actually drink most is iced coffee, which comes in a cold cup like this. If you fancy an iced drink too, draw one by starting with the same basic cup shape but give it just one rectangle for the lid. Add a straw going down through the cup, as well as a line to show where your liquid stops. For more detail, draw some little square ice cubes and a series of detail lines along the lid.

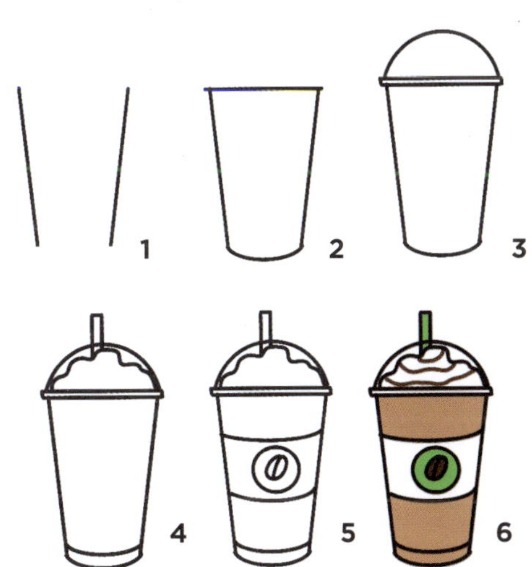

FRAPPÉ CUP

If your favorite coffeehouse treat is a frozen drink, you can draw a frappé by starting with the same cup shape and adding a domed lid. Inside the lid, draw a wavy line to show some delicious whipped cream, then add a straw extending from the top of the whipped cream out above the lid. Sketch a label and/or logo on the front of the cup, and as you add color, feel free to add some mocha or caramel drizzle to that whipped cream.

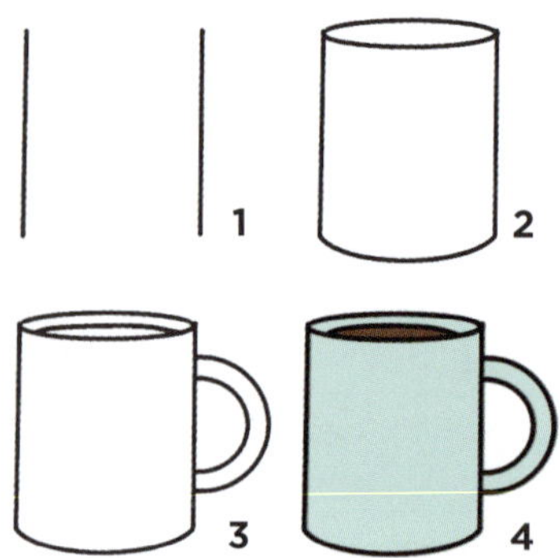

COFFEE MUG

To draw a basic coffee mug, start with two parallel lines connected with a curving line at the bottom. Add an oval on top and a semicircle handle. To show where the coffee is, draw a smaller oval inside the top area, which you'll color in brown. You can leave the mug itself a solid color or personalize it with any pattern, design, logo or phrase.

COFFEE POT

Some days require a cup of coffee, others require the whole pot. To draw this coffeepot doodle, make a rounded "U" shape with a band on top. Draw a spout above the band and a handle extending out to the side. For detail, sketch a series of short lines along the side of the pot, then draw an oval to show where the coffee is inside. Color the coffee and the handle, leaving the rest of the pot white.

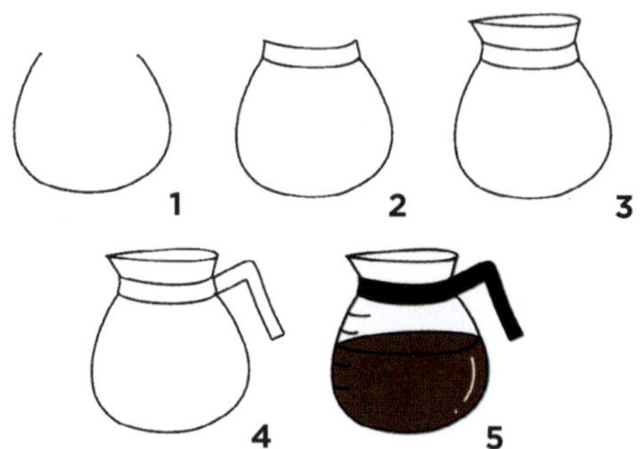

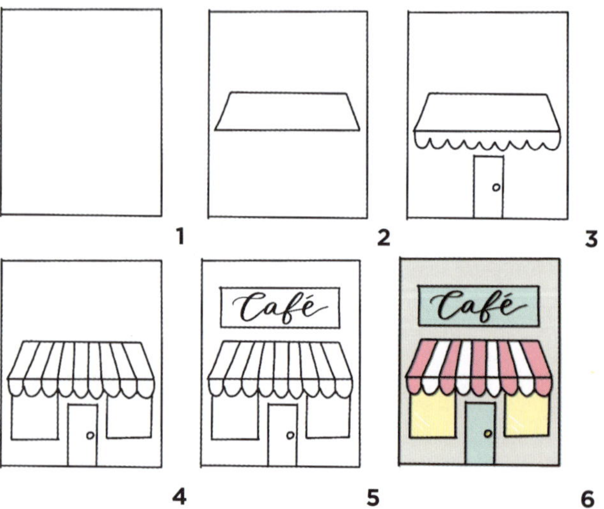

CAFÉ

Now that we have some cute doodles of coffee, let's learn to doodle the café itself. First, draw a rectangle for the building, then sketch a trapezoid shape halfway down for the awning. Add scallops and stripes to the awning and give your café a door. Draw two large square windows, then sketch a sign above the awning. You can label it with the name of your favorite coffee shop or simply write "Café." Then, add color to make the building pop off the page.

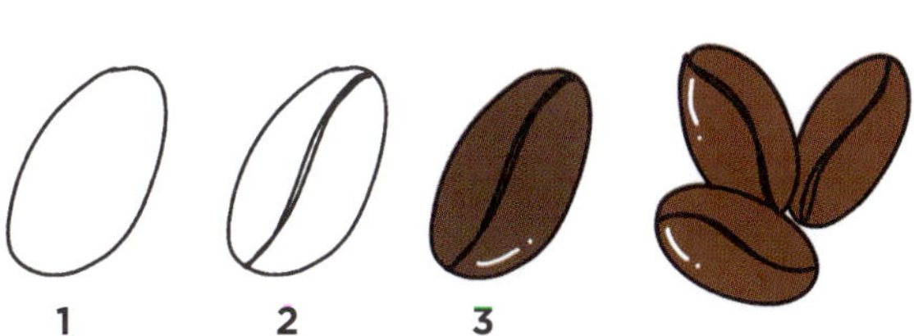

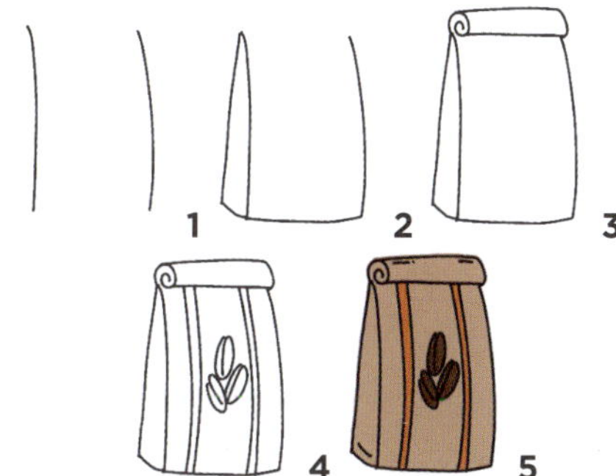

COFFEE BEANS & BAG

Drawing a coffee bean is a piece of cake . . . or should I say coffee cake? Start by forming an oval, then draw an "S"-shaped curve inside. Color in the bean brown, add a highlight and your doodle is complete! These make a fun border and they're also cute in little groups of three or five.

To draw a bag of coffee, sketch a rectangle shape with a small triangle on the side. Then, add a rolled top by drawing a spiral with lines that extend out from the sides across the top of the bag. To indicate what's inside, doodle your coffee beans on the bag's front, along with some stripes.

BISTRO TABLE & CHAIRS

Tables and chairs where patrons can sit are integral parts of a local coffee shop. To doodle a bistro table, start with an oval and add a rim to the bottom half. Next, draw three curving lines below it for table legs and connect them with a small oval. For the chairs, start with a rounded line for the back, then add a seat and four legs. Connect the legs with an "L"-shaped line below the seat and add decorative curving lines to the chair back. Your table and chairs are ready to color!

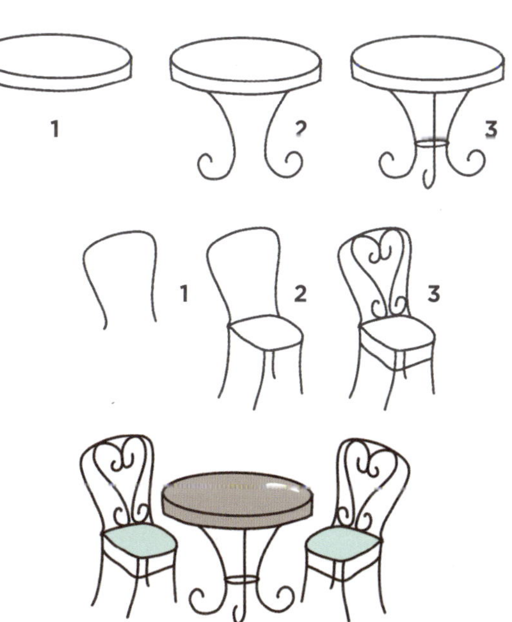

YOUR CUP OF TEA

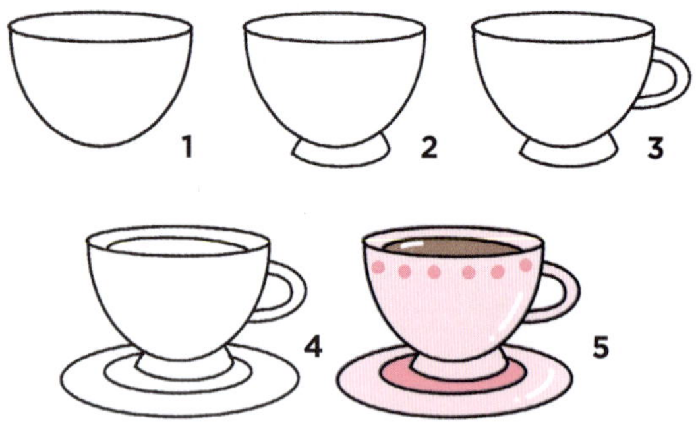

TEACUP

To draw a cute teacup and saucer, first sketch a semicircle with an oval on top. Then, give your cup a base and a handle. Draw an oval below your cup, around the base, for the saucer. Also, draw a small oval in the top of the cup to show where the tea is. As you color your design, you can get creative by adding little flowers, hearts or another dainty pattern to the cup and saucer.

TEA BAG

To draw a tea bag, first make a rectangle shape with diagonal lines in the top corners. Then, make a triangle on one side to show that the bag has depth. Draw two short lines in the top corners to show where the bag is secured and sketch a curving line with a square at the end for the string. Use a wavy line to mark where the contents of the tea bag stop, then add color to finish your doodle.

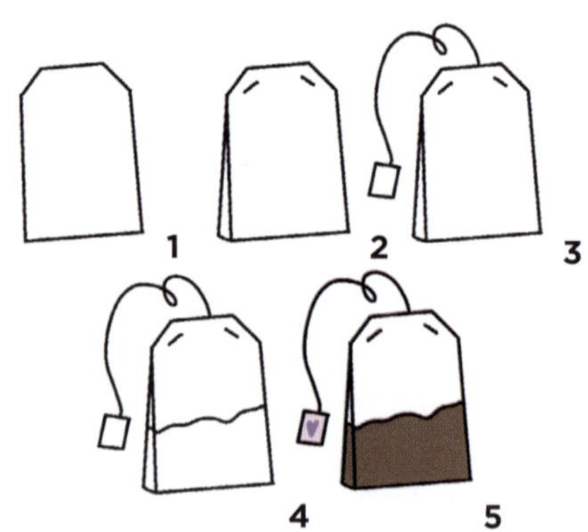

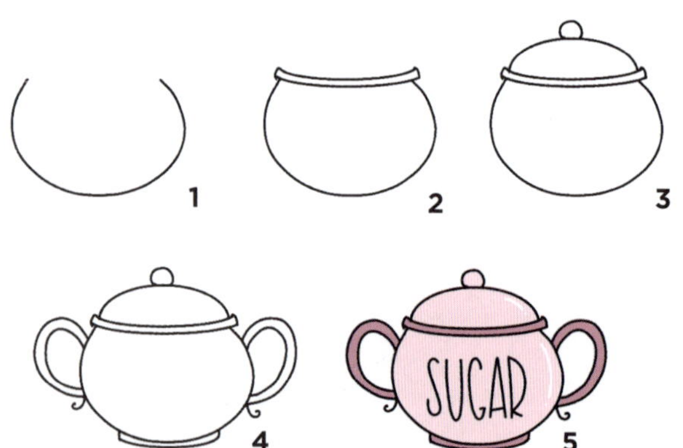

SUGAR DISH

To draw a sugar dish, you'll basically doodle a teapot with two handles instead of one and a spout. Make a rounded shape with a lid, add a base, then draw a handle on each side. Feel free to make the handles simple or slightly more intricate. Finally, color your drawing and add the word "SUGAR" to label the dish.

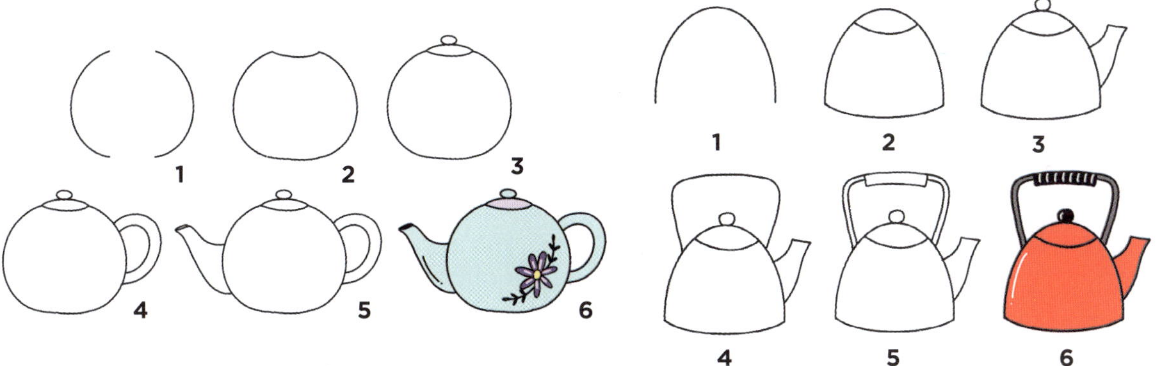

TEAPOT & KETTLE

Draw a rounded shape with a little semicircle lid on top to form the teapot base. Add a handle on one side of the pot and a spout on the other. Once you have the basic shape, it's time to decorate your pot with your favorite design. I chose a flower and vine design, but you can also use hearts, polka dots or another pattern.

A tea kettle is similar to a teapot, but it's flat on the bottom rather than rounded. Make a semicircle shape, add a lid and draw a spout on one side. Then, sketch a handle that attaches to both sides of the kettle and goes up over top of the lid. I have a particular fondness for shiny red tea kettles, but you can color and decorate yours in any way.

LEMON SLICE

A slice of lemon is a perfect complement to a cup of tea. Draw this one by sketching a semicircle with a curved line inside for the outside rind. Add several rounded triangle shapes inside the semicircle to represent the separate sections of the fruit. Then, color in your doodle with different shades of yellow. You can follow these same steps to draw slices of orange and lime—just use orange or green instead of yellow when you color your doodles.

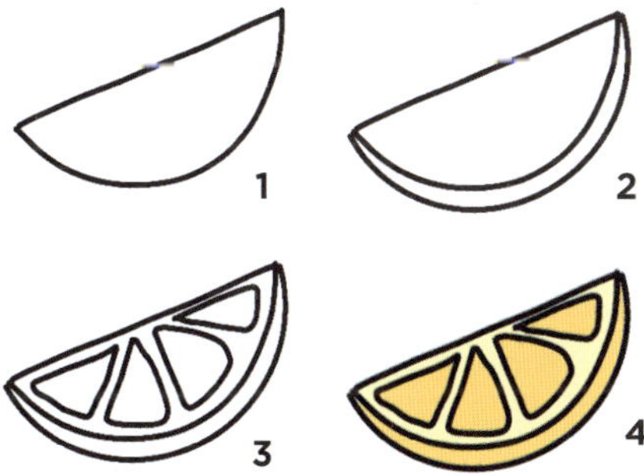

BAKED GOODS

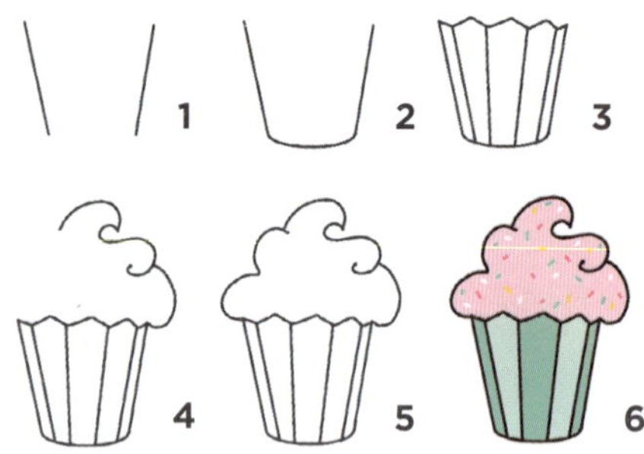

CUPCAKE

Cupcakes are delicious any day of the week, and they're almost as fun to draw as to eat. Start by sketching the liner: two diagonal lines that connect with a rounded line at the bottom and a zigzag line at the top. Draw details on the wrapper by making vertical lines or adding your own pattern. Finally, add the frosting by drawing a series of bumps that comes to a point near the top. Use color to show your favorite icing flavor, and if you're feeling extra festive, top it off with some colorful sprinkles.

DOUGHNUT

To draw a doughnut, simply sketch a small circle inside a larger one (unless it's a filled doughnut, in which case it's just one big circle). The most fun part is adding color for frosting and details like sprinkles, chocolate chips and other toppings.

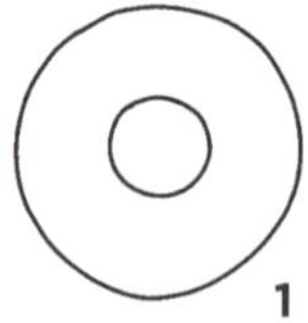

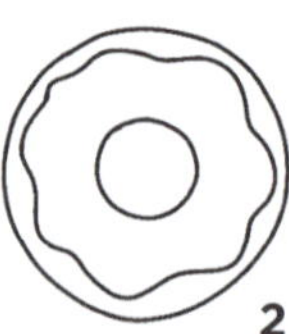

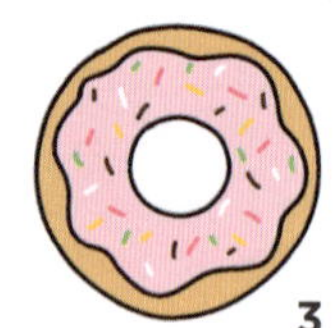

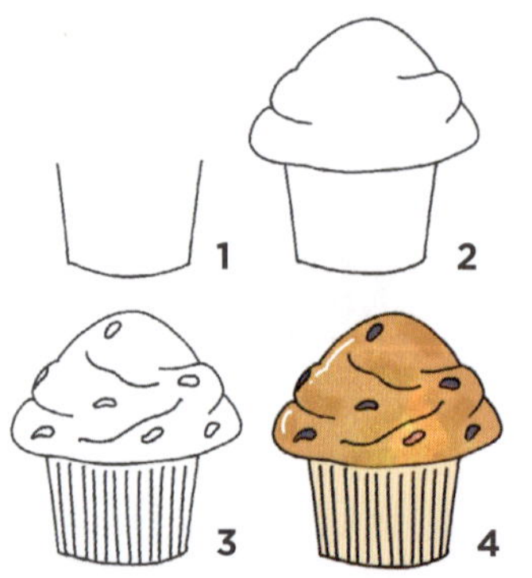

MUFFIN

A fresh-baked muffin pairs wonderfully with a warm drink. Draw this one by sketching the muffin bottom first, then add a rounded top. Draw a few curving lines in the muffin top to show that it's not perfectly shaped and add details like blueberries or chocolate chips. Sketch vertical lines around the base of the muffin for the liner.

CROISSANT

To draw a croissant, start with the center section, then add two more sections on each side, each one slightly smaller than the one next to it. For the final sections, draw a "U" shape on each end. Using shading and highlights to add visual interest, color your croissant.

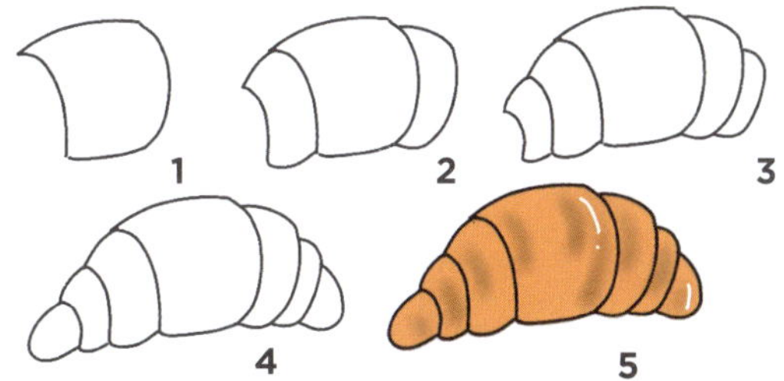

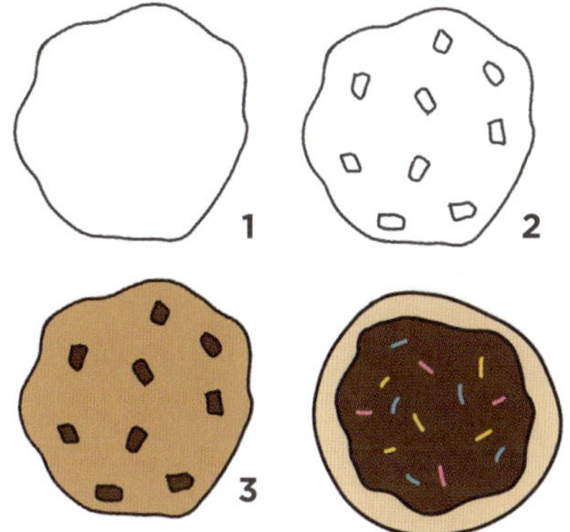

COOKIE

Cookies are always a great choice at a café, or really anywhere, and personally, my favorite kind is whatever I'm eating at that moment! Typically, homemade cookies are not perfectly round, so as you draw the shape, don't worry about making a perfect circle. I added small shapes inside my cookie to represent chocolate chips, but you can draw whatever type of cookies you prefer. Try making a sugar cookie with sprinkles, frosting or other details to make yours uniquely delicious.

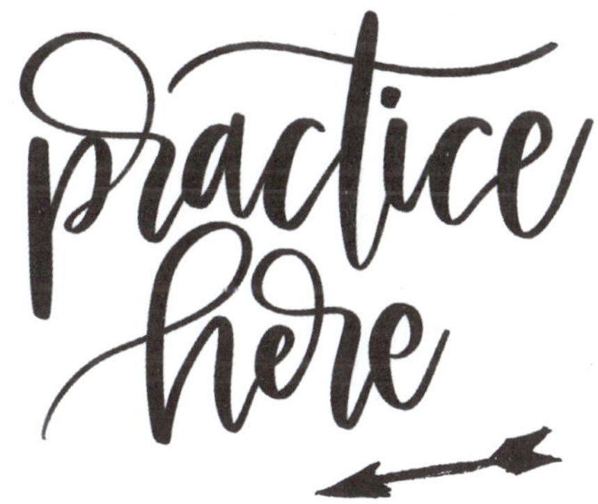

AT School

Love it or hate it, school is an essential part of life. With these cute doodles, it can be lots of fun! In this chapter, learn to draw school supplies and symbols to represent the major subjects. These doodles are great for decorating notebooks and folders, and they make adorable additions to lunchbox notes. You can also use them to create cards and gifts for teachers and other school staff to show them a little appreciation.

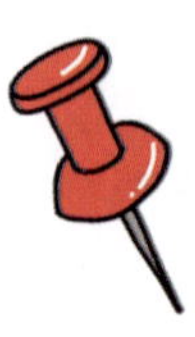

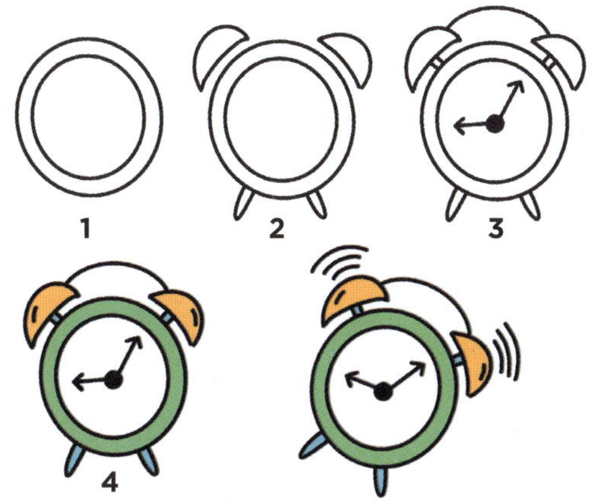

ALARM CLOCK

The first thing that happens in our house on a school day is the alarm going off at 6 a.m. To doodle this little alarm clock, draw a smaller circle inside a slightly larger one. Then, add legs on the bottom and two semicircle bells near the top. Sketch hands on the clock to represent a time (you can also add numbers to the clock face if you like) and color it in. To make the clock look like it's ringing, add short curved lines next to each of the bells and draw the clock at a slight angle.

SCHOOL BUS

The easiest way to draw a school bus is to start with the roof and the hood. Sketch the bottom of the bus, leaving spots where the wheels will go. Add round tires, a windshield and several windows along the length of the bus. Then, sketch details like headlights, taillights, a bus number and anything else you'd like to add. Finally, color it in that famous shade of yellow.

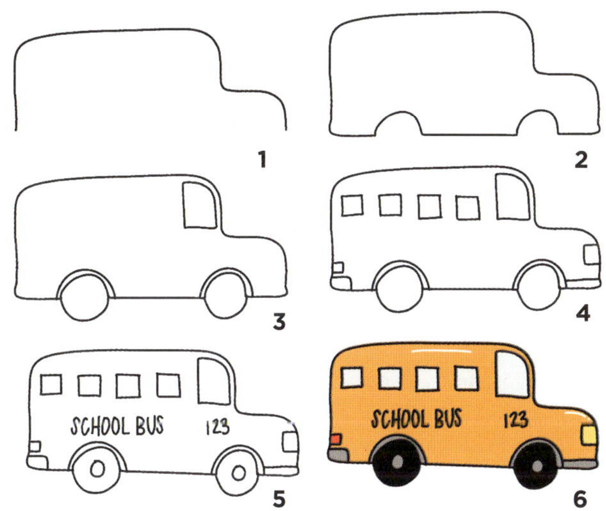

APPLE

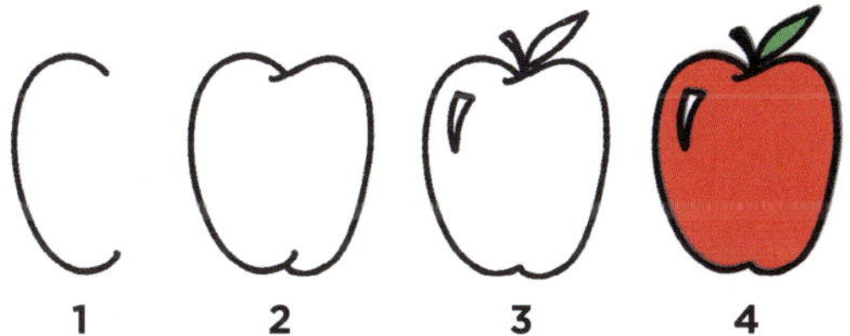

Here's a simple way to draw an apple for the teacher: Start with a "C" shape on the left. Form the other side of the apple with another "C" shape in the opposite direction, extending the top line slightly. Draw a short stem with a leaf on top and a little triangle for a highlight, then color your finished apple.

BACKPACK

Form the base of this backpack doodle by drawing an arch with a line across the bottom. Add a curving line to the left of the shape to give it depth. Next, draw a pocket with a zipper pull and a label. Finally, add a dashed line to represent the main zipper along with straps. Color in your backpack in any way you like.

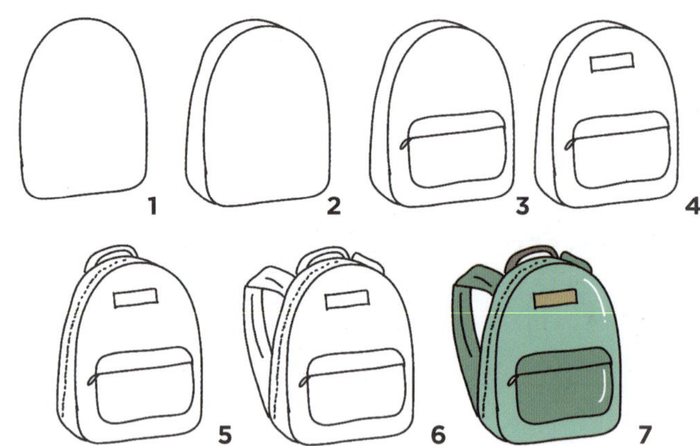

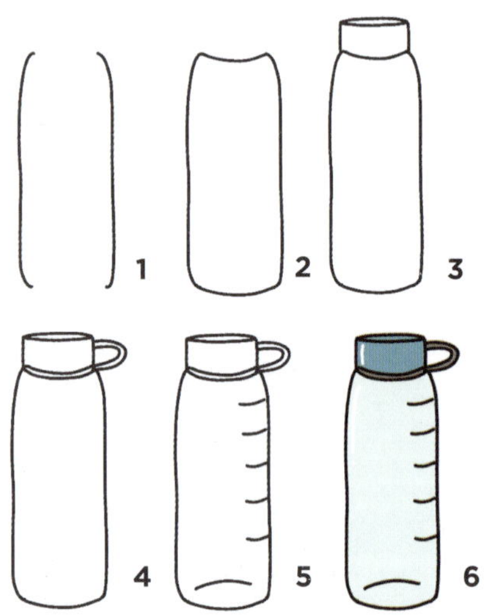

REUSABLE WATER BOTTLE

Draw the main part of the bottle by making two parallel lines and connecting them with a curving line at the bottom. Next, add a cap and a little curving strap to keep it attached to the bottle when it's in use. For extra detail, draw a series of short lines along the length of the bottle.

LUNCH BAG

To sketch a lunch bag, start with a rectangular "U" shape on a diagonal for the front of the bag and draw a triangle to the right of it to show dimension. Then, draw the top flap along with a handle. Feel free to add a design to your bag or fill it in with a solid color.

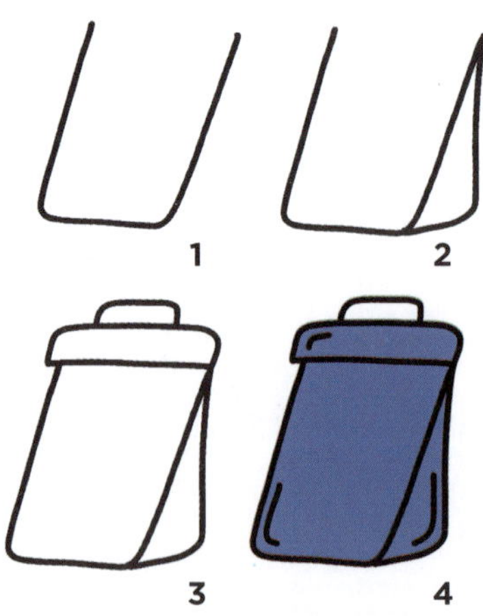

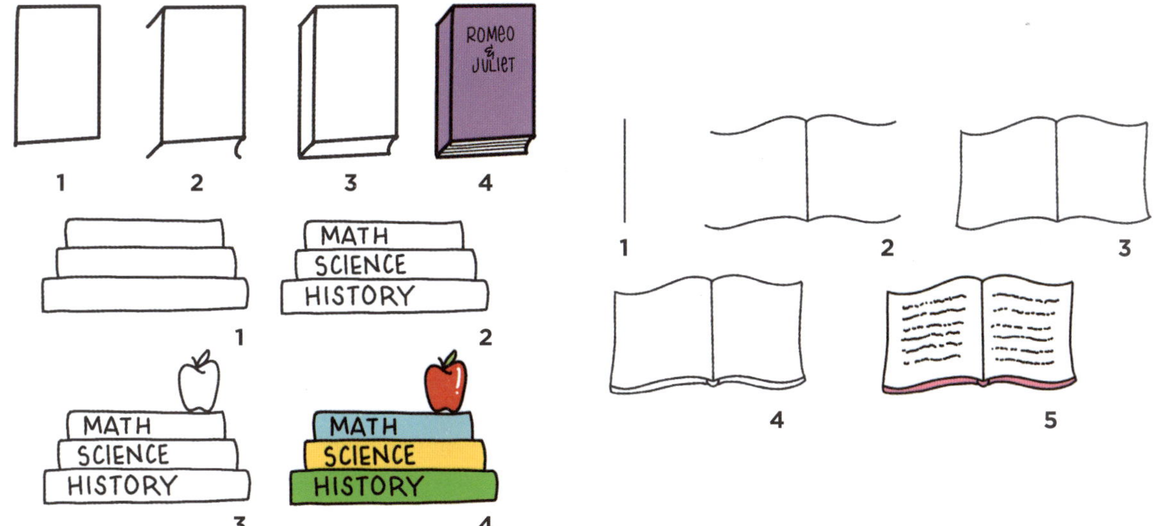

BOOKS

Books are essential when it comes to learning at school, so we're going to look at several different ways to draw them.

This first doodle is a simple closed book. Start with a rectangle cover, add diagonal lines out to the left, and connect them to form the spine. Connect the spine to a curving line coming from the bottom right corner of the cover and fill in that area with lines. Give the book your favorite title and color in the cover.

Doodle a stack of books by making three (or more) rectangles on top of one another, each one slightly smaller than the one beneath it. Label the book spines with subject names or titles, then, if you like, sketch your apple doodle (page 157) on top of the stack before adding color.

The final type of book we're going to draw (above right) is an open one. Sketch a vertical line for the center, then draw waving lines at the top and bottom going off to each side. Connect these lines with two more vertical ones to form your pages. Draw another line across the bottom for depth and fill your pages with either squiggles and dots or tiny words. While the pages will be white, you can color in the cover that's visible at the base of the book.

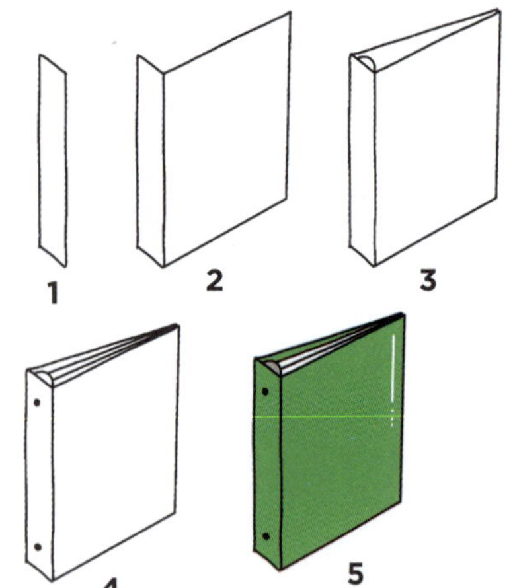

BINDER

To draw a binder, start with a slightly angled rectangle for the spine, then add a large rectangle off to the right side of the spine for the binder's front. Connect the left corner of the spine to the upper right corner of the front to form a triangle. To make it look even more realistic, draw two little circles on the spine and some lines to represent paper inside the triangle area. Now, it's time to have fun decorating your binder in any way you like.

PENCIL

Pencils are a must-have in the classroom, so let's doodle one by drawing two parallel lines and connecting them on one end to form an eraser. On the other end, draw a point that's separated from the body of the pencil with a zigzag line. Add lines for the metal eraser attachment and any other details you want to include, then fill in your image with color.

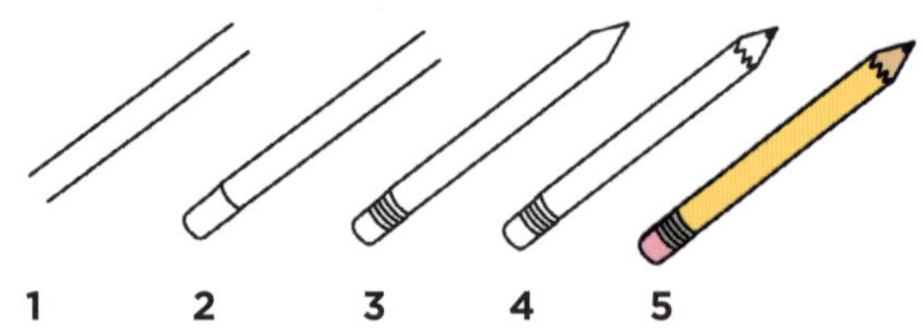

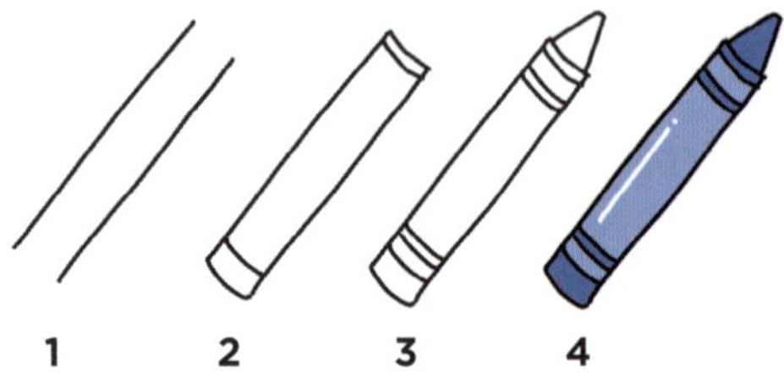

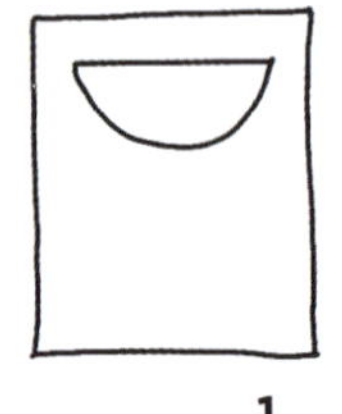

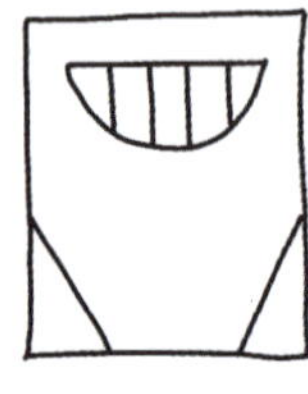

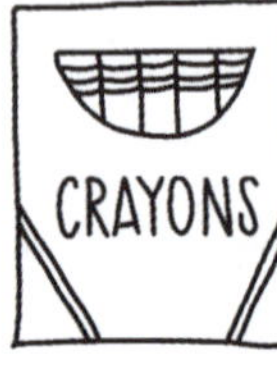

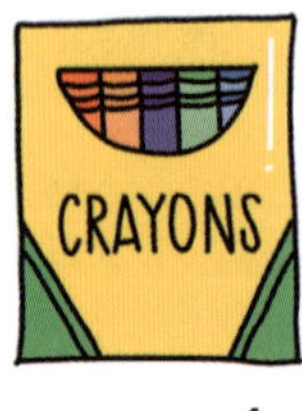

CRAYONS

Crayons are similar to pencils; to draw them, you'll start with parallel lines connected with a curving line on one end and a point on the other. Add some detail lines to create a label, then color your crayon. You can write the name of the color or crayon brand on the label or leave it as is.

Who wants to create with just one crayon? Draw a box of crayons by sketching a rectangle with a half-circle inside. Divide the circle with vertical lines to represent the crayons you can see through the cutout space. Add details to the box, like stripes, as well as to the crayon labels. Finally, add color to each crayon and to the box.

GLUE BOTTLE

Start with a rounded rectangle shape that has a small slightly curving rectangle and a triangle on top. Next, add groove lines on the cap, then draw a smaller rounded rectangle for the label. Write the word "GLUE" and draw a pointed design or give the label a different design. Finish your doodle by coloring in the label and cap.

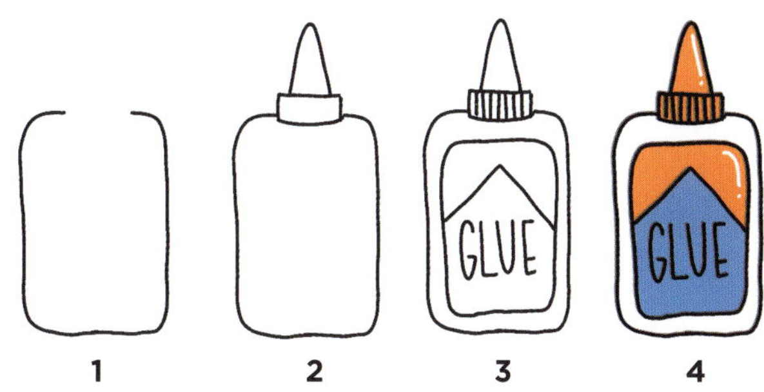

NOTEBOOK PAPER

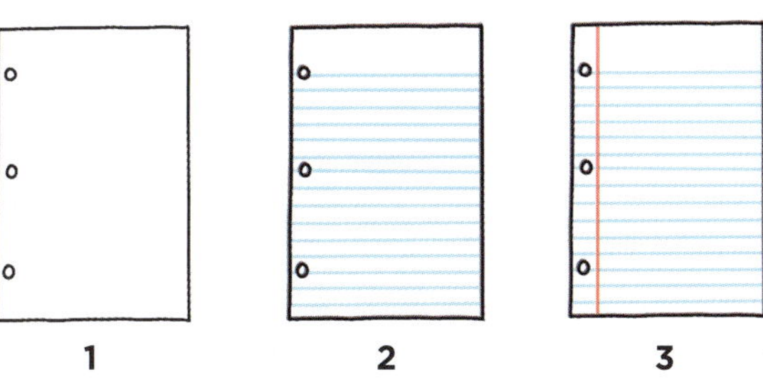

While many things are going virtual in schools nowadays, notebook paper is still a necessary supply. To doodle it, simply draw a rectangle with three small circles going down the left side. Draw a vertical red line just to the right of the circles, then a series of horizontal blue lines all the way down the page.

PAPER AIRPLANE

Give a student a piece of paper and there's a good chance it'll turn into a paper airplane. Doodle yourself one starting with a right triangle that has a "V" shape coming off the corner. Draw a second triangle that connects to the first one at the top point. A dashed line coming from the back of the plane suggests that it's been in flight. Although many paper airplanes are white, shading the inside folds with a light gray or blue can give the effect of dimension and shadow.

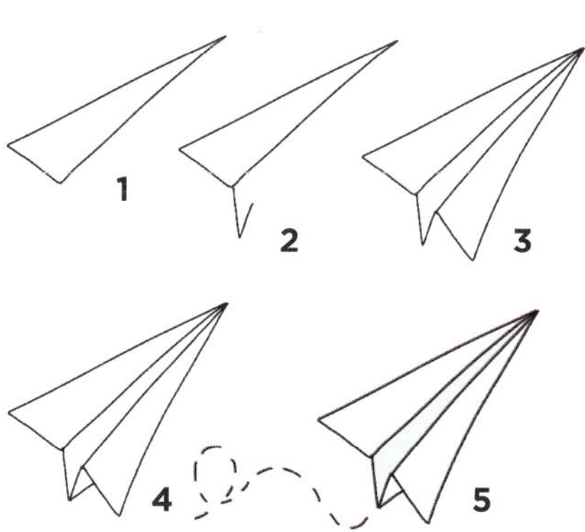

PUSHPIN

This pushpin doodle starts with an oval for the top, then you'll add the other two parts of the head. Finally, draw the all-important pin itself with a sharp point at the end. Add color and highlights to give it a three-dimensional appearance.

RULER

To doodle a ruler, all you have to do is sketch a long thin rectangle. Then, add a series of vertical lines to mark off centimeters and inches along the top and bottom. I also like to draw a line through the center of the ruler. Adding numbers is optional; it's still easy to tell that you've drawn a ruler without them and you don't have to worry about being precise.

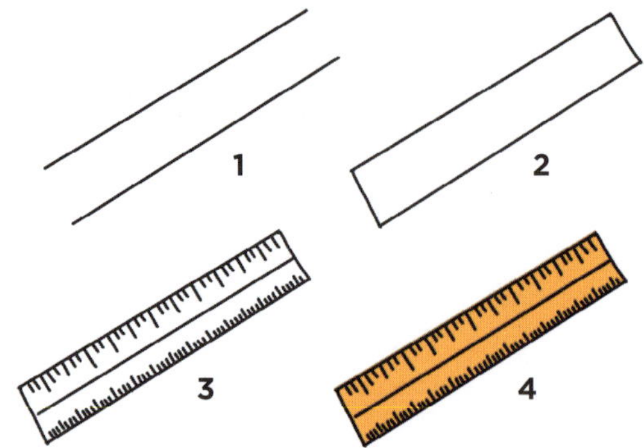

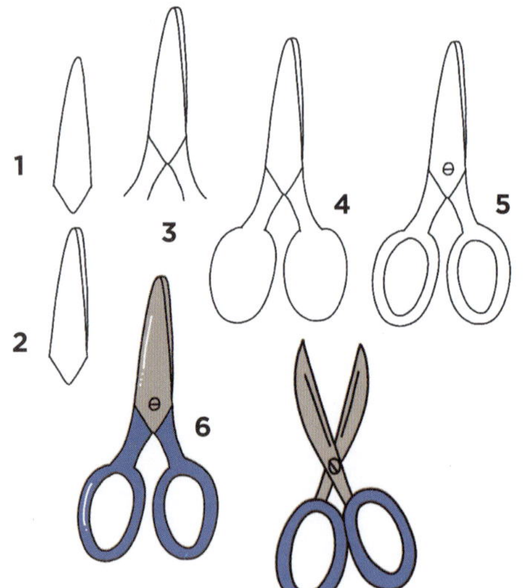

SCISSORS

To draw a pair of scissors, start with the blades. Make a triangle shape with a point at the bottom and draw a second line just to the right to suggest the second blade behind the first. Next, add two handles with double oval shapes on the ends. For extra detail, add a small round screw at the base of the blade, then color your doodle.

For a variation on this doodle, you can draw your scissors in an open position. To do this, draw the blades as more of a "V" shape like we did with the garden clippers on page 24.

CLIPBOARD

A clipboard is just a rounded rectangle base with a clip at the top. To add a piece of paper, draw a second rectangle inside the first one but going under the clip. Then, it's up to you to write or sketch something on the paper itself . . . a list, a chart, a poem, a map or whatever else you can imagine.

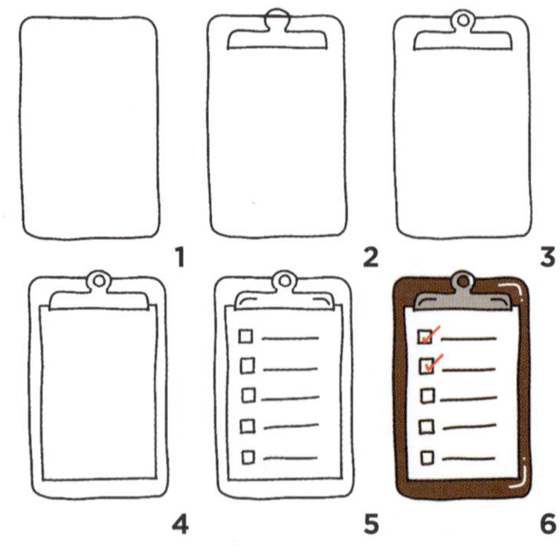

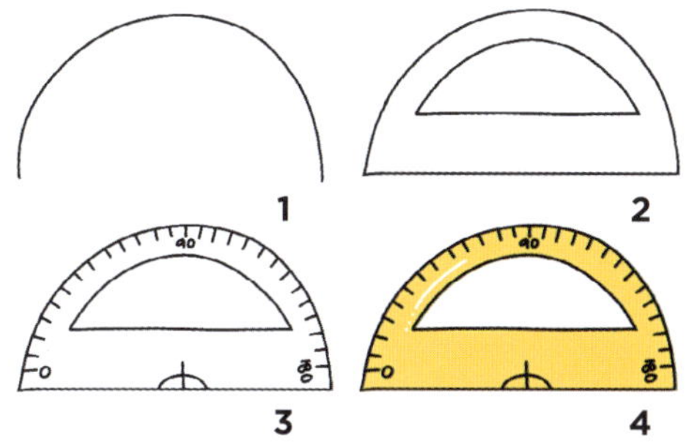

PROTRACTOR

In a math classroom, you might find a protractor, which is just a half-circle with a smaller semicircle inside. Draw a series of short lines around the inside of the arch to show the different angle measurements. You don't have to label them all, but adding "0," "90" and "180" is a good idea.

GLOBE

Draw a globe by sketching a circle with a larger "C" shape to the left side. Attach the "C" to the circle and give it a base to form the globe's stand. Add wavy lines to suggest the shapes of the continents inside the circle. Don't worry about precision; we're just giving the general idea. Color in the ocean blue and the land green or brown, then use any color you like for the stand.

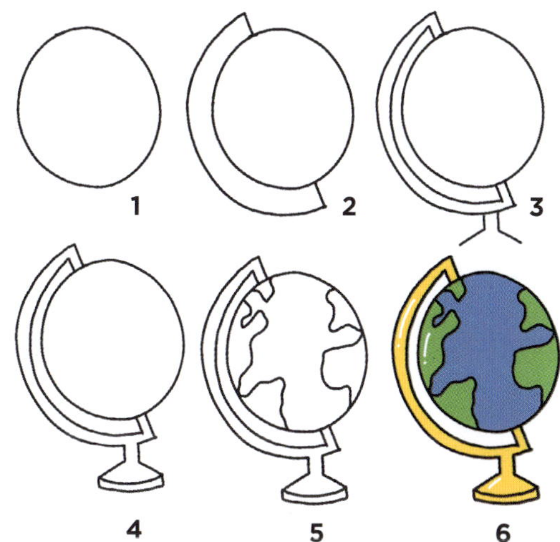

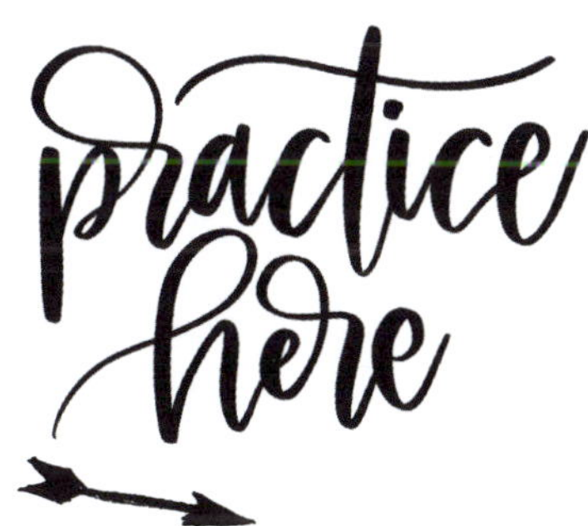

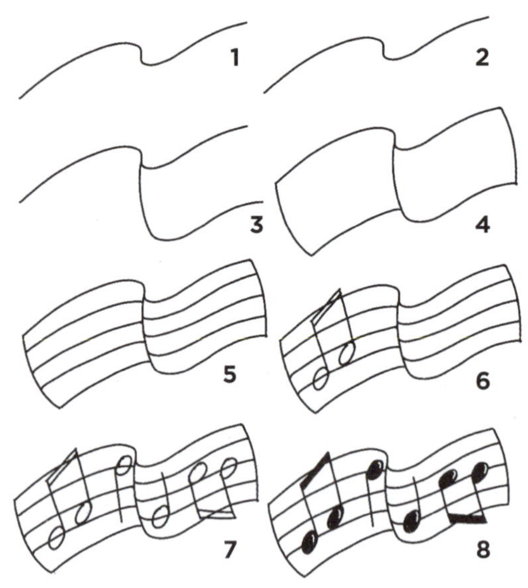

MUSICAL STAFF & NOTES

A music staff can, of course, be absolutely straight across the page, just like it is on sheet music. I like to make this doodle a little more exciting by forming it like a waving banner. Start with a curving line, then divide it in half to give the appearance that the right side is closer forward than the left. Add three more horizontal lines inside the staff (a staff has a total of five), then draw your notes on the lines and spaces. I used a combination of quarter notes and eighth notes, but you can use any type or pattern of notes on your drawing.

PAINTBRUSH & PALETTE

Art is an important part of any well-rounded education, so let's take a moment to doodle a paintbrush! Start by forming the handle shape, then add a small rectangle at the top for the metal piece that connects the brush to the handle. Draw a teardrop shape at the top, then feel free to add some paint on the brush, as well as a few drops to the side, to show that the brush is in use.

Artists also need a paint palette to go with their brushes. Draw a kidney bean shape for the palette itself, with a circle at the top so the artist can grip it. Then, create a series of irregular shapes around the edge of the palette to represent splotches of paint. Finally, color in the palette (usually a neutral shade) and your paints, leaving the circle area white.

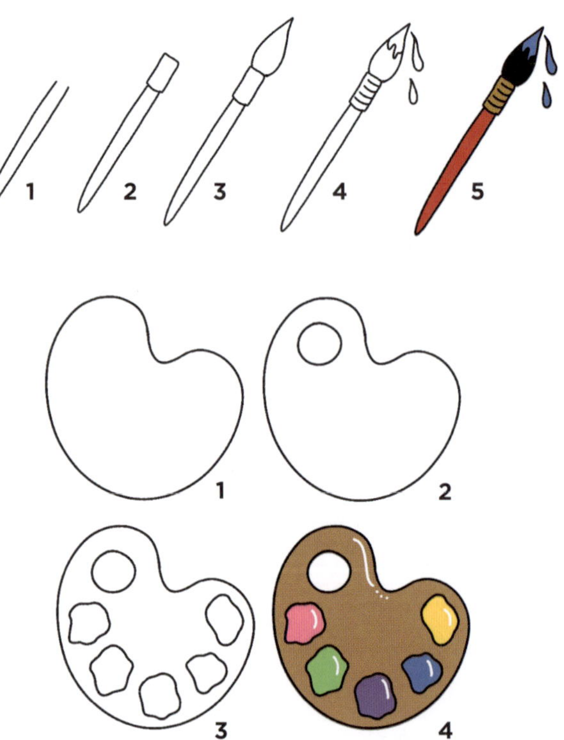

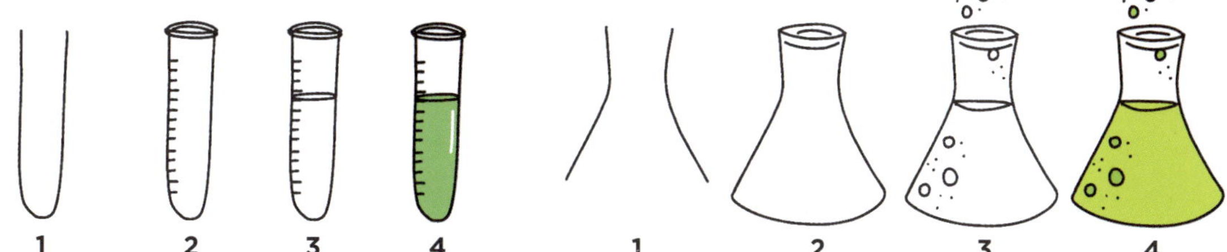

TEST TUBE & BEAKER

Let's sit in on a science class and doodle a test tube. Start with a long thin "U" shape and add an oval top. Label your tube with a series of short horizontal lines, then draw another oval somewhere inside the tube to indicate where your liquid stops.

To draw a beaker, start with two lines curving toward one another that are closer at the top than at the bottom. Connect these lines to form the basic shape, then add an oval top and an oval for the liquid inside the beaker. I like to add some tiny bubbles to suggest that this is an experiment and something interesting is happening!

GRADUATION CAP

Graduation is a major milestone, and this doodle is perfect for graduation cards, gift tags and other celebratory projects. First, draw a diamond, then add the hat's base below it. Sketch a small circle in the center of the diamond and a cord extending out to the side and down to form a tassel. While many graduation caps are black, they can also be the colors of a particular school.

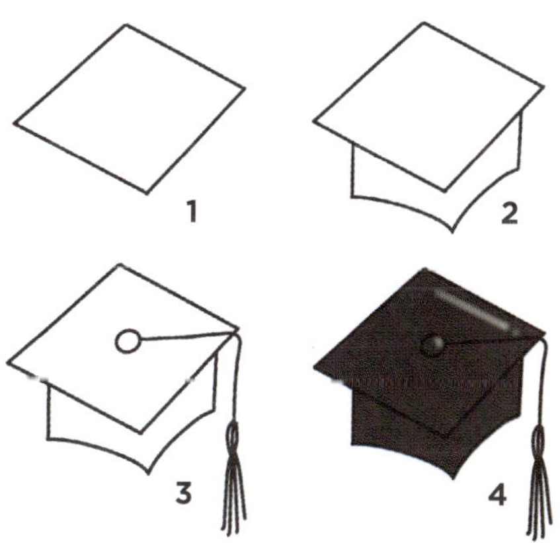

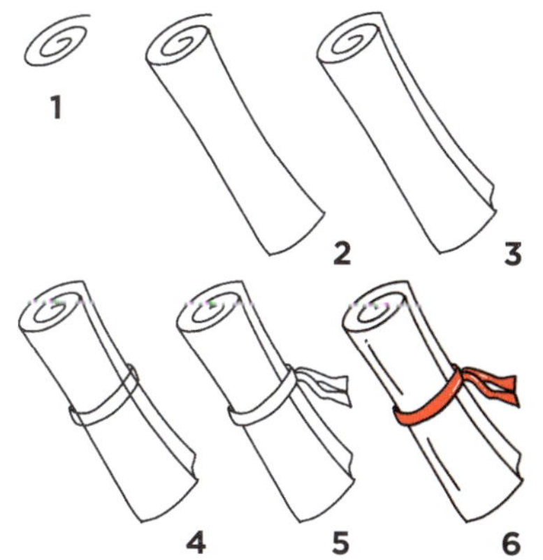

DIPLOMA

A diploma is the perfect complement to a graduation cap doodle. To create this one, draw a spiral, then draw vertical lines extending down from the sides to form the basic shape of a rolled paper. Add a ribbon tie around the center to hold the diploma together. Mine is red, but it can also be fun to use the school's colors for this detail.

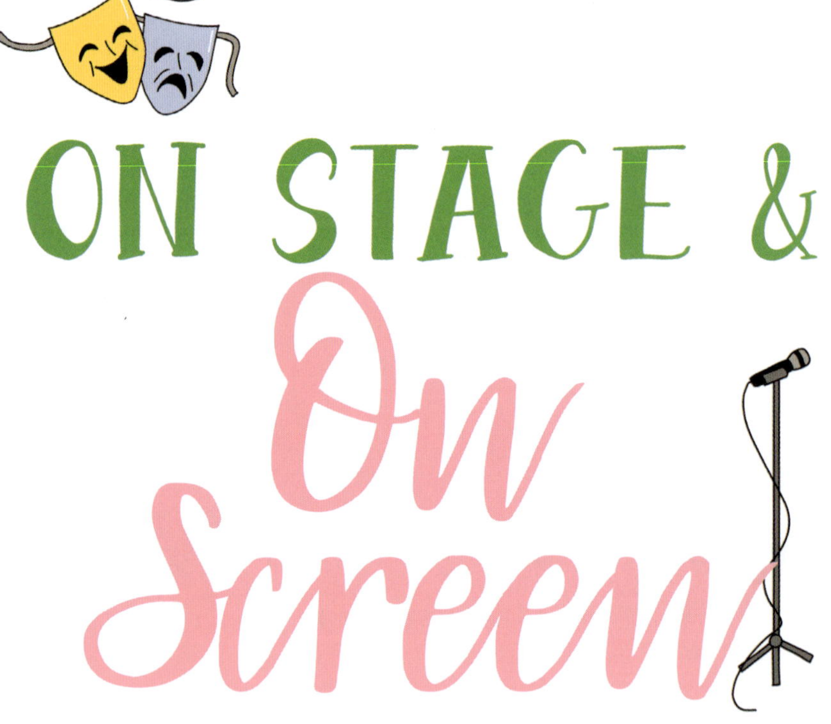

ON STAGE & On Screen

Whether we're watching a movie or viewing a play or a concert live onstage, we love to be entertained. The doodles in this chapter are designed to pay homage to what happens on the stage and the screen. Some are old-style Hollywood, like a strip of film and a star, while others are timeless, like drama masks and ballet slippers. Use these for playbills, cards, movie posters, calendars, journals and any other performance projects.

MOVIES

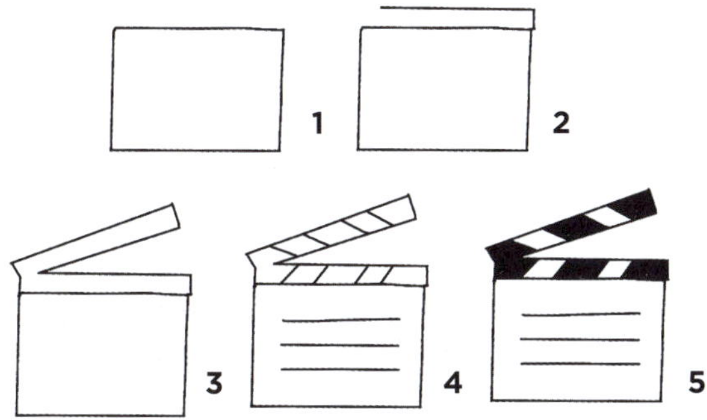

CLAPBOARD

A director would be lost without a clapboard, so let's draw this one by making a rectangle with a "V" shape on top. Add a pattern of diagonal lines on the "V," as well as some lines on the main part of the clapboard where the crew can write the date, scene and take.

DIRECTOR'S CHAIR

Directors and actors need a place to sit when they're not hard at work. Sketch a rectangle for the chair back with two vertical pieces connecting it to a trapezoid-shaped seat. Add arms and "X"-shaped legs, then color the chair. Feel free to personalize the back with a name or the word "DIRECTOR."

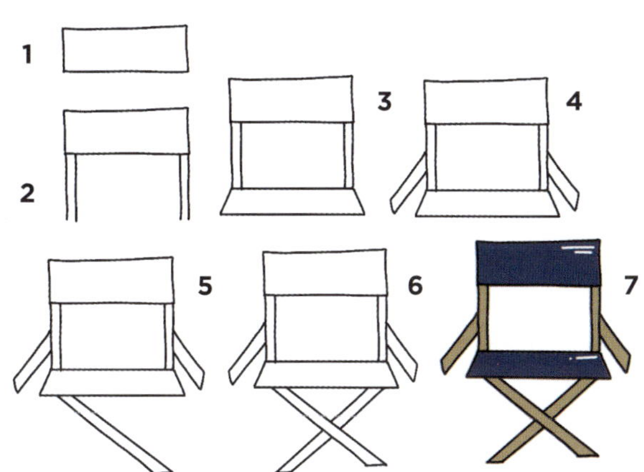

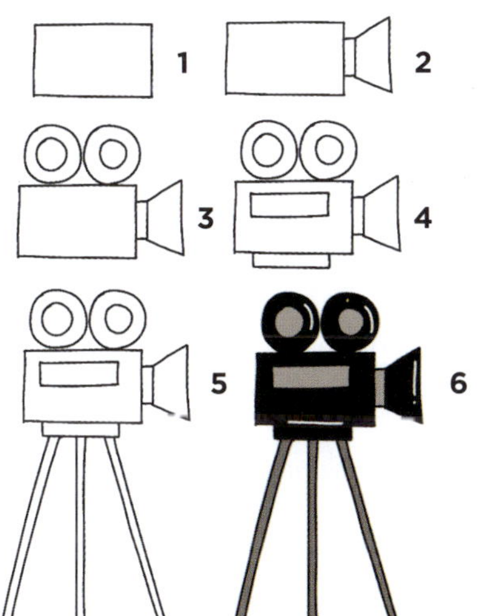

MOVIE CAMERA

To draw an old-fashioned movie camera, sketch a large rectangle for the body and a small rectangle with a trapezoid for the lens. Although modern cameras don't have wheels for film on top, two circles on top make your doodle instantly recognizable as a movie camera. Add a base and a tripod, as well as details and highlights.

MEGAPHONE

This megaphone doodle is basically a cone shape. Add a handle on the bottom and stripes on the sides, as well as a few short lines extending out from the large opening to represent sound. You can also add a team name or other words to the side of the megaphone to make it unique to your project.

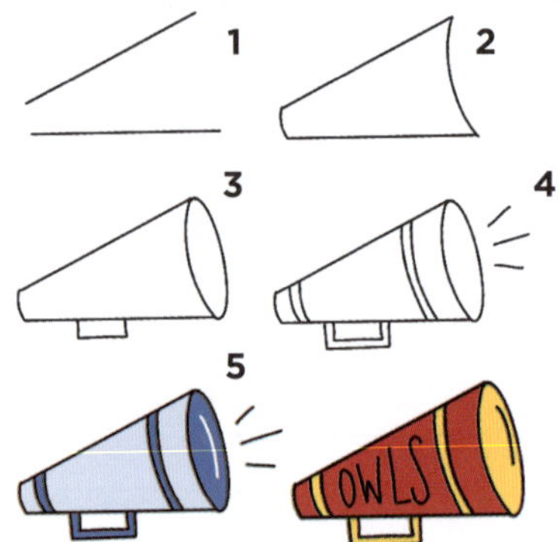

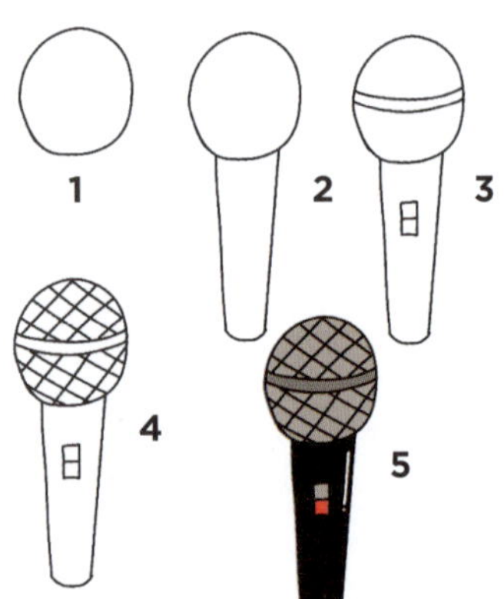

MICROPHONE

Performers of all kinds rely on microphones to sing or speak to the crowd. Draw this one by putting a circle on top of a tapered rectangle handle. Divide the circle in half and give it a checkered pattern for texture. Add a switch on the side of the handle and color in the microphone with shades of black and gray.

STAND MICROPHONE

We've learned to doodle a handheld microphone; now let's look at how to draw a microphone on a stand. First, draw a pair of parallel lines with a circle at the base. Then, draw three rectangles coming out from the bottom of the circle. These will be the legs. Sketch a rectangular shape on an angle at the top of the stand for the clip that holds the microphone. Add the basic microphone shape, along with a few details, like a cord.

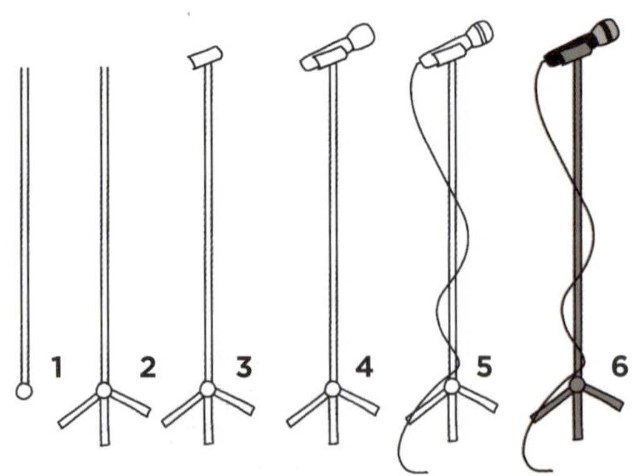

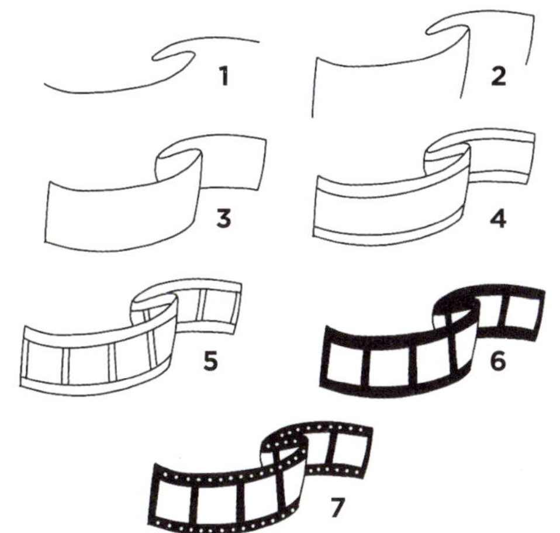

FILM STRIP

If you can draw a banner, you can draw a strip of film. Create an "S"-shaped line, then add vertical lines to divide it into two sections. Connect those lines at the bottom and add another vertical line in the curve of the "S" to show where the film is folded. Divide the film into a series of squares, coloring in the edges and spaces between the squares black, while the squares themselves stay white. For extra detail, add tiny dots along the edges. You can do this using a white gel pen on top of your black ink or you can draw small circles first, then color in black around them, leaving the circles white.

3D GLASSES

Drawing a pair of three-dimensional glasses isn't much harder than wearing them to watch a great film. Start by sketching a rectangle with a small point in the bottom center. Add rectangles for the lenses and sketch an earpiece coming out on a diagonal from each side. You can color in your glasses whatever shade you like, but the lenses are typically red and blue.

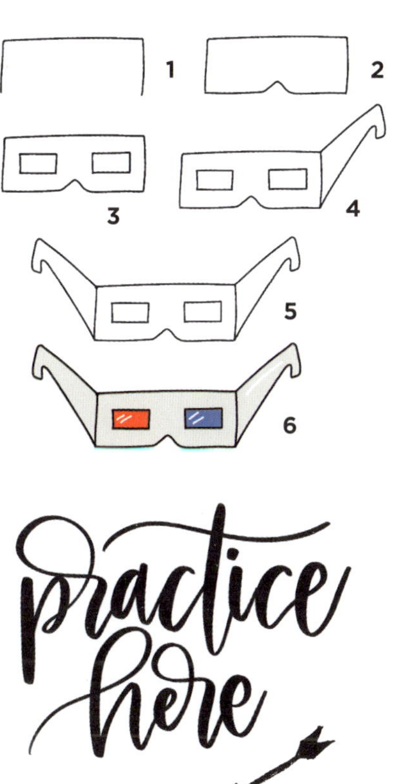

ON STAGE

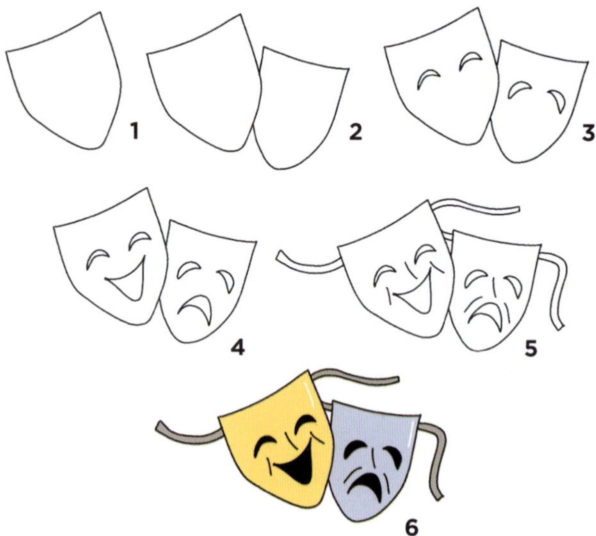

DRAMA MASKS

The side-by-side masks of comedy and tragedy often symbolize drama, which you can doodle by sketching two overlapping mask shapes. For the comedy mask, draw crescent-shaped eyes and a smile. For the tragedy mask, draw slanted eyes and a frown. Add strings on each side of the masks, along with detail lines in the nose and cheek areas. Color in the masks in any way you like to represent the forms of drama.

BALLET SLIPPERS

Let's doodle a pair of ballet slippers! Sketch a thin kidney bean shape, then add a curving line around the outside to form the first slipper. Add a line on the inside to show where the sole of the shoe separates from the side. Then, below the first slipper, sketch a "U" shape with a curving line around it for the second slipper. Draw two ribbons coming from the sides of each slipper. Make sure to erase any overlapping lines, then add color to complete the doodle.

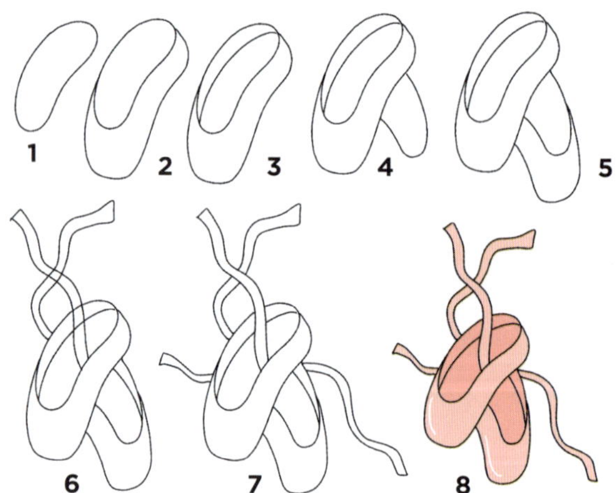

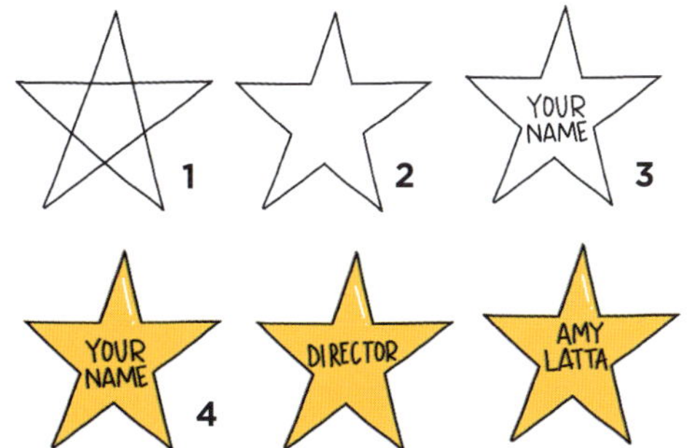

CELEBRITY STAR

If you've ever imagined your name on a dressing room door, you can make it happen with this star doodle. First, sketch a basic five-point star, then erase the lines in the center. Add a name or any other word inside the star, then color it in yellow or gold.

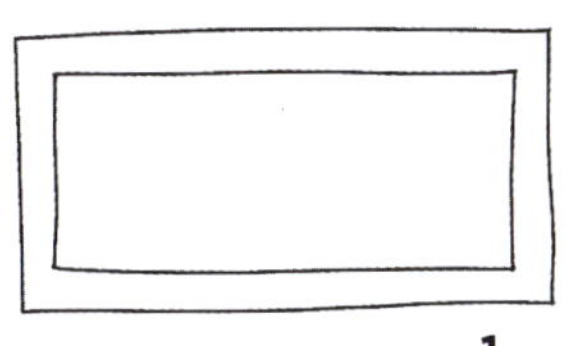

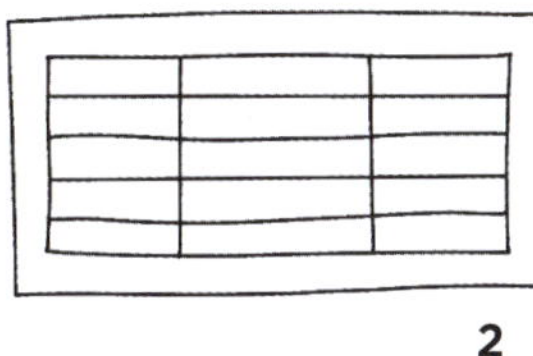

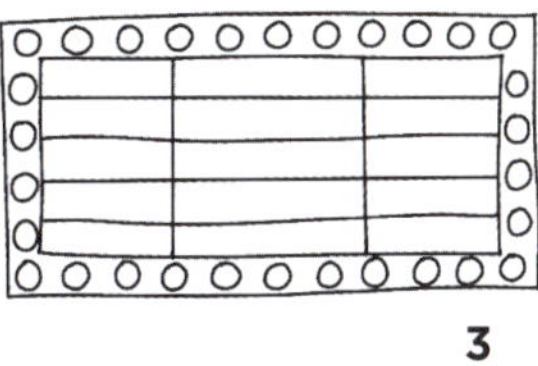

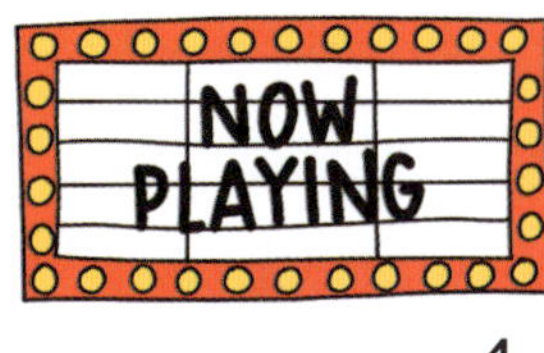

MARQUEE

Imagine your name in lights! Doodle this marquee sign, starting with a rectangle inside a slightly larger rectangle. Divide the center area of the sign with two vertical lines and four horizontal ones. Add circles for lights around the outer rectangle, then add any words you like on the inside, like a name or the title of a movie or a play.

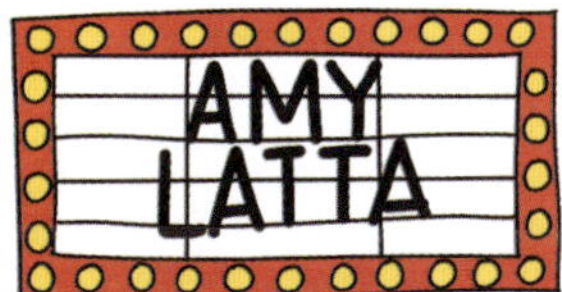

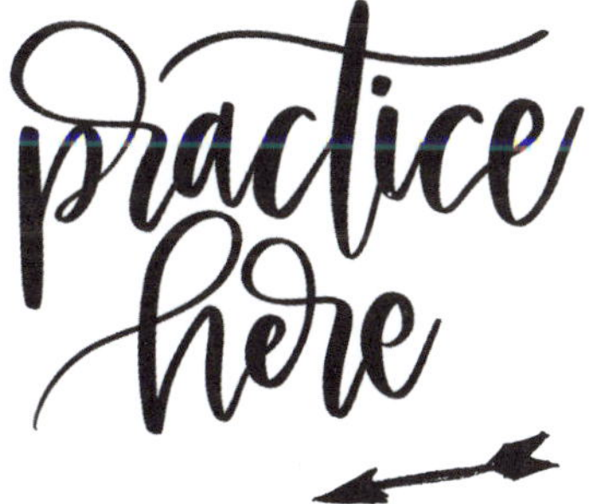

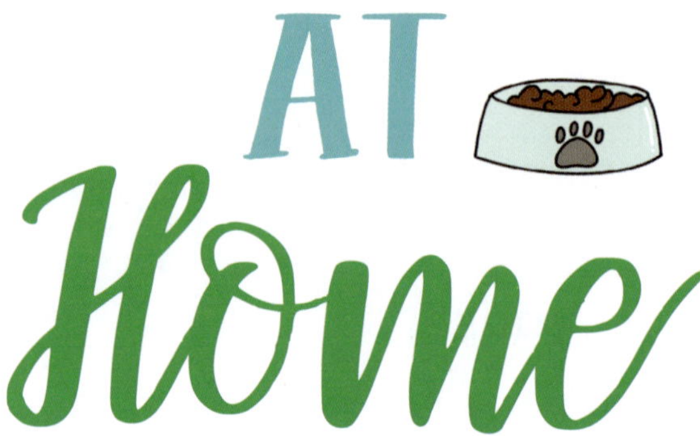

One of the simplest sources for doodle inspiration is what we see around us every day. The things in and around our homes can make great embellishments for our artistic projects. From plants, chairs and lamps to our pets or our kitchen utensils, there are plenty of ideas we can draw. In this chapter, I've chosen some of my favorite things around the house as a starting point to help us doodle the sweet and simple things all around.

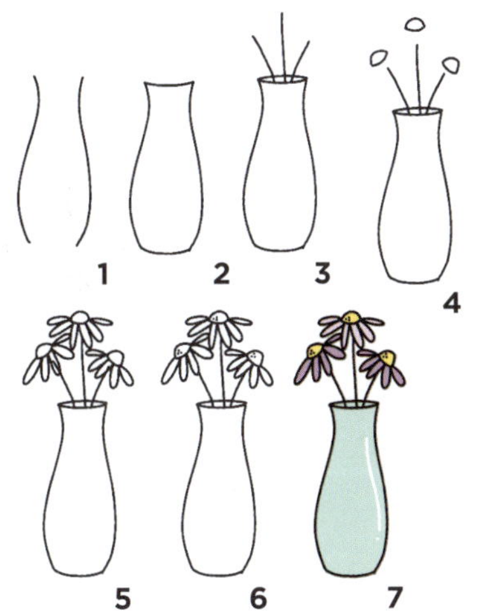

FLOWER VASE

Two curving lines connected at the top and bottom form the base of this cheerful vase. Add an oval on top along with three lines for flower stems, then draw a few petaled flowers peeking at the end of each stem. Using some of the varieties of flowers from the In the Garden chapter (page 11), you can also fill your vase with any other type of flower arrangement you like.

CACTUS HOUSEPLANTS

A cactus is one of the only houseplants I can keep alive, so let's doodle one! Start by sketching a basic pot, then add an upside-down "U" shape with two smaller ones on top. Continue adding more little "U" shapes branching off the existing ones to form the rest of the plant. Draw a few tiny flowers on top, then add detail lines to the cactus. Decorate your pot with any design (I chose a stripe), then add color.

Here's another variation on a cactus plant. Once again, start with a pot, then add a large arch for the main body of the cactus. Give it a curving arm on each side, then draw tiny lines all around the outside for the prickly spikes. Add detail lines on the cactus and a pattern on the pot to complete your doodle.

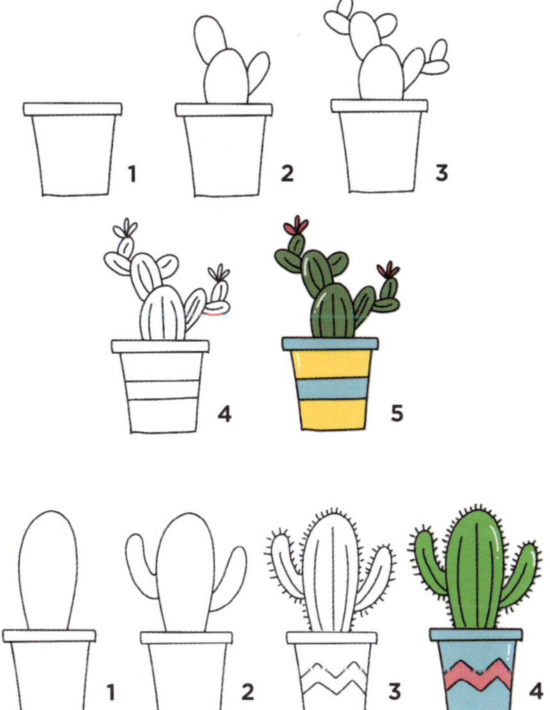

ALOE HOUSEPLANT

Aloe is a particularly helpful plant to keep on hand since it's so good for treating minor burns. Draw a basic pot shape, then add a series of long thin pointed leaves. These will overlap each other, so you'll want to go back and erase those areas to show that some leaves are in front of other ones. I added polka dots to this pot, but you can use any kind of pattern to decorate yours.

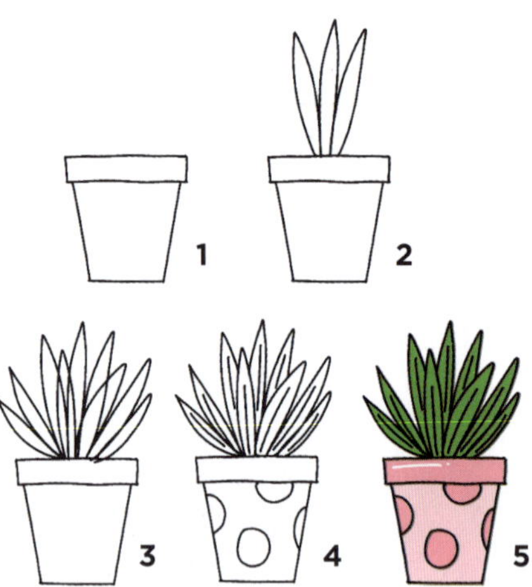

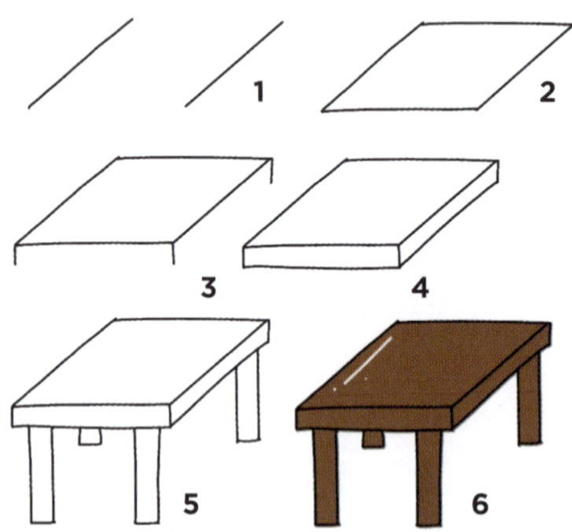

TABLE

To sketch a table, start with the top. Draw a parallelogram with vertical lines coming down from three corners. Connect those lines, which gives your table the look of being three-dimensional. Finally, add four rectangular shapes for legs and color your table.

STOOL

Draw this three-legged stool by making an oval with a rounded rectangle underneath for the seat. Next, add three rectangular legs. Connect the legs with three more rectangles in a triangle pattern. Finally, add color and your stool is complete.

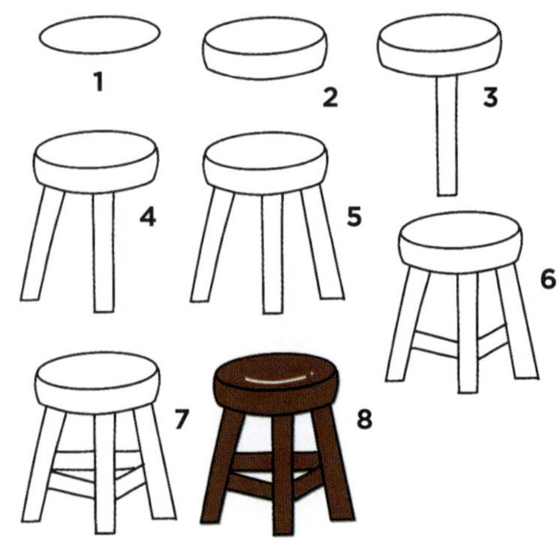

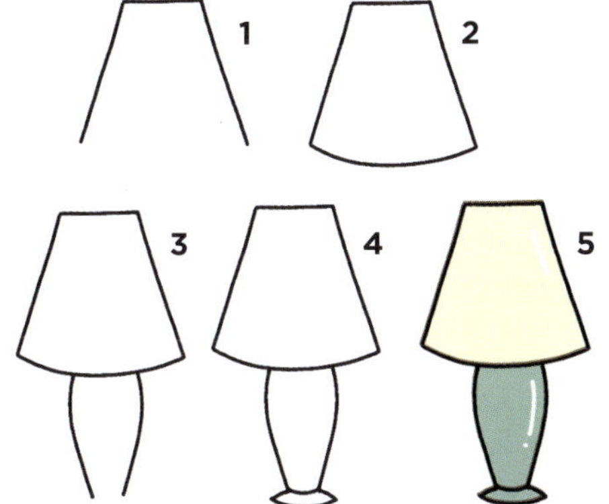

LAMP

Drawing a lamp starts with the shade: a trapezoid shape that's rounded at the bottom. Next, add the body of the lamp, which can be any shape you like. Mine is a set of parentheses with a little base. You can draw your lamp on its own or doodle it sitting on a table.

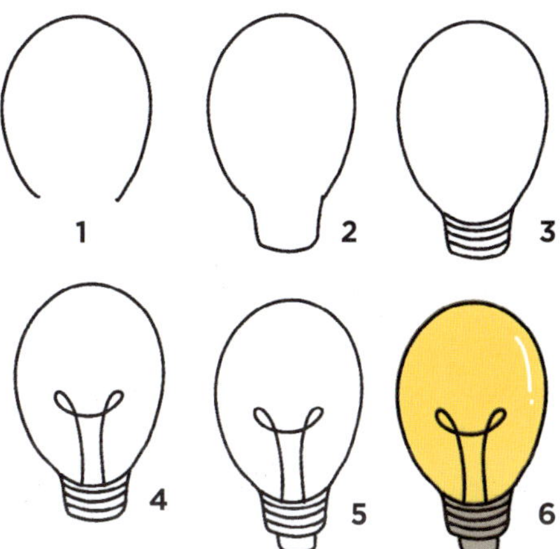

LIGHT BULB

Light bulbs are great doodles to represent ideas and learning in your lettering or crafts projects! To draw one, make an oval with a rounded rectangle base. Add lines across the base to represent the threads where it screws into the socket. Draw the filament inside, then add color to illuminate your bulb.

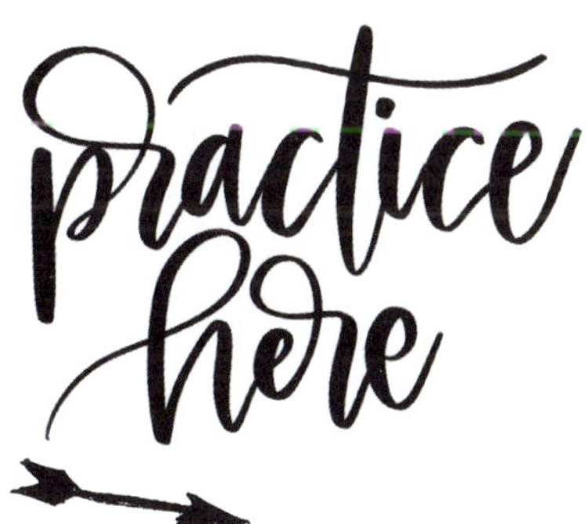

FURRY FRIENDS

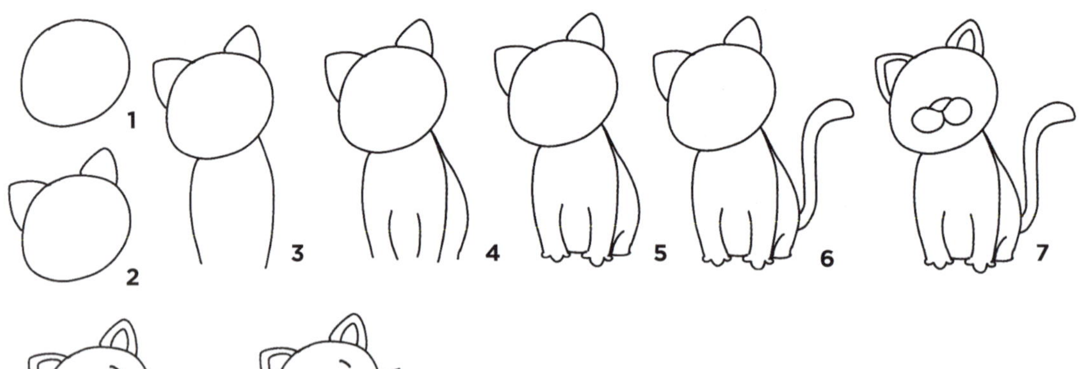

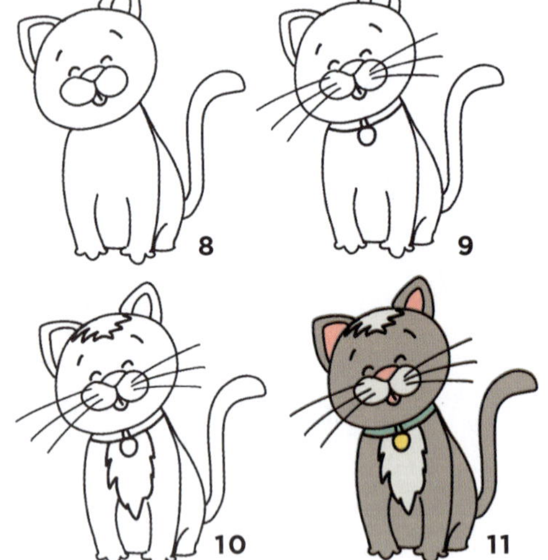

CAT

Furry friends make a house feel like a home. Doodle this kitten by forming a round head with short pointed ears. Next, add a body with front legs and feet and the back of the body off to the right side. Draw a long curving tail, then add details like a face, whiskers and a collar. Feel free to add spots, stripes or splotches of fur wherever you like, then color in your kitty.

DOG

We can't forget to draw man's best friend! This dog doodle starts with a rounded face and short floppy ears. If you have a different type of dog, feel free to make the ears longer, shorter and/or a different shape. Add a body and front legs, then draw a hind leg peeking out from each side. Draw a tail curling around the body and add a face and a collar. Color your dog brown, black, yellow, white or any combination of colors.

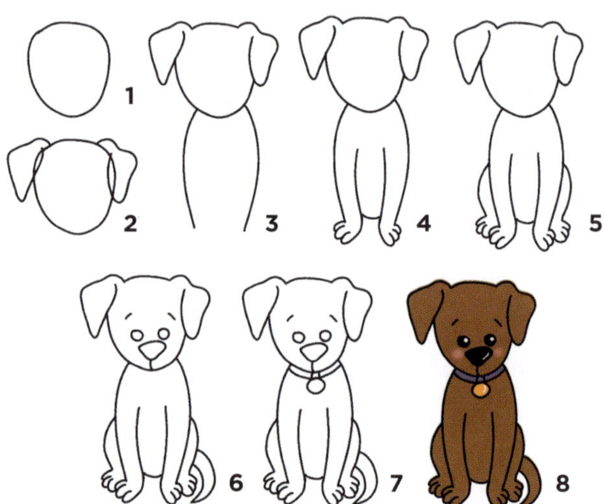

PET FOOD

Doodle your pet some food by making a rounded rectangle dish with an oval on top. Add some bumpy lines (or small ovals) to represent the food itself. Then, label the dish with a little paw print drawing or your pet's name.

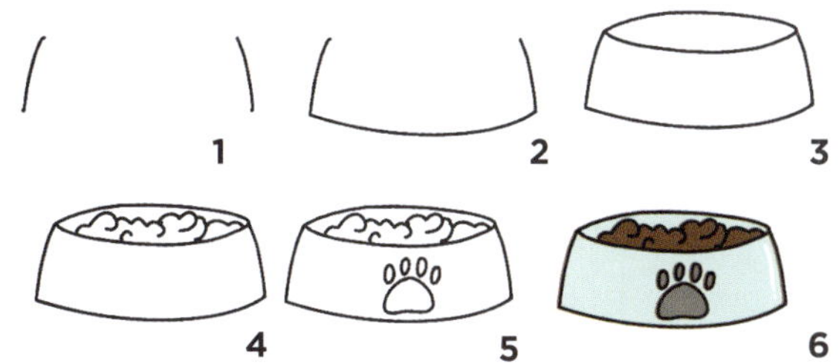

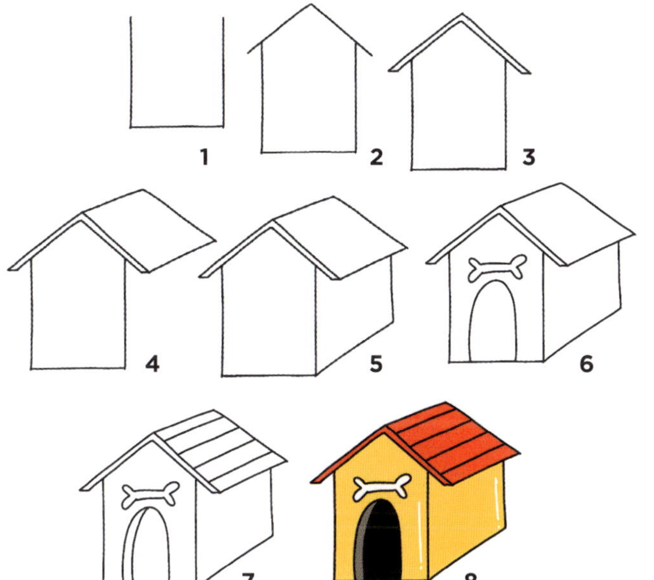

DOG HOUSE

A dog house starts with the same basic foundation as a regular house: a rectangle with a triangle on top. Then, we'll add dimension by extending the roof and the house itself out to the side on a diagonal. Make sure to draw an arched doorway so your pup can go inside and add details like lines across the roof and a bone or the dog's name above the entrance.

MOUSE

While no one really wants to have a mouse in the house, this little guy makes an adorable embellishment. Draw his head first, followed by large rounded ears. Next, draw a curving line for the body and give the mouse a tiny pair of front legs. Sketch a long thin curving tail and add a face to complete your doodle.

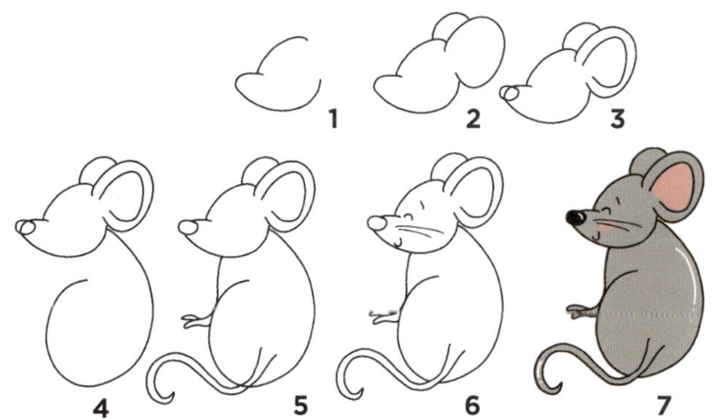

IN THE KITCHEN

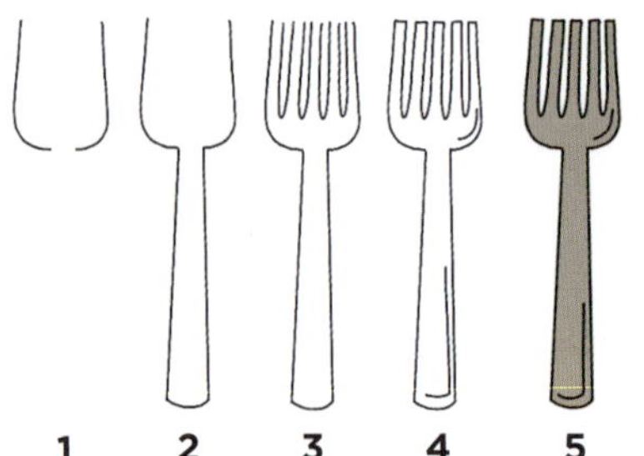

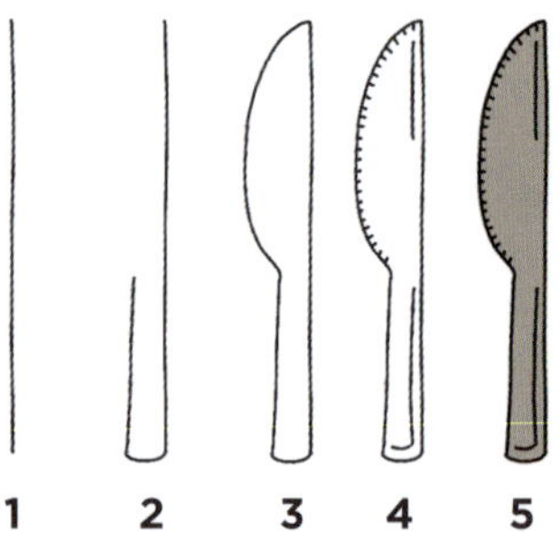

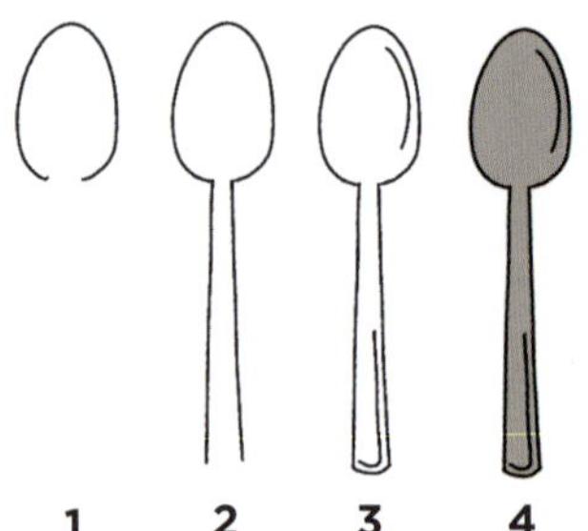

FORK, KNIFE & SPOON FLATWARE

To draw a fork, start with a "U" shape with an opening at the bottom and a long thin handle. Then, divide the "U" into a series of tines. Add detail lines, then color in your fork silver or gray.

Draw a knife by making a vertical line attached to a curving line that stops about halfway. Continue straight down to form the handle and add tiny detail lines to show that the knife's blade has texture.

The first step in drawing a spoon is to make a rounded shape for the bowl. Then, add a long thin handle. Draw any detail lines you like to help add dimension, then color it in.

COOK POT

To doodle a pot, start with a rounded rectangle for the base and a smaller rounded lid. Add a little handle on the top and a long thin handle out to one side. Color in your pot and get ready to cook up something delicious.

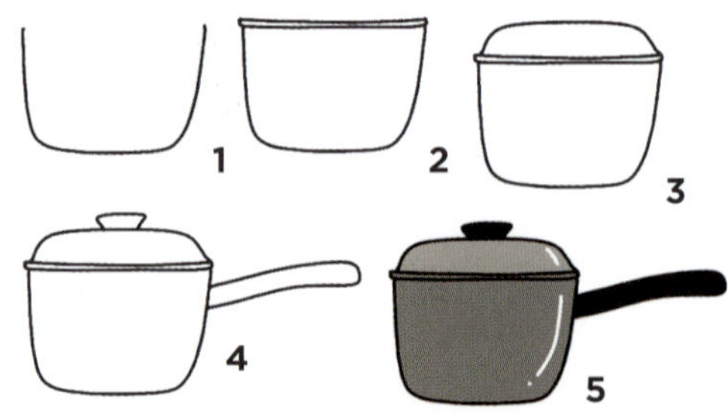

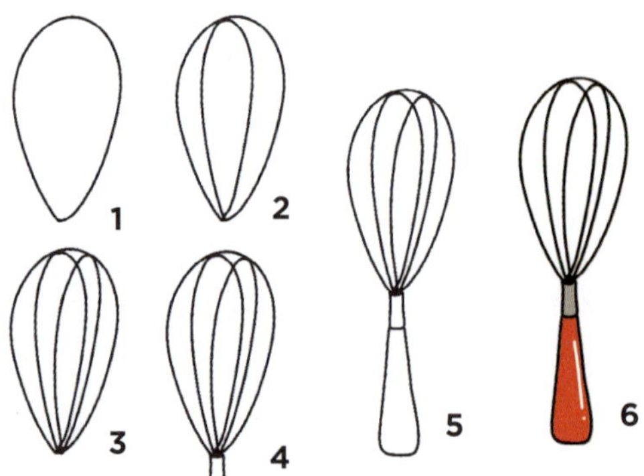

WHISK

The head of the whisk is the first part we're going to doodle, starting with a large teardrop shape. Add two more smaller teardrop shapes inside to represent the different pieces of wire that make up the whisk. Add a handle and some color, then your drawing is complete.

STAND MIXER

It took many years for me to invest in a stand mixer, but now I wouldn't want to be without it. To doodle this kitchen appliance, start by drawing the rounded top and an "L" shape for the arm and the base. Next, add the bowl and draw the top of the mixing paddle coming out of it. Add a speed adjustment on the top and color in your doodle.

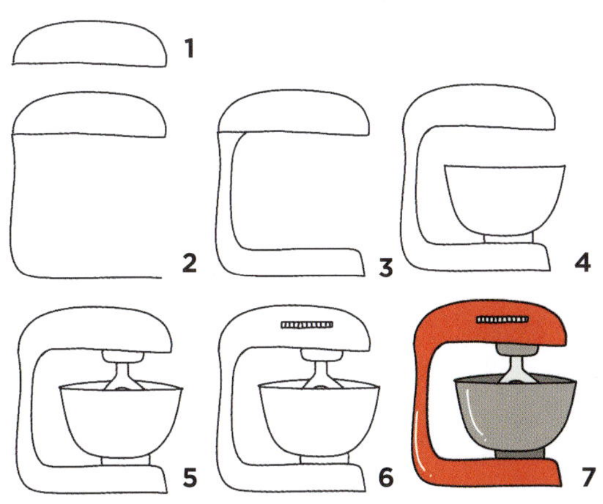

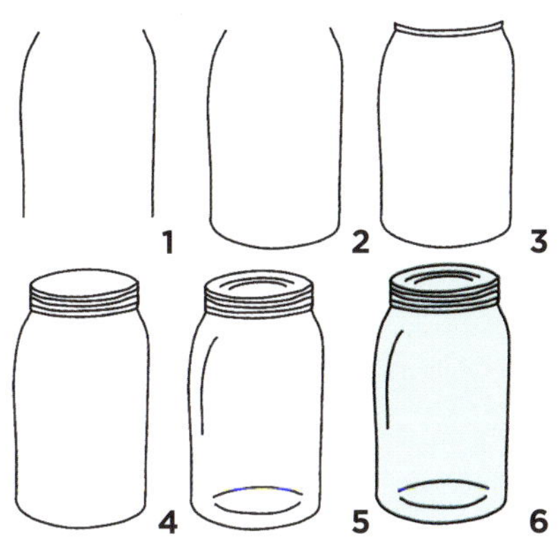

MASON JAR

Draw the sides of your Mason jar first and connect them with curving lines at the top and bottom. Add the neck of the jar and lid, as well as a few detail lines to help show depth and dimension. You can leave your jar white or give it a very light blue tint.

OVEN MITT

Two "U" shapes form the basic outline of an oven mitt. Draw a rectangle across the top and add a loop for hanging it somewhere in the kitchen. For texture, sketch a checkerboard-style pattern or any other design you like to decorate the mitt.

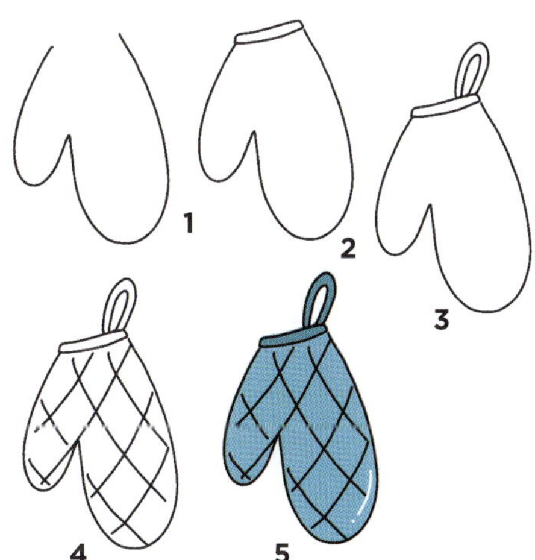

ROLLING PIN

To form a rolling pin, draw parallel lines connected with slightly curving lines on the ends. Draw a long thin handle on each side and add dimension to the end closest to you. Your rolling pin can be any color you like; I made mine brown so it looks wooden like the one I grew up using in my mom's kitchen.

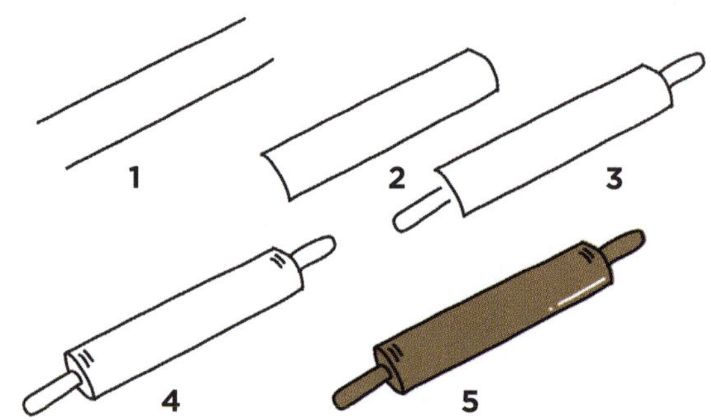

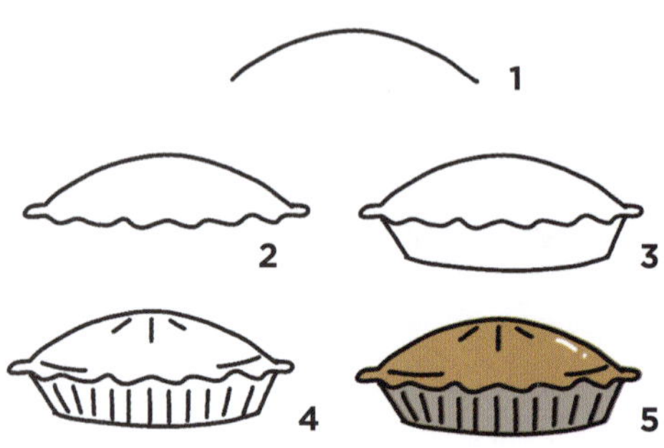

WHOLE PIE

I find pies far easier to draw than they are to bake. Start by making a wide arc with a wavy line across the bottom for the top of the pie. Add a pie plate with vertical lines for texture and draw a few slits in the top of the pie where the steam can vent. Color it in and it looks almost good enough to eat!

MILK CARTON

Doodle this milk carton by drawing a rectangle with a parallelogram on top. Add another rectangle above that, then draw a triangle and a rectangle on the side for a three-dimensional effect. I labeled my carton with the word "MILK," but this doodle could also be used for a carton of orange juice or another type of beverage.

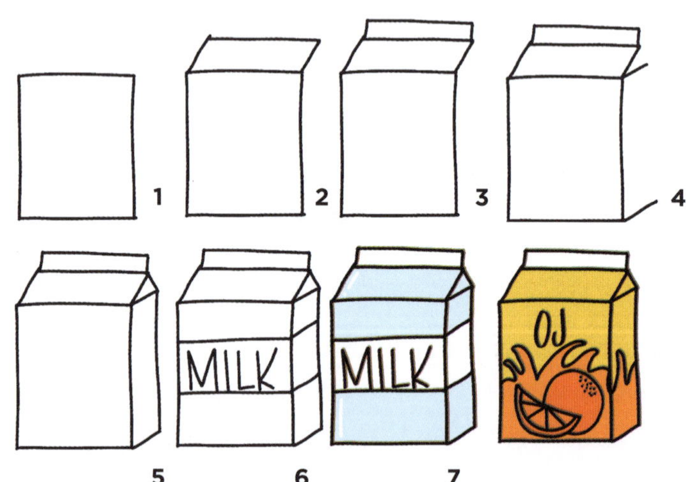

BEAUTY & SELF-CARE

LIPSTICK

To draw a tube of lipstick, start with the sides of the tube and a curving line across the bottom. Then, add a rounded rectangle for the rest of the case. Draw the lipstick itself peeking out of the tube with an oval on top to show the area that applies to the lips.

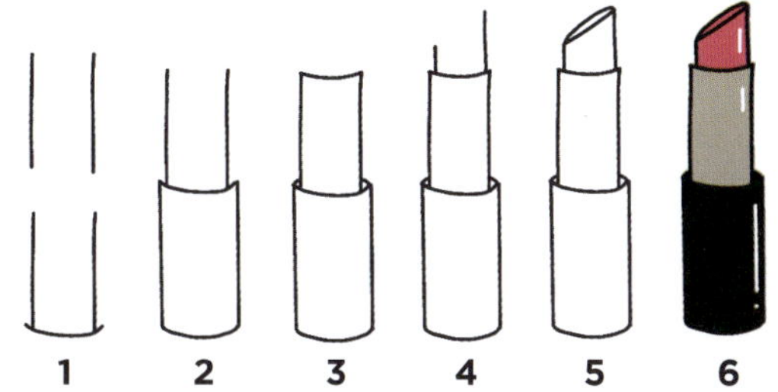

NAIL POLISH

Sketch this bottle of nail polish by drawing the basic bottle shape first. Different brands are different shapes, so you can play around with making it rectangular, rounded, tall or short. Then, add a tall, thin cap on top and a label to the front of the bottle. The funnest part is deciding what color the polish will be!

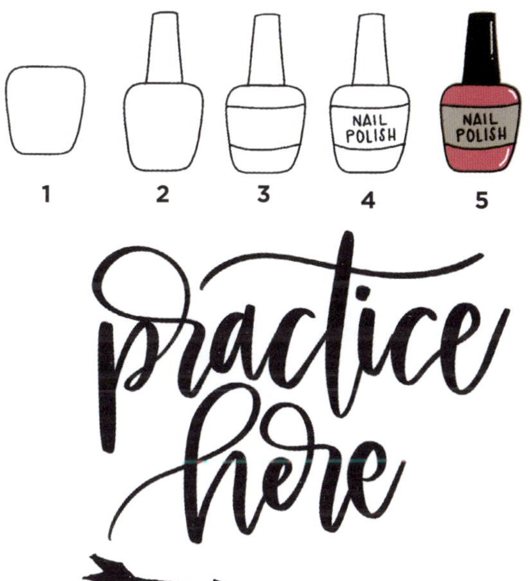

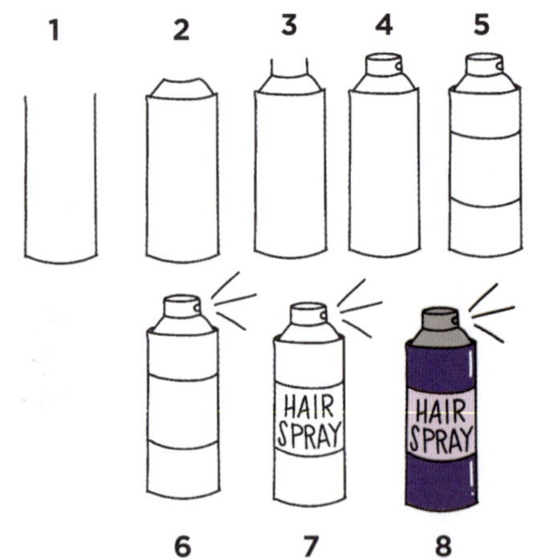

HAIRSPRAY

The first step to drawing some hairspray is making parallel lines for the can's sides. Next, connect them with a rounded line at the top and bottom, then add the spray nozzle on top. Draw a label on the can, along with several lines coming out from the nozzle to represent the spray in action. This shape could easily become a variety of different hair or house products, even a cleaning spray!

MIRROR

To doodle a hand-held mirror, start with an oval inside a slightly larger oval. Then, add a long thin handle. Using a very light gray or blue with a few white highlights to show the mirror's glass, color in your mirror.

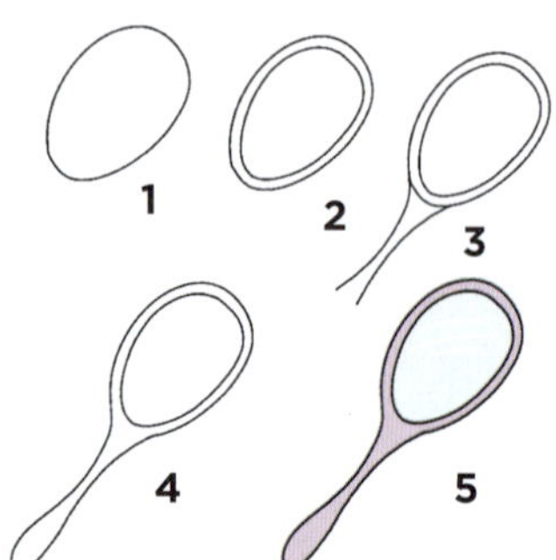

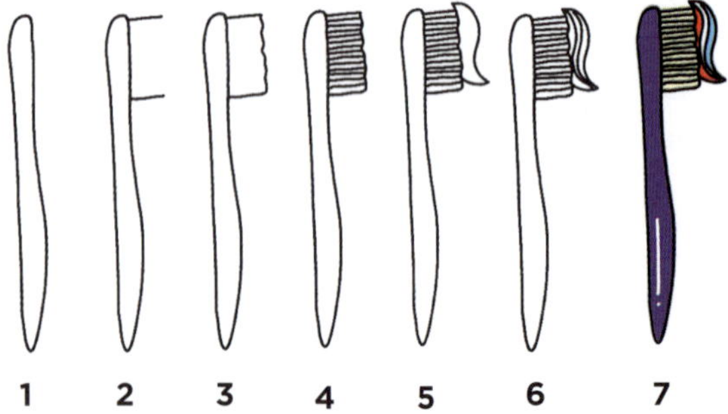

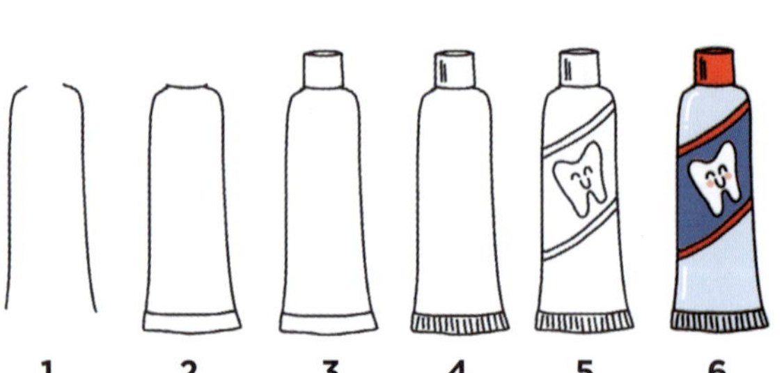

TOOTHBRUSH & TOOTHPASTE

Start this toothbrush doodle by forming the long thin handle. Next, add two horizontal lines for the top and bottom of the bristles, connected by a wavy line. Draw lots of detail lines across the head of the brush to show the bristles, then don't forget a little dollop of toothpaste!

A toothpaste tube is a lot like a tube of sunscreen (page 33). Start by forming the sides of the tube, then add a little cap. Draw some detail lines on the end of the tube, along with whatever you like on the label. I divided my tube into some stripes with a happy little tooth in the center. You could also write the word "TOOTHPASTE" or the name of a particular brand.

EVERYDAY THINGS

GAME CONTROLLER

One of my son's most well-loved possessions is his game controller. To doodle one, draw a "C" shape connected to a backward "C" shape with horizontal lines. Draw buttons for game play, like a plus sign shape and small circles for the various controls. Use mine as an example or look at the controllers in your house for ideas.

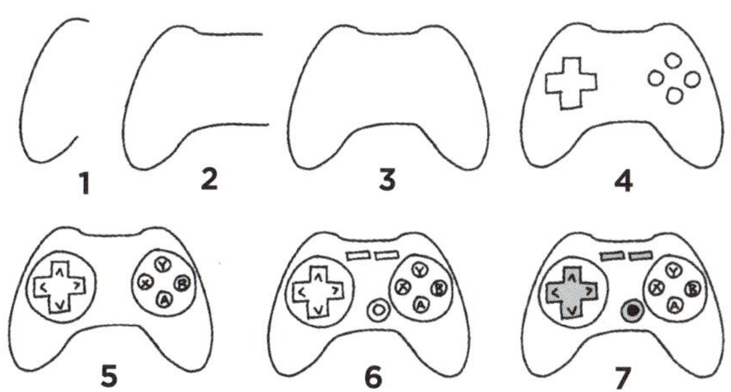

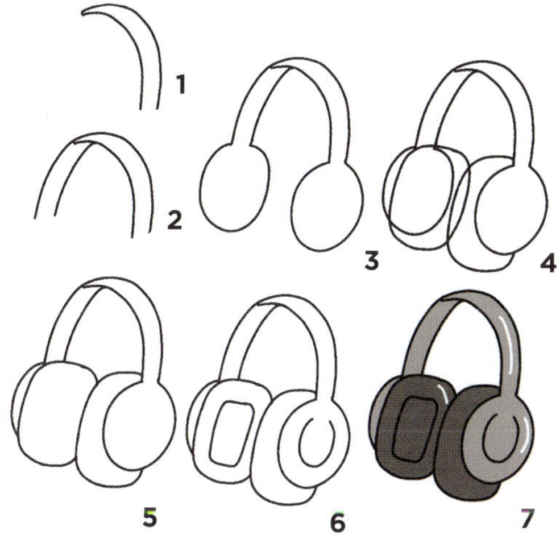

HEADPHONES

Drawing a pair of headphones starts at the top. Draw two curving sections, each with a circle at the bottom. Add rounded rectangles for the padded areas and detail lines for dimension. Color your headphones, and if you like, you can even combine this doodle with some music notes (page 164).

KEYS

Keys can be used in so many projects, not just home-based ones, but also as in the key to someone's heart. To draw a key, start with the top and form whatever type of oval or rounded shape you like. Mine has a bump on top and curves on the sides. Next, draw the shaft, a long thin rectangle coming down from the head. Then, draw a line composed of straight parts, angles and curves for the teeth. Add a key ring and some color to finish your drawing.

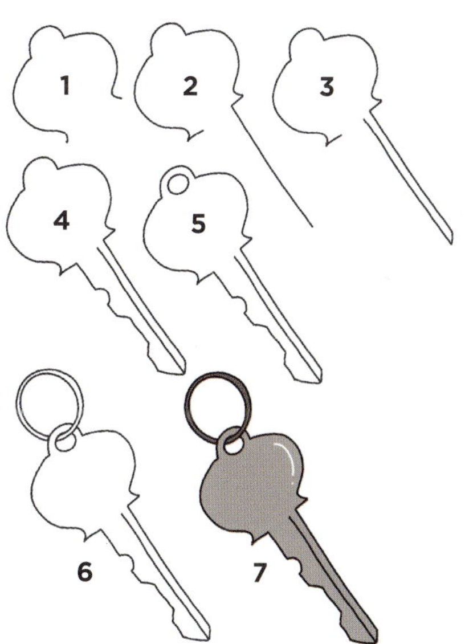

SMARTPHONE

A smartphone (or tablet) is just a rectangle inside a rounded rectangle, often with a little round button at the bottom. Color it in, either making the screen black or adding images and text.

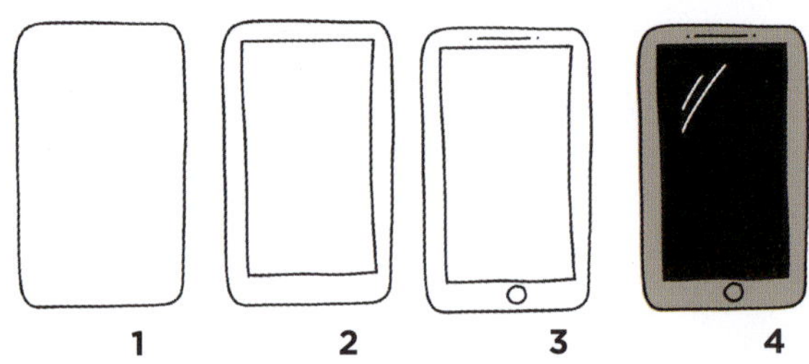

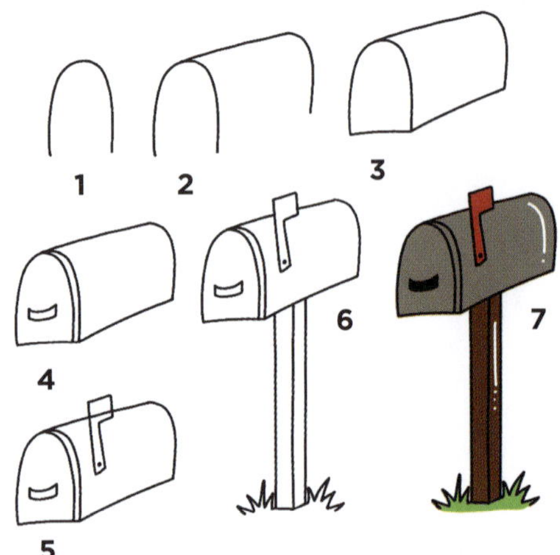

MAILBOX

Doodle a mailbox by starting with an arch and extending it out to the side. Add a handle and a flag, which you can draw up or down, depending on whether or not there's mail inside. Sketch a post below the mailbox with a few blades of grass on either side. Leave your mailbox as is or label it with your house number or last name.

SPOOL OF THREAD & THIMBLE

To draw a spool of thread, start with two parallel lines connected with a rounded one at the bottom. Next, draw a "C" shape around the bottom and an oval on the top for the ends of the spool. Add a hole in the top and lots of little detail lines to represent the thread wrapped around the spool.

This thimble doodle is simply a pair of diagonal lines that are connected with an oval on top and a "C" shape on the bottom. Add tiny oval shapes around the top section of the thimble for texture and color it in, usually silver or gray.

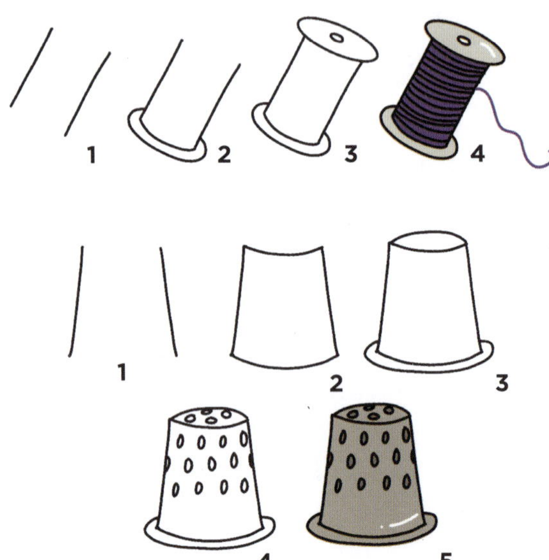

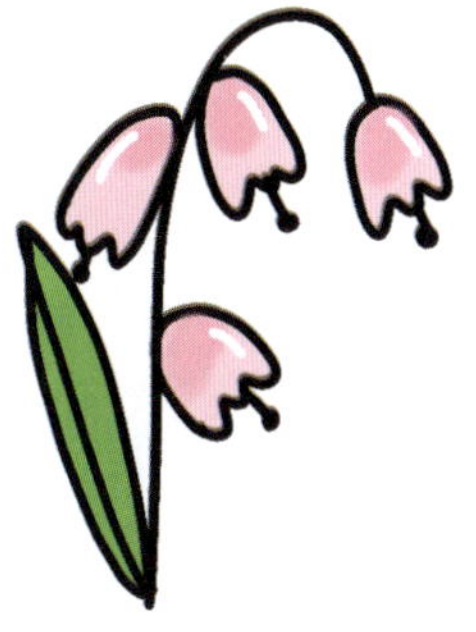

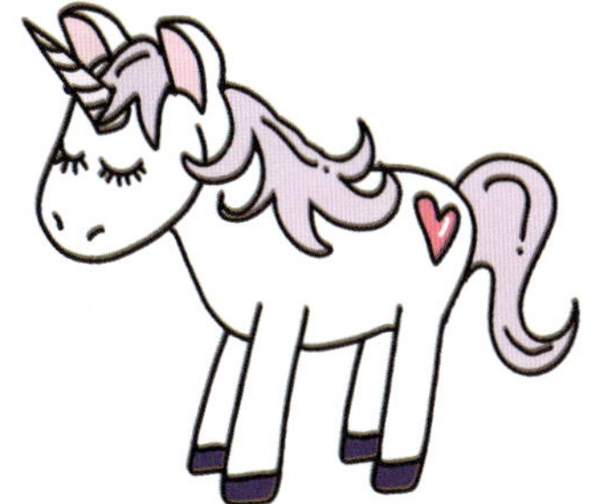

ACKNOWLEDGMENTS

The Page Street Team: Thank you for asking me to create this book and for continuing to partner with me to create amazing things.

Sarah: You are the best editor a girl could ask for and I am so grateful for your insights.

Dan, Nathan and Noah: Thank you for your love and support and for being my doodle testers.

Mom and Dad: Your belief that I can do anything made me believe it too. I love you.

My wonderful readers: It is an honor to be a part of your creative journey. Without you, there would be no meaning in what I do.

ABOUT THE AUTHOR

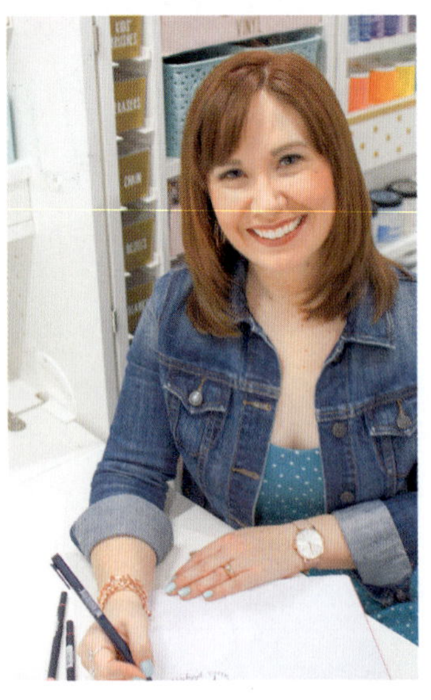

Amy Latta is passionate about inspiring others to discover, explore and express their creativity. On her award-winning website, amylattacreations.com, you'll find tutorials for arts and crafts projects, as well as all levels of hand lettering. She also loves teaching workshops worldwide through Michaels Community Classroom, Pinners Conference and other venues. You can regularly find Amy sharing creative ideas in segments on a variety of local and national lifestyle television shows. And, of course, you can learn from Amy by reading one or all of her six previous books. Amy is happiest when crafting, and when she's not covered in paint, you can find her working on professional collaborations. Her original lettered designs have been featured nationally in Gap stores and Starbucks commercials. Amy is a Maryland girl who runs on iced coffee and loves spending time with her family.

Check out Amy's hand-lettering workbooks and other books at your local bookstore or anywhere books are sold.

Hand Lettering for Relaxation: An Inspirational Workbook for Creating Beautiful Lettered Art

Express Yourself! A Hand Lettering Workbook for Kids: Create Awesome Quotes the Fun and Easy Way!

Hand Lettering for Laughter: Gorgeous Art with a Hilarious Twist

Hand Lettering for Faith: A Christian Workbook for Creating Inspired Art

Hand Lettering Off the Page: Easy Projects to Create Beautiful Décor, Apparel and Gifts

Practice Makes Progress: My Creative Journal

INDEX